Gendered Dynamics
in Latin Love Poetry

ARETHUSA BOOKS

Series Editor: Martha A. Malamud

GENDERED DYNAMICS

in Latin Love Poetry

Edited by
Ronnie Ancona and Ellen Greene

THE JOHNS HOPKINS UNIVERSITY PRESS
Baltimore

For my mother, Ruth Ancona   R.A.

To Jim, as always   E.G.

The Johns Hopkins University Press
2715 North Charles Street
Baltimore, Maryland 21218-4363
www.press.jhu.edu

Library of Congress Cataloging-in-Publication Data

Gendered dynamics in Latin love poetry : edited by Ronnie Ancona and
Ellen Greene.
      p. cm. — (Arethusa books)
   Includes bibliographical references and index.
   ISBN 0-8018-8198-6 (alk. paper)
      1. Love poetry, Latin—History and criticism.   2. Man-woman relationships
in literature.   3. Feminism and literature—Rome.   4. Women and
literature—Rome.   5. Sex role in literature.   I. Ancona, Ronnie, 1951–
II. Greene, Ellen, 1950–   III. Series.

PA6029.L6G46 2005
871'.01093543—dc22   2005009108

A catalog record for this book is available from the British Library.

Contents

III: Female Subjectivity and Silence

Contributors

RONNIE ANCONA is a professor of classics at Hunter College and The Graduate Center, City University of New York. She is the author of *Time and the Erotic in Horace's Odes* (Duke University Press 1994), *Horace: Selected Odes and Satire 1.9* (Bolchazy-Carducci Publishers 1999), and *Writing Passion: A Catullus Reader* (Bolchazy-Carducci Publishers 2004). She is editor of *Latin Scholarship / Latin Pedagogy* (University of Oklahoma Press, forthcoming).

PHEBE LOWELL BOWDITCH is an associate professor and head of the Classics Department at the University of Oregon. She is the author of *Horace and the Gift Economy of Patronage* (University of California Press 2001) and essays on Propertius, Ovid, Horace, and the poetics of translation. Her current research is on love elegy and Roman imperialism.

CHRISTOPHER BRUNELLE teaches classics at St. Olaf College. He has published several articles on Ovid and co-authored an edition of Plautus's *Poenulus*; he also works on ancient music.

TREVOR FEAR is a lecturer in classical studies with The Open University. He was guest editor of *Fallax Opus: Approaches to Reading Roman Elegy* (*Arethusa* 33.2, 2000) and is author of several articles on Roman elegiac and lyric poetry.

ELLEN GREENE is the Joseph Paxton Presidential Professor of Classics at the University of Oklahoma. She is the author of *The Erotics of Domination: Male Desire and the Mistress in Latin Love Poetry* (Johns Hopkins University Press 1998). She has edited two collections of essays on Sappho and one collection on *Women Poets in Greece and Rome*. Her new book, *The Elegiac Hero: Gender and Genre in Propertius Book 2*, will be published by Ohio State University Press.

KERILL O'NEILL is Taylor Associate Professor of Classics at Colby College. His interests and publications range from Greek tragedy to Latin love elegy and ancient magic.

KIRK ORMAND is an assistant professor of classics at Oberlin College. He is the author of *Exchange and the Maiden: Marriage in Sophoclean Tragedy* (University of Texas Press 1999) and articles on Hesiod, Sophocles, Lucan, and Clint Eastwood.

VICTORIA RIMELL teaches Latin literature at the University of Rome, La Sapienza. She was previously a Junior Research Fellow at University College, Oxford and a lecturer at Cambridge. She is the author of *Petronius and the Anatomy of Fiction* (Cambridge University Press 2002), and recently completed a book on the interplay of subjectivity, creativity, and desire in Ovid. Current projects include a monograph on Martial and an edited volume on the ancient novel.

PATRICIA SALZMAN-MITCHELL is an assistant professor of classics at Montclair State University, New Jersey. She is the author of *A Web of Fantasies: Gaze, Image, and Gender in Ovid's Metamorphoses* (Ohio State University Press 2005) and essays on Ovid and gender in Latin literature.

EFROSSINI SPENTZOU is a lecturer in classics at Royal Holloway, University of London. She is the author of *Readers and Writers in Ovid's Heroides: Trangressions of Gender and Genre* (Oxford University Press 2003). She co-edited with the late Don Fowler *Cultivating the Muse: Struggles for Power and Inspiration in Classical Literature* (Oxford University Press 2002). At the moment, she is working on a book on *Selfish Subjects: Self and Society in Late First-Century A.D. Rome*.

ELIZABETH SUTHERLAND is an associate professor and associate head of the Department of Classics at the University of Tennessee. She is the author of *Horace's Well-Trained Reader: Toward a Methodology of Audience Participation in the Odes* (Peter Lang 2002) and of articles on Horace and gender theory.

HÉRICA VALLADARES is a Ph.D. student at Columbia University and currently the Samuel H. Kress pre-doctoral fellow at the

Center for Advanced Study in the Visual Arts, Washington, D.C. Her dissertation is entitled "*Imago Amoris:* The Poetics of Desire in Roman Painting."

TARA S. WELCH is an associate professor of classics at the University of Kansas whose work focuses on the literature and topography of the Augustan era. She has published essays on Horace's *Satires* and Propertius's late elegies. The latter is the subject of her book, *The Elegiac Cityscape*, forthcoming from the Ohio State University Press.

Acknowledgments

We would like to recognize the help and support we received throughout the process of bringing this book to completion. Martha Malamud, series editor for Arethusa Books, expressed interest in and support of the project from our first contact with her. Michael Lonegro, associate editor for humanities at the Johns Hopkins University Press, shepherded the book through the whole publication process at the press. His always prompt and knowledgeable replies to queries made our experience an easy and enjoyable one. Both Madeleine Kaufman, managing editor of the journal *Arethusa*, and Susan Lantz, manuscript editor at the Johns Hopkins University Press, gave careful attention to the manuscript at different stages, while Anne Holmes of EdIndex compiled the index in a timely fashion. Paul Allen Miller offered generous and useful comments as respondent at the Women's Classical Caucus panel from which this book originated. The careful and incisive readings of the manuscript by the two anonymous reviewers for the Johns Hopkins University Press provided us with material that allowed us to make this a better book. We thank our contributors for their patience, good humor, and ability to meet deadlines.

Separately, Ronnie Ancona appreciates the generous contribution of The Pleskow Classics Fund of the Department of Classical and Oriental Studies, Hunter College, for help in production of the index, while Ellen Greene expresses gratitude to the University of Oklahoma for providing generous financial support during her work on this project. On a more personal note, Ronnie Ancona thanks Steve for his computer knowledge and both Steve and David for taking her work as a given and for reminding her continually of life beyond it. Ellen Greene thanks Jim for his humor and computer expertise but most of all for his patience and love. Finally, we, as co-editors, would like to acknowledge the rewards of the collaborative process. Our work together on the book, primarily via email and phone, gave us a valuable opportunity to discuss with each other issues of mutual scholarly interest.

Introduction

Ronnie Ancona and Ellen Greene

This collection of essays grew out of a Women's Classical Caucus panel at the 2001 American Philological Association meeting. We organized that panel and developed this volume because we recognized that, although the consideration of gender dynamics in Latin love poetry has been the focus of much scholarly debate over the last several decades, there are no published collections that specifically examine issues of gender in Roman amatory texts. Our volume, then, is a first, and its essays reflect pressing concerns in the critical discussion of gender in these works. By creating the first anthology of essays on gender dynamics in Latin love poetry, we hope to further stimulate debate about the complex relationship between the notion of gender as a construct (both historical and ideological) and the production of amatory discourse.

While classics has often resisted theoretical and feminist approaches to the study of ancient texts, the last two decades have seen an unparalleled flowering of studies not only on women in antiquity and on ancient conceptions of gender and sexuality but also on the complex dynamics of gender relations represented in Greek and Roman literary texts. Latin love poetry offers perhaps the most fertile ground within Roman literature for examining both the problematization of gender roles and the engagement of literary texts with cultural norms and ideologies.[1] Elegy, for example, with its narrative of a feminized male lover and a masculinized female beloved, raises a host of questions that concern male writers' representations of both masculine desire and female subjectivity. The gender inversion implicit in the trope of *servitium amoris* in elegy has given rise to lively debate over the last thirty years about the extent to which the Latin love poets endorse and/or subvert stereotypical notions of gen-

1

der identity. Likewise, recent studies in Latin lyric draw attention to the ways in which the construction of a gender identity is connected to larger issues of literary and social power.[2]

We can trace the roots of this debate in Judith Hallett's 1973 essay, "The Role of Women in Roman Elegy: Counter-Cultural Feminism." Hallett argues that the elegists indicated their nonconformity with traditional gender roles by portraying women as dominant and men as subservient. Hallett's essay not only reflected the general burgeoning of feminist approaches to literary criticism but also the emerging interest within classical studies in both the recovery of women's voices and representations of women in male-authored texts. This interest is especially relevant to Latin love poetry, given its focus on the lover's engagement with his beloved and the portrayal of relations between the sexes. Two major lines of interpretation have emerged in feminist scholarship on the Latin love poets since Hallett's groundbreaking essay. One sees the female beloved as an objectified other, subject to the rhetorical control of the male narrator.[3] The other, an offshoot of Hallett's argument, regards representations of women in amatory texts as examples of the potential for female power in ancient Rome.[4] Most recently, some scholars have mapped out a territory beyond the dichotomy of these two approaches. In general, the scholarly shift past this polarity is founded on seeing amatory texts as a site for very complicated negotiations concerning traditional notions of gender, sexuality, and power politics. As Maria Wyke argues (2002), Roman love poetry often contests Roman social and political systems through its deployment of gender categories.

The thirteen essays in this anthology (eleven of which are new) reflect in various ways the arguments that have developed since Hallett's essay. They focus, specifically, on the ways in which Roman amatory texts present a complex picture of male desire and female subjectivity. In these texts, the positions of subject and object of desire are susceptible to being undermined and destabilized. While these essays come to a variety of conclusions about gender dynamics in Latin love poetry, what they all have in common is an attempt to avoid reductive approaches that see gender dynamics operating in a simplistic or univocal fashion. Utilizing a variety of strategies, each chapter focuses on a particular aspect of gender dynamics in erotic texts. In addition, an increased focus on gender issues in classical literature has led to a broadening of the definition of love poetry. While several of the arguments made in this collection emerge from the study of Roman elegy in the wake of Hallett's influential article, we have intentionally included essays that involve lyric and epic texts as well. They show not only the more complicated views of gender dynamics emerging in recent scholarship but also how scholars who pursue such issues push the boundaries of what constitutes an "amatory text." For example, Ovid's *Metamorphoses*, clearly marked as epic by meter and other generic characteristics, is nevertheless open to analysis as an amatory text, while Horace's lyrics (not often studied for their erotic potential) are explored along with some of Ovid's less-known works.

In order to present these newer approaches to gender and love poetry (broadly defined) in a way that reflects the major themes of current scholarship on gender and the erotic, we have divided the volume into three sections: Male Desire and Sexuality, The Gaze, and Female Subjectivity and Silence. Despite these categories, readers will discover that our authors deal with overlapping issues. For example, the concerns of female subjectivity are not necessarily separable from issues of the gaze. One conclusion that emerges from all of our essays is that the dynamics of gender in amatory poetry do not map in any single way onto the cultural and historical norms of Roman society. In fact, as several of our authors show, there is a dialectical relationship between the poetry under examination in this collection and Roman cultural practices. Thus, for example, Trevor Fear's analysis of the elegiac narrator focuses on the ways in which the practice of elegy offers opportunities for young males to act out experiences that must be abandoned later upon assumption of mature, appropriate male desire. In a sense, Fear is arguing that elegy is about what a man can't do later when he's a man. Ronnie Ancona examines what happens when Roman social control of marriage cannot contain male desire. Ellen Greene shows that the feminized persona of the elegiac *amator* in Propertius is modified by the epic, masculine persona he also adopts, while Kirk Ormand discusses an allegedly female homoerotic story and concludes that it's really a story about masculinity: how to act like a man. It is our hope that this collection will give readers a more nuanced appreciation of the gender dynamics in Latin love poetry and the Roman cultural context that produced and was affected by it.

The essays in the first section (Male Desire and Sexuality) examine the various ways amatory poetry offers writers the possibility of constructing gender identities for their male narrators that reveal the norms of masculinity in Roman culture. The essays in this section do not take the view (à la Hallett 1973) that amatory texts simply overturn traditional gender categories. Rather, they emphasize the dynamic interaction between biological sex and social gender, and between the appropriation and subversion of conventional gender hierarchies.

Trevor Fear's essay, "Propertian Closure: The Elegiac Inscription of the Liminal Male and Ideological Contestation in Augustan Rome," leads off the collection by arguing that male desire in elegy opens up a ludic space for the male narrator as an escape from masculine responsibility. Fear argues that elegy presents a narrative of the male on the threshold of Roman respectability and normative masculinity, and that elegy provides time and space for socially sanctioned youthful eroticism. As Fear points out, the liminal position of the elegist is also associated with the *amator*'s self-presentation as someone who is socially alienated. Elegiac ideology may thus be seen as a resistance to both maturation and civic responsibility. Moreover, Fear argues, it is important to see a connection between the youthful poetic and erotic dalliances of the elegist and Rome's maturation from republic to principate. Thus it is significant that elegy emerges at a moment of "postwar release" concurrent with Augustus's attempts at cultural hegemony. Fear's examination of Propertius's apparent disavowal of elegiac waywardness in his later poems points up the complexities in elegy's negotiation of the dominant Roman ideologies and the impossibility for either poet or *princeps* to efface resistance and difference.

Ronnie Ancona's essay, based on an intertextual reading of Catullus 61 and Horace *Odes* 2.8, examines male anxiety about gender identity and masculine responsibility, as well as the issue of liminality, by specifically addressing the role of marriage as an institution for social control of the erotic. The social and historical context of both poems is that of a culture anxious about channeling male desire in appropriate directions. She argues that Horace's poem is meant to be a reading of Catullus's marriage poem that explodes the potentially disruptive vision of marriage Catullus's poem already contains. Horace pushes to the extreme the vision of male desire out of control by replacing the bride with a *publica cura* who keeps men from their expected roles. The ode reveals both awe and fear of a female erotic power that might disrupt social expectations for the male.

Ellen Greene's essay on Propertius 2.1 examines the fluctuation between elegy and epic in the poem and the attendant gender dissonance arising from that fluctuation. Greene argues that 2.1 dramatizes the ways in which the Propertian *amator* presents himself in the conventional manner of elegy (i.e., as the passive, soft, slave of love) alongside a more typically heroic masculine version as seen through the incorporation of epic models. The vacillation of the poet-lover between epic and elegiac discourses subverts the polarity of those discourses. More specifically, the Propertian narrator in 2.1 circumvents the putative opposition between epic and elegiac poetry by linking *amor* to images of death and glory, thus suggesting a heroic role for the traditionally disempowered elegist. Greene concludes that the Propertian lover promulgates contradictory images of masculine behavior, thus undermining the possibility of identifying him with either defiance of or adherence to traditional Roman male models.

In his essay, "Impossible Lesbians in Ovid's *Metamorphoses*," Kirk Ormand discusses the story of Iphis and Ianthe, arguing that Ovid's seeming portrayal of female same-sex passion is actually a story of the impossibility of imagining a relationship in which neither lover can take on the expected, dominant, male role. Utilizing current scholarship on homosexuality in ancient Rome, Ormand shows that the centrality for the Romans of the concepts of active and passive behavior in the realm of the erotic makes the mutuality of Iphis and Ianthe unthinkable. Rather than condemning homosexuality per se, Ovid demonstrates the necessity, both linguistically and culturally, for someone in an amatory relationship to act like a man, that is, to play the active part. Ormand argues that Ovid's story is not about female homosexuality, but is, rather, an attempt to envision a love relationship "unmarked by hierarchy and difference." Thus what purports to be a woman's story turns out to be an exploration of what it means to be a male in Rome—not in terms of biological sex but in terms of the semiotics of gender difference in Augustan culture.

The essays in the second section, The Gaze, reflect upon how expectations about male desire are involved in the dynamics of the gaze. Responding in a variety of ways to recent gaze theory, these essays show that the erotic gaze, so integral to the representation of desire in Latin love poetry, is used both as a way for the male lover-narrator to assert his dominance over the female beloved and to explore how the positions of subject and object of desire constantly shift.

Elizabeth Sutherland's essay on Horace *Carmina* 2.5 uses film theory and reader response criticism to argue that Horace associates vision with the male lover's desire for an objectified female other. She teases out the ways in which the speaker of the poem makes (or attempts to make) his audiences complicit in his project of desire. Yet the figure of Gyges, as she argues, by embodying both object and subject of desire as well as by being male (albeit a feminized male), complicates any neat identification of the male with the power of the gaze. Her arguments recall Fear's resistance to identifying elegy as simply reinforcing or challenging Roman expectations of masculine behavior.

Christopher Brunelle's discussion of "ugly sex" in Ovid's *Remedia Amoris* explores the use of satire within elegy to make abhorrent the vision of the female body. Brunelle argues that Ovid, like the Roman satirists, shows how the description of women's bodies as disgustingly moist and malodorous both attracts and repels the male spectator. Thus Ovid emphasizes the reader's complicity in producing misogynistic responses to the female object of male vision. Ovid makes the reader look at things that are meant to disgust, while also presenting him or her with the challenge of imagining what is too disgusting to be represented. Brunelle argues that the *Remedia*'s presentation of the female body is certainly misogynist, but the fact that Ovid's narrator demands the reader's response before giving his own reveals Ovid's strategy of exposing the misogyny of both his male audience and his narrator. In that sense, Brunelle suggests, Ovid may be considered a social critic in the tradition of the Roman satirists.

While Sutherland's and Brunelle's essays see the gaze as primarily an instrument of male control, the next four essays in this section argue that the male gaze cannot be considered a static or entirely stable mechanism of power and that the scene of spectatorship represented in amatory texts reveals a reversibility of gender roles in which women do not necessarily submit to the objectifying gaze of their male lovers. Patricia Salzman-Mitchell discusses the way that the gaze shapes narrative pacing in Ovid's *Metamorphoses* and argues that, while the male gaze stops the narrative and fixes the object with its power, the object of the gaze also exerts power over the bearer of the gaze. While narrative action may be seen as more masculine and description as more feminine, Salzman-Mitchell suggests that the power of the image of the female can induce stupefaction in the male viewer, thus constituting a disruption of traditional gender dynamics. Despite what Salzman-Mitchell would regard as the male author's ultimate control over the female in the *Metamorphoses*, the poem contains feminine moments that have the power to question that control.

Victoria Rimell explores the artistic and erotic implications of the use of female cosmetics in Ovid's *Medicamina*. Working her own magic on Ovid's didactic instructions, Rimell shows how the image of the mirror breaks down simple notions of self and other and how what initially appears to be a female activity (using makeup) ends up revealed as an activity that resembles artistic production and as the new male activity of imperialist *cultus* or cultivation. Thus the made-up *puella*, like the elegiac poet, bedazzles her audience with a series of masks that are removed and reapplied. Yet Rimell points out that the *Medicamina* also performs an "anti-seduction" by revealing to us what women really look like in the mirror. Women's Medusa-like qualities thus threaten to turn the tables on male spectatorship. But by showing women their reflections in the mirror, the Ovidian narrator robs women of their stupefying gazes. Rimell concludes that, although the untamed, Medusan woman of the *Medicamina* turns into the object of the male artist's gaze, Ovid's male audience is also subject to the dangerous glare of the mirror. Or, in other words, the made-up girl rivals men in the pursuit of *cultus*; Rimell argues that the gazes of men and women meet in the mirror, thus creating a strange symmetry between the sexes.

Using comparative material from the visual arts, Hérica Valladares extends Archibald Allen's influential discussion of *fides* as both "sincerity" and "persuasiveness" to Propertius 1.3, examining the manipulation of recognized literary and visual conventions. She argues that the mythological paintings the poem suggests, which focus on enthrallment rather than possession, help create a space for identification with different amatory roles across traditional gender lines. For Valladares, the cause of enchantment exerts power over the holder of the gaze, thus allowing for a destabilization of the expected power and gender relations. More specifically, Valladares argues that Propertius's gaze upon the sleeping Cynthia in 1.3 shifts power from the male subject to the female object of desire, since the Propertian narrator identifies himself with Argus, who can only watch, but not possess, the female beloved. In addition, Valladares contends that Propertius's reference at the end of the poem to Cynthia's lyre playing suggests that the male poet-lover may function as *materia* for *her* imagination.

Kerill O'Neill, using recent scholarly work on the gaze and the novel, sees Cynthia's perception of the lover's gaze in Propertius as containing a transformative power. Utilizing views of the gaze that locate the origin of the gaze in the object viewed rather than with the viewer, O'Neill examines the power gained by intercepting the lover's gaze. He argues that Cynthia's recognition that she is the object of the lover's gaze empowers her to control the object of the lover's desire. For O'Neill, the female object gains power by looking back. Like Rimell, O'Neill points out how the *puella*'s Gorgon-like quality has an emasculating effect on the male lover that renders him incapable of maintaining mastery through his phallic gaze. Even though Cynthia can assume the dominant position and thus disrupt the traditional gender hierarchy, the poet-lover takes pleasure in portraying her as both spectator and spectacle. As O'Neill implies, the struggle between lover and mistress for control of the gaze lies at the heart of Roman elegy.

The third section of this volume, Female Subjectivity and Silence, extends our discussion of the inherent ambiguities and fluctuations of gender identity to an area in which the female self or voice functions to disrupt the gender expectations within amatory texts. In her essay on Ovid's *Ars Amatoria*, Phebe Lowell Bowditch examines the ways in which "woman," as both an object of seduction and *materia* for the poet's verse, undermines and subverts the male discourse of the *praeceptor* through the "runaway" digressions that interrupt the narrative and offer resistance to the putative "objectivity" of didactic verse. Specifically, Bowditch shows how the hermeneutic uncertainties in the Procris and Cephalus digression mark a place where female subjectivity can be found in the figure of Procris who, as an active interpreter of signs, plays a role typically associated with "male" subjectivity. Of course, Procris's reading (or, rather, misreading) tragically destroys her. As Bowditch argues, Ovid's digressions in the *Ars* undermine the poem's discursive systems, suggesting that the feminine in Ovid's text eludes complete control by masculine discourse.

Similarly, in her essay on Propertius's Tarpeia poem, Tara Welch argues that, while Propertius allows Tarpeia to voice dissent in her attempt to join the erotic with the demands of the state, she is ultimately silenced, her subjectivity poetically circumscribed by the voice of the male narrator. Welch shows that Tarpeia, while having a voice, is only allowed to speak within the liminal spaces of the city. Welch's analysis maps Propertius's poem onto the space of the city and shows how female subjectivity, both literally and figuratively, cannot find a "place" within the city of Rome.

Finally, Efrossini Spentzou compares Ovid's exilic *Tristia*, where the male narrator functions as the *exclusus amator* before the door of Rome and Augustus, with the letters of the exiled heroines of his *Heroides*. After a discussion of speech as a signal of presence and writing as inherently uncontrollable, Spentzou argues that Ovid and his letter-writing heroines have areas of difference and commonality. Both turn to writing, but for the male, once accustomed to speech and a physical presence in Rome, the turn shows a kind of powerlessness, while for the heroines, it signals a hopeful move out of the silence of their traditional "official" myths. Ovid comes to exile writing having lost his voice; they come to it to find a voice. Yet when Ovid uses silence and reticence to keep secret those things that might prove harmful to him or his friends, the seeming divide between controlling male speech and female, powerless silence breaks down. Subversive silence is learned from heroines.

Notes

1. The publication of special issues of *Classical World* (1999) and *Arethusa* (2000) on Roman elegy not only attests to the continued interest of scholars in the genre but also reflects the current engagement of scholars with feminist approaches to Latin love poetry. In addition, the recent collections *Roman Sexualities* and *The Roman Gaze* make important contributions to the wider study of women, gender, and sexuality in Roman culture. See also Skinner 1993, Wyke 1987b, 1989a, 1994b, 2002, Keith 1994, Gamel 1998, James 1998, and Greene 1999.

2. See, especially, Ancona 1994, Janan 1994, and Miller 1994.

3. For different versions of this view, see Wyke 1987b, Ancona 1989, Sharrock 1991, Gold 1993, Greene 1998, and Sutherland 2003.

4. See, especially, Janan 1994 and 2001. James 2003 implicitly acknowledges the potential for Roman female power by reading elegy from the perspective of the *docta puella* ("learned mistress").

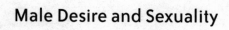

I Male Desire and Sexuality

1 Propertian Closure

The Elegiac Inscription of the Liminal Male and Ideological Contestation in Augustan Rome

Trevor Fear

I'll so offend to make offence a skill,
Redeeming time when men think least I will.
—*Henry the Fourth, Part One*, act 1, scene 2

Much scholarly energy focuses on Roman elegy's representation of its leading female figures.[1] Somewhat less attention is paid to the inscription and representation of the leading male figures of elegy, the narrators who bear the poets' own names.

In this essay, I want to examine the representation of the elegiac narrator. In particular, I wish to examine how this figure is characterized as a male on the threshold of adulthood and to argue that such masculine liminality is an essential ingredient of elegy. To this end, I consider a variety of sources dealing with issues of youthful excess and maturation and suggest how this builds up a picture of a permissible temporal space of youthful aberration for the elite Roman male that precedes adult responsibility. I then proceed to an examination of elegiac discourse and the behavior of the elegiac narrator in light of this Roman cultural concept. Having formulated a general impression of elegiac ideology, I attempt to situate the ideological ramifications of elegy's liminal narrative more closely in its socio-historical context.

I then shift focus onto the conclusion of Propertius's Book 3 and consider how this particular act of elegiac closure ties in with the cultural concept of the ludic space of liminal male adulthood. Finally, I consider how the end of Propertius Book 3 might affect our understanding of the idiosyncrasies of the elegiac vision and the extent to which we are bound to process elegiac narrative along set lines.

13

The Carnival of Youth

In chapter 26 of his life of Nero, Suetonius describes some of the nocturnal antics of the youthful emperor: wandering through Rome's taverns in disguise, assaulting in the streets those returning from dinner, stabbing those who resisted and dropping their bodies in the sewers, and breaking into shops and proceeding to auction off the stolen goods from the palace. Suetonius prefaces his narrative of Nero's shoplifting habits and homicidal tendencies by explaining that, in others, such a veritable cocktail of vices could be simply attributed to "youthful misdirection" (*iuvenalis error*), but, unfortunately, in the case of Nero it was an indication not of juvenile delinquency but of his true nature.[2]

Nero is thus represented by Suetonius as a type of *enfant terrible*, a male member of the elite who never outgrew youthful self-indulgence. It is only Nero's innate deformed character and his inability to mature in an acceptable fashion that stops his behavior from being condoned as nothing more than excusable youthful high jinks. Nero is a playful, if not entirely innocent, youthful prankster who never grows up.[3]

Nero, of course, is a rather egregious and idiosyncratic example of youthful excess. Another example, nearer in time to the Augustan era, contains an erotic element that brings us a little closer to the elegiac world. Cicero, in his defense speech for Marcus Caelius Rufus in 56 B.C.E., spends a great deal of time dwelling on issues of youthful elite male behavior. Although at one stage in his speech, the orator states that he has no intention of constructing a plea based on a consideration of Caelius's age (Caelius was nearly twenty-six at the time of the trial and charged with various counts of public violence, murder, and attempted murder), he does, nevertheless, proceed to identify the grounds for such a defensive strategy by referring to a *vacatio adulescentiae* ("youth's holiday") and the *perfugia aetatis* ("excuses of age"). The orator argues that such notions would form a legitimate defense of his client (should he choose to use them) as they are *concessa omnibus iura* ("rights conceded to all").

Needless to say, in the time-honored manner of ancient forensic practice, Cicero does proceed to do what he has denied having any interest in doing; he embarks on the path of misdirecting the jury by aiming to recuperate his client precisely on the basis of his age, while also indulging in a vicious character assassination of Clodia Metelli. Thus this particular Ciceronian plea depends in large part on constructing a hybrid: impressionable youth crossed with a capricious older woman.

Caelius had simply been going through a period of youthful acting out under the malignant erotic influence of Clodia.

As he develops his argument, the orator asserts that a certain degree of indulgence is the due of youth: "detur aliquid aetati; sit adulescentia liberior; non omnia voluptatibus denegentur" ("Let some allowance be given to age; let youth be a little freer; let not pleasure be denied entirely," *pro Caelio* 42). He proceeds, perhaps more daringly, to argue that adolescent aberrations could almost be seen as prerequisites to later civic distinction. Thus he argues (*pro Caelio* 43) that both in the present and past, "famous and distinguished men" ("summi homines et clarissimi cives") displayed their "great capabilities" (*eximiae virtutes*) only after "adolescent desire fizzled out" (*cum adulescentiae cupiditates defervissent*) and they were "mature" (*firmata iam aetate*).

In this manner, Cicero sets out a case for what he presents as a natural process of maturation whereby dalliance in the ephemera of adolescent desire should serve only as a prelude to civic integration and responsibility. Preoccupation with the *ludus aetatis* ("game of youth") and *inanes adulescentiae cupiditates* ("frivolous adolescent desires") should be brief; a young man should sate himself, turn away in disgust, and get on with proper business: "cura rei domesticae, rei forensis reique publicae" ("the care of domestic, legal, and state affairs," *pro Caelio* 42).

To bolster his point, the orator argues (*pro Caelio* 44) that, in Caelius's case, erotic indulgences (*amores, deliciae*, "love affairs," "flirtations") were never too much of a factor in the first place: for those with "resolve" (*firmiore animo*), they are not "troublesome" (*molestae*) but "wither early and quickly" (*mature et celeriter deflorescunt*).

Caelius is thus presented by Cicero as a positive developmental paradigm: a youthful elite male whose capacity for self-indulgence and antisocial behavior "withered early and quickly" and served only as the proper basis for adult maturity. Numbered among what should be the passing indulgences of youth, *inanes adulescentiae cupiditates* are precisely the sort of erotic dalliances (*amores, deliciae*) that figure as central preoccupations in elegiac poetry.

In a passage in Seneca's *Controversiae*, there is a reference to a permissible period of indulgence and misdirection for elite youth dubbed the *tirocinium adulescentiae*, "the apprenticeship of youth," that would seem to tie in with Suetonius's *iuvenalis error* and Cicero's *vacatio adulescentiae*. In the Senecan passage, a Roman *iuvenis* ("young man") pleads that his *luxuria* ("wantonness") is simply an allowable and transitory symptom of his youth: "Concessis aetati iocis utor et iuvenali lege defungor; id facio quod pater meus fecit cum iuvenis esset. Negabit? Bona ego aetate coepi; simul primum hoc tirocinium adulescentiae quasi deb-itum ac sollemne persolvero, revertar ad bonos mores" ("I am taking ad-vantage of the fun allowed to youth and employing the law of the young; I am doing that which my father did when he was young. Will he deny it? 'I began at a good age; as soon as I have got through this necessary and customary apprenticeship of youth, I shall return to good ways,'" *Controversiae* 2.6.11). The references here to *ioca aetatis* ("youthful pranks") and a *lex iuvenalis* ("the law of the young"), as well as to the *tirocinium adulescentiae*, all point to an approved temporal space of youth-ful carnival: a sort of societal safety valve for the liminal adult. This ap-pears to be generally symptomatic of a professed tolerance in Roman so-ciety for youthful aberration on the part of elite males. However, it should also be noted that, as the speaker makes clear, this period of life is viewed as an excess that leads to conformity, responsibility, and proper behavior, *boni mores* (just as Cicero argues is the case with Caelius).

The connection between this youthful period of life and erotic ini-tiation and amorous indulgence is made clear when Cicero manages to reduce virtually the entire case against Caelius to a matter of his rela-tionship with Clodia Metelli. This is also evident in Persius *Satires* 5. In this poem, the ceremonies that indicate the end of boyhood and the onset of puberty, the assumption of the *toga virilis* and the dedication of the *bulla* (*bulla donata*), are swiftly followed by a now permissible visit to the "red-light" district of the Subura.[4] In a similar fashion, Martial suggests handing over a male sexual novice to an instructress in the Subura (78.11–12):

> ergo Suburanae tironem trade magistrae.
>   illa virum faciet; non bene virgo docet.

> Therefore hand over the recruit to an instructress of the Subura.
>   She will make him a man; a virgin doesn't instruct so well.

The characterization in Persius of this time of life as an *iter am-biguum* ("uncertain journey") and of the narrator as being led by an *error vitae nescius* ("a mistake based on ignorance of life") serve to define this as a period of youthful experimentation that gropes forward to the per-ilous acquisition of the experience that will serve as the foundation for future maturity.

The *tirocinium adulescentiae*, then, and the *vacatio adulescentiae* sug-gest that the Romans would expect a period of anti-social and self-indulgent behavior on the part of a liminal adult elite male to precede mature adult status. Such a period of youthful acting out could be generally tolerated, seen as normal, and even rhetorically promoted by an orator like Cicero to seem almost a good and necessary foundation for civic integration. This phase of life also coincided with an induction into sexuality, giving the indulgences of this period a distinctively erotic bent.

Situating the Elegiac Narrator

Having set out the general framework of Roman attitudes to youthful male elite behavior, I want to consider now how the literary genre of Augustan elegy might relate to this notion of the *tirocinium adulescentiae*. First of all, mainstream Roman elegy[5] constructs a narrator who can be placed within the time frame understood in Cicero's *vacatio adulescentiae* or Seneca's *tirocinium adulescentiae*. Reference to his own youth on the part of the narrator is a commonplace in Roman elegy and, in the discourse's more self-reflexive and professedly autobiographical moments, a time frame for elegiac composition is also set out that places the author's literary endeavors specifically within the transition from boy to man.

In Propertius 4.1B, Horus relates a biography of the narrator. It locates the narrator's first attempt at poetic composition (analogous to his elegiac poetry) at the moment of the removal of the *bulla* and the assumption of the *toga virilis*, the ceremonies that marked a boy's transition to manhood (Propertius 4.1B.131–34):[6]

> mox ubi bulla rudi dimissast aurea collo,
> > matris et ante deos libera sumpta toga,
> tum tibi pauca suo de carmine dictat Apollo,
> > et vetat insano verba tonare foro.

> Presently, when the golden locket was removed from your inexperienced neck and the toga of a man[7] had been donned before your mother's gods, then Apollo dictated to you a few words from his own poetic oeuvre and forbad you to thunder out words in the mad forum.

Similarly, in the biography that Ovid presents for himself in *Tristia* 4.10, the initial recitation by the poet of his work is dated to soon after the ritual of the *depositio barbae:* "barba resecta mihi bisve semelve fuit" ("when my beard had been cut once or twice," 4.10.58).[8] The events referred to in these poems place the professed inception of elegiac composition during precisely the youthful phase of life that seems to underlie the concept of the *tirocinium adulescentiae*.

The elegiac narrator also appears to be an elite member of Roman society.[9] Ovid's narrator, for instance, stresses that he is an *eques* of entrenched social pedigree, not an upstart social climber (*Amores* 3.15.5–6):[10]

> siquid id est, usque a proavis vetus ordinis heres,
> non modo militiae turbine factus eques.

> If it counts for anything, the ancient heir of a rank stretching back to distant ancestors, not an *eques* fashioned just now in the whirl of war.

No explicit mention of status is made in Propertius and Tibullus, but there are references in the works of both authors (Tibullus 1.1.19–20, Propertius 4.1.127–30) to a diminution of inherited material resources. These references may indicate a narrator who should be understood as an elite member of Roman society (that is to say, an equestrian or from the Italian gentry) impoverished by unnamed circumstances.[11] Such professed poverty, of course, also serves a rhetorical function within the discourse of elegy as the basis for the narrator's inability to provide material rather than poetic benefits for his *puella* ("girl, young woman").[12]

The combination of youth, elite status, and erotic initiation as part of the elegiac economy reveals a strong parallel between the narrative of elegy and the scene in Persius *Satires* 5 where the narrator and his *blandi comites* ("wheedling companions") venture for the first time into the Subura. Elegy's earlier exploration of this theme is evident in Propertius 4.7 with the recollection the poet puts into the mouth of Cynthia (Propertius 4.7.15–16):

> iamne tibi exciderunt vigilacis furta Suburae
> et mea nocturnis trita fenestra dolis?

> Have our erotic antics in the sleepless Subura and my windowsill worn down by stealth in the night so soon slipped from your memory?

The reappearance of Cynthia in Book 4 has been read as a strategy of demystification, where the potential realities behind the elegiac text are allowed to peep through, and the words of the dead elegiac *domina* ("mistress") read as the metafictional revenge of a misrepresented character from beyond the literary grave (though one should bear in mind that it is the poet who exhumes her).[13] From this perspective, the affair of Propertius and Cynthia in the text could be viewed retrospectively as a shadowy and allusive dramatization of the sexual initiation of a Roman elite male who casts aside his *bulla* and heads for Rome's red-light district.

Elegiac Disaffection

The presentation of the elegiac narrator as a youthful elite male is allied to a self-portrait of social alienation and erotic motivation. He is staged as a young man suffering from, and complaining profusely about, a compulsion that leads him to debase himself before a female figure.[14] This seemingly masochistic and unfulfilling lifestyle becomes a kind of elegiac creed or ideology that, in its own sense of self-importance, rejects the possibilities of civic integration and the norms of Roman society.[15]

I would like to stress, however, how the aberrant nature of elegiac ideology is tied to the specific representation of the narrator as a youthful Roman elite male. The speaker in elegy raises to almost a matter of principle his resistance to maturing in a timely fashion and becoming a productive member of Roman society. Elegy is thus presented as the tale of a youthful male narrator on the liminal threshold of adulthood who turns his back on the two traditional routes to a productive Roman adulthood (*tirocinium militiae* and *tirocinium fori:* "military apprenticeship" and "forensic apprenticeship") and, instead, plunges with a vengeance into the youthful wildness of the *tirocinium adulescentiae*, while also seeing it as a permanent rather than temporary way of life. Note also that the composition of this narrative, in itself, also signifies such youthful indulgence (*amores* represent frivolous poetry as well as erotic indulgence).

Both the Ovidian and the Propertian narrators expressly turn their backs on forensic oratory (and civic life in general) and, instead, indulge in elegiac careers that both incarnate and represent youthful dissonance. Hence Apollo simultaneously inspires the Propertian narrator with poetry and debars him from the forum (4.1B.133–34, quoted above). In similar fashion, in *Amores* 1.15 the narrator rejects the assessment of his poetry as "the product of an idle intellect" (an *opus ingenii inertis*) and, instead, devalues the traditional activities of young manhood (*strenua aetas*, "the vigorous time of life"): *praemia militiae pulverulenta*, "dusty military honors" and *verbosae leges*, "wordy laws." Forensic activity, from the narrator's perspective, is reduced to an act of verbal prostitution before a thankless audience. One should note in these instances how an apparent rejection of traditional values is tied to the composition of elegy itself.

The normal career paths for an elite Roman male are rejected and vilified. Instead, the narrator pursues an elegiac lifestyle that, he declares, forces him to remain static in an erotically fixated state. Hence in Propertius 1.6, the narrator presents his erotic affair with Cynthia as preventing him from accompanying Tullus to Asia and so from making a timely transition into manhood and civic service. In this manner, the poet develops a sharp contrast between himself and Tullus. The latter attempts to live up to and surpass his family's tradition of public service, his *cura* ("concern") is for the state (*armata patria*, "fatherland under arms") and not a *domina*; he has not wasted time in love: "tua non aetas umquam cessavit amori" ("Your youth has never dallied in love," 1.6.21). The former, however, conceives of *militia* ("military service") differently, he is not a soldier dependent on weapons, nor is he concerned with *laus* ("praise," "reputation"): "non ego sum laudi, non natus idoneus armis" ("I am not concerned with reputation, nor was born suited to military service," 1.6.29), he will die for love, not Rome.

In this manner, elegy engages in a strategy of recuperation and appropriation that attempts to enhance the value of its own activities. The elegist attempts to trope elegiac *inertia* ("idleness") and *otium* ("leisure") as an alternate and more demanding form of *negotium* ("business," "affairs").[16] This strategy is most elaborately expressed in *Amores* 1.9, where the narrator expounds in detail the parallels between traditional *militia* and the *militia amoris* ("the military service of love"). This analysis leads, with a degree of seeming inevitability, to the conclusion that the charges of *desidia* ("inactivity") that are leveled against the lover are baseless. Love is found to be a demanding activity: *ingenii est experientis amor* ("Love is the province of an enterprising character," 1.9.32). The elegiac lifestyle is paradoxically troped as providing the *duritia* ("hardness," "rigor") that it is generally supposed to lack: a soul, *segnis . . . in otia natus*, "slothful and born for leisure" (1.9.41), softened by the couch and the shade (1.9.42), has been whipped into shape by a strenuous *formosae cura puellae*, "concern for a beautiful girl" (1.9.43). In other words, an elegiac lifestyle is itself the solution to its own problematic *mollitia* ("softness") and *inertia*: "qui nolet fieri desidiosus, amet!" ("Let him who doesn't wish to be idle, love!" 1.9.46).

However, while there appears to be proud defiance in this stance of social deviance, there also appears to be an element of helpless coercion (the narrator is a pawn in the grip of an irresistible compulsion: *amor* in the form of the *puella*) and an acknowledgment of the price to be paid for such indulgence. Hence all the narrators point to the social stigma that attends upon an elegiac lifestyle. The Propertian narrator describes himself as the *caput nequitiae*, "fount of worthlessness" (2.24.2), and insists that he is on display as an object of *infamia* ("ill repute") throughout the city: "per totam infamis traducerer urbem" ("I am on display throughout the city as an object of ill repute," 2.24.7); the Tibullan narrator similarly begs Marathus in poem 1.4 to allow him not to become a *turpis fabula*, "a shameful source of gossip." The first poem of Sulpicia[17] likewise revolves around the potential impropriety of revealing an erotic attachment and the narrator's desire both to do so and her weariness with the proprieties of social reputation: "sed peccasse iuvat, vultus componere famae / taedet" ("Having sinned gives me pleasure, and donning a mask for the sake of rumor is irksome," 1.9–10).

The Ovidian narrator, not surprisingly, displays the most ebullient embrace of such stigma. He cheerfully proclaims himself to be the bard of his own depravity at the opening of *Amores* Book 2: "ille ego nequitiae Naso poeta meae" ("I am that Naso, poet of my own depravity," 2.1.2). He professes in *Amores* 2.17 indifference to questions of propriety, though not to those of erotic servitude; hence if it is shameful (*turpis*) "to be a slave to a woman" (*servire puellae*), he stands readily condemned (2.17.1–2) and will likewise be happy to be judged *infamis* provided he is erotically roasted a little more mildly (2.17.3).

At the beginning of the final book of the *Amores*, the narrator, caught in the middle of an awkward literary threesome, is accosted by the personification of Tragedy and confronted with the consequences of his writing habits and lifestyle. Tragoedia comments on the manner in which the *nequitia* ("depravity") of the narrator is discussed at drunken dinner parties and crossroads, how he is shamefully pointed out as he goes on his way, and how he is a feature of gossip over the whole city: "fabula . . . tota iactaris in urbe" ("You are a theme of gossip the whole city over," 3.1.21), all apparently with no sense of shame on his part, *praeterito . . . pudore*, "with shame cast aside" (3.1.22).[18]

The elegiac narrator's sense of worth appears, to some extent, to be based on society's sense of his or her worthlessness. The speaker is validated by precisely the behavior that society in general deems to be inappropriate and demeaning. The violation of traditional decorum is, for the narrator, a defining and positive characteristic of his lifestyle.

The narrator also professes to being beyond redemption and to seeing his behavior not as a passing fad but as a lasting choice. Hence no temporal boundary or limit can be set on irrational excess (Propertius 2.15.29–30):

> errat, qui finem vesani quaerit amoris:
>   verus amor nullum novit habere modum.

> He is mistaken, who seeks to impose a limit on mad passion: true love doesn't know how to have any boundary.

Hence the Tibullan narrator tells Delia that they should be an *exemplum amoris* ("a paradigm of love") when they are both white haired (1.6. 85–86). This notion again finds its culmination in its Ovidian treatment. Here the narrator projects a form of elegiac closure through sex, a fitting climax to his career (*Amores* 2.10.35–38):

> at mihi contingat Veneris languescere motu,
>> cum moriar, medium solvar et inter opus;
>
> atque aliquis nostro lacrimans in funere dicat:
>> "conveniens vitae mors fuit ista tuae!"

> But may my fate be to grow slack in the very act of love when I die, to be loosed mid act; and someone might say, weeping at my funeral: "That was a death in keeping with your lifestyle!"

The elegiac life will consume its follower in his prime or is envisioned as extending forward in time without any essential change in its preoccupations: an apparent manifesto of youthful difference, defiance, and morbid self-preoccupation.

Unlike the passages from Seneca's *Controversiae* and Cicero's *pro Caelio* on the need for a limit to youthful transgression and a timely progression to adult maturity, the elegiac narrator is presented as seeing no possibility of change. He is the way nature intended him (Propertius 2.22A.17–18):

> uni cuique dedit vitium natura creato:
>> mi fortuna aliquid semper amare dedit.

> Nature has given a vice to everyone at birth: fortune allotted to me the fault of always being in love.

The elegiac narrator is not portrayed, like Cicero's Caelius, as going through a temporary phase on the way to redemption and integration, but rather, like Suetonius's Nero, as a lost cause with an inherently flawed character.

Flawed Manhood

It is clear that the behavior of the elegiac narrator constitutes a failure in terms of normative Roman masculinity. If Roman masculinity can be conceived of as fundamentally a matter of control over oneself and others, then the elegiac narrator falls far short of this cultural ideal (see Williams 1999.132ff.). The period of youth and early manhood (corresponding to the *tirocinium adulescentiae* and the dramatic setting of ele-

giac narrative) was "a period of transition" when normative male adulthood had to be established (Richlin 1993.534). Thus all Roman youths
were, in a sense, effeminate, positioned in a kind of gender limbo sand-
wiched between the womanly *mollitia* that characterized pre-pubescence
and pubescence and the *duritia* of achieved adult manhood. The failure
to move successfully from the one to the other, to be able to temper oneself, was to risk being labeled effeminate.

The elegiac narrator runs the risk of being taken as an effeminate
male. Thus Maria Wyke comes to the following conclusion concerning
the sexual identity of the "narrating ego" of Propertian elegy:

> In the genre of Propertian love elegy, however, the narrating ego is consti-
> tuted as an effeminate voice. Paradoxically, it is sexual impotence rather than
> potency that marks the figure of the male lover of elegy, for he is represented
> as languishing almost perpetually outside his beloved's door. He submits,
> not imposes, is weaponless rather than armed, soft not hard, and feminine
> not masculine. Even the elegiac couplet itself can be inscribed with the con-
> dition of sexual impotence, as when the Ovidian lover/poet opens his first
> book in such a way as to associate that verse form with the erection and de-
> tumescence of the penis.[19]

Hence the notion of *mollitia* encompasses both the essence of elegy's narrator and the genre of elegy itself; form and content are symbiotically entwined.[20] After all, elegiac deviance lies not only in the projected immaturity of the narrator but also in the poetic immaturity of the elegist.[21]

The elegiac narrator's *mollitia*, which signals his effeminate character, is variously manifested. It can be seen as a natural attribute of his liminal adult status, it is generally apparent in his lack of control over himself and others, and, more specifically, it is apparent in his pursuit of
women (including, it seems, married ones—demonstrating a type of sexual *incontinentia*, "lack of control"), in his inability to control a woman,
and in his toleration of her sexual activities with other men.

In this manner, the elegiac narrator is assimilated to socio-sexual categories demonized in Roman culture: he is represented as akin to the
stereotypical figure of the *cultus adulter* ("refined adulterer"—similar, as
Holt Parker notes, to our "ladies' man").[22] In addition, the acceptance of
both a subordinate position in a sexual relationship and of the *domina*'s
alleged infidelities place the narrator in a role akin to that of a *pathicus*.[23]
On a more general level, as noted above, the narrator is portrayed as dis-
playing the signs of *mollitia* and hence characterized as effeminate and a
kind of *cinaedus*.[24]

Contextualizing Elegiac Discourse

Cultural products are inevitably entwined with their socio-historical contexts.[25] If elegy, therefore, is a youthful discourse of disaffection, we must try to situate its particularity in Augustan Rome. Why did this specific literary genre flourish at this precise moment, and how did elegy manage to "say the right things in the right way at the right time"?[26] These are, of course, big questions, and it is doubtful that even a radical contextualization will ever fully explicate the intricacy of the connection between a literary form and its context, but that is no excuse not to at least explore the issue.[27]

On one level, elegy can be related to a general increase in literary activity and the raising of its public status in Augustan Rome. The establishment of the *pax Augusta* and the principate led to an increase in, and a re-evaluation of the value of, elite *otium*.[28] In this context, literary production can be viewed as both a symptom of the establishment of the principate and a validation of its capacity to produce *pax et quies* ("peace and quiet"). Hence the space of *otium* became proportionately more important and developed as an alternate arena for aristocratic display and distinction and, simultaneously, a means of social advancement.[29] One does not have to take Horace's comments on an Augustan *scribendi studium* ("writing craze") at face value (*Epistles* 2.1.108–10), but one might see in such a comment an attempt to outline an equation between stability and prosperity and literary production. In this cultural context, one can view the flourishing of literary patronage and literary production as a means of both renegotiating the boundaries between *otium* and *negotium* and also, perhaps, of consciously (or unconsciously) promoting and internalizing an emergent ideological model of a *Roma otiosa* ("Rome at leisure").

If such a historical situation might account for the general flowering of literary activity in the Augustan period, there are also ways of seeing elegiac narrative as particularly suited to this moment. On this level, elegiac discourse might be seen as a response to a general concern in Roman culture that is particularly intense in the early Augustan period: the ramifications of victory and its aftermath. What was an appropriate response to the cessation of civil wars and Augustan victory? Craig Williams, in his discussion of Maecenas and effeminacy, notes the attempts of the author of the *Elegiae in Maecenatem* to excuse Maecenas's lifestyle with the general argument "that there is a time and place for everything and that among the perquisites of victory one may include a certain relaxed leisure" (1999.158 and note 133). Williams quotes the following passages from the *Elegiae* (1.93–94, 49–50):

> sic est: victor amet, victor potiatur in umbra,
> 　　victor odorata dormiat inque rosa;

> This is how things are: let the victor make love, let the victor drink in the shade, let the victor sleep among sweet-smelling roses.

> pax erat: haec illos laxarunt otia cultus:
> 　　omnia victores Marte sedente decent.

> There was peace, these leisurely pursuits have loosened those cares: all things are befitting to the victors when war has subsided.

The theme is familiar from its famous incarnation in Horace *Carmina* 1.37: *nunc est bibendum*, "Now is the time to drink."

However, there is a flip side to such indulgence, and Williams rightly points out the contrasts with such passages as Sallust *Catiline* 10, where victory and the resulting leisure are seen as precipitating moral decline.[30] Where does the well-earned respite and relaxation of the victor end and the moral torpor of self-indulgence begin? This was surely an Augustan conundrum. Hence elegy as a literary form that idiosyncratically celebrated Augustan *pax et otium* in a narrative of erotic self-indulgence can be viewed as a manifestation of the tensions inherent in the Augustan settlement. For part of the problem facing the *princeps* was how a Rome at carnival in the wake of the release from civil war "could be harnessed to the legitimation of a programme of social conservatism."[31]

One can also see that aspects of elegiac discourse are entwined with specific themes and actions in the emergent political and cultural hegemony of Augustanism. For instance, the social policy of the *princeps* and his promotion of marriage and procreation among Rome's social elite is a contemporary reality against which elegiac behavior can be measured.

The liminal aspect of masculinity that is a part of elegiac discourse might also be related to an apparent Augustan concern to educate and integrate the youth of Rome's elite (to which the elegiac narrators appear to belong) into the ideological paradigms of the emerging principate. For instance, Zvi Yavetz argues that if the *Res Gestae* had a dedication it would have been *pro iuventute* ("for the youth"), as this work was intended by Augustus to promote an image that could usefully be emulated by the youth of the elite.[32]

Augustus also took pains to integrate the traditional ceremony of the

Roman passage into manhood into his refurbishing of Rome's civic space. Hence with the dedication of the new Augustan forum and Augustus's assumption of the title *pater patriae* ("father of the fatherland") in 2 B.C.E., the centerpiece temple of Mars Ultor (Mars the Avenger) was designated as the place where, in the future, Roman youths would assume the *toga virilis*.[33] Augustus's newfound paternal standing, in combination with the temple's integration into the military life of the principate, made this an obvious symbolic spot for the new *iuvenes* to take their place in the civic order under the watchful eye of the father of the state.[34]

Elegiac discourse can also be assimilated into the general anxieties and ideological arenas of contestation of its day through a process of analogy.[35] If elegy is a narration of a liminal adult masculinity, then such a literary disquisition can be seen to take place on the threshold of a general climate of ideological, political, and cultural change and consolidation. If the rise of the principate at Rome is viewed as the establishment of "a broadly based cultural hegemony,"[36] then elegiac discourse is both part of the soundtrack to this process and also an integral element of such a cultural shift. In this manner, issues of liminality and maturation seem to be fundamental Augustan concepts. The coming-of-age throes of the elegiac poet can be set beside the "maturation" of Rome from republic to principate. In the same way, elegy's controlling metaphor of *servitium amoris* ("the slavery of love") could also be translated into a symbolic manifestation of anxiety over the ramifications of the establishment of the principate for Rome's elite. The "enslavement" of the narrator to an imperious *domina* could be read as an allegory for the perceived disempowerment of Rome's elite by the new *princeps*.[37]

The above analysis suggests some of the reasons why elegiac discourse might have had a particular impact in its immediate context and been a particularly Augustan cultural product. Elegiac narrative, with its tale of indulgent youthful excess and exuberance, can be tied thematically and through analogy to a historical context of postwar release and celebration and the emergence and attempted imposition of a chastened self-discipline. Elegy emerges at a moment both of societal carnival and its containment in an Augustan "revenge of Lent."[38]

Recuperating Youthful Misdirection

How, then, should we assess the ideological ramifications of elegiac poetry, if such poetry can properly be understood as a youthful discourse of disaffection? The apparent rejection of the ideological paradigms of mainstream Roman culture and the occupation of a subject position outside the approved parameters of the Roman sexual economy may make the stance of the elegists seem non-conformist and confrontational. Given the erotic fixation and self-indulgence, the rejection of civic duty, responsibility, and "proper" masculine deportment that is to be found in elegiac narrative, it might be tempting to see the discourse as ideologically challenging in the socio-political climate of Augustanism.

The closural sequence of Propertius Book 3, however, appears to present a containment of elegy's youthful challenge. These poems form an ostensible frame for the original Propertian collection and deliberately engage their higher profile poetic cousin, 1.1.[39] In these poems, the narrator confesses to a final change of perspective that causes him to renounce Cynthia, an elegiac lifestyle, and elegiac composition. The engagement of the closural sequence with 1.1 appears systematic and deliberate; it is encapsulated by the deliberate echo of the famous Propertian opening line: "Cynthia prima suis miserum me cepit ocellis" ("Cynthia first captured wretched me with her eyes") by 3.24.2: "olim oculis nimium facta superba meis" ("made at one time excessively arrogant by means of my eyes"); a line that, as G. P. Goold notes (1990.347), sets up 3.24/3.25 (which he combines) as "a designed repudiation of 1.1, which it echoes in themes and structure, even to the number of lines."

In 3.24, the disabling erotic infatuation and madness that formed the kernel of the collection's opening poem are cured (Propertius 3.24.9–19):

quod mihi non patrii poterant avertere amici,
    eluere aut vasto Thessala saga mari,
hoc ego non ferro, non igne coactus, at ipsa
    naufragus Aegaea (vera fatebor) aqua.
correptus saevo Veneris torrebar aeno;
    vinctus eram versas in mea terga manus.
ecce coronatae portum tetigere carinae,
    traiectae Syrtes, ancora iacta mihist.
nunc demum vasto fessi resipiscimus aestu,
    vulneraque ad sanum nunc coiere mea.
Mens Bona, si qua dea es, tua me in sacraria dono!

What family friends were unable to deflect from me or Thessalian witches wash away in a vast sea, this I have effected myself, not by the knife, not forced with fire, but (I will tell the truth) shipwrecked in a very Aegean sea of love. Venus, having taken hold of me, was roasting me in a savage cauldron; I was bound with my hands tied behind my back. But look! my garlanded ship has reached the harbor, the Syrtes are past, and my anchor has been cast out. Now, finally, weary from the vast tide, I have regained my senses, and my wounds have healed into sanity. Good Sense, if you are a goddess, I dedicate myself in your sanctuary.

The appeal for assistance from friends, magic, surgery, and cautery are all found in the opening poem of the collection, and so the resolution reached in 3.24 is the literary denouement of this initial theme. The furor and irrational lifestyle, *nullo vivere consilio*, "to live with no judgment" of 1.1 are answered by the *resipiscimus*, "I have recovered my senses" and the *devotio* ("dedication") to *Mens Bona* (Good Sense) of 3.24.

The metaphor of the Propertian narrator emerging safely from the tempestuous waters of love, "nunc demum vasto fessi resipiscimus aestu" ("Now, finally, weary from the vast tide, I have regained my senses," 3.24.17), is the same one that Cicero uses in the *pro Caelio* to demonstrate how illustrious citizens of the past have risen to the surface from the excesses of youth to become responsible adult citizens: "emersisse aliquando et se ad frugem bonam, ut dicitur, recepisse gravesque homines atque illustres fuisse" ("They surfaced in time and turned over a new leaf, as they say, and became serious and notable men," *pro Caelio* 28). Thus the Propertian and Ciceronian strategies of recuperation through maturation can be seen to cohere with one another.

In the final poem of Book 3, the narrator continues his resolution and resigns his courting of notoriety to the past (Propertius 3.25.1–2):

risus eram positis inter convivia mensis,
    et de me poterat quilibet esse loquax.

I was a laughingstock among the banquets when the tables were set in place, and anyone was free to gossip about me.

The description of the narrator's past predicament here recalls his statements in 2.24 that he is called the *caput nequitiae*, "fount of worthlessness" (2.24.6) and that his *infamia* is discussed *per totam urbem*, "through the whole city" (2.24.7). The original Propertian text, then, comes full circle from the narrator's induction into irrational erotic passion in 1.1 to his recovery from erotic illness in 3.24 and 3.25.

At the beginning of Propertius 3.25, the narrator also declares "quinque tibi potui servire fideliter annos," "I was able to serve you faithfully for five years." The time frame for the fictionalized relationship between Cynthia and the narrator that forms the core of the first three books of Propertius is thus set at five years. This span of time could then, in turn, be taken to correspond to that period of youth and incipient manhood that makes up the *tirocinium adulescentiae*. Hence the end of the affair and the rejection of Cynthia in 3.25 are analogous to the return to *boni mores* after the indulgence of the *tirocinium adulescentiae* as set out by the youthful narrator in *Controversiae* 2.6 or to the alleged rehabilitation of Caelius after the *vacatio adulescentiae*.

The frame, then, of the fall into and out of madness that encloses the Propertian collection would seem to give this discourse a conformist rather than a subversive feel. Ultimately, the narrator appears to proclaim a newfound maturity and consigns his previous indulgent, youthful excess to the scrapheap of past immaturity. If one chooses to read the discourse as teleological, then any subversive content can be read, in light of this act of closure, as contained.

In this way, elegy represents a narrative of youthful waywardness that, much in the manner of Roman comedy, indulges a period of youthful inexperience that finds its way home to traditional respectability in the end. Hence the generational conflict that is represented at the beginning of Propertius 2.30B can be reassessed through a consideration of the manner in which the collection ends (2.30B.1–3):

> Ista senes licet accusent convivia duri:
>> nos modo propositum, vita, teramus iter.
> illorum antiquis onerentur legibus aures:

> Let stern old men denounce these revels of ours: let us, my darling, keep down the same path we have started regardless. Let their ears be burdened with old-fashioned strictures.

In retrospect, it turns out that the *duri senes* ("stern old men") were probably right all along, and elegiac discourse only serves finally to demonstrate the propriety of a traditional moral perspective.[40]

While the elegiac narrator is immersed in his youthful excesses, he naturally claims not to see beyond them and actively resists evaluating his behavior in conventional terms. However, the final poems of Propertius's collection break this frame and allow conventional morality to return and evaluate past behavior in an ideologically normative way as a youthfully aberrant and passing phase. In this manner, too, the sexual characterization of the youthful narrator is finally recuperated. For ultimately in Roman culture, deviancy resides not in youthful sexual indulgence but in the prolongation of such behavior into adulthood.

One might also be tempted to see in the opening of 3.25 a deliberate blurring of the lines between the theme of a literary fiction and the actual circumstances of its production. In other words, the length of the relationship with Cynthia, said to have lasted five years, could also be understood to be the amount of time the poet took to compose and publish this serial affair. Hence a farewell to youthful erotic excess is also, inevitably, a farewell to elegiac composition.

Elegy is not only a form of youthful erotic indulgence and misdirection on the narrative level, it is also an example of poetic immaturity and excess. Hence elegiac discourse is a conflation of youthful erotic and poetic exuberance that (in)appropriately features a Roman male on the threshold of adulthood. Rejection of the subject matter of elegy, the *domina*, must be matched by an analogous farewell to the literary form within which she is contained. Just as a young man must learn to move past infatuation and erotic preoccupations, so, too, a young poet must move from the frivolity of elegy into more mature genres of poetry. This would explain why, when the Propertian elegiac narrator returns for a fourth book, his literary persona changes to accommodate his increased years (inside and outside of the text): etiology is apparently privileged over erotics, and Cynthia's appearances seem like cameos deliberately designed for a past elegiac diva. An elegiac narrator who returns to compose from outside the parameters of the *tirocinium adulescentiae* must display an appropriate degree of personal and literary maturation. So, too, the Ovidian narrator of the *Ars Amatoria* and the *Remedia Amoris* must now be characterized as a *praeceptor* ("instructor") of, rather than a participant in, youthful erotic misadventure.

To summarize, the conclusion of Propertius Book 3 suggests that the collection can be seen as a literary dramatization of the elite male *tirocinium adulescentiae*. From this perspective, elegiac discourse can be understood as reinforcing, rather than challenging, the dominant ideological paradigms of its day. Elegy thus might be understood as taking place in a marginal but conceded space for such aberration: the dramatic time is youth, the setting, the Subura. The concluding gesture of Propertius's collection mirrors the proclamation of the youthful speaker in Seneca *Controversiae* 2.6 that, after his allotted period of adolescent waywardness, he will revert to the expected pattern of adult maturity, *boni mores*. In this manner, the marginality of an elegiac lifestyle, and its professed deviance, only exist as a prelude to integration, as the elegiac narrator presents his past behavior as a product of *iuvenalis error*.

Re-evaluating Elegiac Discourse, Part One: Authorial Intent

Propertius's act of closure attempts to impose a frame of interpretation on his work; it picks up the already negative imagery of madness, bewitchment, and disease of 1.1 and rejects the former poem's masochistic embrace of *amor* as misguided and destructive. Does this closural sequence offer the reader an authorially sanctioned and privileged key to evaluating elegiac discourse? Does this gesture mean that elegy should properly be understood as a narrative of youthful folly, "a tale told by an idiot, full of sound and fury, signifying nothing"?[41]

Even if the closure of Propertius Book 3 does suggest that elegiac discourse could be processed so as to minimize its ideological disruption, this does not, of course, necessarily mean that it had to be processed this way. Authors might try to control the reception of their work and rewrite the impact of its ideological parameters, but signification is notoriously difficult to control, and the construction of authorial intent is perilous ground on which to build the potential ideological significance of a discourse. Readers have a habit of processing texts in line with their own ideological preoccupations rather than those of the author.[42] Neither speakers nor authors are allowed a totalitarian control over their utterances and texts. As Shakespeare's Hamlet demonstrates in an exchange with the king, words are not subject even to regal authority: the king comments about a typically opaque statement of Hamlet by saying: "I have nothing with this answer, Hamlet, these words are not mine," to which Hamlet replies, "No, nor mine now" (act 3, scene 2).

Thus it would be perilous to suggest that the apparent authorial intent of the closural sequence of Book 3 inevitably circumscribes the ideological ramifications of elegiac discourse and contains within it a normative model of cultural maturation. It does, however, raise the question of why Propertius chose or felt the need to frame his work in this way. Was this gesture an aesthetically formalist one masquerading as pseudo-autobiography (a poet's farewell to a genre understood as the narrative of the young and foolish whose poetic closure could be troped as an act of maturation and renunciation)? Was it intended as not only a formalist but also an evaluative gesture framing elegy as a morality tale based on an authorial embrace of a culturally normative model of maturation? Or maybe it was not the literalization of an already internalized ideological position but rather a response to emergent ideological pressure, an act of Augustan-induced censorial reassessment? The discernment of authorial intent is not in itself an ending but only another beginning, another piece of over-determination to be unraveled.[43]

Re-evaluating Elegiac Discourse, Part Two: Ideological Contestation

As noted above, this reading of the discourse suggests a way that any ideological challenge elegy posed could be negotiated and contained. Such a process of containment could be theorized in a number of ways. If, for instance, elegy was read as a literary analogue of youthful carnival, then the closural strategies of Book 3 represent the limits of such excess. If carnival is nothing more than an officially sanctioned (or tolerated) expression of difference, then it can be ultimately assessed as a tool of normalization rather than of alterity.[44] As Terry Eagleton, quoting Shakespeare, argues in a critique of carnival as a positivist means of ideological disruption: "There is no slander in an allowed fool" (1981.148). Is the exuberance of permitted dissonance a form of revolution or a means of social control? Along these lines, Francis Cairns reads Propertius 2.7, with its apparently antagonistic rejection of Augustus's marriage legislation, as a "hysterical response," an effect that promotes rather than undermines, Augustus's moral and social legislation (1979.188). Thus Propertius's narrative confirms "the existence in society of those pernicious attitudes which justified Augustus's proposal of his law in the first place" (Cairns 1979.191). Hence elegiac narrative must be viewed as constructing a youthful narrator who is purposefully a negative paradigm; far from posing a threat bristling with positive alterity, elegiac narrative is implicated in the construction of a "necessary negative" whereby dominant ideological values are confirmed.[45] In this way, elegiac narrative may be taken to represent a specific literary manifestation of a persistent but containable feature of Roman social practice, a "culture of delinquency" on the part of elite adolescent males.[46]

Such acts of containment are also discussed in studies of modern subcultures. In these instances, the process whereby the potential ideological threat of such groups is contained is seen as one of active recuperation, incorporation, and normalization on the part of the dominant ideology. Hence what might appear as radical and challenging alterity can be trivialized and the participants "*returned* . . . to the place where common sense would have them fit."[47] Thus the punks and glitter rockers of the 1970s are "just kids dressing up" and "daughters just like yours" (Hebdige 1997.131). At this level, elegiac narrative might be viewed, as Cairns appears to view it in his analysis of Propertius 2.7 or as the narrator encourages us to in 3.24/3.25, as intentionally engaging in a process of undermining its own potential for disorder.

However, a reader could choose to conceptualize elegiac discourse otherwise, to resist the inducements to normalize elegy. The Augustan, and, indeed, the modern reader, when faced with elegiac narrative was/is enmeshed in a process of encoding/decoding the signification of this youthful discourse.[48] The way in which this was/is done is inevitably variable and maps out a whole spectrum of potential responses ranging from acquiescence to resistance in reading a text in line with a dominant ideological agenda.[49]

Instead of choosing to read a text in such a way as to minimize its ideological challenge, one could instead make the decision to maximize it.[50] In this manner, the ideology inscribed in Propertian elegiac discourse would not be seen as contained by the gesture of its frame but rather remain as an ineradicable difference. Thus, for instance, Judith Hallett's reading of elegy saw the discourse as a literary counterculture that challenged the entrenched norms and traditional patterns of Roman life and disdained "accepted social practices" (1973.108–09).

The readings of Hallett (elegy as conscious counterculture) and Cairns (a deliberate narrative of youthful misdirection) demonstrate two plausible ways of responding to this discourse of youthful disaffection. The fact that their analyses produce two such opposed readings of Roman elegy's ideological impact may indicate the variety of responses that the elegiac text can and could elicit.

This theorization of the variable reception of elegiac narrative can also be applied to its production. The ideology of the emerging principate involved the incorporation and negotiation of culturally resonant terminology (such as *pax*, *otium*, *libertas*, etc.). Such culturally and ideologically laden concepts can be viewed as "multiaccentual," that is to say, they are open to variable interpretation and emphasis.[51] The manner in which these concepts were consolidated into the ideology of the principate was not natural but rather a process of naturalization.

In this context, we might consider elegiac narrative as a literary strategy for negotiating a response to the emerging cultural hegemony of the principate and Augustanism with an analogous process of mediation and appropriation.[52] For elegy as a contemporaneous cultural practice necessarily was part of the process by which such a hegemony was articulated, negotiated, and contested.

Work on the youth subcultures of postwar Britain maintains that such groups are "seen as collective solutions to collectively experienced problems."[53] Such subcultures address the various problematics of contemporary social experience and attempt a resolution "in an imaginary way."[54] The ideological dimension of such symbolic processes of resistance is seen as particularly pronounced in times of crisis, upheaval, and social change (such as the immediate postwar years in Britain).

The means of resistance, or of negotiation, employed by such groups is often one of creative and adaptive appropriation. Where such a strategy involves the adoption, modification, and symbolic appropriation of material goods, it has been labeled *bricolage*.[55] However, material objects are not the only ground on which ideological contestation can take place. Values and ideas can also be appropriated and serve as a basis for the negotiation and articulation of competing ideological viewpoints.

Hence the importation of such culturally resonant concepts as *otium*, *pax*, and *amor*, and such ideologically charged metaphors as *militia* and *servitium amoris* might all be seen as part of elegy's own form of symbolic *bricolage*, as the discourse incorporates and appropriates emergent aspects of Augustan ideology in a (de)constructive act of literary negotiation.

As the studies of modern subcultures demonstrate, such symbolic forms of youthful resistance are most likely to arise and proliferate in times of crisis and social and ideological turmoil. Such was the situation when elegy was produced, as Rome's political, social, and cultural discourses were subject to a process of articulation, negotiation, and consolidation that established the principate as a new hegemonic ideology.[56]

The establishment of the principate and its attendant hegemonic ideology was not an inevitability, and it necessarily left traces of resistance and difference that could be appropriated, marginalized, or demonized, but not entirely effaced. Elegiac discourse can be read as indicative of such an ideological challenge, producing a youthful discourse that represented a negotiated version of an emerging dominant system whereby the values of such a system were not simply rejected or opposed but incorporated and appropriated to produce an idiosyncratically different, but related, ideology.[57]

If a model of ideology is constructed that is not monolithic but dynamic, for instance Raymond William's threefold distinction (1977.121–27) between the "residual," "dominant," and "emergent" aspects of a dominant ideology, then a culture's subversive, or apparently subversive, practices cannot simply be viewed as ultimately contained or benignly propping up the status quo (even if the narrative in the end says this is the case). For the production of alternate subject positions to those approved by a dominant ideology inevitably introduces the possibility of change and contradiction: these emergent aspects of a culture once put into play cannot simply be erased. A dominant ideological paradigm must either adapt itself to take them into account or it must face the possibility of being eventually replaced. In either event, such emergent aspects of a culture ensure that ideology is an evolutionary process rather than a static given. In such circumstances, the intentions of an author, whether constructed correctly or not, are ultimately as important as the way in which an audience processes the narrative.[58]

Notes

1. Roman elegy as a literary genre was at its height during the turbulent period of history that saw the demise of the Roman republic and the establishment of the principate under Augustus. It is particularly associated with three authors: Tibullus (born c. 55–48 B.C.E.), Propertius (born c. 54–47 B.C.E.), and Ovid (born in 43 B.C.E.). Tibullus composed his two books of elegies c. 27–19 B.C.E., Propertius wrote his initial collection of elegies c. 28–23 B.C.E., and Ovid likely composed and published his *Amores* c. 26–21 B.C.E.

2. "sed ut tunc quoque dubium nemini foret naturae illa vitia, non aetatis esse," "so even then no one doubted that those were the vices of his nature and not just his age," Suetonius *Nero* 26. All translations are my own.

3. "ludibundus nec sine pernicie tamen," "playful but nevertheless destructive," Suetonius *Nero* 26.

4. The *toga virilis* was a white wool toga that was adopted in place of the purple-bordered *toga praetexta* by a boy coming of age; the *bulla* was an amulet Roman children of both sexes wore around their necks.

5. By mainstream Roman elegy, I mean the first three books of Propertius, the two books of Tibullus, and Ovid's *Amores*. In each of these works, there is a first-person narrative whose narrators are poets and lovers who are part of similar dramatic situations to comparable effect. This coherence on expressive, pragmatic, structural, and mimetic grounds serves as a basis for genre classification.

6. The age at which the assumption of the *toga virilis* took place seems to have been variable (as puberty tends to be), and generally fell in the range from fourteen to seventeen; see further Rousselle 1988.59, Richlin 1993.546–47.

7. *Toga libera* is used synonymously with *toga virilis*; see also Ovid *Fasti* 3.771.

8. The *depositio barbae*, an event of Greek origin that helped mark the transition from child to man, seems to have taken place at around the age of twenty; see Richlin 1993.547–48, Wiedemann 1989.116–17.

9. On the social status of the elegists, see further Lilja 1965.10–16, Hubbard 1974.96ff., Syme 1978.182–83, White 1993.211–22.

10. This detail is matched by assertions elsewhere in the Ovidian corpus: *Epistulae ex Ponto* 4.8.17–18, *Tristia* 2.89–90, *Tristia* 2.541–42. An *eques* ("knight") was a member of the equestrian order, the second highest social order at Rome after senators.

11. Such professed circumstances would suit the context of the proscriptions of 43 B.C.E. in which numerous members of Rome's elite were murdered and/or their property confiscated: this process served both to eliminate the political enemies of Octavian, Antony, and Lepidus and also to enhance their financial resources. Other evidence external to the narrative but perhaps indicative of what a Roman audience may have brought to the texts are the *Vita* of Suetonius on Tibullus, Horace *Carmina* 1.33 and *Epistles* 1.4, and the identification of Postumus in Propertius 3.12; see further Hubbard 1974.97, Syme 1978.182–83. The importation of external material to explicate a discourse's idiosyncrasy is, of course, always a potentially hazardous procedure, but it is, nevertheless, one that I think elegy encourages.

12. On this theme in elegy, see James 2001, 2003.

13. See Wyke 1994b and Myers 1996.

14. As Maria Wyke has well elaborated, elegiac narrative is more to do with male debasement than female empowerment; as she says, it is "not the concern of elegiac poetry to upgrade the political position of women, only to portray the male narrator as alienated from positions of power and to differentiate him from other, socially responsible male types" (1989a.42). However, elegiac discourse has also been presented as ideologically challenging rather than normative on the level of gender; see, for example, Gold 1993, Wyke 1994b, and Greene 1998.

15. Conte 1989 refers to the construction of this idiosyncratic elegiac ideology as a process of "transcodification." Such an elegiac creed has been interpreted as willfully confrontational; see, for instance, Hallett 1973, Stahl 1985, and Sullivan 1972, who writes: "The professed aims and ideals of the elegists, however playfully they are interpreted, clearly and consciously fly in the face of accepted Roman standards of seriousness, sobriety, public service, and personal ambition" (23).

16. See Stahl 1985.93: "Here a reversal clearly takes place and a reevaluation of one of society's points of honor, a reevaluation which must shock the normal Roman mind. For, by assigning the term of honor to his own miserable condition, Propertius gives the impression of upgrading it to the level of (or valuing it as high as) the official career."

17. Sulpicia is the only female elegist whose work survives. She was the niece of the statesman and patron Valerius Messalla Corvinus and a rough contemporary of Ovid. Her work was attached to the collected works of Tibullus: the number of poems authored by her in this collection is disputed. Traditionally, only six epigrammatic length poems have been thought hers, but some would argue for her authorship also of some of the longer elegies in Book 3 of the corpus Tibullianum.

18. For a more detailed analysis of this complex poem, see Wyke 1989b.

19. Wyke 1994b.120, drawing on the earlier work of Gamel 1989 on the *Amores* and, more particularly, Gold 1993 on Propertius.

20. See also Kennedy 1993.59.

21. Hence the *Amores*, for instance, are constructed as a poetic space always

under siege by the impending necessity of a poetic talent being applied to the more mature and socially significant genres of epic and tragedy.

22. Parker 1997.58. As Parker notes, "Paradoxically from our point of view, the man obsessed with women is passive"; see also Williams 1999.43: "Roman audiences were not predisposed to find anything anomalous in the figure of a womanish man sexually pursuing women."

23. Parker 1997.57 notes that the "*pathicus*, if anything, approaches more closely our concept of the masochist than of the homosexual." Clearly the elegiac narrator is scripted into a pattern of such masochistic behavior as he not only endures hardship but even contrives to ensure that such hardship should continue. See also McGinn 1998.192 on how the *patientia* ("tolerance") of a cuckolded husband produces a "feminized male."

24. The definition of the Roman word *cinaedus* is problematic: one aspect of what a Roman would have understood by the term is effeminacy. For more detail on what were typically denoted as effeminate traits, see Richlin 1992a.258 n. 3, Edwards 1993.63–97, Gleason 1995.67–70, Corbeill 1996.ch. 4, 1997, Williams 1999.ch. 4. On the evidence for, and manifestations of, the *cinaedus*, see Richlin 1993, Corbeill 1996.ch. 4, 1997, Parker 1997.60–62, Williams 1999.172ff.

25. Such a premise lies at the heart of the theoretical models used by the "new historicism" and "cultural materialism," which, in turn, draw on a Marxist tradition of literary criticism. For some thoughts on how, and to what effect, such theoretical models are becoming increasingly mainstream in classical studies, see Myers 1999.196–98.

26. Hebdige 1997.142, discussing why certain postwar youth subcultures flourished in a particular socio-historical context.

27. Nor will such a contextualization delimit a work's potential to be contextualized otherwise over the course of its historical reception.

28. On the entwining of *otium* and elegy, see the final section of Fear 2000: "The Ambivalence of *Otium*."

29. On literature as an emergent means of self-promotion and an arena for elite ambition, see the chapters by Bloomer, Dupont, and Oliensis in Habinek and Schiesaro 1997.

30. One might also add Juvenal *Satires* 6.292: "nunc patimur longae pacis mala" ("Now we are enduring the evils of a long peace"); see also Galinsky 1996.138 on the manifestations of Roman anxiety towards *pax et otium*.

31. Wilson 1992.150; the author here is discussing the appropriation of carnival elements in the England of Elizabeth I and James I as background to the themes and performance of Shakespeare's *Julius Caesar*. The harnessing and control of leisure time is always a problem for an autocrat (or those in charge of any governmental structure).

32. Yavetz 1984.20. There also seem to have been plans to revitalize and train the youth of the Roman aristocracy, in particular, those of the equestrian order (Yavetz 1984.15–20). Augustus revived and introduced various practices in

this regard: the review of the *turmae equitum*, "troops of knights"; the *Lusus Troiae*, "Trojan games"; the *exercitatio campestris*, "exercises on the plain" (exercise taken on the *Campus Martius)* (Suetonius *Augustus* 38.3, 43.2; Dio 48.20.1, 51.22.4, 54.26.1, 55.10.6; Vergil *Aeneid* 5.550, 575; Ovid *Tristia* 3.12.7–22). He also allowed the sons of senators to attend meetings of the senate after the assumption of the *toga virilis* and gave them additional command responsibilities at the commencement of their military careers to ensure that each youthful member of the Roman elite would be *expers castrorum*, "experienced in military life" and not in the elegiac sort (Suetonius *Augustus* 38.2). On a more paternal note, he banned the beardless at the Lupercalia (a Roman festival celebrated in February) and enforced adult supervision for youthful participants in the night entertainments at the Secular Games (Suetonius *Augustus* 31.4; the games were held by Augustus in 17 B.C.E. as a celebration of a new era).

33. On the temple of Mars Ultor as the new site of the *toga virilis* ceremony, see Rawson and Weaver 1997.215.

34. This integration of youth into an emergent political system can also be seen in the assertion in the *Res Gestae* (14.2) that the whole body of Roman equestrians presented Gaius and Lucius Caesar with silver shields and spears and hailed them as *principes iuventutis* ("leaders of the youth"). A dominant ideology must, after all, provide for its perpetuation as well as its consolidation.

35. Analogy is an important part of new historicist analysis. On its strengths and pitfalls, see Jonathon Hart's review (1991.429–48) of Greenblatt's *Shakespearean Negotiations*.

36. Habinek 2002.46; such is also the general thesis behind Habinek and Schiesaro 1997.

37. Hence Habinek 2002.47 explains the use of this particular metaphor by the early elegists as an attempt "to negotiate the position of male aristocrats newly subordinated to a system and an emperor not entirely beholden to their whims" or, as I have written elsewhere (Fear 2000.238): "Elegy's image of elite *adolescentes* subjugated and emasculated through the agency of an imperialistic seductress would have served as a powerful allegorical rendition of the dangers for Rome's aristocracy of *pax et principes*."

38. This term is taken from Wilson 1992.150; the asceticism of Lent follows the exuberant indulgence of carnival. The promotion of the latter serves to enhance the acceptance of the former.

39. The Propertian manuscript tradition is somewhat troubled (Goold 1990 gives a succinct summary at the beginning of the revised Loeb edition). There cannot be certainty, but it seems a reasonable surmise that 3.24 and 3.25 mark the end of the original Propertian collection to which our present Book 4 was a later addition.

40. In a similar fashion, Catullus, an epigrammatic/lyric poet actively composing c. 60–55 B.C.E. and generally assumed to be one of the poetic precursors of the elegists, ruminates on the potential destructiveness of *otium* ("leisure,"

"idleness," "inactivity") in the final stanza of poem 51. *Otium* was a state that both enabled Catullus's own poetic composition and served as a theme in his poetry. This negative mediation can be seen as the promotion of traditional Roman values that the poet elsewhere professes to hold in contempt (Catullus 51.13–16):

otium, Catulle, tibi molestum est:
otio exsultas nimiumque gestis:
otium et reges prius et beatas
    perdidit urbes.

Leisure, Catullus, is bothersome to you; you revel and engage excessively in leisure: previously leisure has destroyed both kings and prosperous cities.

41. Shakespeare *Macbeth*, act 5, scene 5.

42. Thus Fredric Jameson 1981.58 argues with respect to reading methods that "the working theoretical framework or presuppositions of a given method are in general the ideology which that method seeks to perpetuate."

43. The assessment of the ideological ramifications of Propertian discourse based on an examination of the author's personal development lies at the heart of Stahl's 1985 analysis. Stahl resists a framework of maturation that sees the author move from rebel to conformist; he believes such a reading would be an internalization and acceptance of Augustan ideology both on the part of the poet and the reader. However, at the same time as Stahl resists the eventual essentialization of Propertius as a "good Augustan," he also seems to embrace the opposite essentialism of the poet as dissident. This reduces both the complexities of the composition of the subject and the process of ideology formation. For a critique of Stahl along these lines, see Kennedy 1993.37–39.

44. Carnival is one of the main concepts in the work of Mikhail Bakhtin; see, in particular, Bakhtin 1973.100–49.

45. The phrase "necessary negative" is taken from Williams' 1999.183 analysis of the *cinaedus* as a foil for "true" Roman masculinity.

46. The term "culture of delinquency" is taken from Clarke, Hall, Jefferson, and Roberts 1997.100–01; such behaviors on the part of working-class adolescent males are "regular and persistent features of the 'parent' class-culture."

47. Hebdige 1997.131–34, quoting Hall 1977; emphasis in original.

48. The phrase "encoding/decoding" is taken from the title of Stuart Hall's 1980 study of the responses of television audiences.

49. Hall identifies three main positions: the "dominant-hegemonic" ("preferred") position, the "negotiated" position, and the "oppositional" position; in a similar fashion, Michel Pêcheux 1977 maps out three positions a subject might adopt towards dominant ideological paradigms: the "good subject," who responds in an act of "total identification," the "bad subject," who refuses the identity offered in an act of "counter-identification," and what is described by Pêcheux as a "third modality" that falls somewhere in between, an act of "disidentification."

50. Thus the narrator's subjugation by the *domina* might be read as a pointed

political allegory on elite disempowerment; but then how might one interpret the ultimate rejection of the *domina* in Propertius 3.24/3.25? Is it the acceptance of a culturally normative model of maturation (and Augustanism) or an act of disidentification with the emergent principate?

51. The term "multiaccentual" is taken from Valentin Volosinov 1973.

52. Hence in his study of Augustan culture, Galinsky argues that elegy is not "an antiworld (*Gegenwelt*) of constant provocation and inversion of Augustan society and values" but rather "includes a wide variety of reactions to that 'real' world and, especially, a wide and complex range of appropriations from that world" (1996.270). This second statement seems to me to be an accurate assessment of the complexity of a cultural product's insertion into a socio-political context. Nevertheless, the "fluidity" that Galinsky detects in elegy and Augustanism generally has a tendency in his analysis to congeal into a somewhat homogeneously solid body of values. Thus the elegists may express their Augustanism idiosyncratically, but their hearts and minds are essentially imbued with the same values and ideals. They form a literary microcosm of an Augustan macrocosm. This privileges a homogeneous view of culture and occludes the contestation and struggle upon which the appearance of such unity rests.

53. Clarke 1997.175, although one must bear in mind the limitations of applying modern subcultural theory to a Roman literary discourse. Modern studies of subcultures can be informed by empirical data that is inevitably lacking in the case of ancient Rome. The study of modern subcultures typically focuses on those composed of working-class youths. The numbers involved, the social positioning of the participants, and the cultural products used and fashioned are all quite different from what we find in the case of elegy.

54. Clarke, Hall, Jefferson, and Roberts 1997.104.

55. The concept was originally developed in the field of anthropology, but has been applied, notably by Dick Hebdige, to the stylistic ensembles of youth subcultures, ensembles that serve, as Hebdige 1997.136 puts it, "to erase or subvert their original straight meanings."

56. Hence, Kennedy 1992.35: "The emergence of the principate might be viewed as the progressive re-organization of a fragmented discourse, whose previous centre was provided by the institutions of the Republic, around the *princeps* as the new focus of stable meaning in society."

57. "Negotiated version" is taken from Parkin 1971.92.

58. Thanks to the editors of this volume, Ronnie Ancona and Ellen Greene, for their comments and encouragement.

2 (Un)Constrained Male Desire

An Intertextual Reading of Horace *Odes* 2.8 and
Catullus Poem 61

Ronnie Ancona

Despite the fact that the Roman poet Horace lived a generation
after his predecessor Catullus, many of the Roman cultural assumptions
and social practices that inform Catullus's poetry also inform Horace's.
More specifically, the cultural expectations for marriage remained stable
in their most general outlines.

Two somewhat contradictory ideals or assumptions coexisted with
regard to what we might call "male fidelity" (although the modern notions that underlie this phrase do not map onto the ancient world with
complete accuracy). One ideal saw the marital sexual relation as the only
one acceptable for the husband. Craig Williams notes that the generic
expectations of the marriage poem entail the convention that the man
would forsake all other sexual activity when he is married. On the renunciation of the slave-boy relationship after the groom's wedding in
Catullus poem 61, Williams argues that it is not a homosexual renunciation per se. "The comment is generically conditioned, coming as it does
in the course of a marriage hymn whose very purpose is to celebrate a
certain ideal, namely the mutual and exclusive love between husband and
wife" (1999.274).

The other ideal allowed for non-marital sexual activity for the husband that would not bring ill repute to either the husband (whose reputation had to be maintained) or the sexual partner (whose status and,
therefore, reputation were already low). In this model, the husband
might have sex with the same individuals, male or female, as before the
marriage, namely those of lower status (for example, slaves and non-cit-
izens). Under this ideal there was a different standard of behavior for
husband and wife, a kind of double standard, but one that nevertheless

41

required the husband's sexual activity to be restricted in specific ways.[1] For example, Horace *Satires* 1.2.31ff. is often cited for its commentary on the dangers of using married women for this non-marital variety of sex and its recommendation of freedwomen. For a wife's excusing her husband's marital "infidelity," one can cite Valerius Maximus *Facta et Dicta Memorabilia* 6.7.1–3, written in the first century C.E. Valerius recounts the virtuous behavior of Tertia Aemilia, who tolerated her husband's sexual involvement with a slave girl.[2] Tertia Aemilia was the wife of the famous general and conqueror of the Carthaginian Hannibal, Publius Cornelius Scipio Africanus (236–184 B.C.E.), and mother of the famous Cornelia, who was mother, in turn, of the politically important Gracchi brothers.

These, then, were two somewhat different ideals; the second, perhaps, reflecting the more common social practices and expectations. Despite these differing ideals and the perceived necessity for keeping respectable women away from non-marital sexual relations, our sources for the first century B.C.E. suggest a world in which even upper-class women at times engaged in socially tolerated affairs. Indeed, some of the love poetry of Catullus, namely that addressed indirectly or directly to "Lesbia" (the girlfriend who, in poems 68 and 83, is identified as having a *vir* or husband), attest to that cultural phenomenon. Indeed, as Susan Treggiari states (1991.307):

> Catullus and his successors portray a world in which the poet and his friends can regard extra-marital affairs with women of the upper class as a romantic ideal. The reality of such a world is confirmed by the gossip of Cicero and Caelius, the slanted attacks of Cicero in his speeches or Sallust in his history, the moralizing of Horace, the gibes of Antony and Octavian, and the reaction of Augustus the legislator. It is possible to believe that the Roman upper classes of the late Republic were able to absorb and tolerate a degree of sexual licence for married women as well as married men.

How such affairs or relationships were to be negotiated had been of great interest to Catullus. Indeed, the extra-marital romantic ideal imagined by Catullus may have, in some ways, exceeded even the ideal of an actual marriage. According to Treggiari (1991.303): "Catullus had neatly set the pattern for confusion of categories of relationships when he demanded the quasi-contractual loyalty of Roman friendship and played with the idea of fidelity in a relationship which was clearly extra-marital and, at least for a time, adulterous."

Thus one can see in Catullus's poetry an elaborate and not necessarily consistent interplay of social practice and romantic ideal.[3] While Catullus may be best known for his love poems that involve an extra-marital affair with a woman, he, of course, wrote love poems to men and poems celebrating marriage as well. Likewise, while Horace can be the "moralizer" Treggiari suggests when he chastises the young married woman who is unfaithful at the end of *Odes* 3.6, and when he warns men against the dangers of sex with married women and urges them to seek out partners who will provide no danger in *Satires* 1.2 (noted above), he can also be the somewhat bemused ironist who is both disturbed by and in awe of a threat to marriage, as we will see in *Odes* 2.8.

These preliminary remarks on the social and larger cultural context of Roman marriage are meant to make clear that neither Horace nor Catullus is to be labeled as pro- or anti-marriage in any simple way. Rather, these poets are writing in a Rome that both values marriage and is interested in the counterclaims of non-marital love and desire. Catullus's literary influence upon Horace is undeniable, despite the fact that Horace mentions Catullus only once by name in his writings (*Satires* 1.10.19). This influence has been traced by many scholars, although it may be even greater than has been realized.[4] In what follows, I hope to expand discussion of that influence by showing that an intertextual reading of Catullus 61 with Horace *Odes* 2.8 reveals a shared interest in and fascination with the institution of marriage and elucidates Horace's ironic, if anxious, response to his predecessor. Specifically, my focus is on the ways in which the two poems address the issue of constraining male desire.

Catullus's poem 61 is a wedding song celebrating the marriage of Manlius Torquatus and his bride Junia (line 16), also called Aurunculeia (line 82).[5] The groom, Torquatus, is likely the historical figure of that name who held the office of praetor in 49 B.C.E. The historical identity of the bride remains unknown. It is unlikely that the poem was written for actual performance in connection with the couple's marriage.[6] The poem's structure includes an invocation to Hymen, Greek god of marriage, praise of Hymen, praise of the bride, a *deductio* (escorting the bride from her old home to her new), the *Fescennina iocatio* or native Italian Fescennine bantering directed at the bridegroom, as well as an encouraging address to the bride, and, finally, the *epithalamium* proper: the song sung outside the *thalamos* or bedchamber of the new couple. Catullus's wedding song stands in a long tradition dating back at least to Sappho, who was known in antiquity for having written a whole book in this genre.[7]

Some interpreters of poem 61 see it as holding forth unambiguously a vision of faithful marital love. T. P. Wiseman (1985.112–16), for example, sees the poem as celebrating marriage and the production of children and condemning adultery, and thus as sharing in the same values that Augustan moral legislation promotes in Horace's generation, while others see, especially in the poem's eroticism, a playful hinting at the precariousness of sexual fidelity.[8] In fact, Craig Williams goes so far as to say: "Even in a hymn in his honor, Hymen bows before Priapus," thus suggesting the primacy of the erotic over the marital.[9] What we can see in these two different approaches to the poem is the centrality of the issue of fidelity. Is the groom's fidelity assured and celebrated through the injunction to him to put aside the male slave who had served as the object of his erotic interest and the warning to his bride that she must satisfy him sexually lest he stray, or does the mention of these very issues warn of the fragility of the groom's sexual fidelity?

The particular response of Horace to this poem anticipates some modern interpretations, for depending on how one interprets Catullus's poem, one can see Horace either as ironizing what was un-ironic in Catullus or as taking Catullus's potential irony about marriage and pushing it to the limit. In a sense, then, it is useful for us to see Horace as one of the first interpreters of Catullus 61 and one whose interpretation we still possess. Horace, clearly attracted to this poem for its depiction of certain anxieties surrounding marriage, creates as a result a poem that shows the disturbing way in which adult male desire remains susceptible to sexual diversion, an unacceptable (if enticing) situation when it interferes with the socially sanctified and public demands of marriage. While Barine, the object of erotic attention in *Odes* 2.8, may represent the kind of woman who, *in theory*, might be an acceptable sexual diversion for a married man, the effect she *actually* has is to disrupt the social framework as embodied in marriage. Her disruption of the social order suggests that men acting upon their desires must be controlled if the social order is to be maintained. However, despite the seeming unacceptability of her effect, she nevertheless holds a certain fascination for the speaker of the poem.

In an earlier work (Ancona 1994.82–83), I briefly developed the idea first suggested by E. Ensor in 1902 (and little noted) that *Odes* 2.8 lines 21–24 parodied lines 51–55 of Catullus 61. I now argue for a far more pervasive intertextual reading of Catullus on Horace's part. In order to see in detail how Horace in *Odes* 2.8 is responding to poem 61, I outline the elements of poem 61 that seem to provoke and inform Horace's response. Then I examine the nature of Horace's response to his Catullan material. I hope to show both continuity with regard to cultural anxieties about male desire and marriage in the two poems as well as a self-conscious reading on Horace's part of his predecessor's work. I argue that the bemused, yet anxious, speaker of *Odes* 2.8 inhabits a world in many ways culturally and socially continuous with Catullus's, but his often ironic stance with regard to desire makes it interesting for him to somewhat nervously explore the anxieties about marriage and male desire inherent in Catullus 61.

Within and surrounding the larger theme of marriage, Catullus develops numerous intertwining sub-themes in poem 61. The marriage of bride and groom occasions thoughts of beauty, family, and the production of children, chastity/fidelity, legitimacy, home, slavery, temporality, liminality, Venus, desire, constraints, movement, and reluctance, to name the most important. Since my concern will be Horace's response to Catullus's poem, I will limit my discussion here to those elements of poem 61 that Horace responds to in *Odes* 2.8.

Poem 61 celebrates a marriage. Bride and groom are characterized in various ways, as are the circumstances surrounding their marriage. Each of the elements mentioned above helps to shape the particular vision of marriage that emerges from poem 61. Within the celebration of marriage lie references to its potential disruptions, and, as I have already mentioned, scholars have responded variously to these potentially disruptive elements, seeing them either as successfully banished or as unconquered. I will try to outline here in general terms the presentation by Catullus of these interrelated themes. I will return to the poem later to give additional details of theme and language that will make more sense in the context of Horace's response. However, an outline will help us to see how Horace is answering his predecessor.

Perhaps the broadest theme in poem 61 is that of liminality.[10] Both bride and groom are in transition from one stage of life to another. In addition, on a literal level, the bride is about to cross the threshold (*limen*) to enter her new home. Each shows reluctance to leave the past—the bride weeps and the groom is fearful—but the groom is also described as, and the bride is encouraged to be, eager and desirous of the future. Temporality is a closely related and pervasive theme. There is an insistent push toward the future marriage initiated by the invoking of the marriage god, Hymen. A future child from the marriage is imagined, and the marriage is to last until old age. The elderly parent invokes Hymen to assist in the production of legitimate children on whom one can depend and through whom one's family line continues. Mapped onto this diachronic temporality is repetition:[11] the repetition of individual words (for example, forms of *bonus*), as well as the repeated hymnic refrain invoking the god Hymen and the repeated refrain addressed to the bride. The final injunction to the married couple that they spend their youth in "uninterrupted or constantly recurring sexual activity/duty," *munere assiduo* (line 227), reinforces this theme.[12]

The family functions in the poem both diachronically and synchronically. Over time, the young couple will become parents and produce a son, while the single image of a child moving from the mother's lap is both the movement of the bride away from *her* mother and the stretching forth from *her* lap, in turn, of her own new baby boy. Hymen is important because he ensures that the purpose of marriage, the production of children, can be fulfilled legitimately. In other words, when Hymen does his duty (*suum munus*, 42–43), the couple can legitimately do theirs.

Venus, or love, is *bona* ("good, noble") only in the context of marriage. Venus/love cannot take reputable pleasure without marriage. And the bride herself is compared to the goddess Venus, so, in a sense, the respectability of both the bride and sexual activity must be affirmed. While the bride and groom are described as beautiful, it is the bride alone whose beauty gets detailed attention. She is compared not only to Venus but to myrtle shining (*enitens*) with its flowering little branches (21–22) and to flowers, because she is shining (*nitens*, 186) with her little flourishing face. The bride need not weep because she has no competition for her beauty; there is no woman more beautiful (*pulcrior*, 84) than she.

While both bride and groom are attractive, it is only the bride who bears the "burden" of attractiveness. It is she who, having had her mind bound by love (*mentem amore revinciens*, 33) as clinging ivy entwines a tree, will, in turn, constrain her husband in her embrace as the vine entwines the trees (102–05). Thus marriage, to which she must be released (cf. *mitte*, 174), and the loosening of the *sinus* or folds of clothing/breasts from the girdle (*zonula*, 53) endow the bride with a constraint in the form of love. She, then, is to prevent her husband from turning to adultery by entwining him in her (loving) embrace. The husband will not want (*non . . . volet*, 97–100) to lie apart (*secubare*, [105]) from her tender breasts. Thus her embrace is the force that is needed to limit, specifically, her husband's desires (not his actions). The poem vividly imagines his possible adultery, with the word *non* ("not") the only control on very pejorative language: *levis* ("fickle"), *mala . . . adultera* ("wicked adulteress"), *probra turpia* ("shameful scandals") (97–99). Just as the bride is to constrain this activity, so the word *non* constrains (or attempts to constrain) the image of the husband engaging in shameful sexual infidelity.

The bride's role in containing her husband's desires is made more explicit when she encounters a male rival. And rather than imagined future competition, this competition is present. The groom is told to give up his *concubinus* or male slave sexual companion. (Note the same verb root, *cub-*, "to lie with, have sex with" is used for his relations with the bride, *secubare*.) While he is told that, of course, his activities with the slave boy have been "licit" (and this would be so because of the boy's status), he is also told that even such licit activities are not acceptable for a husband (139–41). The husband, we are told, will abstain with difficulty (*male*, 134) from his hairless (slave) boys (*glabris*, 135). The bride is then admonished to beware of denying to her husband what things he will seek from her, lest he seek them elsewhere (144–46). Here the needed constraining role of the bride is emphasized. It is with difficulty that her husband will abandon his future pleasures (like his former pleasure) with slave boys, and the plural broadens the threat to sexual exclusivity from the particular *concubinus* he has been enjoying up to the present to the group of slave boys as a whole. In addition, the groom's not seeking sexual activity elsewhere is now specifically tied to the bride "not saying no" sexually. Thus while the groom in the poem is expected to have a sexually exclusive relationship with the bride, it is her attractiveness (cf. the tender breasts) and her submission to his sexual demands that are established as the constraining power that creates his fidelity.

The language of mastery belongs, in one sense, to the bride, whose job is to constrain her new husband sexually. And in line 31, she is called to her new home as its mistress (*domum dominam*). Yet the issues of mastery and slavery are more complicated, for the *concubinus*, whose sexual activity with the groom is to be abandoned (*desertum . . . amorem*, 122–[130]), plays a structural role that is intertwined with that of both bride and groom. He is the one who must scatter nuts for the wedding, an activity typically performed by the groom.[13] The language of "not denying" with which the task is mentioned (*nec . . . neget*, 121) echoes that used of the responsibility of the bride (*ne neges*, 145) not to deny her husband's demands for sexual activity, thus confounding the relationships. The importance of the *concubinus* is highlighted by his performing in place of the groom an activity associated with the groom's own liminality. It is the groom's leaving behind of childhood and proceeding to fertile sexual activity that makes the former slave-boy lover "obsolete."

The *concubinus* himself is a liminal figure. He is described as *iners*, a significant word in the context of a wedding poem, for it can mean "impotent" (cf., e.g., Horace *Epodes* 12.16). In what sense might this figure be impotent? He is about to have his hair or (according to some commentators) his beard cut, signifying physical maturity.[14] The significance of hair is evident in lines 77–78 and 94–95, where *comae* ("hair") is used of the light of the wedding torches. The cutting of the hair of the *concubinus* signifies that he is getting too old to be a hairless, feminized object of desire.[15] But as he grows older, there could easily be other younger boys to replace him. So in a sense, he himself, ironically, becomes "impotent" as a love object for his master just as he becomes more physically mature and more of a "man."

The purpose, as we recall, of marriage is the production of children, and for this the groom needs a fertile bride. While the bride's *pudor* ("modesty, chastity," 79) slows down her procession to her new home, it is her production there of a male child who will resemble his father that will confirm her married chastity (*pudicitiam*, 217). Her chastity, like that of Penelope, the prototypical faithful wife, will assure her son's *fama* ([230]) or good reputation. This comparison, which clearly locates the burden of chastity and legitimacy with the female wife and mother, leaves the husband and father unmentioned. While the poem points in many ways to a sexually exclusive relationship for the marrying couple, this final image (final except for the injunction to sexual activity that follows) speaks as much through what it does not say as through what it does. The reader is left to supply the missing Odysseus, whose presence necessarily undercuts, to some extent, the ideal of a sexually exclusive marriage. While the recognition and reconciliation scene between Penelope and Odysseus in Homer's *Odyssey* Book 23 is an amazingly moving commentary on maturity, knowledge, and marriage, Odysseus does not work as an ideal model for marital sexual exclusivity. Poem 61, I would argue, is caught between the two competing ideals or assumptions about marriage mentioned at the beginning of this article, that of sexual exclusivity for both partners and that which allows additional non-disreputable sexual activity for the male. By leaving Odysseus absent, Catullus finesses this issue. Horace, reading Catullus, recovers the eclipsed Odysseus and explores the anxieties and social disturbances surrounding the attractions of non-marital sex.

If Catullus's poem 61 is concerned with the channeling of the erotic, and, especially, the channeling of male desire, into acceptable love in the context of marriage that leads to the production of legitimate offspring,

Horace's *Odes* 2.8 examines that same male desire when it has spun out
of control. If the social institution of marriage and, more specifically, the
beauty and sexual compliance of the bride are the vehicles through which
the husband is to have his desires controlled, then Horace's poem shows
us the nightmarish, awesome, but somewhat amusing, social chaos that
ensues when unacceptable love takes over because of the exciting and
frightening attraction of (female) sexuality outside of the controls of marriage. While in Catullus, the "social" in the form of marriage and the circumscribed role of the bride is supposed to put limits on the "erotic" for
the male, guiding his desire into faithful sexual activity and the production of children, in Horace, the "erotic" definitively takes precedence
over the "social," revealing the fragility of marriage's supposed control
of male desire.

   Odes 2.8, a poem of twenty-four lines, is addressed to Barine, whose
name alludes to the port city of Barium (modern Bari), located in Apu-
lia, Horace's native region in Italy. The Greek termination of her name
is suggestive of freedwoman status and separates her from conventional
expectations for respectable Roman women.[16] In the poem, the speaker
says that if Barine had ever received punishment for an oath falsely sworn
or were becoming uglier with one blackened tooth or nail, he would believe her (1–5). He continues (lines 5–8) to state that as soon as Barine
has bound her faithless head in vows, she shines much more beautifully
and goes forth as the public love object of the young men. She profits,
he says, from swearing falsely on the buried ashes of her mother, the
stars, and the gods (9–12). Venus herself, he continues, laughs at this, as
do the nymphs and Cupid (13–16). In addition, the young, a new group
of "slaves," "grows for her," while earlier admirers don't leave her although they've often threatened to (17–20). Mothers and old men fear
her, as do brides who worry that her "aura" will slow their husbands
down (21–24).

   Odes 2.8 has attracted little attention from Horace scholars, and I
think this is largely due to the fact that the poem has not been seen in
its larger literary, cultural, and historical contexts.[17] The poem, however,
is far more interesting than my reductive summary would suggest, and,
as I have anticipated in my discussion above, I hope to show how the
poem can be seen to function as Horace's "reading" of Catullus poem 61.
I owe my interest in the poem's Catullan connection to the very brief remarks written in 1902 by E. Ensor in "Notes on the *Odes* of Horace."
There he argued that the last four lines of *Odes* 2.8 parodied Catullus 61,
lines 51–55. In my discussion of *Odes* 2.8 in *Time and the Erotic in Horace's*

Odes, I expand upon that Catullan connection, arguing that the parody of poem 61 cuts deeper than a "malicious burlesquing" of Catullus (Ancona 1994.83). Pointing to additional echoes of poem 61 in Horace's ode, I argue that the bride and Barine are structurally identical because it is through their sexuality that male desire is (or is not) controlled. The present discussion will elaborate upon my previous analysis in two ways: first, by detailing further the ways in which the language of Horace in this poem echoes that of his predecessor, and, second, by placing the ode in the context of a larger Roman cultural discourse on marriage and desire.

In *Odes* 2.8, Horace ironically critiques his literary predecessor, Catullus, by taking anxieties about channeling and constraining male desire into the socially sanctioned institution of marriage and pushing them to their furthest extreme through the creation of a multigenerational, servile band of men that "grows" for Barine and, once under her spell, cannot depart. The attitude of the speaker in *Odes* 2.8, humorous yet disturbed, can be explained as emerging from the competing and potentially conflicting discourses in first-century b.c.e. Rome discussed above concerning the socially responsible and necessary institution of marriage for a man and the non-marital satisfaction of desire.

In our reading of *Odes* 2.8, it is helpful to look at the disjunction Catullus's contemporary Cicero outlines between a respectable married woman (or widow) and a disreputable prostitute in his speech *pro Caelio*. Of course Cicero's speech has as its rhetorical and practical goal the freeing of his defendant, Caelius, from the legal charges against him. (And Cicero was perfectly capable of arguing contrary things for different oratorical purposes.) Nevertheless, Cicero's strategy of helping Caelius by defaming the "respectable" Clodia Metelli is a relevant one, for it shifts the burden of guilt and responsibility away from the man he is trying to defend onto a woman whose status will determine whether her word has any legal standing. If her actions make her out to be a *meretrix* ("prostitute"), then he and the court can dismiss her accusations.[18] Cicero imagines a *non nupta mulier* ("not married woman") who opens up her own house (*domum suam*) to the desire of all (*omnium cupiditati*) and is therefore a whore or *meretrix* (*pro Caelio* 49). And it is this image that we are to identify with Clodia Metelli. (Whether or not the Clodia of Cicero's speech is the Clodia pseudonymously identified as Catullus's poetic "Lesbia" is not significant for this discussion, it is the social and sexual tensions she embodies that are apt.[19]) While Cicero's purpose is to condemn Clodia, he acknowledges elsewhere in his speech that young men are allowed to indulge in sexual affairs as long as they bring no dishonor. Thus it is not so much that the erotic apart from marriage is to be banished for the respectable Roman male as that it is to be confined both temporally (love affairs are the business of the young man) and socially (they must not harm those who have a reputation capable of being harmed). After he has safely indulged his youthful pleasures, let the good upper-class Roman male "call himself back to the care of his home, the Forum, and public life" ("revocet se aliquando ad curam rei domesticae, rei forensis reique publicae," *pro Caelio* 42).

This rhetoric, which calls upon shared values accepting harmless youthful male sexual indulgence before taking on the burden of public and domestic responsibility, is useful for analyzing Horace's response to Catullus 61. For Barine becomes the "anti-bride" (the Clodia?) who disrupts all the categories that poem 61 attempts to establish. Horace's poetic discourse "deifies" Barine while simultaneously making her a whore. It confuses public and private. It makes men slaves to their desire. It defies normal temporal expectations. It mocks the power of marriage and reproduces the anxieties of a world in which male desire is out of control. The tone of the poem, though, is certainly not that of a moral diatribe against Barine. The speaker reflects a kind of grudging admiration for Barine's powers, as well as a sense of his good luck in being immune from them. The word *crederem* ("I would believe, trust [you]") is the one-word apodosis to the contrary-to-fact protases that begin the poem. It is the speaker's lack of trust in Barine that allows him the distance to stand back in awe at the chaos she creates. The social and cultural context in which both Catullus and Horace wrote produced an uneasiness about the competing demands of desire and social responsibility. *Odes* 2.8 explores the attractive yet nightmarish world in which men do not "call themselves back" (to use Cicero's phrase) to their domestic, forensic, and public responsibilities.

How does Horace in a twenty-four-line ode write a "response" to Catullus's lengthy poem of over two hundred lines? The answer is through condensation. (For example, the *concubinus* and the future hairless boys are gone, subsumed under the one female Barine.) However, all of the major themes discussed in relation to Catullus 61 are here, as well as language that recalls and counters the sense of the earlier poem. The themes of marriage, beauty, family, and the production of children, chastity/fidelity, legitimacy, home, slavery, temporality, liminality, Venus, desire, constraints, movement, and reluctance all reappear transformed.

Poem 61, as a marriage poem, of necessity involves liminality. Bride and groom are poised between their unmarried and future married state.

Each is in transition from immaturity to maturity, for both bride and groom are depicted as young. In actual experience, many upper-class Roman marriages would have involved couples in which one or both partners were older than Catullus's pair due to such factors as divorce, remarriage, and death from illness, war (in the case of men), or childbirth (in the case of women), etc.[20] However, it is a youthful marriage that is celebrated in this poem for Torquatus and his bride. The physical threshold or *limen* to be crossed is that of the bride's new marital, as opposed to natal, home. In Horace's poem, the young men (and young women) have crossed the threshold to marriage, but the husbands have not united successfully with their brides alone. The brides are described as *nuper virgines* ("recently maidens, virgins," 22–23), but their husbands are already off at Barine's house, and the wives are anxious about their return. Barine, described as a mistress (*dominae*, 19), has control over both her home (*tectum*, 19) and the men who visit her and fail to leave. The bride, in Catullus, called to her new home as a mistress (*dominam*) desirous of her new husband ("ac domum dominam voca / coniugis cupidam novi," 31–32), has been supplanted by a new *domina*.

Thus the image of liminality as presented by Catullus in terms of marriage in both its temporal and physical sense is disrupted by Horace, who takes the grooms away from the physical place where they belong (home with their wives) and extends their non-marital sex into the time of marriage. The control that the new bride was to exert over her husband in order to keep him away from non-marital sexual activity in the Catullus poem is ineffective in the poem by Horace. While, in Catullus, the liminal figure of the *concubinus* and other female or feminized objects of desire were to be banished by the power of the new wife, in Horace, Barine, a female object of desire who is not a wife, has taken control.

In fact, Barine acts as an almost "anti-liminal" figure, for while others age over time and typically grow less attractive as objects of desire, she actually becomes more beautiful. In poem 61, it was the bride's physical attractiveness and sexual availability that was to serve as a control upon her husband's desires. She was to provide the sex he wanted. In Horace, Barine's beauty, increasing with each false oath, is what draws her band of lovers. Barine and the bride are linked through the language used to describe their beauty. While the bride is "shining" (*enitens*, 21, and *nitens*, 186), and no woman is more beautiful than she (*pulcrior*, 84), Barine shines much more beautifully (*enitescis / pulchrior multo*, 6–7) every time she swears a false oath about love. Barine and the bride of Catullus 61 also have identical structural functions. It is their sexuality that car-

ries the burden of men's fidelity or lack of fidelity. In poem 61, it is a failure of female attractiveness if the husband wanders. There the wife, released into marriage, binds her mind with love and then binds her husband in her loving embrace. The wife's role is to exert constraint upon
unconstrained male desire. Whereas the bride's beauty is intended to
"snare" her husband, and she has already bound her own mind with love,
in Horace's poem, Barine binds (*obligasti*, 5) her faithless head (*perfidum
caput*, 6) in false vows. The binding and the false swearing are connected
temporally (5: *simul*, "as soon as") with her growing beauty and with her
going forth as public care/worry/love object of the young (*iuvenumque
prodis / publica cura*, 7–8), perverting the image of fidelity and constraint
found in poem 61. The use of the comparative *turpior* ("if you were becoming uglier") in the protasis of the condition that is "answered" by *pulchrior* ("more beautiful") recalls the description of shameful scandals (*probra turpia*) the bride in poem 61 is supposed to ward off. This verbal echo
makes Barine's lack of physical ugliness in the light of her faithlessness
all the more striking. It is disturbing when physical beauty and "beautiful" acts are not automatically linked.

   The disruption to the natural order found in a woman whose outer
beauty does not guarantee inner beauty or fidelity also functions in terms
of issues of power and mastery. The bride's role as *domina*, earned
through her chastity and marriage, is mocked when Barine, the new *domina*, controls the men who do not leave her presence, even when they
have threatened to do so. Barine's role as *domina* suggests not only her
supplanting of the marital *domus* but also her taking on the role of mistress, in the sense of female master, over her slavish admirers. The fact
that the female object of desire in the genre of elegy is referred to as *domina* adds to the sense of social chaos, for the elegiac lover cannot be a
dominus, a socially responsible, adult, married male.[21] In poem 61, the
issue of slavery was intimately connected with desire. The groom had
to abandon his male slave lover, and his bride was to keep him from similar liaisons in the future as well as from adultery. Thus Horace picks up
on the idea of slavery and removes the bride from a position of control
or mastery, replacing her with Barine. Barine's location in a house and
her attendance by slaves (*servitus nova*) turns inside out the "proper"
functions of home, master versus slave, and husband versus wife. What
compounds the image is the "pileup" of males who have been drawn as
if by a magnet to Barine and are unable to leave her. Barine creates temporal as well as physical disorder. Not only are men physically with her
when they should be with their wives, but men become temporally

"stuck" with her when they should be progressing through their adult male lives. Horace replaces Catullus's focus on the liminal pair on the threshold of marriage with a continually growing group of men stuck on (or past) the literal *limen* or threshold of Barine's house. Lines 17–20 present a capsule image of enslaved men: from all the young men growing up for her, to a new group of slaves growing up for her, to the earlier ones (*priores*) who do not leave. Time progresses, but once they arrive, those in her thrall do not leave.

That the men threaten to leave but don't suggests that their sexual capacity is creating a social incapacity. The repetition in the Catullus poem of forms of the word *bonus* ("good, noble"), of the refrain to the god Hymen, and, finally, of the injunction to the married pair to spend their life *munere assiduo*, in "uninterrupted or constantly recurring sexual activity/duty" is perverted here into a repetition of uncontrolled male sexual excitation that runs counter to any sense of marital and social duty. The word *nova* ("new"), used repeatedly by Catullus of the bride in the refrain, *prodeas, nova nupta*, is transferred to Barine's "new" group of slaves (*servitus . . . nova*, 18) who are "growing up" for her, and this new group recalls the group of male slaves away from whom the bride was to keep her new husband (cf. *glabris*). Thus the attention given to the fresh new bride is switched to the fresh new crop of all the young (*pubes . . . omnis*, 17) who will become slaves of Barine. "*Crescit*, the verb used to describe the activity of this new generation, suggests both the normal maturation of young men (they are 'growing up'), and their literal sexual response to Barine (they are 'growing big'). (The latter, more literal, sense is mimed by the repetition of *crescit* in lines 17 and 18, which imitates in language the build-up of the young men's desire)."[22] The idea of slavery applied to the young men growing up for Barine is extended to the older men who, because they threaten to leave but remain, become "lesser men." Their out-of-control male desire becomes incapacitating with regard to social obligations like family.

Of course, the function of marriage as seen in Catullus 61 is the production of legitimate children to carry on the family line. Married sex, while entailing pleasure, has as its goal the creation of the next generation. The physical similarity between the son to be produced and his father confirms the child's legitimacy and the chastity of the wife. In *Odes* 2.8, however, sexual activity becomes dangerously divorced from procreation. The conventional language used of the bride's sense of modesty or chastity "slowing down" her movement towards marriage in poem 61, *tardet ingenuus pudor* (79), is ironically recalled and transformed by Horace into the new brides' fears that their new husbands will be "slowed down" or "detained" by Barine: "tua ne retardet/aura maritos" (23–24).[23] It should be noted that the groom delays as well, but not for long. (Cf. *ne remorare*, "do not delay" [200] and *non diu remoratus es*, "you have not delayed long,"194.)

The sexual nature of the delay is further supported by the word *aura*, the subject of the verb *retardet* ("slow down"). While the word can mean "breeze" or "allure," it is also used in Latin to refer specifically to the sexual emanation or smell that attracts male animals to females. A particularly powerful example of this use of *aura* can be found in Vergil's *Georgics* 3.250–51: "nonne vides ut tota tremor pertemptet equorum/corpora, si tantum notas odor attulit auras?" ("Don't you see how a tremor affects deeply the entire bodies of the male horses, if only the smell has brought the famous breezes?"). The context of the Vergilian passage is the inability of the male to resist this sexual attraction. As Ensor notes (1902.110), Horace's *aura* plays aurally on Catullus's *aure* in poem 61, line 55. In Catullus, the new husband timidly listens for (*captat*) Hymen, god of marriage, *cupida . . . aure*, "with eager, desirous ear." In Horace, *aure* becomes *aura* and, rather than eagerly awaiting marriage, wives fear their husbands, like animals, are dangerously attracted to a non-marital love. Issues of marriage, fidelity, potency, and the production of legitimate offspring all combine in these lines. And the attraction of the men to Barine in an animal-like fashion suggests the powerlessness of social constraints over male sexual desire.

While the focus in much of the poem is on Barine's allure for the young—the mothers fear for their young (*iuvencis*) who may become Barine's next slaves (*iuvencis* is used in its primary sense of young animals)—"sparing" old men (*senes parci*, 22) fear her as well. The placement of the *senes* between the mothers and the brides and the lack of a specific object for their fear—in some sense it may be that of the mothers, in some sense that of the brides—makes the adjective *parci* of special interest. I would suggest that their fears may be both financial and sexual. Financially, Barine poses a threat to young men who may waste their family money on her. (Such wasting of money on love affairs by young men is a common theme in Roman comedy, as well as in speeches like the *pro Caelio*, mentioned above.) In addition, if we extend the notion inherent in *priores* ("the earlier ones"), who is to say that the old men are not still captives of Barine and in danger of financial and sexual ruin themselves? Their "sparing" nature may refer to their diminished sexual capacities after continued contact with Barine. The shameful sexual infidelity imaged but seemingly controlled by the negative word *non* ("not") in Catullus 61, breaks free from its restraints in Horace *Odes* 2.8.

Barine's enigmatic and disturbing status is perhaps best seen in lines 7–8: *iuvenumque prodis / publica cura* ("And you go forth as the public worry, love object of the young"). This clause is worthy of extensive discussion, for its highly evocative language helps to position Barine in terms of both her appeal and her production of worry and fear. The Latin words themselves operate on several levels, but they also allude to earlier Greek poetry in some significant ways. We have already discussed Barine's appeal to the young. Let us now examine the rest of the language of the passage.

In Catullus 61 (92, 96, 106, 113), the bride is repeatedly asked in a refrain to go forth (*prodeas nova nupta*) to her new home. The verb *prodeo* seems to echo a traditional formula used in relation to the bride.[24] In addition, it has been noted that the repeated *prodeas*, directed towards the bride in Catullus 61, may echo the triple call for Athena's appearance in Callimachus's Hymn 5, lines 33, 43, and 55 (ἔξιθι, "go out, forth").[25] This use of traditional language for the bride and the echo of Callimachus's call to the goddess Athena draw attention to both the virginal and the goddess-like aspects of the bride. This makes all the more striking Horace's use of the verb "go forth" in relation to Barine. In addition, as one critic states: "The generalizing present tense of *prodis* conveys endless repetition of this process" (Sutherland 2002.109). What is the process Barine is engaged in? The *Oxford Latin Dictionary* cites this Horatian passage under the meaning "appear in public, show oneself in a particular fashion" (2b), while the use of the verb in the Catullan refrain is listed under the meaning "come out of doors, come out" (1b).[26] This distinction is a useful one, for it points to the very different connotations of the verb. While the bride is being called forth from her home to go to her new one, Barine is described as appearing in public in a certain way. What does it mean to go forth or appear in public as a *publica cura*? That Barine is simultaneously sex goddess and whore accounts for her ability to produce awe, desire, and fear, and both of these roles emerge from the phrase *publica cura*.

The linking of the word *publica* with *cura* raises Barine to the status of a "public object of anxiety, concern." The first meaning of the word *cura* in the *OLD* is "anxiety" or the "object of anxiety or care." However, *cura* is a standard word in Latin love poetry specifically for the lover's object of desire.[27] The beloved functions as a *cura* because of what the lover invests in the beloved. The beloved is the focus not only of love and desire but of concern and anxiety as well. While the word *iuvenum* ("of youths") suggests that Barine's effect may be primarily on the young, this modifying genitive loses some of its limiting power in a sense with the word *publica*. As a *cura*, Barine is simultaneously an object of worry and of desire. That *cura* is described as *publica* extends both worry about her and desire for her to the public at large. As one scholar notes: "Whores are sometimes called 'women of the people, public, common' for the obvious reason that in a sense they belong to everyone" (Adams 1983.343). In addition, the feminine noun *publica* appears in Latin with the meaning of "prostitute."[28] Still further, the phrase *publica cura* has a Greek antecedent that, to the best of my knowledge, has not been noted. In Alcman fragment 3, the female leader who is the object of amorous attention on the part of the girl members of the chorus is named Astumeloisa ('Αστυμέλοισα) or "city object of care/anxiety/desire" and is described as an "object of care/anxiety/desire to the people" (μέλημα δάμωι, 74), which, of course, contains a pun on her name. In addition, in fragment 163, Sappho (who is a major influence on Catullus) uses the word μέλημα for "object of desire." I would argue that these Greek intertextual echoes in the Latin phrase *publica cura* enhance the positive erotic potential of Barine. In addition, the echo of Alcman, in particular, brings out the complicated issues of public and private in relation to desire because of Astumeloisa's status as an object of individual (female) desire as well as as an object for the "people."[29] Nisbet-Hubbard's comment (1978.127) that the phrase *publica cura* calls to mind sentiment that is undermined by suggestions of promiscuity gets at the rather uncomfortable mix of public and private at work in the poem. Their note that the phrase "suggests that Barine causes a national crisis" (1978.127) looks to the way in which interpretation of Barine is a social as well as a private "affair."

This double nature of Barine—goddess and whore—is perhaps reflective of the split to be seen in the goddess Venus. In Catullus 61, "Venus and love become 'virtuous' because of the legitimizing role of Hymen, suggesting the illicit potential of Venus/love in the absence of marriage" (Ancona 1994.84). In Horace's ode, where marriage is threatened by the allure of non-marital sex, Venus is tied not to marriage but to the awe-inspiring and treacherous love of Barine. And unlike poem 61, where Venus is connected with the bride, here Venus's interests run counter to those of the new brides. She is an amused supporter of an object of male desire out of control. Allied with her in her amusement is the figure of her son, Cupid, who is described as *ferus* ("wild"), just like the groom (*fero iuveni)* in poem 61, line 56. While in Catullus 61, it is the (wild) young groom who receives the bride into his hands from the mother's embrace, in *Odes* 2.8, the "wildness" of Cupid is framed outside of the context of marriage. And, of course, it is this very sense that desire is something potentially out of control for (young) men that creates both excitement and social discomfort in *Odes* 2.8. In poem 61, "good" Venus is found in the context of marriage. Here, she just laughs.[30]

I hope to have shown how an intertextual reading of Catullus 61 and Horace *Odes* 2.8 can contribute not only to our understanding of the common cultural anxieties that inform both poems but to our appreciation of the very different literary treatment Horace gives to these anxieties. In both poems, male desire and its need to be controlled for the sake of social order is central. In Catullus's poem, marriage is held out as the vehicle for that control, and the liminal male is shown the way to a channeling of his desire into legitimate marital eroticism that will produce children to carry on the family line. Yet even in Catullus's poem, the potential threats to such channeled male desire are hinted at. In *Odes* 2.8, Horace assumes the role of reader and reviser of his literary predecessor by taking anxieties about channeling male desire into the socially sanctioned institution of marriage and pushing them to their limit. Parodying Catullus, who focuses in poem 61 on the liminal figure of the man about to marry and the consequent changes required upon marriage for the direction of his desires, Horace creates a somewhat comical, but also disturbing, image of successive generations of men (those coming to maturity, the newly married, and the older) unable to comply with the necessity of channeling their desires in socially acceptable directions. Despite Horace's special focus on the liminal male, Barine's multigenerational lovers suggest the continuing challenge posed by unrestrained male desire. Both Catullus and Horace in these two poems engage the notion of the precariousness for the male of the social ideals and practices surrounding marriage and desire in first-century B.C.E. Rome. That Horace could and did develop the latent disturbance to marriage lurking in Catullus 61 shows how his reading of poem 61 is both a creative act in itself and a tribute to its original.

Notes

1. In both scenarios, the woman, of course, was expected to enter her marriage as a virgin unless she had been married previously.

2. Shelton 1998.296–97, who cites this passage as an example of the marital double standard.

3. See Janan 1994 for a Lacanian analysis of the "gaps" in Catullus and for the necessity of abandoning a search for "consistency."

4. For Catullus's influence on Horace, see, e.g., Lee 1975, Mendell 1935, and, more recently, Hubbard 2000–01, Ancona 2002, and Woodman 2002.

5. See Fedeli 1983 for a very complete discussion of poem 61. See Thomson 1997.347–48 on its structure. Line numbers cited for poem 61 are those of Thomson 1997.

6. See Thomson 1997.348–49, but, for another view, Wiseman 1985.199, cited by Thomson.

7. See Fedeli 1983.83 for discussion of the history of the genre.

8. See Katz 2002 and Williams 1999.52–54 and 31, 73, 284.

9. Williams 1999.54. Williams' analysis of poem 61 points out both the exclusive marital ideal to be found there as well as the threat to it of the power of the erotic.

10. Cf. Skinner 1997 for a discussion of Attis as the liminal male in Catullus 63.

11. That Catullus was interested in the idea of repetition is particularly obvious in his echoing use of the word *identidem* ("again and again") in poems 11 and 51.

12. All translations are mine.

13. Fedeli 1983.89–90. The significance of the scattering of the nuts was unclear even to the Romans. The activity may have connections with fertility or the giving up of childhood (nuts were used in children's games). See Thomson 1997.357 ad loc. 121.

14. See Thomson 1997.358 ad loc. 131–32.

15. On hairless or depilated boys as desirable and specific references to them including Horace *Odes* 4.10, see Williams 1999.73.

16. See Nisbet and Hubbard 1978.125 ad loc.

17. For treatments of the poem, see Esler 1989, Ancona 1994.76–85, West 1998.56–60, and Sutherland 2002.108–13.

18. See the *Oxford Classical Dictionary* under *infamia*.

19. See Dixon 2001.ch.9: "The Allure of 'La Dolce Vita' in Ancient Rome" for recent bibliography on this issue as well as an excellent examination of the attractions of identifying Cicero's Clodia with Catullus's Lesbia despite problems with the evidence.

20. See, e.g., Gardner 1986.ch.3: "Marriage."

21. Sutherland 2002 argues that Horace in *Odes* 2.8 creates a masculine lyric mastery over effeminate, elegiac, disorder.

22. Ancona 1994.81. Minadeo 1982 also notes the phallic excitation in the repeated *crescit*. For *cresco* in a sexual sense elsewhere, cf. Vergil *Eclogues* 10.54 (where it is repeated) and 73.

23. See Fedeli 1983.70 on delay as a likely conventional motif in wedding ceremonies and songs. For support for the sexual pun in *retardet*, see, e.g., Col-

umella *de Re Rustica* 10.109, where *tardus* is used of "slow" husbands who need an aphrodisiac: "excitet ut Veneri tardos eruca maritos."

24. Fedeli 1983.70–71 and Plautus *Casina* 806, cited there.

25. Fedeli 1983.70. For another Callimachaean echo in poem 61, cf. Wiseman 1985.113 n. 71 on Hymen as son of Urania.

26. It is worth noting that the form *prodis* can also be derived from the verb *prodo*. I would suggest that the meanings "publish" and "betray" of this alternate verb may be seen as possibly lurking in the Horace poem as well.

27. Cf., e.g., Vergil *Eclogues* 10.22 and Propertius *Elegies* 2.25.1.

28. Cf. the *OLD* for *publica* listed as a feminine noun with citations from Seneca *Epistles* 88.37 and Propertius 4.7.39.

29. There are gaps in the Alcman fragment that make some issues less than clear in the poem. However, I do not think that they affect my argument here. Cf., e.g., Campbell 1982.213–15 and Hutchinson 2001.103–09.

30. On alternate visions of love (marital, non-marital, etc.) in Horace *Odes* 4.1, cf. Habinek 1986.

3 Gender Identity and the Elegiac Hero in Propertius 2.1

Ellen Greene

The elegiac lover's well-known stance of sexual servitude and his characterization of both himself and his verse as *mollis* ("soft") establish a feminine persona for the male lover that becomes one of the chief topoi in elegiac poetry.[1] Of the elegiac poets, Propertius is often considered to be the inventor of the image of *servitium amoris* ("the servitude of love"). Throughout the first three books of the *Elegies*, the Propertian lover appears hopelessly enslaved to a woman he describes as *domina* ("mistress," with connotations of "dominance"). The elegiac enterprise in general, especially in Propertius's amatory texts, seems to subvert Roman conventions of masculinity by assigning to the male narrator traits typically associated with women: *servitium* ("servitude"), *mollitia* ("softness"), and *levitas* ("levity, light-mindedness"). The male lover thus presents himself as devoted, dependent, and passive, and, in turn, often depicts his mistress as *dura* ("hard"). The gender inversion implicit in the narrator's stance ostensibly allows the Propertian lover to embrace a philosophy of life that overturns traditional gender roles and violates the principles by which women are under male authority.[2]

Indeed, one of the most striking features of Propertian elegy, as both Maria Wyke and Barbara Gold argue, is the way the male narrator often takes "the woman's part," adopting what seems to be the woman's conventional attributes of subservience and softness.[3] While, in his first book, Propertius largely maintains the fiction of gender reversal, the *amator* ("male lover") often undermines his own rhetoric of subservience by constructing mythical stories (*exempla*) that depict him in the role of rescuer, protector, and hero before a defenseless and captive mistress.[4] In this paper, I argue that the heroic persona the male lover *implicitly* imag-

61

ines for himself in Book 1 becomes more overt in the second book. My study will focus on Propertius's programmatic poem 2.1, a text that offers a dramatic example of the ways in which the speaker in Book 2 constantly vacillates between an image of himself as the soft poet of elegy and an identification with the values and ideals associated with masculine epic.[5]

Throughout Book 2, the narrator identifies himself with the images of disease and vulnerability characteristically associated with the Sapphic and Catullan traditions of portraying eros as disintegrating and disabling to the lover.[6] Propertius carries on this tradition not only by having the male lover explicitly characterize himself as subject to the violent ravages of desire but also by dramatizing the experience of fragmentation through the conflicting gender identities he associates with the male lover. Unlike the Catullan lover, the speaker in Propertius's poems does not try to overcome his "feminine" powerlessness and vulnerability by using arguments on himself to exert the manly self-control and *dignitas* ("honor, self-respect") expected of any Roman male citizen wishing to live up to his social and moral obligations.[7] The Propertian *amator*, instead, expresses gender dissonance in the way he shifts subtly between epic and elegiac discourses and between conflicting images of himself and his mistress. Moreover, the more emphatic association of the elegiac mistress with literary production in Book 2 heightens the ambivalent nature of the speaker's gender identity and dramatizes more forcefully the amator's vacillations between lover and poet.[8] Despite the narrator's repeated declarations that he rejects the more lofty occupation of epic poet, he, nonetheless, often identifies himself with the ideals and discourses of that manner of writing. In so doing, I argue, the Propertian speaker not only circumvents the feminine persona that he establishes for himself in the first book, he also reveals a discourse that can elude categorization. To be sure, the fact that Propertius's elegiac discourse constantly resists precise formulation coincides with the problematization and destabilization of traditional generic categories in Augustan poetry.[9]

Propertius's opening programmatic poem of Book 2 takes the form of a *recusatio* ("refusal"), a form that traditionally rejects engagement with other kinds of discourse such as epic or encomium.[10] As Paul Allen Miller argues (2001), Propertius's opening poem shows that his project in Book 2 is based on both his refusal to embrace "normative Augustan discourse" and his acceptance of it. The speaker in the poem begins by describing his book as *mollis*, soft and effeminate, and links this characterization with the announcement that his *puella* ("girl"), rather than Calliope or the Muses, inspires him (1–4):

Quaeritis, unde mihi totiens scribantur amores,
    unde meus veniat mollis in ora liber?
non haec Calliope, non haec mihi cantat Apollo.
    ingenium nobis ipsa puella facit.

You ask how love poems are written so often by me,
    how my book comes soft on the lips?
Neither Calliope nor Apollo sings these songs for me.
    The girl herself creates my talent.

At first, the speaker accords his mistress blanket authority by asserting that she herself (*ipsa puella*) gives rise to his poetic talent. The *amator*'s conventional stance of passivity is reinforced by the passive *scribantur* in line 1, while the mistress's active role is emphasized by the agency ascribed to her in *facit* at line 4.

Indeed, the distinct roles of active and passive, traditionally associated with the mistress and the male lover, seem to be reinforced by the speaker's use of *nobis* in line 4. In depicting himself as a passive recipient, the speaker uses the personal pronoun *mihi* but then switches to the more impersonal *nobis* to describe the *ingenium* arising from *ipsa puella*. To be sure, the use of the first-person plural to refer to the speaker is a convention in Roman elegy. But here the abrupt change from *mihi* to *nobis* is striking and suggests a public dimension to the *puella's* role in the production of literary discourse. This public dimension may recall the association of the elegiac mistress with the poet's *fama* in Book 1. In poem 1.11, for example, the figure of the beloved Cynthia is inextricably tied to her role as narrative *materia* in the poet's writing.[11] The speaker in 1.11 makes clear that the poet's place in posterity is dependent on the mistress's own *fama* (in the double senses of Cynthia's "reputation" and the "fame" that results from continuing to be the subject of the poet's elegies). While in 2.1 the speaker attributes agency to the *puella* in making her the "cause" of his poetic talent, the use of *nobis* in line 4 hints at an image of her as a vehicle for the speaker's artistic fame. The *puella* provokes an *ingenium* not only for the speaker but, as *nobis* suggests, for the benefit of present and future audiences. It may also be argued that *nobis* alludes more specifically to the speaker and Maecenas, since the "you" of *quaeritis* ("you ask") refers to the speaker's immediate addressee: Maecenas. If that is the case, then the speaker implicitly privileges *amicitia* over *amor* here.[12] The speaker suggests that the *puella*, cast in the conventional role of *domina*, is herself the medium for an exchange between men.

In lines 5–8, the speaker goes on to provide a seemingly logical litany of cause and effect relationships between the mistress and the poetic skill she inspires.

> sive illam Cois fulgentem incedere vidi,
>> totum de Coa veste volumen erit;
> seu vidi ad frontem sparsos errare capillos,
>> gaudet laudatis ire superba comis;

> If I have seen her step forth gleaming in Coan silks,
>> a whole book will emerge from her Coan garment;
> if I have seen her scattered locks wandering on her brow,
>> she, proud, enjoys walking with praised hair.

That logic dissolves at line 8 when the narrator tells us that once he has seen Cynthia's scattered locks and has praised them, she walks proudly with "praised hair." The speaker's act of gazing at his mistress seems to be the cause of her *laudatis comis*. The speaker asserted earlier that Cynthia "creates" his poetic talent, yet here it appears that the image of the mistress as *superba* depends on the poet's *ingenium* to praise her. The images of Cynthia as both joyful and *superba* derive syntactically from the speaker's actions of looking at her and being able to describe what he sees. It turns out, in fact, that the poet-lover is most inspired when the mistress is asleep, only then does he discover *causas mille novas* for his verse (11–14):

> seu compescentis somnum declinat ocellos,
>> invenio causas mille poeta novas;
> seu nuda erepto mecum luctatur amictu,
>> tum vero longas condimus Iliadas:

> or if, requiring sleep, she lets her eyelids fall,
>> I, poet, discover a thousand new themes;
> or if, her dress torn off, she struggles naked with me,
>> then, truly, I compose long *Iliads*.

In addition, after he describes Cynthia with her clothing torn off, presumably by him, he proclaims that then he is able to compose *longae Iliadae*. In both instances, the *puella's* position of vulnerability, either asleep or naked, leads to an intensification of the narrator's poetic talent—or at least to fantasies of such talent arising in him. But despite his declarations that the *puella's* words and deeds inspire him to write verse, he admits finally that a "maxima de nihilo historia nascitur" ("A great story is born out of nothing," 16). Given the authority and agency earlier accorded to the *puella*, the narrator's statement here seems paradoxical. The logic of the speaker's argument requires us to equate the nothing (*nihil*) that generates the speaker's verse with the mistress herself.

Interestingly, the word the *amator* uses to describe his new poetic inventions is *causas*, implying that he, rather than the mistress is the *causa* of his own creations. In addition, we can observe a division in the speaker's presentation of himself: he shifts from speaking in the first person (*vidi*) to referring to himself in the third person as a *poeta*. The personas of fictive lover and elegiac poet seem to be split off from one another and to be linked with gendered modes of speech. The lover who speaks in the first person (*mihi* and *vidi*) identifies himself with the *mollis* mode of speech associated with elegy, while the *poeta* in line 12 implicitly imagines himself in a position of dominance over a sleeping and naked mistress. It is that dominance that apparently gives rise to his grandiose fantasies of literary production. Moreover, the poem's seemingly univocal elegiac discourse is quickly disrupted by allusions to epic. They begin with references to amorous violence in line 13 and continue with the announcement that such violence provokes the narrator to write his own long epics (Miller 2001). Despite his avowed rejection of epic poetry, the speaker, in his identity as *poeta*, links himself not only to the masculine genre of epic but also to the traditional gender hierarchies associated with that genre. As *poeta*, the speaker constructs a *maxima historia* out of a woman, or *de nihilo*.

Further, by describing his slender verse in epic terms, the speaker undermines his own claim that epic lies beyond his grasp. Casting elegy in terms of epic diminishes the distance between these seemingly opposite modes of composition and, moreover, calls into question the autonomy of the very categories of epic and elegy, *durus* and *mollis*, that his *recusatio* is predicated upon. More generally, elegy's resistance to traditional values and its blurring of generic categories emphasize its multivocal nature.[13] It may also be argued that genres in general are constituted through a dialectical relationship with other genres.[14] Indeed, throughout 2.1, Propertius identifies elegy as a generic category precisely by means of its opposition to epic, thus suggesting that elegy derives its meaning, its "borders," through constant references to what is *other*. In line 14, the speaker asserts that amatory struggle gives rise to the production of epic; his *longae Iliadae* are not offered as *analogies* to elegiac verse. Rather, the speaker states that amatory experience—in particular the defenseless position of the *puella*—leads directly to epic composition.

The *amator* thus elevates his own long tale of amatory troubles to epic proportions, implying that *amor* is as worthy a subject of commemoration as military conquest. Not only, as Duncan Kennedy suggests, does the *puella* stand in as the *hostis* of elegy, but the male lover also reconfigures himself as a hero worthy of confronting an adversary he describes here and throughout the elegies as *dura*: the elegiac mistress.[15]

The conflation of epic and elegiac discourses and of the speaker's position as lover and poet is reinforced when the speaker addresses Maecenas directly in line 17 and provides him with a list of epic subjects he cannot undertake. Naming Maecenas, however, in the context of the speaker's *recusatio* explicitly introduces another relationship that ostensibly aligns the speaker with a rhetoric of subservience. As Ellen Oliensis argues, the asymmetry in the client-patron relationship mirrors the fiction of gender reversal in the bond between lover and beloved depicted in elegy.[16] The mention of Maecenas's name not only evokes the "network of relations between men" in Roman society but also underscores Maecenas's superior status as well as the speaker's avowed position of erotic subjection. Oliensis argues, however, that the client's subordinate status links him with the beloved rather than the lover, since the lover only feigns subservience while the client experiences it (Oliensis 1997b.152). On the surface, the association of Maecenas with male public culture is reinforced by the inclusion of his name in the speaker's list of masculine subjects for song, subjects he rejects. Indeed, the narrator's long excursus on the history of epic themes, from the battle of the Titans through Augustus's glorious feats, sustains the speaker's identification with epic ideals implicitly expressed earlier in his description of the elegiac enterprise in terms of masculine epic. Moreover, the highly embellished language with which the speaker presents these epic themes, ironically, attests to his ability to memorialize epic achievements with as much skill as he describes his amorous exploits.

After his demonstration of poetic virtuosity, the speaker assures his patron that, if he were to write encomiastic epic, his muse (*mea Musa*) would interweave (*contexeret*) Maecenas into his epic themes (25–26, 35–38):

> bellaque resque tui memorarem Caesaris, et tu
>   Caesare sub magno cura secunda fores.

> I would commemorate your Caesar's wars and deeds, and you,
>   after the great Caesar, would be my second care.

te mea Musa illis semper contexeret armis,
  et sumpta et posita pace fidele caput.

Theseus infernis, superis testatur Achilles,
  hic Ixioniden, ille Menoetiaden;

My Muse would always weave you into these exploits,
  you, loyal soul, in taking up or rejecting peace.

Theseus in the underworld, Achilles in the world of men
  bore witness, the one for Pirithous, the other for Patroklos.

Earlier, the speaker identified *ipsa puella* as his source of inspiration in place of the Muses. The reference here to *mea Musa* thus weaves an image of the elegiac mistress into images of war, again linking the production of elegy with that of epic and also conflating the normative gender roles associated with those genres. This conflation is reinforced by the speaker's promise to Maecenas that any commemoration he might offer to Augustus would also celebrate Maecenas. Ellen Oliensis points out (1997b.154–55) that "*amicitia* and *amor* are not only cognate," they have analogous hierarchical structures. She argues, rightly, that what matters most in the sexual ideology of Rome is not the gender of the participants but their positions as active or passive partners. Oliensis also argues that the asymmetrical client-patron relationship often has a sexual component, and we can see hints of this in Propertius's presentation of the speaker's relationship to Maecenas.

Any supposed subordination in the speaker's relationship to his patron is called into question in a number of ways. W. A. Camps asserts that Propertius had adequate enough means so as not to need a patron (1967.68). If that was true, then it is possible that the relationship implied in the speaker's address to Maecenas is of a more intimate nature than that between client and patron—or at least we may say that the relationship, particularly its hierarchical structure, is indeterminate. Indeed, unlike Tibullus, who specifically celebrates Messalla's military exploits in the context of his *recusatio*, the Propertian poet-lover imagines Maecenas only in the context of his verse: a fiction within his creative universe.[17] The speaker tells Maecenas that after he commemorates the wars and deeds of Caesar, he (Maecenas) will be his *secunda cura* ("second care, concern"). The use of the word *cura* to describe what Maecenas means to the speaker seems to emphasize a more personal bond between them. Although *cura* can signify an object of literary study, it also often implies concern and devotion. The word stands out, especially in contrast to the list of the abstract, impersonal glories of the epic heroes and Augustus. Moreover, the affectionate manner with which the speaker refers to Maecenas in line 36 as *fidele caput* heightens the personal nature of his address to his putative patron.[18] Such a personal address has a disruptive quality in the context of the speaker's litany of Augustus's achievements—all of which involve the impersonal destruction of people and places (27–34):

> nam quotiens Mutinam aut civilia busta Philippos
>   aut canerem Siculae classica bella fugae,
> eversosque focos antiquae gentis Etruscae,
>   et Ptolemaeei litora capta Phari,
> aut canerem Aegyptum et Nilum, cum attractus in urbem
>   septem captivis debilis ibat aquis,
> aut regum auratis circumdata colla catenis,
>   Actiaque in Sacra currere rostra Via;

> For as often as I sang of Mutina or Philippi,
>   that citizens' graveyard, or the naval battle,
> the rout at Sicily, the ruined hearths of Etruria's
>   ancient race, and the captured shores near Ptolemy's
> lighthouse, or I would sing of Egypt and the Nile,
>   when dragged into Rome, it went feebly with its
> seven streams captive, or the necks of kings circled with golden chains,
>   or beaked ships running along the Sacred Way.

The speaker's reference to Maecenas as *fidelis* ("faithful"), an attribute associated in elegy with the ideal relations between the lover and his mistress, further links *amor* and *amicitia*. It also conflates distinctions between the masculine power relations implicit in the client-patron relationship and the more disreputable (feminine) sphere of amatory relations. The manly pledges between client and patron contained in the concept of *fides* are closely tied to the vows lovers make to one another. In addition, as Oliensis points out (1997b.153), the presence of a patron's name in elegiac verse adds a public dimension to the poetry and also calls to mind the extraliterary reality of the social and sexual subordination at the heart of the client-patron relationship. However, the speaker in 2.1, while personalizing his address to Maecenas, makes it clear that Maecenas exists in his poems as a *name in a text*. Like the elegiac mistress, Maecenas, as another theme in the poet's verse, is subject to the rhetorical control of the speaker. The patron's future reputation, like the *puella's*, would depend on the poet endowing him with the heroic attributes worthy of inclusion in commemorative verse.

Indeed, the speaker's mythological comparisons between his would-be celebration of Maecenas and the commemorations of Achilles and Theseus for their companions seem to reinforce the speaker's privileging of *amicitia* over *amor* and to underscore the hierarchies in the client-patron relationship. Yet the speaker's implicit comparison of himself to Theseus and Achilles positions the speaker as a figure of heroic proportions whose own fame guarantees the fame of his comrade. As a Theseus or Achilles, the speaker clearly imagines himself in a position not of subordination to his patron but of superiority in terms of his ability to confer *fama*.

The allusion to Achilles, however, also carries with it more ambiguous implications regarding the speaker's gender identity. The interpolation of strong homosocial bonds into epic encomium links the *amator* to a mode of speech that may be identified as feminine. In the *Iliad*, Achilles' withdrawal from battle signifies his alienation from warrior culture. Achilles only returns to battle as a result of his passionate devotion to Patroklos and not out of a sense of civic duty. Achilles' chief mode of commemoration for Patroklos is lamentation, a form of discourse that aligns him with the marginalized position of women in Greek society.[19]

Further, the theme of lamentation in the *Iliad* also implicitly contests the dominant ideology of Homer's poem, which celebrates the *kleos* achieved by the warrior in battle. The identification of the Propertian speaker with Achilles thus may connect the *amator* not only with modes of speech associated with women but also with a form of discourse that suggests criticism of the prevailing social order. Although the speaker lists Augustus's conquests in order to tell Maecenas the subjects about which he will *not* be writing, the lengths he goes to do that suggest that perhaps he wants to remind his audience of the destruction and losses perpetrated by the emperor. Further, the emphatic position of *te* in line 35 reinforces a contrast between the bellicose exploits of Augustus and the peaceful activities of Maecenas. The *amator's* promise to interweave a commemoration of Maecenas into a tribute to Augustus suggests the intrusion of a celebration of personal bonds into public praise. It also reinforces the paradoxical nature of the speaker's discourse—exemplified by his refusal to perform the traditional emcomiastic function of the poet at the same time as he demonstrates his poetic skill in celebrating heroic exploits—including those of Maecenas.[20]

Although the speaker vows that Maecenas would be his *secunda cura*, he ends his litany of heroic accomplishments not by mentioning Augustus but by praising Maecenas's *fides*. The emphasis on personal loyalty, presented in the context of epic discourse, furnishes a link between the epic subjects rejected by the speaker and the production of elegy. Maecenas's *fides* is the very same attribute the elegiac lover perpetually calls for in his mistress. In lines 39–46, the speaker renews his commitment to the more personal subjects typically treated in elegy:

> sed neque Phlegraeos Iovis Enceladique tumultus
>   intonet angusto pectore Callimachus,
> nec mea conveniunt duro praecordia versu
>   Caesaris in Phrygios condere nomen avos.
> navita de ventis, de tauris narrat arator,
>   enumerat miles vulnera, pastor oves;
> nos contra angusto versamus proelia lecto:
>   qua pote quisque, in ea conterat arte diem.

> But Callimachus with his slender breast would not
>   sound the strife of Jove and Enceladus at Phlegra,
> nor is my temperament fit to put into the harsh strains
>   of epic verse the name of Caesar among his Phrygian ancestors.
> The sailor tells of winds, the ploughman of oxen,
>   the soldier counts his wounds, the shepherd his sheep;
> but I wage my own battles on a narrow bed:
>   let each man spend his days in whatever art he is able.

The speaker invokes Callimachus in order to reaffirm his aversion to epic poetry. But the narrator's statement that his temperament (*praecordia*) precludes him from preserving the name of Caesar seems ironic in light of his earlier highly descriptive poetic catalogue of Augustus's epic feats. Moreover, the description of epic as *durus versus* resonates with the amator's characterization of the *puella* as *dura*. That the speaker attributes the same trait to his mistress as he does to epic suggests not only an intertwining of public and private discourses but also a subversion of the speaker's avowed feminine stance. While he claims that the *durus versus* of epic is beyond the capability of the "soft" poet, the chief subject of his elegies (the *puella*) is *dura*. How soft, then, can the soft poet be?

Despite his protestations, the speaker continues to characterize effeminized elegy in terms of masculine epic. In line 45, he uses a military metaphor to describe his amorous exploits: "But I wage my own battles on a narrow bed" ("nos contra angusto versamus proelia lecto").[21] Although the speaker insists that every man, no matter what his occupation, has only one subject to tell ("the sailor his winds, the ploughman his oxen," etc.), his own discourse remains decidedly indeterminate. The implicit characterization of his verse as *angustus*, the same adjective used of Callimachus, marks the elegiac lover as *mollis*. But the representation of amatory activity as *proelia* and the use of a verb denoting vigorous manly exertion (*versamus*) to describe the particular occupation of the elegiac poet identify the speaker with the *durus* style of epic.[22] In the next stanza, however, the speaker seems to offer a positive affirmation of his commitment to love poetry—to the *levis* style of poetic discourse (47–56):

> laus in amore mori: laus altera, si datur uno
>> posse frui: fruar o solus amore meo,
> si memini, solet illa levis culpare puellas,
>> et totam ex Helena non probat Iliada.
> seu mihi sunt tangenda novercae pocula Phaedrae,
>> pocula privigno non nocitura suo,
> seu mihi Circaeo pereundum est gramine, sive
>> Colchis Iolciacis urat aena focis,
> una meos quoniam praedata est femina sensus,
>> ex hac ducentur funera nostra domo.

> To die in love is glory: and a second glory, if it is given
>> to be able to enjoy one love: oh may I alone enjoy my love.
> If I recall, she used to blame fickle girls, and,
>> because of Helen, disapproves of the whole *Iliad*.
> Even if I am doomed to taste the potion of stepmother
>> Phaedra, a potion not destined to harm her stepson,
> or if I must die of Circe's herbs, or if the Colchian witch
>> should heat her cauldron on the hearths of Iolcus,
> since one woman has plundered my senses,
>> from her house my funeral will set out.

The speaker circumvents the putative opposition between epic and elegiac poetry by linking *amor* to images of death and glory. The repetition of the word *laus* and its emphatic position in line 47 give greater prominence to the epic goal of glory in death than to the elegiac aspiration to possess the beloved expressed in line 48. What is most intriguing about the speaker's characterization of his mistress in this stanza is the way he describes her as implicitly condemning the very style of verse in which she is the chief subject. The kind of girls the mistress finds fault with are described as *levis*—the same adjective used of the poet's own elegiac verse. In addition, the speaker tells us that Cynthia censures the "whole *Iliad*." Earlier in the poem, the *amator* referred to his own poetic compositions as *longae Iliadae* and declared the *puella* to be the source of his inspiration for these poems. The mistress ostensibly repudiates the *Iliad* because she disapproves of Helen's infidelity. This is highly ironic in light of the fact that, throughout the *Elegies*, Cynthia's own infidelity is constantly bemoaned by the *amator*. It is also ironic that, as the *levis* subject of elegy, the mistress castigates other *levis puellas*. On the one hand, the speaker depicts his mistress here as *dura*, as implicitly rejecting the style and substance of his poetry—and hence him as well. But on the other hand, the contradictions in the mistress's attitudes call into question her role as the poet's Muse. The speaker's exposure of Cynthia's hypocrisy here suggests that the image of the *amator* as a man ravaged by desire is a rhetorical stance adopted by the speaker in service to his art. Furthermore, the speaker's association of Cynthia with mythical female sorceresses, each one more diabolical than the next, invokes stereotypical views of women as themselves incapable of controlling their sexual desires.

In light of this implied invective toward women in general and Cynthia in particular, the speaker's expression of fidelity in lines 55–56 seems not only hyberbolic but also part of his continued strategy to ally the elegiac enterprise with the heroic values of epic. On the one hand, the speaker links himself to the tradition of love lyric by describing his emotional condition as an incurable disease. On the other hand, the speaker again evokes an image of glory in death through an association between his fidelity to one woman (*una femina*) and his future funeral rites. In lines 57–70, the speaker catalogues the legendary cures of famous epic heroes, apparently in order to highlight, by contrast, the incurability of love:

> omnis humanos sanat medicina dolores:
> > solus amor morbi non amat artificem.
> tarda Philoctetae sanavit crura Machaon,
> > Phoenicis Chiron lumina Phillyrides,
> et deus exstinctum Cressis Epidaurius herbis
> > restituit patriis Androgeona focis,
> Mysus et Haemonia iuvenis qua cuspide vulnus
> > senserat, hac ipsa cuspide sensit opem.
> hoc si quis vitium poterit mihi demere, solus
> > Tantaleae poterit tradere poma manu;

dolia virgineis idem ille repleverit urnis,
    ne tenera assidua colla graventur aqua;
idem Caucasia solvet de rupe Promethei
    bracchia et a medio pectore pellet avem.

Medicine cures all human sorrows:
    only love does not love the healer of disease.
Machaon cured the lame legs of Philoctetes,
    Chiron, son of Phillyra, the eyes of Phoenix,
and the Epidaurian god with his Cretan herbs
    restored lifeless Androgeon to his father's hearth;
and the Mysian youth from the Haemonian spear from which
    he felt his wound, he then felt his cure.
If anyone can remove this defect from me, he alone
    can put fruit into Tantalus's hand;
he, too, will fill the vessels from the maidens' jars,
    lest their delicate necks be weighed down with constant water;
and he, too, will free Prometheus's arms from the Caucasian cliff
    and drive the bird from the middle of his chest.

The speaker emphasizes in these lines the incurability of *his* affliction compared with those of famous heroes. The use of the word *vitium* ("fault, vice") to describe the speaker's ailment appears to accentuate its irremediability, since it is a word sometimes used to characterize a defect that cannot be eradicated. It seems that the speaker presents himself here in the Catullan tradition of portraying the lover as someone whose moral failings prevent him from achieving the *sanitas* ("sanity") he claims to desire.[23] Like the Catullan lover, the speaker in Propertius's poem also reveals ambivalence in his attitude toward his supposed shortcoming. While Catullus correlates the sickness of the lover with the detrimental effects of unrequited love, Propertius refers to the lover's *vitium* in the context of a *recusatio*, the incapacity of the poet to take up the more challenging strains of epic poetry. The moral distress of the lover often evinced in Catullus's poems seems to be completely absent in Propertius's poem. Thus the use of *vitium* to describe what is little more than an aesthetic deficiency suggests melodrama rather than moral ineptitude. In addition, the credibility of the speaker's reference to his condition as a *vitium* is undermined by his earlier statement that *laus in amore mori* ("To die in love is glory"). It is clearly a contradiction for the speaker to say that *amor* constitutes a defect of character but also that it engenders virtue (*laus*)—or is at least worthy of praise. How can a *vitium* produce glory or even praise for the speaker—considering the connotations of moral depravity contained in *vitium*? The association of *amor* and glory is also evident in the mythological *exempla* the speaker uses to support his claim that his "defect" is supposedly incurable.

The speaker attests to the hopelessness of his situation by saying that if he can be cured, then surely the impossible dilemmas of Tantalus, the Danaids, and Prometheus can be solved. The speaker seems to reinforce his own *vitium* by comparing himself to figures in myth who are notorious for the price they pay for their *vitia*. The punishments of both Tantalus and the Danaids represent frustrated human endeavor, perpetual but futile attempts to satisfy human desire. That particular aspect of their situations clearly mirrors the speaker's own often fruitless efforts to win Cynthia's love. The implicit identification of the speaker with the Danaids, who are presented sympathetically despite their crime of killing their husbands, underscores, on the one hand, the speaker's avowed position of feminine powerlessness and vulnerability. But, on the other hand, the image of the Danaids reinforces the implicit invective against women in the earlier images of mythical witches whose powers constitute a threat to masculine sexuality and authority.

Tantalus and Prometheus both resisted divine authority, and thus the images of them here may call to mind the elegiac lover's oppositional stance toward Augustan ideology.[24] In particular, the association of the speaker with Prometheus suggests that there is irony in the speaker's characterization of his condition as a *vitium*. First, the fact that Prometheus is freed from his bondage by Heracles undercuts the speaker's implicit argument that his situation is more impossible than that of Prometheus. Second, Prometheus is known in antiquity not for his moral failings but for his courageous defiance of the gods and his association with the origins of fire. Indeed, the most prominent (surviving) portrait of Prometheus comes from Aeschylus, who depicts him as a culture hero, responsible for expanding man's skills and spheres of knowledge. The speaker's identification with Prometheus seems to emphasize the glory that comes from heroic action, in particular, from action that claims for man an individual voice in the face of arbitrary authority. The speaker's abject status as lover, his choice to write elegy rather than epic, thus can hardly be considered a *vitium* in light of his identification with Prometheus. Rather, the *amor* that constitutes the *amator*'s seemingly incurable disease is what defines his place in posterity and guarantees for him, as for Prometheus, mythical status. Indeed, in the last stanza of the poem, the speaker expresses intense concern for what posterity will say of him (71–78):

quandocumque igitur vitam mea fata reposcent,
    et breve in exiguo marmore nomen ero,
Maecenas, nostrae spes invidiosa iuventae,
    et vitae et morti gloria iusta meae,
si te forte meo ducet via proxima busto,
    esseda caelatis siste Britannia iugis,
taliaque illacrimans mutae iace verba favillae:
    "Huic misero fatum dura puella fuit."

When, therefore, the fates claim my life,
    and I will be a brief name on meager marble,
Maecenas, the hope and envy of Roman youth,
    and the rightful boast of my life and death,
if by chance your path should bring you near my tomb,
    halt your British chariot with its carved yoke,
and, weeping, lay these words on my silent ashes:
    "A harsh girl was the doom of this wretched man."

This last stanza conveys the poem's characteristically oxymoronic style. The speaker begins by identifying himself with the *levis* style of elegy: like his slender verse, the speaker's name will be *brevis* and his tomb merely *exiguus*. The invocation to Maecenas, however, once again brings into focus the world of male public culture, but it also underscores the close association of *amicitia* and *amor*. The description of Maecenas as "the hope and envy of Roman youth" recalls the sexual connotations in the speaker's earlier affectionate personal references to his patron. Moreover, in the process of declaring the *dura puella* to be the defining feature of his life, the speaker calls Maecenas his *iusta gloria* in life and death. Such an approbation suggests that the speaker regards Maecenas at least as much the source of his potential *fama* as the mistress herself. Indeed, the fact that the *gloria* Maecenas brings to the speaker is described as *iusta* suggests symmetry between the speaker and his addressee. Further, the double images of Maecenas as warrior (in his British chariot) *and* lover (the envy of Roman youth) in this stanza resonate with the poem's conflation of epic and elegiac discourses and also with the speaker's own vacillations between the personas of abject lover and masculine hero. Although the speaker assumes a posture of self-effacement at the beginning of the stanza, his use of imperatives in his address to Maecenas (*siste, iace*) again suggests that it is the speaker—*qua poeta*—who endows his addressee with the praise that ensures his *kleos* ("glory"). It is also the speaker who composes his own epitaph, an epitaph that appears simply to commemorate the *dura puella* and to sustain the speaker's position as the effeminate poet-lover.

While the speaker evokes the characteristically unstable emotional condition of the lover by referring to himself as *miser* and also by attributing to the *puella* the cause of his *fatum*, the logic of the poem depends on equating the *puella* with the poet's *ingenium*, and thus with the praise and glory the speaker explicitly links to both love and death. Although the speaker rejects the *durus versus* of epic, he embraces the epic ideal of glory in death. The speaker's last characterization of Cynthia as *dura* not only identifies elegy with epic, it also suggests that the style and substance of the elegist's preferred mode of poetic composition cannot be reduced to neat classifications of genre. If the mistress, as Wyke argues, is to be equated with the narrator's poetics, then the characterization of her as *dura* also suggests that elegy is as rigorous a form of discourse as epic. Despite his protestations, the speaker implicates himself in the world of Maecenas. Although the speaker appears to reinforce his identity as the soft poet of elegy, the image of Maecenas proclaiming over the speaker's ashes in his chariot of conquest imparts an air of epic grandiosity to the imagined death scene. And although the speaker tells Maecenas to pay tribute to his "silent ashes," the speaker's voice is anything but silent. While elegy itself is defined as *mollis* and is thus discursively aligned with the feminine, the *puella* herself (*ipsa puella*) has been rendered subject to the poetic control of the speaker, who begets his *maxima historia* from the raw material (*de nihilo*) she supplies. Further, the assertion that the *dura puella* is the speaker's *fatum* echoes his earlier association of *amor* and glory ("To die in love is glory"). At the end, the speaker imagines himself fulfilling this dictum, achieving the glory worthy of a great epic hero. It is Maecenas and the male audience he represents who confer on the speaker his *iusta gloria*. That the speaker describes the *fama* Maecenas brings to him as *iusta* suggests a reciprocity between the two men that is nearly always lacking in the imagined relationship between the lover and his mistress. The image of the *puella*, it seems, merely provides the means through which one man may pay tribute to another. The true *fama* the speaker envisions for himself issues from the homosocial bonds that not only constitute the fabric of Roman society but also comprise an aesthetic space in which the elegiac poet can define himself as a "hero" in a set of shifting discursive relations of both gender and genre.

Notes

1. For discussions of the image of the *servitium amoris* in Roman elegy, see Copley 1947, Day 1938, Kennedy 1993, Lyne 1979, McCarthy 1998, Veyne 1988.

2. See Hallett 1973, Wyke 1987a and 1989a.

3. See, especially, Wyke 1994 and Gold 1993. Gold argues that Propertius destabilizes traditional Roman categories of gender by putting the male narrator "into play as the feminine."

4. In Greene 1999, chapter 3, see my argument about how the *amator* in Book 1, despite his protestations of passivity and subservience, treats the elegiac mistress as a pictorial object that arouses the lover's erotic fantasies and serves as a vehicle for his artistic fame. See also McCarthy 1998; McCarthy argues that the elegists' assumption of a feminine persona allowed them a "vacation" from the vigilance and control required of them as members of the Roman male elite. While McCarthy's paper offers some interesting insights about the way elegy plays with the hierarchies in Roman culture, her essay does not explore the ways in which the *domina*'s apparent "autonomy" is part of a poetic strategy to reassert the authority of the male poetic voice. I attempt to argue for such a view in this paper.

5. Miller 2001 has an insightful discussion of Propertius's tendency in Book 2 to vacillate between the discourses of elegy and epic.

6. On the topos of erotic disease in Greek poetry, see, especially, Cyrino 1995 and Carson 1986.

7. In Greene 1999 (chapters 1 and 2), I discuss moral discourses in Catullus. See also Edwards 1993.

8. See Wyke 1987a and 1989a on the image of Cynthia as a literary construction in Book 2 of Propertius's *Elegies*. Wyke argues persuasively that the elegiac mistress becomes equated with the elegiac book, and that "Cynthia's attributes and activities reveal her to be a 'written women' (a *scripta puella*, 2.10.8), the marker of a Callimachean poetic practice." In other words, Cynthia's body constitutes the poetic corpus of the male narrator. On this point, see Keith 1994 and Fredrick 1997.180ff. Also, see James's discussion (2003) of the *docta puella* ("learned mistress") as a literary construct.

9. This instability of genre in Augustan literature may be, in part, a function of the transition from republic to principate—a transition that seriously undermined many of the traditional values of the *mos maiorum*. For recent discussions of a cultural "revolution" and the attendant *mutatio morum* in the wake of the establishment of the principate, see Habinek and Schiesaro 1997 and Habinek 1998.

10. For discussions of the *recusatio* in Roman elegy, see Cahoon 1985, Lyne 1980, Ross 1975, Wyke 1987b.

11. For more on the elegiac mistress as *materia*, see Wyke 1987b and Greene 1995b.

12. In Oliensis 1997b, see the discussion of the triangulation among client, patron, and *puella* in Tibullus 1.1.

13. I thank the anonymous reader for suggesting a greater emphasis on the ways in which elegy constantly calls into question the terms of its own generic category. On this point, see Edwards 1996.53–63.

14. See, especially, Derrida 1991 and 1992. Derrida argues that genre can never belong merely to the genre it mentions, that it always exceeds the limits that bring it into being. "Every text," Derrida writes, "*participates* in one or several genres, there is no genreless text, there is always a genre and genres, yet such participation never amounts to belonging . . . In marking itself generically, a text unmarks itself" (1992.230; emphasis in original).

15. For a discussion of the elegiac lover's characterization of his mistress as *dura*, see Kennedy 1993.31–33, Greene 1995b, Miller 2001.

16. Oliensis 1997b. Oliensis argues that the fictional subjection of the elegiac lover provides compensation for and escape from the realities of the poet's subordination to a patron.

17. In *Elegy* 1.1.53–58, Tibullus refuses Messala's invitation to join him on a military campaign, yet praises his excellence in battle and predicts his inevitable success.

18. In Book 4 of Propertius's *Elegies* (11.55), the speaker refers to his mother as *dulce caput*. Camps 1967.70 points out that, in the *Aeneid*, Dido refers to Aeneas as *infandum caput* (*Aen.* 4.613).

19. On Achilles' association with "feminine" lamentation in the *Iliad*, see Foley 1993 and Murnaghan 1998.

20. See Gale 1997. Gale argues that Propertius misreads the *Iliad* as a work of love poetry and thus undermines his assertion that elegy is as good a genre as epic. As I have been arguing in this paper, however, the Propertian speaker's identification with masculine epic underscores the indeterminacy of Propertius's elegiac discourse.

21. See Cahoon 1988 for a discussion of the use of military metaphors in Ovid's *Amores*. Cahoon's analysis may be usefully applied to Propertius as well.

22. Camps 1967.72 points out that Propertius's use of *versamus* here is equivalent to the meaning in *agitamus*—a word that connotes forceful activity, even hunting.

23. In poem 76, the Catullan lover explicitly links mental and physical health with giving up unrequited desire. See a discussion of this in Greene 1995a.

24. See Miller and Platter 1999b for a discussion of Roman elegy's resistance to traditional Augustan values. See also Platter 1995 and Edwards 1996.

4 Impossible Lesbians in Ovid's *Metamorphoses*

Kirk Ormand

I mean the term *lesbian continuum* to include a range—through each woman's life and throughout history—of woman-identified experience, not simply the fact that a woman has had or consciously desired genital sexual experience with another woman . . . including the sharing of a rich inner life, the bonding against male tyranny, the giving and receiving of practical and political support.—A. Rich, *Compulsory Heterosexuality and Lesbian Existence*

Lesbian is the only concept I know of which is beyond the categories of sex (woman and man), because the designated subject (lesbian) is *not* a woman, either economically, or politically, or ideologically.—M. Wittig, *One Is Not Born a Woman*

Ovid's *Metamorphoses* will not be considered love poetry by most modern readers. The work contains, however, a great many stories that can only be described as erotic (though most are not romantic), and a number of these borrow directly from elegiac poetry when presenting the lovers' complaints. One of the most striking of these is the story of Iphis and Ianthe in Book 9, a story of impossible love miraculously redeemed.[1] The poem tells us of a relationship between two young women—though one is disguised as a boy—and of the unusually equal passion that they share for one another. The story ends happily, as most scholars would have it, when Iphis is transformed into a boy, allowing the two star-crossed lovers to marry. This mutually successful ending makes the story unusual in the *Metamorphoses*. But what makes this story unique, not only for Ovid's poem but for extant Latin literature, is that it presents same-sex passion between two women and treats that passion with considerable empathy.[2] The young lover, Iphis, does deliver an over-wrought and despairing monologue in which she explores and regrets the unusual nature of her passion. Unlike the invectives of Martial or Juvenal, however, Ovid's narrator does not condemn either of the young women in his story for wanting to sleep together.[3] The story presents this atypical love not as a moral failing but as a thorny and near-tragic problem for a young woman who is in every other regard admirable.

As virtually the only text in the extant Latin corpus to treat in such detail and with such empathy the subject of female-female relations, the story has naturally attracted the attention of scholars working on sexuality in the ancient world.[4] In general, however, analyses of this passage take Iphis's monologue at face value and argue that it represents a typical Roman attitude towards female homoeroticism, an attitude that we might label homophobic. Here lies the interesting problem of this unique text. For in the past twenty-odd years, there has been a virtual explosion of work on ancient Greek and Roman understandings of sexuality, and the dominant view now argues that neither the Greeks nor the Romans divided the world into categories of homosexual and heterosexual. Iphis's condemnation of her own love for Ianthe would seem to fly in the face of this formulation. When we read the story in its full literary and social context, however, we see that the Romans were not concerned with homosexuality (male or female) *per se*. The story does, indeed, aid our understanding of Roman sexual categories and practices, but not in the straightforward and unmediated way that most previous scholars have assumed.

The Current State of Affairs

Our understanding of male sexual norms in ancient Rome is reasonably sound. Fully adult men were, if normal, expected to play the active role in sex. The sex of the erotic object was unimportant in determining the lover's personal character or social and sexual identity: whether lusting after a boy or a woman, a man earned no shame for desiring or acting on that desire, so long as the man kept his desires under control. What was shameful was to be mastered by one's desires, to be unable to control one's sexual urges. Such a lack of control could lead to socially deviant desires, one of the most contested of which was to want to be penetrated—and again, it did not matter by whom. To be penetrated was to be passive, and hence effeminate, a denial of manhood generally. In Rome, a man who did so was said to *pati muliebria*, that is, play the part of the woman. And as Jonathan Walters has recently shown, following Francesca Santoro L'hoir, the term *vir* in Roman discourse means specifically a man who cannot be penetrated.[5]

There were prohibitions against having sex with freeborn boys—notably the notoriously slippery *lex Scantinia*—but this seems to stem not from a concept of homosexuality but from a concern with the boys' future as *viri*. As Craig Williams shows, the Romans were more restrictive in this regard than the Greeks: sex with any freeborn citizen (other than a man's wife) was always strictly forbidden.[6] The prohibitions against sex with citizen boys are consistent, moreover, with restrictions against having sex with freeborn women to whom one was not married.[7] As Williams argues, sex with a freeborn boy was considered *stuprum*, a significant offense, but was, if anything, a less serious offense than *stuprum* with a married woman.[8] No shame fell on the man who desired such a boy, even though serious penalties could be brought for having damaged a free boy's future if he acted on that perfectly normal desire.[9]

If Rome was more restrictive than Greece about allowing sex with freeborn boys, however, it was somewhat less restrictive about men desiring other (fully adult) men. Certainly many texts suggest that boys were highly desirable; but where Greek men are assumed, under normal circumstances, to find the secondary-sex characteristics of mature masculinity a distinct turnoff, there is some evidence that fully adult men were acceptable objects of desire in Rome (Williams 1999.77–86). It is important to note, however, that such sexual practices are still not a mutual exchange of pleasure between equals: only those males who were socially marked as non-men could be legitimate objects of desire. Indeed, only a man's wife or slaves (of either sex) could be penetrated with absolute impunity. In other words, the sexual objects of desire, regardless of physical sex, were understood to be of a fundamentally lower social status—we may even say of a different gender—than the men who penetrated them: "Normative sexual experience is regularly portrayed in Roman texts less as loving intercourse between two partners and more as a series of penetrative encounters in which one party (a *man*) acts upon another (a *non-man*, whether a female, a boy, an effeminate man or *cinaedus*, or a slave)" (Williams 1999.163; emphasis in original).

So Holt Parker writes in a recent overview: "The ancient world, both Greek and Roman, did not base its classification on gender, but on a completely different axis, that of active versus passive . . . Simply put, there was no such emic, cultural abstraction as 'homosexuality' in the ancient world."[10] Parker here confirms what Dover, Veyne, Halperin, Winkler, and others have been saying for some time.[11] Although it would be simplistic to deny that the ancient Greeks and Romans did draw distinctions between homoerotic and heteroerotic relations, these distinctions are not the ones that are seen as constitutive of a person's internal character.[12] In so far as a man in ancient Rome can be said to have a "sexual identity," that identity is characterized by his activity or passivity.[13] The greater problem, however, is that even identities like that of the *cinaedus* are difficult to pin down as specifically sexual; the range of behaviors that identifies the *cinaedus* moves out of the sexual into the social and is generally characterized by effeminacy. It is difficult to find here a specifically *sexual* identity, and so Williams and others argue that this sort of deviance is best understood as *gender* deviance.[14]

One of the strongest challenges to this view is put forth by Amy Richlin, who argues that the ancient Romans, at least, did have a notion of sexuality comparable to our own.[15] In her important "Not Before Homosexuality," she argues that "men identified as homosexuals really existed at Rome and . . . their existence was marked both by homophobia within the culture and by social and civil restrictions" (Richlin 1993.530). A careful reading of her article, however, reveals a surprising fact. In the myriad of examples that she adduces, there is not a single case in which a man is criticized, prosecuted, or insulted for homosexuality per se. On the contrary, case after case is highly critical of the person who seeks out or willingly accepts the *passive* position. It appears that what Richlin means by "homosexual" is "passive," a view consistent with that presented in her groundbreaking work of 1983 (1992a, revised): "To a Roman reader there was no practical difference between desiring a thousand kisses from your mistress or from your *puer*" (39). Thus for Richlin, ancient sexual identity is not a question of object choice, any more than it is for those authors she disagrees with.

Richlin slips between the terms "homosexual," "passive homosexual," and "passive," however, and this has sometimes led to the erroneous conclusion that she does not recognize the importance of activity versus passivity in constituting sexual identity for the Romans.[16] Richlin agrees that the two groups (ancient and modern) that she calls homosexual consist of individuals who have entirely different sexual proclivities and are criticized for different things and in different ways. Moreover, she concedes that the category of passive excludes individuals who would today be considered gay and that "homosexual" includes individuals who would not have been stigmatized by the category of passive in antiquity.[17] As Richlin correctly states, however, the interpretation of sexual practice in antiquity is an activist project. The result of abandoning the term homosexual is, for Richlin, that "homophobia tends to disappear along with homosexuals" (1993.571). For her, it is politically useful to ally the two groups as victims of social discrimination on the basis of sexual practice.[18] Richlin's objections to Foucault, Winkler, and Halperin on these grounds, then, do not contradict their formulations of pre-modern sexual identity.[19]

Nonetheless, the Romans did impose restrictions on civil rights for acts of gender deviance when these acts took the form of passivity. Richlin, arguing for a legally defined sexual identity, suggests that passives in Rome were subject to the broad social disqualification of *infamia*. She is probably incorrect. Williams points out that passives are only subject to less dire social restrictions, but in any case, it does appear that some civil restrictions could be applied to them.[20] The people who fall under the praetorian edict in question (*Digest* 3.1.1.5) are unfit as full citizens or have misbehaved socially in a variety of ways: "All women; any man who was blind in both eyes, who had been convicted of a capital offense (*capitali crimine damnatus*), or of calumny in a criminal court (*calumniae publici iudicii damnatus*), who had hired himself out to fight against beasts, or who had 'submitted to womanly things with his body' ('qui corpore suo muliebria passus est')" (Williams 1999.194). It is tempting to see in this list some sort of social homogeneity, as both Richlin and Edwards do: "*Infames* are people who have done something bad, usually involving fraud; or who habitually do something bad, usually involving the public use of bodies (actors, pimps, gladiators)."[21] Such homogeneity allows us to think of certain types of individuals as identified, and penalized, by the law. Even here, however, it is difficult to see in such a loose association a coherent notion of sexuality, and in so far as the *Digest* does specify sexual activity as improper, it uses, again, the language of passivity, not homosexuality. To cite Parker once more, "By the fifth time one has made the qualification, 'The passive homosexual was not rejected for his homosexuality but for his passivity,' it ought to become clear that we are talking not about 'homosexuality' but about passivity."[22]

Our understanding of the ideology of women's sexual life in ancient Rome is, however, considerably less clear. To be sure, this is in large part due to the fact that the ancient Romans theorized less explicitly about women's sexual lives and identities than they did about men's.[23] This is true of most aspects of women's lives, since, for Roman women, *gender* determines a necessarily subservient social position. Still we can sketch out some norms based on a wide variety of sources (see discussion of Brooten, below).

First, we should note that women were considered to be *objects* of desire, as nearly all sources make relentlessly clear. Any time that a woman expresses desire of her own—even if her desire is to be conventionally penetrated by a man—she represents a threat to the masculine order and lies open to moral condemnation.[24] This is particularly the case because women were assumed to lack the self-control that characterized successful masculinity, so that expression of their passions tends toward morally reprehensible extremes, especially adultery and promiscuity. So to take one extreme example, Cicero viciously attacks Clodia for her sexual forwardness in his defense of Caelius, saying that she deports herself "not only as a prostitute, but as a forward and brazen prostitute" ("non solum meretrix sed etiam proterva meretrix procaxque," *pro Caelio* 49.8–10). Similarly, as Richlin shows in an extensive treatment of Juvenal's sixth satire, "The many sections all concern women who in one way or another exceed the limits of the role of the Roman *matrona*, thereby threatening the husband. Their behavior is excessive or contradictory, that is, they do things women are not supposed to do; frequently they take on overly aggressive or traditionally male roles" (1992a.203). Among those so offending, not surprisingly, are women who are adulterous and excessively promiscuous (Richlin 1992a.205). As we will see below, women who are morally reprehensible in this way are often grouped with those who are conceived of as sexually deviant.[25]

If women are supposed to be demure and retiring in public, then when it comes to sex itself, the normal woman is passive; she can be passive vaginally, anally, or orally, and still be quite normal.[26] To be active (that is, penetrating) in sex is the deviant position, and such a woman is usually described as a *tribas*. Again, it is important to note that the sex of her object is irrelevant. As Williams points out, Martial (at least) imagines *tribades* as penetrating boys as well as women; the *tribas* is monstrous in either case, because not passive.[27] Such women, moreover, are often assumed to also exhibit the failings of less specifically role-oriented deviance: quite frequently women who are *tribades* are characterized as adulterous and promiscuous as well.[28] In other words, there is a zero-degree mapping between gender and ancient sexual ideology. To be active is to be masculine; to be passive is to be feminine. A woman who is not passive is assumed to have none of the virtues of a good Roman woman. Though we can define a set of rules that we might call Roman female "sexuality," these sexual categories tend to be subsumed under the larger category of gender.[29]

As a result, it is nearly impossible to uncover what sexual relations between two women might have been like. Unlike the case of male-male sexual relations (which took place under normal circumstances), there is no juxtaposition of normal roles that results in two women having sex. Because ancient Rome perceived sex as *essentially* predicated on an asymmetry of power, one of the two parties must be active and, if a woman, therefore monstrous.[30] Thus nearly all our sources about relations between women are hostile. It is important to recognize, however, that where a clear target can be discerned, this hostility is not directed against same-sex unions per se but rather against women assuming the *active* role in such unions.[31]

Bernadette Brooten has issued an important challenge to the scheme set out above, however. A canny and sensitive reader who has amassed much (largely hitherto unexplored) evidence, Brooten sees her Roman sources as opposed to female homoeroticism per se, not as opposed to the gender deviance of an active (masculine) woman. It is necessary, therefore, that I address Brooten's evidence and formulations at some length.[32]

Brooten recognizes from the start that the ancient world organized sexual roles along the lines of active and passive, calling it at several points in her work "fundamental" (1996.126–27). But for Brooten, "female homoeroticism" remains a distinct pre-social category, one on which the active versus passive distinction acted, but which it does not supersede. So, on page 1, we read: "Because a strict distinction between active and passive sexual roles governed the prevailing cultural conceptualizations of sexual relations in the Roman world, it shaped the way that people viewed female homoeroticism."[33] Female homoeroticism here has a curious status as a pure biological fact, not constructed by culture, that the Romans sometimes chose to view through their idiosyncratic lens of activity versus passivity.[34] At the same time, however, Brooten wants female homoeroticism to be a fully functioning cultural category, akin to modern lesbianism: to take only one of Brooten's four types of evidence, she says of the astrological texts that they "deemed female homoeroticism a plausible category for describing a woman's sexual behavior" (1996.116).

Such a reading of Roman sexual norms is not, however, supported by Brooten's examples. Brooten does students of ancient sexuality a great service by collecting evidence from four areas: erotic magic spells, astrological texts, medical texts, and dream analysis. I will discuss at length only the astrological texts, which certainly seem to postulate something like a sexual identity. Indeed, certain astrological configurations (at birth) can cause those born under such signs "to be oriented towards their own sex" (Brooten 1996.120). A careful reading of Brooten's examples, however, reveals that these "orientations" have more to do with active versus passive than with homo- versus heteroerotic. Dorotheus, for example, puts three categories of women into one section: adulterous women, women who "do in women the act of men" (which Brooten calls homoerotic), and promiscuous women. Clearly it does not make sense to consider the women under this section as linked because of their common homosexuality; only one of the three types refers to homoerotic activity. The grouping of adultery, promiscuity, and the active role in sex, however, is a familiar one. As Brooten recognizes, the constellation that results in each of these is "strikingly masculine," and "Dorotheos may have grouped them together because they share an active sexual desire" (1996.120–21). In other words, these are active women, the first and the third types because they act as erotic subjects rather than objects, and the second because they go the further step of imitating men in sex. Dorotheus does not tell us why these three types should fall under a single grouping, but Brooten's interpretation is consistent with typical Roman thinking about women's proper place. Even if we do not wish to accept the three types as belonging to a coherent social category (as Dorotheus evidently does), we must admit that these three types do not correspond to our sexual categories (as pointed out by Halperin 2002.64–68).

Similarly, the astrologer Manetho speaks exclusively of *tribades*, who are "culturally masculine" (Brooten 1996.123). Ptolemy, again, speaks of *tribades* who "take the active sexual role with women and perform male functions" (Brooten 1996.125–26). So also Vettius Valens. Firmicus Maternus changes the terminology, using *virago*, which Brooten also takes as meaning a masculinized woman.[35] Similarly Hephaistion of Thebes. Given this predominance of evidence, it seems reasonable to conclude, against Brooten, that the Romans did not conceive of female homoeroticism as an important classificatory principle onto which they clumsily grafted the image of the active woman, but rather that they conceived of some women as sexually active, which in most cases (but not all) resulted in two women having sex. And indeed, the evidence from Brooten's other three categories confirms this reading: women are criticized for playing the active role.

That is undoubtedly too simple a model, and we can trouble it some. The ancient Greeks and Romans did recognize that homoerotic relations

were different from heteroerotic, even if they did not think of these categories as constitutive of sexual types.[36] More to the point, women's homoerotic relations do fall under a curtain of obscurity. Sometimes, as in
the elder Seneca's *Controversiae* 1.2.23, both women in a same-sex relationship are referred to as *tribades*.[37] Even more difficult, the astrological writings in the corpus attributed to Hermes Trismegistus "envisages
both female partners in a sexual act as *fricatrixes*, as if there were no active or passive partners" (Brooten 1996.131). Clearly the sexual life of
women in ancient Rome was under-theorized.[38] But while Brooten assumes that this lack of distinctions is the outgrowth of an understanding of the sexual world as homo- versus heteroerotic, I believe, on the
contrary, that it is simply the result of male authors writing for a male
audience who do not care to think with nice precision about the sexual
desires and acts of women. If there are two women in bed, one must be
a *tribas*, monstrous; of what importance is it to identify which one?

In support of this view, we might consider the odd but important fact
that no contemporary of Sappho mentions her (literary) preference for
love affairs with other women.[39] By the period of Augustan Rome, however, her "homoeroticism" has apparently become a problem, as the discussion of Pamela Gordon has now made clear. In theorizing this problem, however, the author of the controversial fifteenth epistle of the
Heroides did what nearly every Roman author does: he portrays Sappho
as occupying a masculine erotic subjectivity as compared to her lover
Phaon's untypical passivity and inactivity.[40] Our sources do not speak out
against female homosexuality per se, any more than they do against male
homosexuality. Again, that is not a category the Romans thought with.
Rather, the sources—primarily invective—speak out against women
being manly and, in extreme cases, being *tribades*, desiring to be active
and penetrating (Parker 1997.58–59).

A Test Case: Iphis the Lesbian?

In the context of these assertions, I would now like to turn to
the story of Iphis and Ianthe in Book 9 (lines 666ff.) of Ovid's *Metamorphoses*. It is an anomalous story in many ways, even in the wild "pastiche"
of Ovid's epic.[41] It provides us with a difficult test case, as we will see, for
in the middle of the story, Iphis speaks a monologue that certainly reads
like a denunciation of female homosexuality based on natural law.

The story in brief: a poor man in Crete, Ligdus, informs his pregnant wife, Telethusa, that they cannot afford to raise a girl and instructs
her, if her baby is born female, to expose the infant. A dream comes to

Telethusa, however, in the guise of the goddess Isis, who tells her to raise
the infant no matter what. She does so, disguising the young girl as a boy.
As luck would have it, Ligdus gives the girl the name Iphis from his (Ligdus's) father, a name that can apply to either sex. And Iphis, too, seems
to partake of a bisexual nature, with good looks that would fit either a
boy or a girl (9.708–13):

> vota pater solvit nomenque inponit avitum:
> Iphis avus fuerat, gavisa est nomine mater,
> quod commune foret nec quemquam falleret illo.
> inde incepta pia mendacia fraude latebant:
> cultus erat pueri, facies, quam sive puellae
> sive dares puero, fuerat formosus uterque.

> Her father paid his vows and named her after her grandfather;
> Iphis had been her grandfather, and the name made her mother happy,
> since it could go either way, and she would deceive nobody with it.
> Begun from this deception, the pious lie lay hid:
> Her clothing was a boy's, and her form, whether you gave it to a girl
> or a boy, either one was beautiful.[42]

Iphis is, at this point, thirteen; and somewhat surprisingly (by
Roman standards) the time has come for her (him?) to marry. She is betrothed to Ianthe, a beautiful but poor girl, and they are madly in love.
The day of the wedding comes. Iphis is beside herself with anxiety, and
here she speaks her famous monologue, which I will treat in detail
shortly. Finally, she and her mother go to the shrine of Isis, loosen their
hair, and pray for help. The statue moves, a sign of acceptance. And as
Iphis and her mother leave the temple, Iphis becomes, miraculously, a
boy (9.785–91):

> non secura quidem, fausto tamen omine laeta
> mater abit templo, sequitur comes Iphis euntem
> quam solita est, maiore gradu; nec candor in ore
> permanet, et vires augentur, et acrior ipse est
> vultus et incomptis brevior mensura capillis,
> plusque vigoris adest, habuit quam femina. nam quae
> femina nuper eras, puer es.

> Not yet sure, but happy with the favorable omen,
> her mother leaves the temple and Iphis follows as her companion
> with a longer stride than she was accustomed; nor does her pale complexion

remain, and her strength increases, and her face becomes sharper,
and the measure of her loosened hair shorter,
and she has more energy than she had as a woman. For you who
were just now a woman, are now a boy.

In this passage, Iphis acquires the signs of masculine gender: her step lengthens, color darkens, hair grows shorter, and so on.[43] And so the two are married, and for once, at least as most scholars take it, we have a happy ending.[44]

In the middle of this episode, which John F. Makowski calls "a tale of lesbian passion, confusion of gender, and trans-sexualism,"[45] Iphis speaks forth a remarkable monologue. I will treat it in two major sections. In the first, Iphis draws on parallels from the natural world to declare the impossibility of her love (9.726–63):

> vixque tenens lacrimas "quis me manet exitus," inquit
> "cognita quam nulli, quam prodigiosa novaeque
> cura tenet Veneris? si di mihi parcere vellent,
> parcere debuerant; si non, et perdere vellent,
> naturale malum saltem et de more dedissent!
> nec vaccam vaccae, neque equas amor urit equarum;
> urit oves aries, sequitur sua femina cervum;
> sic et aves coeunt, interque animalia cuncta
> femina femineo correpta cupidine nulla est.
> vellem nulla forem! ne non tamen omnia Crete
> monstra ferat, taurum dilexit filia Solis,
> femina nempe marem: meus est furiosior illo,
> si verum profitemur, amor; tamen illa secuta est
> spem Veneris, tamen illa dolis et imagine vaccae
> passa bovem est, et erat, qui deciperetur, adulter!"

Holding back tears with difficulty, "What escape is there for me," she said,
"me whom an unheard-of heartache holds, a monstrous
heartache of novel Love? If the gods wanted to spare me,
they ought to have spared; if not, and they wanted to destroy me,
at least they ought to have given me a natural destruction, a customary one!
For love of cows doesn't burn cows, nor love of mares, mares.
The ram follows the ewe, and his own female follows the (male) deer,
so even the birds come together, and among all the animals,
no female is caught by love for female.
I would that I were not [a woman?]! So that Crete should bring forth

every sort of monster, moreover, the daughter of the Sun loved a bull,
at least a female after a male: mine is a more rabid love than that,
if I confess the truth; at least she followed
a hope of Love, at least she, by trickery and the shape of a cow
suffered a bull, and he who was deceived was an adulterer!"

Iphis's speech is indeed unparalleled in Roman poetry: she tells us explicitly that the problem is that she, a woman, is chasing after a woman. The careful juxtaposition of gendered terms, *vaccam vaccae, femina femineo*, emphasizes this crucial lack of difference.[46] This "monstrous" (*prodigiosa*) new love is demonstrated to be contrary to nature by means of several examples. And finally, we are told that even Pasiphaë's love for a bull was less remarkable. At least there we had a male and a female. Later, towards the end of the soliloquy, Iphis tells us that only nature stands in the way of her desire (758–59). It is hardly surprising that modern scholars have read this, as Makowski does, as a "damning denunciation of homosexuality."[47]

For Makowski, indeed, the organizing feature of 9.666–11.66 *is* homosexuality, in the modern sense of the word. That is, he reads the story of Iphis and Ianthe as an introduction to the homoeroticism of the stories about (and by) Orpheus that follow. The point of these stories is to reveal Orpheus as "an effeminate, gynophobic pederast" (Makowski 1996.27). While Orpheus's pederasty is not in question, Makowski's terminology makes it clear that he is not reading in terms of a sexual identity that is defined by activity or passivity; because Orpheus eschews the love of women, Makowski sees him as "effeminate," a notion quite foreign to our Roman sources (as discussed above).

Even more remarkable, Makowski depends on a generalized notion of homosexuality in order to make his arguments. For, as it turns out, the Orpheus sequence contains no negative comment on Orpheus's proclivities for sex with boys.[48] As Makowski argues, "Further remarks on unnatural passion would be redundant with Iphis's monologue still fresh in our ears" (1996.32–33). But this presumes both that the Romans saw pederasty as unnatural (which they did not)[49] and that they would have linked female-female sexual relations to male-male sexual relations as being qualitatively similar, if not identical. Such an abstract structural parallel finds no support in secular discussions of ancient sexual practice.[50]

Makowski's argument falters on one other important ground. He reads the passage cited above as anti-homosexual in large part because he sees Ovid as opposed to same-sex relations. I make no argument here about Ovid's personal sensibilities; I do not take it as given that, even if Ovid's narrator were homophobic in one poem or section of a poem, he would necessarily be so elsewhere. But we should discuss briefly one of the passages that Makowski cites in favor of this view, *Ars Amatoria* 2.683–84: "odi concubitus, qui non utrumque resolvunt:/hoc est cur pueri tangar amore minus," "I hate that sleeping together that doesn't satisfy both parties: this is why I am touched less by love of boys." Of course, this statement of preference does not constitute a sexual identity.[51] Rather, Ovid (or better, the narrator of the *Ars Amatoria*) is commenting on his particular likes and dislikes from among the available options. More importantly, the narrator here bases his judgment on the lack of mutual desire in man-boy relations. This inequality is explicitly lacking in the story of Iphis and Ianthe, as we will see. Thus the story of Iphis and Ianthe can hardly qualify as a denunciation of homosexuality *in general*, as Makowski's biographical reading would have it.[52] But what of the more specific question? Can it be a denunciation of specifically *female* homoeroticism? Is that a category the Romans thought with? The equality of Iphis and Ianthe's love will prove to be of some importance in answering this question, and we will return to it shortly.[53]

Iphis's Monologue: Some Literary Aspects

It has long been recognized by feminist critics that Ovid is a problematic source for information about the lives of women in the ancient world.[54] His narrators are shifty, his poems highly literary and stylized, and Ovid's "own" views are as difficult to discern as they are unlikely to be representative of the thoughts of everyday Romans. This story, however, has regularly been taken at face value as a straightforward expression of homophobia. Even Judith Hallett, a canny reader who recognizes that the voice of Iphis contrasts with that of the primary narrator, does not place Iphis's monologue in any specific literary context; instead it (and the resulting sex change) merely become evidence for the Roman elite's denial of "reality" (cf. Hallett 1997.263, 267).

We should note the difficulty that arises when we assume that Iphis's story is a comment on the social reality of female homoeroticism per se. What exactly is Iphis's problem? What is all this talk about new, revolutionary, unheard of love? As W. S. Anderson comments, "Ovid's audience surely knew the odd facts of life and had heard about what we today call 'lesbianism'. . . Thus all the emphasis on novelty must have amused the Roman audience" (1972 ad 726). Anderson is partly right. Ovid's audience had heard about such sexual types as *tribades*, which Anderson (in

1972) is probably equating with lesbians. What is particularly curious about this story is that *tribades* are never mentioned.[55] Nor, in fact, is Iphis's love for Ianthe structured as tribadic. On the contrary, their desire for each other is characterized by an unprecedented equality and mutuality, as 9.718–21 (discussed below) shows. Whatever else this story is, then, it is not a transparent representation of everyday attitudes. Instead, Iphis lives in a curious literary world, a world in which love between women is not so much morally reprehensible as imaginatively impossible because there is no asymmetry of power between them. Tribadism is apparently simply not an option. Ovid has created a situation in which his lovers are, startlingly, equal. What Iphis finds unthinkable is not the typical Roman category of tribadism (to say nothing of "lesbianism"), but a romance of equal partners.[56]

Ovid has gone to some trouble to create this mutuality and equality, and the result is that some seams are left showing. To begin, the two lovers are the same age. We might well ask why Iphis, if presumed a boy, is marrying at the age of thirteen rather than twenty-five or thirty?[57] To some extent, of course, we can answer by pointing to the comic structure of the story: a young man, poor but noble, overcomes obstacles in order to marry the woman who is his match.[58] Like a good comic couple, they are said to have an *aequum vulnus*, something like an "equal passion" for one another.[59] Note, however, that the comic reading presumes that Iphis is somehow destined to play the man's role (see further below). Moreover, what Ovid has done in writing this comic motif is to transform the very thing that attracts the two lovers—their similarities—into their greatest difficulty. This is a fairly common technique in the *Metamorphoses*; so Myrrha complains of the one thing that keeps her from love with her father (10.339–40): "Nunc, quia iam meus est, non est meus, ipsaque damno / est mihi proximitas," "Now, because he is already mine, he is not mine; and closeness itself is my destruction."[60] Similarly here, Ovid has made these two lovers even more than usually equal and is highlighting the difficulty that this absolute equality creates. To take this comic twist as a straightforward comment on Roman attitudes towards female homoeroticism is more than a bit naïve. Rather, Ovid's Iphis demonstrates a verbal dexterity and a sense of melodrama played for humor in a fantastic construction of female homoeroticism—fantastic because non-hierarchical.

We should recognize here Ovid's penchant for playing with categories of thought in rhetorical display. Iphis's reliance on the natural world to describe the impossibility of her love is something of a topos in love poetry. A little bit later in the epic, in fact, we will find a very similar argument, used this time by Myrrha (10.323–31):

> sed enim damnare negatur
> hanc Venerem Pietas, coeuntque animalia nullo
> cetera dilectu, nec habetur turpe iuvencae
> ferre patrem tergo; fit equo sua filia coniunx,
> quasque creavit, init pecudes caper, ipsaque, cuius
> semine concepta est, ex illo concipit ales.
> felices, quibus ista licent! humana malignas
> cura dedit leges et, quod natura remittit,
> invida iura negant.

> The other animals have intercourse
> with no discrimination, nor is it considered disgraceful for a heifer
> to carry her father on her back; his own daughter may be a wife for a horse,
> and the goat goes into whatever [female] goats he has created, and the bird
> conceives from the [male] bird from whose seed she was conceived.
> Happy, those to whom these things are allowed! Human worry
> has given spiteful laws, and what nature allows,
> jealous laws forbid.

In this passage, however, Myrrha uses the animal world to argue in favor of father-daughter incest. It is a funny world, indeed, if we take Myrrha's and Iphis's speeches at face value: sex between two women is so unnatural as to be unthinkable, but incest is just a matter of human convention.[61] Indeed, even within Iphis's speech, we learn that bestiality is more acceptable than the female-female union she contemplates (9.735–40). Clearly the rhetoric is excessive here, and Iphis's bombast is meant to be taken as amusing, coming as it does from a thirteen-year-old.[62]

To say all this, however, does not alter the fact that Iphis seems to be thinking with modern categories: she seems worried specifically about the homosexuality that her situation requires. But is she? Even in the remarkable statement that Pasiphaë's love for a bull was less crazy than Iphis's for Ianthe, we see evidence of a passive versus active typology of sex. As Iphis puts it, "illa dolis et imagine vaccae / passa bovem est, et erat, qui deciperetur, adulter!" ("She, by trickery and the shape of a cow, suffered a bull, and he who was deceived was an adulterer!" 9.739–40). Though Pasiphaë was possessed by desire for a bull, when it comes to the act of sex, she "suffers" it as a woman should.[63] It is not just that the bull is male, then, but that he is *masculine*: active to Pasiphaë's passivity.

We should note, further, that Iphis's love is *furiosior* than Pasiphaë's not for reasons of moral reprehensibility but because Pasiphaë, at least, had some hope (*spes*) of fulfilling her love (9.737–40).[64] Again, Iphis's desire for Ianthe is not so much immoral as impossible.

I suggest, moreover, that one of the reasons Iphis has been taken as representative of lesbianism is the very equality of her and Ianthe's passion for one another. Though the proper social forms of modern lesbianism are highly contested, one of our narratives about it is that it consists of an equal, mutual desire uninterrupted by the violence of gender difference.[65] It is exactly this sort of narrative that we see in Iphis's relation to Ianthe: contrary to all Roman erotic expectation, nearly everything about their love is marked by equality (9.718–21):

> par aetas, par forma fuit, primasque magistris
> accepere artes, elementa aetatis, ab isdem;
> hinc amor ambarum tetigit rude pectus et aequum
> vulnus utrique dedit,

> Their ages were equal, their beauty equal, and they learned the first
> skills, the basic curriculum, from the same teachers.
> From here love touched the simple breast of each, and gave
> an equal wound to both;

Though their social status, physical status, and even their education are strikingly equal, however, we must recognize that Iphis and Ianthe's passion is not, in modern terms, "lesbian" or even "female homoeroticism." The continuation of lines 718–21 reads as follows (9.721–25):

> sed erat fiducia dispar:
> Coniugium pactaeque exspectat tempora taedae,
> Quamque virum putat esse, virum fore credit Ianthe;
> Iphis amat, qua posse frui desperat, et auget
> Hoc ipsum flammas ardetque in virgine virgo.

> but their hopes were unequal:
> Ianthe hoped for marriage, and the day of the promised wedding
> and whom she thought to be a man, she believed would be *her* man.
> Iphis loved one whom she despaired of ever enjoying, and this itself
> increased the flames, and the maiden burned for maiden.

Despite the supposed equality of their upbringing, Iphis's passion and Ianthe's are marked, even at this stage in their relationship, by difference.[66] Ianthe loves Iphis *as a man*, and her desire is carefully feminine, concealed behind a hope for marriage and wedding torches.[67] More importantly, what Iphis despairs of here is not the shame of "unnatural" homoeroticism but, specifically, the fact that she is not a man. As Stephen Wheeler points out, the verb *fruor* is a standard erotic term for a man's role in sex.[68] The passage does, to be sure, find female same-sex relations unthinkable. Not, however, for the usual reason, that *tribades* are "unnatural," but because, in the highly literary romance that Ovid has constructed, there is no active (masculine) partner.

Finally, we should note that Iphis ends her soliloquy in exactly these terms (9.762–63): "pronuba quid Iuno, quid ad haec Hymenaee, venitis / sacra quibus qui ducat abest, ubi nubimus ambae?" "Why, Juno of marriages, why Hymenaeus, would you come to these rites, at which he who leads is missing, and where both are veiled?" It is inappropriate for Juno and Hymenaeus to attend a wedding where there is nobody who leads— i.e., no *man*—and both parties are to play the passive part. Indeed, the word *ducat* at 763 suggests the common Roman wedding formula, *uxorem ducere*.[69] Similarly, *nubere* in the last line is a verb nearly always used of women that seems to have as its original meaning "to be veiled."[70] In brief, this is not a question of sexuality but of gender. The conundrum facing the reader of Ovid, then, is not "how can two women sleep together" (for which, in any case, the Romans had an answer), but "what do two passives do in bed together?"

This reading is further supported by a close reading of the second half of Iphis's monologue. Iphis here is not so much opposed to same-sex love as she is psychologically transgendered. That is, she is a woman who wants to play a man's role. At 9.745–59, Iphis says:

> quin animum firmas teque ipsa reconligis, Iphi,
> consiliique inopes et stultos excutis ignes?
> quid sis nata, vide, nisi te quoque decipis ipsam
> et pete, quod fas est, et ama, quod femina debes!
> spes est, quae capiat, spes est, quae pascit amorem;
> hanc tibi res adimit: non te custodia caro
> arcet ab amplexu nec cauti cura mariti
> non patris asperitas, non se negat ipsa roganti;
> nec tamen est potienda tibi, nec, ut omnia fiant,
> esse potes felix, ut dique hominesque laborent.
> nunc quoque votorum nulla est pars vana meorum
> dique mihi faciles, quidquid valuere dederunt,
> quodque ego, vult genitor, vult ipsa socerque futurus;

at non vult natura potentior omnibus istis
quae mihi sola nocet!

Will you not gird your spirit and get a hold of yourself, Iphis,
and put out these stupid fires, lacking in counsel?
Look at what you were born, lest you deceive even yourself,
and seek what is allowed, and love what a woman ought.
It is hope that would seize love, hope that feeds love.
The matter itself denies her to you: no guardian keeps you
from her dear embrace, nor the care of a cautious husband,
nor the harshness of a father, nor does she deny herself to you as you ask,
but nonetheless she will not be had by you, nor, even if everything should
    happen,
are you able to be happy, not though the gods and humans work [for it].
Indeed, now no part of my prayers are in vain,
and the gods easily have given whatever they wished
and what I wish, my father wishes, and she wishes, and my future father-
    in-law wishes,
but nature does not wish it, nature more powerful than all these,
nature who alone harms me!

Hallett sees here "revulsion at female homoerotic passion" on the part
of Iphis, as well as "self-condemnation" (1997.263), particularly in lines
747–48 and in Iphis's earlier wish that she were dead (line 735).[71] But this
straightforward reading overlooks the elegiac overtones of the passage.
When Iphis asks, "quin animum firmas teque ipsa reconligis, Iphi, / con-
siliique inopes et stultos excutis ignes?" (745–46), she positions herself
squarely as a (male) elegiac *amator*.[72] In the following lines, she expresses
herself in typical elegiac form, caught in a passion she cannot control.
Like any *amator*, she is at a loss for what to do: her love is *furiosus*, and so
she tries to bring her passions under control and direct the energy to
more productive pursuits.[73] Iphis may despair of the possibility of her
love, but if she expresses self-condemnation, it is the ironic self-abase-
ment of a lover at his mistress's door.[74]

    Here we see Ovid at perhaps his trickiest. For as Diane Pintabone
eloquently argues, the feature that makes Iphis into a conventionally
moral woman is the fact that, as a woman (despite her desire for another
woman), she remains thoroughly passive. She never acts on her desire,
never contemplates becoming a *tribas*; she simply regrets the fact that she
does not have the equipment to "enjoy" (*frui*, 9.724) her beloved. But
now we are left to wonder: is her passivity that of a conventional woman

(as Pintabone 2002.275–78 has it), or that of the (ironically) self-abased male *amator*? There is a triple-layering of gender here: Iphis is a woman, culturally marked as a man, and, as a male lover, taking on a feminized role that is generically and literarily appropriate. This, I suggest, is the culminating example of Ovid "[having] it almost all ways" (Pintabone 2002.259).

The image of Iphis as *amator* continues in the rest of the passage. At 750 and following, Iphis runs through a catalogue of things that are *not* keeping the two lovers apart: no guardian, husband, father, nor the bride herself, and so on.[75] Thus although at line 744 Iphis suggests—briefly— the possibility that *Ianthe* could change genders,[76] in this long catalogue, Iphis clearly figures herself in the masculine role in this relationship. When she complains of the impossibility of her love, then, she does not regret an internal sexual identity but rather despairs of being able to play the masculine gender. Iphis finds herself in the traditional position of a man, but she is not stopped by the impediments that usually obstruct such men. Rather, it is nature that impedes her; not, as most modern readers have taken it, a nature that objects to female-female sex per se, but a nature that requires asymmetry in sexual relations.[77] Iphis's role as failed *amator* both prefigures her eventual transformation and posits its necessity.

Some comparative material from the *Metamorphoses* will help to establish this consistency. *Tribades* do not appear in the pages of Ovid's epic. That is not surprising, given the strictures of genre. We can look, however, at passages that hint at female-female relations and that confirm the general understanding of sex as predicated on the asymmetry between active and passive. On several occasions, gods find it handy to take on the form of a female (mortal or immortal) in order to get close enough to rape an unsuspecting young woman.[78] Jupiter rapes Callisto after disguising himself as Artemis to win her trust (2.424–38), Sol rapes Leucothoë after appearing as her mother (4.218–320), Apollo rapes Chione still cloaked as an old woman (11.310), and, most famously, Vertumnus tries to win the favor of Pomona by appearing to her as an old woman and singing his own praises (14.654–766).

In each of these cases, the god appears as a woman older than the love object, and, in the case of Callisto, holding great power over her. The disguise as a woman allows the god carefree access to the object of his lust, suggesting something like a community of women, a regularity of homosocial bonds between members of the same sex. The sexual act that follows in each case, however, destroys that community, indeed marks the difference between female-female relations and male-female relations. While still disguised as Artemis, for example, Jupiter kisses Callisto (2.430–31): "oscula iungit / nec moderata satis nec sic a virgine danda," "He kissed her not quite modestly, nor as a maiden kisses." Jupiter's true nature is hidden in those immodest kisses, and it will be fully revealed momentarily when he rapes Callisto. Similarly, Vertumnus (disguised as an old woman) kisses Pomona (14.658–59): "paucaque lau-datae dedit oscula, qualia numquam / vera dedisset anus," "To her, praised, he gave a few kisses, such kisses as never a true old woman gave." Again there is no "lesbianism" here, particularly in that sense that sees lesbians as partaking in a love unmarked by hierarchy and difference. Rather, in these female-female scenes, the disguise hides—imperfectly— exactly the one thing on which the Roman sexual scheme is predicated: gender difference.

From Symmetry to Difference

This bit of comparison brings us back to the aspect of Iphis and Ianthe's relationship that is, in fact, so unique: their mutuality. In a sense, as I have argued, this story *is* about homoeroticism. But it is not about female homosexuality as a known and derided sexual identity, rather it is an exploration of the fantastic conundrum presented by two lovers who are not different. This, then, is the feature that Ovid makes Iphis describe as a *prodigiosa novaeque cura Veneris*, a "monstrous heartache of novel love."

This reading is supported by a recent (1997) article by Stephen Wheeler treating wordplay in this story. Wheeler notes that Ovid has taken the story from Nicander (preserved in the mythography of An-toninus Liberalis),[79] but, in the process, he has changed the names of all the characters.[80] Most significantly, Wheeler sees the name Iphis as a bit of wordplay on the word *vis*, "strength," which, as he notes, "calls atten-tion to the missing element of male sexual potency" (1997.195–96). *Vis* is often used in the *Metamorphoses* as a marker of rape; to take one of the examples I just described, it is what Vertumnus prepares, but does not have to use, when all seems lost in his bid for Pomona (14.769–70). Iphis does not have *vis* before her transformation; that is why she cannot be a *vir*. (Wheeler also notes that wordplay on *vis* and *vir* is frequent in this story.)[81] Iphis is not a *tribas*, and still less a lesbian; she is "a man marked by the lack of virility advertised by her name."[82]

And that, of course, is what Iphis's miraculous transformation solves. She ceases to be a young woman and gains the marks of masculine ac-tivity: not only a longer stride and darker color but increased *vires* (787) and *vigor* (790). But here we run into a curious difficulty: at the end of his transformation, Iphis is a *puer*, not a *vir*. This should give us pause, because we learned earlier (712–13) that Iphis's looks were appropriate—even *formosus*—for a *puer*. Why, then, does he need a longer stride, shorter hair, and sharper features in order to become a *puer*? In part, this contradiction highlights the fact that the love presented here is a thoroughly literary construct. Ovid wants both to emphasize the lovers' equality and to successfully transform Iphis into a real man; the result is that some of the machinery is left showing. At the age of thirteen, Iphis can hardly be a *vir*, or even an *adulescens*.

What makes the story possible, however, is the ambiguous status of the *puer* at Rome. The *puer*, as an object of both male and female desire, is passive, but, if freeborn, he must eventually grow into the active impenetrability of a *vir*.[83] Iphis cannot be more than a *puer*, but what this transformation from *puella* to *puer* marks is a move from passive to active. The rather careful ambiguity of Iphis's new position is reflected in the verbal dexterity of line 791: "femina nuper eras, puer es" ("You who were a woman, are now a boy"). The line between what Iphis was and what he becomes is awfully thin, emphasized here by the fact that *puer es* is almost an anagram of *nuper eras*. But, in some sense, Iphis has crossed that line. In the first instance, describing Iphis's beauty as a young boy (712), the term *puer* is contrasted with *puella* ("girl"). After the transformation (790), the contrast is with *femina* ("woman"). As a *puer*, then, Iphis moves from that period when his/her looks are indistinguishable from those of a girl (712–13) to that period in which, by virtue of being a *puer*, he is distinguished from women. In other words, Iphis's transformation represents the transition from a *puer* living with other children of indeterminate gender, to a *puer* beginning his life as a *vir*.[84] The story has never been concerned with female deviance. It has focused on masculinity (or its lack) from the start.[85]

What is fascinating about this masculinity, however, is that it has less to do with biological *sex* than social *gender*. Unlike his predecessor Nicander, Ovid never mentions the growth of male genitalia.[86] Rather, we are drawn to the distinguishing marks that guarantee masculinity in the public streets of Rome: a longer stride, shorter hair, sharper features, and the like. This is of some importance because, as much recent scholarship has shown, the Romans viewed masculinity as an embattled position: not a biological fact but a hard-won social position that had to be continually bolstered and reinforced.[87] This reinforcement took place via a series of external signs meant to represent a never-quite-stable biological identity. To take a famous example, a man who scratched his head with one finger could be identified as a *cinaedus*, a male passive.

In the course of our story, then, Iphis changes his gender; whether or not his sex changes is not addressed. In fact, Ovid has carefully changed the narrative in such a way as to maintain this perhaps disquieting silence. In Nicander's version of the story, the deity responsible for the sex change is Leto Phutiê, etymologized in the story as Leto who helps grow genitalia.[88] And indeed, we are told specifically that Leucippus grows male genitalia in the course of the miracle. In Ovid, Leto has been replaced by Isis, much to the consternation of modern editors and critics.[89] Why these changes?

I see an answer in the shifty relation between gender, a set of arbitrary external signs, and sex, gender's supposedly stable signified. In Egyptian mythology, Isis's consort Osiris is ripped apart after death and his body parts scattered over the globe. Isis spends her eternal life looking for bits and pieces of him. Alas, one part, eaten by fishes, is never found: his penis. And so, as Plutarch tells it, Isis creates a copy, around which the Egyptians hold a festival "even today."[90] In Ovid's text at 9.693, Osiris is described as *numquamque satis quaesitus Osiris*, "never fully found Osiris," a periphrastic reference to this story.[91] Here with characteristic brilliance, Ovid presents the marks of gender with near total silence about what that gender is supposed to represent. Even the reference to Osiris's missing "part" fails to name that part. But at the same time, he hints at the signified—that is, male genitalia—by bringing in a goddess whose story represents its lack. Isis is the perfect emblem for the ideology of gender, an external pointer to something that is never quite there, that can only be represented by an indirect reference to the search for it.[92]

Conclusion: The Category of the *Tribas*

As we read this narrative, it can tell us something about how the Romans organized their thoughts about women's sexual practices. It also tells us something important about how we relate to the ancient world, engaging as we do in the activist project of interpreting those sexual practices. Over the past fifteen years or so, one of the central preoccupations of those scholars who would like to locate sexual identities—and individuals identified by those identities—in ancient Rome has been "the materiality of the *cinaedus*."[93] Good reasons exist for seeking out the material *cinaedus* and for trying to discover what his life was like. Good reasons also exist for wanting to see, in the invective against *cinaedi*, the roots of modern homophobia. But in all this talk of materiality, there has been a stunning silence about the materiality of the *tribas*. We are not so impelled, it appears, to prove that (to paraphrase Richlin): "Women identified as *tribades* really existed at Rome." Rather, when it comes to women who were sexually deviant, scholars have tried to conceptualize them as lesbians and to see the category of *tribas* as part of the oppression of that deviance. In other words, *cinaedi* look to us like oppressed gay men, *tribades* look like a masculine fantasy that reproduces patriarchal hierarchy.

Brooten is the most important representative of this line of reasoning. For Brooten, female homoeroticism is the basic category of thought, and the division between active and passive women represents male fantasy: "While ancient female homoerotic behavior probably included a full range of sexual expression, the ancient . . . male imagination seems limited to postulating a physical substitute for the penis" (1996.154). Here Brooten is in agreement with an important essay by Hallett, who argued in 1989 (reprinted 1997) that Roman literature tends to deny the "reality" of female-female sexual relations by Hellenizing, anachronizing, and distancing them.[94] In particular, Hallett attacks the image of the *tribas* as a penetrating woman as "unrealistic" (1997.266–67). But neither Hallett nor Brooten ever explicitly defines the "reality" of the female homoeroticism that the Romans have thus distorted. We may note, however, that Brooten finds it disturbing when the evidence points to Roman women thinking of sex in hierarchical terms. Speaking of erotic magic, for example, she says, "We may find it even more difficult to understand a woman calling for the sexual enslavement of another woman" (Brooten 1996.103). Perhaps. Perhaps this is not the model of female homoeroticism that classicists and feminists would like to find.[95]

As example after example demonstrates, however, the category of the *tribas*, of an active, penetrating woman, is the one that Romans used to conceptualize female-female sexual relations. That is the way that they thought about women who were sexually deviant. In other words, Hallett and Brooten exactly reverse the relation of fantasy and reality in Ovid's story. For Iphis, a non-hierarchical love, a love between two *equal* women with no person "who leads" is not just monstrous but utterly unthinkable. Iphis literally cannot imagine such a thing. Her dilemma is solved not through sexuality but through gender when she takes on the active traits of a man, much as, in the world of invective poetry, a *tribas* does.[96] Tribadism is not a denial of reality, any more than an ahistoric lesbianism is reality; it is merely contrary to a modern (perhaps idealized) view of female-female relations. Only by seeing the *tribas* or "active woman" as *the* category of female sexual deviance in Rome and recognizing its curious absence in this story can we understand what makes Iphis's love a violation of "nature." Hers is not the love that dare not speak its name; it is a love that has no Roman name to speak.[97]

Notes

1. I became aware of Pintabone 2002 after my piece had already been accepted for this volume. Though we differ in some key arguments, Diane Pintabone and I reached many of the same conclusions independently. My own thinking on this passage has been sharpened considerably through reading her fine essay. I point out our major differences in footnotes throughout. I would also like to mention here a perceptive and lucid unpublished manuscript, Deborah Kamen's "Compulsory Heterosexuality and the Metamorphosis of Isis." Kamen and I cover much of the same ground, and I am grateful for the generous offer to see her work.

2. Satirists such as Martial do mention such possibilities, but always with scorn and disapproval. See below.

3. Pintabone 2002 points out that only Iphis finds fault with her passion for Ianthe, and the narrator of the poem never speaks against it; see, esp., 263–64, 270–73.

4. See Pintabone 2002 (the most extensive treatment of the passage), Hallett 1997, and Makowski 1996. Most recently, Raval 2002 reads the story as exemplifying Butlerian "gender trouble"; see 158–67 on Iphis and Ianthe.

5. Walters 1997.30–32 and passim, Santoro L'hoir 1992, Richlin 1993.537. Pintabone 2002.275–76 discusses this productively with regard to the story of Caenis/Caenus in the *Metamorphoses*.

6. Williams 1999.18–19 and ch. 3.

7. Richlin 1993.537–38, 570, Williams 1995.531–36, Williams 1999.96–110, Walters 1997.34–35.

8. Williams 1995.531–37, Williams 1999.ch. 3, esp. 113, 120–21.

9. Some earlier arguments suggest that this picture did not hold as true for Rome as for Athens. With Williams 1995, we can put these objections to rest. Williams refutes the assertions of MacMullen 1982 and demonstrates that the Romans did not view "homosexuality" as an importation of Greek, and therefore debauched, sexual mores. Williams is followed in this regard by Parker 1997. See also Williams 1999.ch. 2.

10. Parker 1997.47. Parker seems here to mean "sex," though he says "gender," a rare slip. *Cinaedi*, as he shows, are *gendered* female. Parker's work has been anticipated throughout by Williams's 1992 dissertation, now revised as Williams 1999.

11. The bibliography on this item is huge and expanding. On Greece: Dover 1978.16, 81–91, 168–70; Foucault 1985.46, 85, 210–11; Halperin 1990.5, 15–40, 100–04; Halperin 2002.104–37; Winkler 1990.45–70. On Rome: Housman 1931.408 n. 1; Veyne 1978.50; Veyne 1985.26, 29–30; Brooten 1985. Richlin 1992a makes the same point, esp. at 220–26, but is inconsistent in her terminol-

ogy. See the discussion below and Richlin 1993.530–31, 534, 537–38, 570. Parker 1997.64 n. 5 lists most of the sources above, but fails to cite both Halperin and Winkler, whose work on Greece has been highly influential. Parker 2001 provides a useful discussion of the problem and a rigorous anthropological model with which to approach the Greek and Roman sources. Williams 1999 is now the most comprehensive work on the topic as it refers to Roman culture. Pintabone 2002.256–58 provides a useful brief summary.

12. See, e.g., Halperin 1990.15–40; *pace* Richlin 1998.148. Gleason 1995 is a brilliant and extensive treatment of the construction of masculine character. See also Williams 1999.ch. 4, esp. 141–43. Parker 2001 emphasizes that the existence of people with sexual preferences is of little import unless society sees those preferences as constitutive of meaning.

13. Halperin 1998 argues forcefully that Foucault's *History of Sexuality* has been misconstrued as distinguishing "acts" from "identities," and points out that the term "identity" never appears in Foucault's text (109); see, especially, 99–104, 109. Williams 1999.141 notes: "Masculinity was not fundamentally a matter of sexual practice; it was a matter of control."

14. Williams 1999.175–78, 209–15; cited (then forthcoming) in Halperin 1998.103.

15. See, most notably, Richlin 1993.

16. It is difficult not to be confused by statements like the following: "The homophobia of this poem [Juvenal 2] is undeniable . . . what primarily bothers him is that these men are penetrated by other men" (Richlin 1993.544).

17. Richlin 1993.529–30: "It is true that 'homosexuality' corresponds to no Latin word and is not a wholly adequate term to use of ancient Roman males, since adult males normally penetrated both women and boys."

18. Richlin 1993.530: "There was a concept of sexual deviance in Roman culture, which was not homologous with the modern concept 'homosexuality' but partook of some of the same homophobic overtones"; 571: "An analysis from the perspective of gay history, such as the one here, which stresses continuity rather than difference, would emphasize what ancient invective has in common with homophobia and would focus on real *cinaedi*, both on their oppression and on their possible subculture." See also Richlin 1992a.xxvii; duBois 1998.89, 94 is critical of Richlin's ahistoricism.

19. Richlin's other objection, that Foucault, Halperin, and Winkler have failed to cite feminist criticism, is more damning, although I do not agree with every aspect of Richlin's critique. See Richlin 1991 for the argument.

20. Richlin 1993.558–59 reads the list at the Julian *Digest* 3.1.1.5 of *personas in turpitudine notabiles* ("those notable for their moral degeneracy") as referring to those who come under the category of *infames*. Williams 1999.194, by contrast, argues that only the more limited restriction of being "excluded from appearing before a magistrate to make an application on behalf of someone else" applies here, and that the list of those marked by *infamia* is a different list (*Di-*

gest 3.2.1): "soldiers who had been dishonorably discharged; actors; brothel-keepers; those convicted of theft, robbery with violence, *iniuria*, or fraud; and those who had entered upon agreements of betrothal or marriage with two different people other than at the order of their legal guardian. There is no mention of those who 'played the woman's role' in this or any comparable list."

21. Richlin 1993.559. See also Edwards 1997.77: "Yet, those who followed these professions, in addition to their déclassé legal status, shared an association with various forms of sexuality constructed as deviant in ancient Roman texts."

22. Parker 1997.47, quoting Veyne 1985.30.

23. Usefully discussed by Brooten 1996.49, 52–53, 128, 161. In particular, the role of the (presumably passive) woman who slept with a *tribas* is ambiguous and unexplored: Hallett 1997.269. Williams 1999.211–12 argues, however, that the "women who might be penetrated by the *tribades* are implicitly normal."

24. See the brief discussion at Williams 1999.50.

25. A less extreme example can be found in Sulpicia's opening poem ([Tibullus] 3.13). There the speaker must carefully negotiate the fact that her expression of desire in traditional elegiac poetry might be cause for *pudor* ("shame"). See the useful discussion of Keith 1997.299–303.

26. The best treatment is Williams 1999.197–203; see also Parker 1997.55–59. Cf. the important challenges by Williams in his review of Hallett and Skinner 1997 (Williams 1998), particularly with regard to the *tribas* who performs cunnilingus. Now see also Pintabone 2002.256–58.

27. Williams 1998, citing Martial 7.67.1–3. Williams 1999.214–15 treats Seneca *Epistulae Morales* 95.20–21 on the same subject. See, in addition, Brooten 1996.45, who also cites Seneca *Epist.* 95.20.

28. See, for example, Martial 1.90. After exposing Bassa as a woman whose "huge Venus feigns masculinity" (*mentiturque virum prodigiosa Venus*), he closes by saying that she has accomplished an amazing feat: "Here where no man is, there is adultery!" ("hic ubi vir non est, ut sit adulterium").

29. So Williams argues that both the *cinaedus* and the *tribas* are "gender deviants." Cf. Williams 1998 and 1999.ch. 5, esp. 210–11.

30. Konstan 1994 argues that no Greek or Roman literature is predicated on a romance of *mutual* and *equal* desire before the Greek novel; see, esp., 57–59, 139–41.

31. Brooten 1996.25 notes: "We may have difficulty discerning when a woman suffers an act of hatred or discrimination as a lesbian and when the same act is directed toward her simply as a woman." See also the extended discussion in Halperin 2002.74–77.

32. I am indebted to Halperin's discussion of Brooten in Halperin 2002.ch. 2.

33. Brooten 1996.1. Halperin 2002.57 critiques Brooten for seeing female homoeroticism as "a *thing* . . . rather than a social and discursive production in its own right, a culturally constituted category of both erotic arousal and social organization" (emphasis in original).

34. Brooten 1996.6, for example, states: "Social reality was, however, more complex than ideology." To some extent, Brooten is following Hallett 1997 in this regard, particularly in her treatment of Iphis and Ianthe; see Brooten 1996.50. Pintabone 2002 seems close to this formulation as well; cf. esp. 258: "Faderman suggests that love between women occurs naturally, but that responses to it are culturally constructed." See also p. 277.

35. Brooten 1996.132–37. Here we see another difference from our sexual categories: Maternus seems to view *viragines* as a subcategory of prostitutes; see 136.

36. See, e.g., the pseudo-Lucianic *Erotes* and Halperin 1994. This text is entirely concerned with the sexual tastes of men.

37. Hallett 1997.269 points out that the two partners in female same-sex relations are often "undifferentiated." See also Gordon 1997.286.

38. A theme in Brooten 1996; see 49, 52–53, 59, 76, 154.

39. I first learned this from David Halperin, who credits Peter Dorcey with the observation. See now also Gordon 1997.227 n. 12, Brooten 1996.34–36.

40. Gordon 1997 passim. Some of Gordon's arguments are problematic: I see little connection between Sappho and Newton's "mannish lesbian." Nor do I see any reason to suppose that Sappho has grown a penis (281), which would make her a full-blown *tribas*. See the comments of Williams 1998. In any case, there is considerable doubt as to the date and authenticity of the fifteenth epistle. Tarrant 1981, arguing primarily on metrical grounds, suggests that it is the work of a later imitator. Brooten 1996.34–40 also provides considerable evidence that Sappho was initially viewed as inappropriately masculine, and/or a prostitute. It is not until the seventeenth century that she is explicitly criticized as homoerotic.

41. The only full-scale studies of the episode are Pintabone 2002 and Wheeler 1997. Otis 1970 sees the story as one of piety rewarded (as opposed to the stories of Byblis and Myrrha that frame it), and also as championing heterosexual over homosexual relations (184, 186, 225, 389). Galinsky 1975.86–92 also reads the story as a counterpart to that of Byblis and a parallel to the story of Pygmalion (an impossible love made possible by the gods). Hallett 1997 reads the transformation as a denial of "reality" (see discussion below), and is largely followed by Brooten 1996.44–45. Makowski 1996 interprets the story as setting up the implicit homophobia of the story of Orpheus in Book 10. Boswell 1980.83 notes it briefly as denouncing lesbian passion. On the term pastiche, see, especially, the useful discussion in Johnson 1996.9 n. 2.

42. Pintabone 2002.276–77 wonders how it is that Iphis has passed for male all this time, since her transformation into a boy requires an extensive change in appearance (cf. 9.786–91). I see this as one of the sutures that belie the existence of Iphis as a "real" girl (or boy); s/he is a literary conundrum, fashioned to make possible her strange, mutual passion with Ianthe. See further below.

All translations in this essay are my own, and are meant to be literal rather than elegant.

43. See Gleason 1995 for an extensive discussion of the traits of masculinity in men. Corbeill 1997.113–15 also provides a brief overview. Raval 2002 sees this depiction as supporting the notion that gender is performative. See further below.

44. E.g., Otis 1970, who sees Iphis as rewarded for her piety. Hallett 1997.263 also sees the ending as happy, though she sees this happiness as homophobic. Pintabone 2002.279 points out that Ovid here "shows Iphis destroyed in the sense that she is no longer a woman."

45. Makowski 1996.30–31. One of the weaknesses of Makowski's article is his imprecise use of terms defining sexual roles. "Lesbianism" is not equivalent to "trans-sexualism" in the ancient world any more than in our own.

46. Noted by Makowski 1996.31.

47. Makowski 1996.30. Cf. Otis 1970.187, 270.

48. Boswell 1980.83 takes 10.78–215 as evidence that Ovid did not regard male homosexuality as abnormal.

49. See, for example, 3.353–55, 402–03. There Narcissus is desired by both men and women. *His* position is somewhat ambiguous as a *puer* still young enough to be thought of as passive (and hence "feminine"), but there is no suggestion that such desires are shameful either for Narcissus or for the men who desire him. Makowski 1996 seems unaware of Williams 1995. He refers repeatedly to pederasty as "Greek love," e.g., on 25.

50. Williams 1995.537: "Nor is there any evidence in the ancient sources for the creation of any significant parallel between male and female homoerotic experience." Boswell 1980.83 cites Iphis and Ianthe as evidence that the Romans did *not* see male and female homoerotic experience as equivalent, since "he [Ovid] appears to regard homosexual love between males as perfectly normal (e.g. 10.78–215)." A possible example of such equivalence occurs at Paul's Epistle to the Romans 1.24–27; there, however, we hear only that the women practiced sex that was "contrary to nature" (παρὰ φύσιν), which may or may not refer to same-sex relations. Williams 1999.234–35 suggests that the story of Iphis demonstrates the Romans' negative view of female-female relations as opposed to their neutral view of male-male relations.

51. Williams 1995.536–37 and 537 n. 107; on the type of statement generally, see, esp., Halperin 1994 passim, Parker 1997.55 (without reference to Halperin or Williams).

52. We should also note that the other passages cited as evidence of Ovid's attitude against homosexuality, esp. lines 19 and 21 of *Heroides* 15, portray Sappho as sexually avaricious. The invective here (as in every other case) is against women who are *active*, not women who are *homosexual*.

53. Pintabone 2002.279 briefly discusses the strangeness of the "mutuality and equality" of their relationship.

54. See, for example, Culham 1990 (with references); Hallett 1990 suggests some ways in which Ovid can be used to discern contemporary Roman attitudes. The shiftiness of the Ovidian narrator is highlighted throughout Pintabone 2002.

55. Thus Makowski 1996.32 is mistaken when he says that Iphis's transformation is a "comment on the superiority of . . . marriage over tribadism." Pintabone 2002.263–75 has it right: not only is Iphis never called a *tribas*, she never acts on her passion while a girl, thus conforming to Roman standards for female behavior.

56. Konstan 1994 argues that mutual desire is a development unique to the ancient Greek romance novels. I would argue that Iphis and Ianthe prefigure that development, if only in a contrary-to-fact condition.

57. Treggiari 1991.39–43, 399–400 argues that Roman men generally married around the age of twenty-five to thirty, although they may have been legally able to marry as early as fourteen. Augustan marriage legislation may have lowered the expected age of marriage by a few years (402–03). Pintabone 2002.276 notes that Iphis marries at an age normal for girls.

58. See Anderson 1972 ad 673, Pintabone 2002.279–80.

59. Vertumnus experiences *mutua vulnera* (14.771) for Pomona, but this is after he has revealed his masculine self and prepared force (*vis*) (which he then does not have to use). Their love may be mutual, but is not equal.

60. Similarly Narcissus at 3.466: "quod cupio mecum est: inopem me copia fecit," "What I desire is with me: abundance makes me poor."

61. Boswell 1980.152–53 notes these parallels and concludes that these two speeches are mere rhetorical displays. Winkler 1990.20–22, 64–70 is particularly good on the shifting value of "nature" in rhetorical claims that a particular behavior is "unnatural." In *Epistle* 122.7–8, for example, Seneca lists "hot baths, potted plants, and banquets after sunset" as *contra naturam* ("against nature"), and Winkler concludes that for Seneca, "contrary to nature," means "going AWOL from one's assigned place in the social hierarchy" (Winkler 1990.21). Similarly, in discussing Aristotle's fourth book of *Problems*, on the question of why some men enjoy being penetrated, Winkler argues that "in this text nature is both the norm and the culprit, for it is nature who (in one way of speaking) has made certain men unnatural" (Winkler 1990.68).

62. Pintabone 2002.271–75 makes the perceptive point that Iphis's ravings here are not borne out by the story. Despite her despair that the gods cannot help her, in fact they do.

63. See now the useful discussion by Pintabone 2002.265–66, 268–69. Pintabone argues further that, in Pasiphaë's relationship, she is active (and even a "female rapist," 269) because she deceives the bull (9.740). While it is true, as Pintabone points out, that deception is often employed by male rapists in the poem, I do not see Pasiphaë as active here, except insofar as she "acts" (by setting up her passive role) on her desire (which Iphis does not).

64. If anything, Pasiphaë's passion is the one that is morally reprehensible; her bull is an adulterer in line 740. What is contrasted here is the possibility of fulfillment with a (male) animal and the impossibility of fulfillment by a woman.

65. See, for example, the epigraph from Adrienne Rich that prefaces this

essay. For a recent argument that lesbianism *should* have this sort of character, see S. D. Walters 1996.

66. Raval 2002.159 sees the equality in lines 718–19 as emphasizing "the role of performance in determining gender identity." But as the following lines show, there is a difference between the two lovers, even with any definite action absent.

67. Pintabone 2002.277 wonders whether we can call Ianthe's passion homoerotic, since she does not know the "true" sex of Iphis, and asks the productive question: "Is it [homoeroticism] desire of a woman for one known to be a woman or for one who *is* a woman?" (277). We, of course, can define modern homoeroticsm however we like. But the emphasis in Ovid's poem is on the difference between their passions: "unequal," *dispar* (9.721). As far as Ianthe knows, her passion is not homoerotic.

68. Wheeler 1997.198. See further below. Bömer 1977 similarly takes the word to be erotic, like *potiri* in 753 and 796. Pintabone 2002.267–68 is again quite perceptive here: "Iphis focuses on *exempla* that are concerned with sexual desire rather than, say, laws concerning marriage"; see in addition 276–81. Raval 2002.164–65 also draws on Wheeler's work.

69. So Bömer 1977 ad 762. Raval 2002.161 argues that "institutions like marriage play a pivotal role in the identification of gender." While the impending wedding has set up this crisis, however, we should note that Iphis speaks of the act of sex, not of marriage, as the thing that she cannot accomplish with Ianthe.

70. Cf. *Oxford Latin Dictionary* s.v. *nubes* 6, *nubo* 1–3.

71. Anderson 1972 argues that the first half of 735 can be translated: "I wish I were no woman," which would support the argument I am making here. Bömer 1977 ad 735, however, denies that the line can have this meaning and draws a number of parallels from comedy and elegiac.

72. Cf. Catullus 76.11: "quin tu animo offirmas atque istinc teque reducis?" Bömer 1977 points out the links to elegiac here, ad 745, and in his introduction to the passage on p. 473.

73. So, for example, Catullus in poem 8 urges himself to let go of his beloved, since she has apparently left him.

74. Oliensis 1997b provides a useful discussion of this topos, and particularly the relation between client-patron *amicitia* and the eros expressed by a lover for his mistress; see, esp., 152–57 and Williams 1999.154–55. Kamen's unpublished piece is particularly strong on Iphis's adoption of a masculine role here.

75. Bömer 1977 ad 750–52 points out several parallels from erotic poetry.

76. The suggestion is dropped as soon as made. In any case, as Wheeler 1997.194 notes, Ianthe's role in the drama is secured by her name, which means "violet." Iphis's name similarly foreshadows her masculinity; see further below.

77. I am reminded here that Artemidorus seems to qualify dreams as containing "unnatural" erotic content when they fail to create a social hierarchy; see Winkler 1990.38–40, Brooten 1996.184–85. Same-sex erotic dreams fall into all three of his categories: natural, unnatural, and illegal (Brooten 1996.181).

78. See the discussion of Johnson 1996 and 1997, both responding to Richlin 1992b.

79. Antoninus Liberalis *Metamorphoses* 17.

80. For a full-length treatment of Nicander's version as it relates to male initiation rites, see Leitao 1995. Bömer 1977.469–72 discusses Ovid's dependence on Nicander and the significance of the change of patron deities (from Leto to Isis).

81. Wheeler 1997.195. See also Raval 2002.165–66.

82. Wheeler 1997.200. Here I disagree with Raval 2002.166, who sees Iphis as constituting a "third term" to the binary of gender. Unlike modern instances of cross-dressing, this story does not focus on a positive gender identity for Iphis in her cross-dressed state. Instead, it presents her as a man whose masculinity is not yet—but must be—fully realized.

83. See, especially, Williams 1995.525.

84. So Konstan 1994.185 reads the story in terms of male initiation rites. Leitao 1995.147 argues that this is exactly the transition that Nicander's story emphasized, a "transition between these separate feminine and masculine domains."

85. Here I differ from Pintabone 2002.280, who would have Iphis as "essentially female but a woman who loves a woman." As I see it, Iphis's overriding *cultural* masculinity explains why, as Pintabone points out (277, 280), Ovid gives us so few clues as to what sort of internal changes might have accompanied Iphis's physical transformation.

86. See, especially, the discussion of Wheeler 1997.199–200; also Raval 2002.159–61, 163–64, Anderson 1972 ad loc.

87. E.g., Williams 1999.ch. 4, Walters 1997, Gleason 1995, Raval 2002.166.

88. Leitao 1995.136 points out that the epithet Phutiê in cult refers to the productivity of the community in general, and that Leto Phutiê is involved in the enrollment of adult citizens. See also the discussion in Wheeler 1997.191 and 191 n. 11. Graf 1988 sees the *aetion* of Leto no longer relevant to Ovid's audience.

89. For discussion, see Bömer 1977.471.

90. For the story, see Plutarch *Moralia* 351Cff. The story about the missing penis is at 358B.

91. Bömer 1977 ad 693. Bömer traces the establishment of the cult to the Ptolemaic era.

92. So Zizek 1989.45 defines the function of ideology: "In its basic dimension it is a fantasy-construction which serves as a support for our 'reality' itself: an 'illusion' which structures our effective, real social relations and thereby masks some insupportable, real, impossible kernel." I see here a more ambivalent ending than Raval 2002.166–67, who sees the end of the story as fully resolving Iphis's earlier gender ambiguity.

93. The most important example is Richlin 1993. See also Parker 1997.60–63.

94. See, however, the important response by Williams 1995.521 n. 27 and Williams 1998.

95. Some queer feminist thought, however, sees an asymmetrical model for erotic relations as useful and defensible; see, especially, Case 1993.

96. The difference, of course, is that Iphis really becomes a man, so that, in her case, these characteristics are not considered deviant.

97. This paper has a history. I delivered the earliest version of it at the conference on feminism and the classics at Princeton in 1996. A somewhat revised version appeared at the twenty-fifth annual panel of the Women's Classical Caucus of the American Philological Association in 1999. Questioners at both of those talks have contributed to the final product in significant ways; I would especially like to thank Joy Connolly, Karen Bassi, and Yopie Prins. I also owe a great debt to Nancy Sorkin Rabinowitz, who encouraged me to speak at the 1996 conference and who has provided much-needed suggestions and support. An anonymous reader for this volume provided sharp and incisive criticism. The editors, Ronnie Ancona and Ellen Greene, have my sincere thanks for their suggestions, comments, and encouragement. The reader should not hold the people mentioned above responsible for the views I express here or for any errors or infelicities. Much of the work on the final version was completed while I enjoyed a fellowship at the Institute for Research in the Humanities, University of Wisconsin–Madison.

II The Gaze

5 | Vision and Desire in Horace *Carmina* 2.5

Elizabeth Sutherland

In the six stanzas of *nondum subacta* (*Carmina* 2.5), Horace's speaker explains to the poem's addressee that the "heifer" they are watching (a young woman, Lalage, represented metaphorically as a farm animal) is not yet sexually mature, but that she will soon be able to return her admirer's passion. She will then be more cherished than any of the addressee's previous beloveds. Such has been the traditional summary of the ode. This approach, while a correct reading of one level of the poem, has limited the questions that critics have been able to ask. However, by considering how the speaker presents us with information, we obtain a very different reading. We must first appreciate the fact that Lalage is not a real person. She functions as the focal point of the addressee's vision (literally) and of his desire (symbolically). Lalage and Gyges (who closes the ode) reveal the degree to which both desire and the lyricist's self-presentation as male are calculated literary constructs.

Horace develops the relationship between speaker and addressee so as to represent, in a complicated nexus, the connections among vision, absence, and desire. If we read *Carmina* 2.5 with help from audience-oriented theory and feminist film theory, we find that the young woman in the ode is beautiful and desirable entirely because she is watched and commented upon. Those who watch her are identified as men and as powerful insofar as they possess what film theory calls "the gaze." Finally, the ambiguous Gyges challenges the status, and the visual authority, of those who see him on stage: a male who is on display, watched and feminized, he also recalls Herodotus's Gyges, whose act of watching was a manifestation of his own ambiguous relationship to power.

As a starting point, I consider the poem's most conspicuous generic elements (*Carmina* 2.5.1–12):

113

Nondum subacta ferre iugum valet
cervice, nondum munia comparis
    aequare nec tauri ruentis
        in venerem tolerare pondus.

circa virentis est animus tuae
campos iuvencae, nunc fluviis gravem
    solantis aestum, nunc in udo
        ludere cum vitulis salicto

praegestientis. tolle cupidinem
immitis uvae: iam tibi lividos
    distinguet autumnus racemos
        purpureo varius colore.

She is not yet able to bear the yoke
on bent neck, not yet able to match up
    to the duties of an age mate nor endure
        the weight of a bull as he rushes toward love.

The mind of your heifer is concerned
with green fields, as she now relieves
    the heavy heat in the rivers, now
        longs to play with the bull calves

in the damp willow. Dismiss your desire
for the unripe grape: soon autumn,
    dappled in its purple coloring, will
        mark out for you dark clusters of fruit.[1]

Horace begins with two topoi common to erotic poetry, in each of which a young woman (sexually inexperienced up until now) is described as ready to enter a sexually active adult life.[2] The poet first represents Lalage as a young, unbroken farm animal, using the pattern according to which a male pursuer hopes to "tame," euphemistically speaking, the lively young woman whom he desires. We next see Lalage as a grape, currently unripe and not appropriate for consumption, but soon to ripen into juicy edibility.[3]

While these conventions are well established for *Carmina* 2.5, there is a range of suggestions as to what force they have in the poem. Implicitly or explicitly, scholars ask whether or not the addressee will win Lalage and whether he is seeking marriage or a more informal sort of relationship.[4] Another concern that has dominated much scholarship on

2.5 is the identity of its addressee. The earliest extant articulation of this problem appears in pseudo-Acro's commentary on the ode: "incertum est quem adloquatur hac ode, utrum amicorum aliquem an semet ipsum" ("It is uncertain whom he addresses with this ode, whether one of his friends or himself"). Critics fall into two camps here: either the speaker himself is the addressee (leaving us with a soliloquy), or the addressee is a person whom the poet assumes is outside the poem.[5] Why is the poet so unclear as to where he locates the addressee? Why does the text permit such a division between critics who assume that the lover will succeed and critics who do not?

These problems are more closely related than one might expect, and audience-oriented theory proves a useful tool in treating both. Among other benefits, it enables us to move away from two common scholarly assumptions: first, that the ode's central concerns are with a relationship and its eventual consummation and, second, that the poet had in mind an individual (fictional or not, invisible or present) to whom his address was of particular concern. Rather than trying to identify an actual person to whom the poet speaks, we will instead look beyond the world of the poem and its limited cast of characters to consider how an audience, any audience, might respond to the text. We can thus consider, for example, how an educated audience (as opposed to a naïve audience) might respond, and how the text's speaker seems to encourage us to respond.[6]

Because of the genre's characteristics, audience-oriented theory is particularly applicable to lyric poetry. We frequently see in the *Odes*, for example, that Horace's *ego* can manipulate addressee and audience with lyric modes of address. As Ralph Johnson observes, the sense of direct address so prevalent in traditional lyric encourages us to think of the lyric poem as a dialogue between speaker and audience. Johnson terms this "I-You" lyric and argues that if such a poem opens with an address to an unnamed "you"—either explicit or implied—its audience is likely to identify with that "you."[7] Our lyricist encourages the audience of 2.5 to accept this identification and to imagine itself part of the verbal exchange implied by the ode. The sense of intimacy thus produced can make even a modern reader of Horace feel immediately involved in the world represented in the poem. This reader can, as a result, be subject to considerable manipulation by the poet.

The speaker of *Carmina* 2.5 also gains influence over his audience with his use of visual and sensory imagery. We see this early in the text, where the speaker expounds on Lalage's current setting and behavior. While the premise behind these comments is that they are part of a conversation with the poet's fellow observer, they serve, of course, to familiarize the ode's external audience with the scene. These factors have a great impact on an external audience's reception of the ode. The terms associated specifically with Lalage (*virentis*, *udo*, and *gravem . . . aestum*) give us in the audience an immediate and tactile impression of the environment in which Lalage moves. We are aware, through these descriptors, of Lalage's pleasure in the fresh grass, and we appreciate her enjoyment of the contrast between cool stream and oppressive summer. Sharing her surroundings, we find it easier to believe that Lalage romps in her field before our very eyes.

The imagery surrounding the heifer also gives the audience information about her sexual status. Horace's language makes it clear that the heifer's relationship to her world is sensual and unthinking. She is a creature of the body, one whose sexual decisions will not be choices as such, but will, instead, develop naturally (the poet implies) as her body matures. We observe her in the spring or summer; like many classical authors, Horace links spring or summer with sexual ripening. The use of seasonal imagery to dictate appropriate human behavior is a particular feature of Horace's lyric.[8] Because Lalage is represented as a heifer, both her maturation and her acquiescence seem inevitable to the audience. This maneuvering through literary tropes, along with Horace's skillful use of visual effects, encourages the external audience to become immersed in the scene. The combination has contributed to scholarly claims that the heifer-turned-maiden will eventually pursue her lover.

I begin with the ode's visual elements. By combining strong visual elements with lyric address, the poet of *Carmina* 2.5 contrives to produce a certain intimacy and cooperation between himself and his audience. This dynamic, in turn, contributes to the production of *enargeia*.[9] Used by literary critics at least as early as the second century B.C.E., the term *enargeia* refers to the effect of visual intensity that a text (historical or literary) can have upon a reader; by extension, it refers to a quality of the text that produces such an effect. Dionysius of Halicarnassus, writing on Lysias, tells us that (7):

ἔχει δὲ καὶ τὴν ἐνάργειαν πολλὴν ἡ Λυσίου λέξις. αὕτη δ᾽ ἐστὶ δύναμίς τις ὑπὸ τὰς αἰσθήσεις ἄγουσα τὰ λεγόμενα, γίγνεται δ᾽ ἐκ τῆς τῶν παρακολουθ-ούντων λήψεως. ὁ δὴ προσέχων τὴν διάνοιαν τοῖς Λυσίου λόγοις οὐχ οὕτως ἔσται σκαιὸς ἢ δυσάρεστος ἢ βραδὺς τὸν νοῦν, ὃς οὐχ ὑπολήψεται γινόμενα τὰ δηλούμενα ὁρᾶν καὶ ὥσπερ παροῦσιν οἷς ἂν ὁ ῥήτωρ εἰσάγῃ προσώποις ὁμιλεῖν.

The speech of Lysias also contains a great deal of *enargeia*. This is a certain capacity that brings things that have been said close to the senses [of the audience], and develops from [the author's] grasp of detail. Indeed, the person who applies his intelligence to the writings of Lysias will not be so clumsy or fastidious or slow of mind that he will not think that he sees happening the things being described and that he mingles, as if they were present, with the people whom the rhetor addresses.

The same concept appears under a different name in the *Rhetorica ad Herennium*, as follows: "demonstratio est cum ita verbis res exprimitur ut geri negotium et res ante oculos esse videatur" ("It is *demonstratio* when a situation is expressed by words in such a way that the business seems to be carried out and the matter seems to be before one's eyes," 4.68).[10]

Carmina 2.5 has no narrative frame or preamble that might maintain some distance between poem and external audience. We in the external audience are therefore encouraged to respond to the second-person address that dominates this ode and to identify ourselves with the ode's addressee. This is true despite the fact that, within the dramatic fiction of the poem, a shadowy figure lurks behind the speaker's *tu*. Combined with the poem's visual impact, Horace's use of lyric address makes us feel that we are watching Lalage side by side with the speaker who describes her behavior. Our assimilation to the addressee makes us more likely to believe in the authenticity or immediacy of the material presented to us.[11]

A full identification with the ode's addressee is problematic, however, for a variety of reasons. The first difficulty is that both speaker and addressee are apparently men. The image of the *taurus ruens* (a stand-in for the addressee) indicates that the addressee is male. The poet must be male as well: Horace's *ego* (when clearly gendered) is invariably male, and there is no reason to expect anything different here. The two participants in this one-sided conversation are watching a young woman. At the end of the text, however, a young man (albeit one who is feminized) becomes the object of vision. What might the response be of a woman who encounters the poem, or of a man who prefers not to share the speaker and addressee's questionable position? What questions does watching the effeminate Gyges raise for the normative Roman male's gender identity?

Judith Fetterley, writing on American fiction, argues that canonical literature encourages the audience of such literature to identify as male. Women readers, she argues, commonly experience what she calls "immasculation," in that they are "taught to think as men, to identify with a male point of view, and to accept as normal and legitimate a male system of values." The ideal response to this situation is for a woman reader (or spectator, or audience member) to adopt a position in which she "resists" the position offered her by the male-dominated text.[12] Applying Fetterley's principles to Horace's ode requires that we identify with a desiring male spectator. A woman reader would therefore find herself in the challenging situation of adopting the poet's point of view and contributing to the objectification of Lalage.

The terminology of feminist film criticism overlaps significantly with Fetterley's position. Proponents of this method return again and again to the question of women viewers' responses to male-dominated films, particularly the so-called "classical [Hollywood] movie." This body of scholarship addresses the question of who, in either a literary or a cinematic situation, gets to do the watching, and who has to be watched. Women in conventional movies are described as having "to-be-looked-at-ness," the quality that makes them objects of vision. The discussion begins with Laura Mulvey's 1975 article on "visual pleasure," in which she argues that a "woman displayed as sexual object . . . holds the look, plays to and signifies male desire."[13] Mulvey arrives at the conclusion (similar to Fetterley's) that the woman spectator is able to enjoy a male-oriented movie only by assimilating herself to a male viewing position. Mary Ann Doane approaches the same problem from the opposite direction, claiming that "one can readily trace, in the women's films of the 1940s, recurrent suggestions of deficiency, inadequacy, and failure in the woman's appropriation of the gaze."[14] Men in classic films are able to "look," while women are not.

In short, Fetterley, Mulvey, and Doane all conclude that a conventional text or conventional movie anticipate a spectator who is fundamentally masculine and an object of desire that is fundamentally feminine.[15] If we adhere to this system, we must assume that any man encountering *Carmina* 2.5 will have his masculinity and his power as viewer reinforced; a woman audience member will become immasculated, will identify with Lalage as an object of the gaze, or will choose to become the cinematic equivalent of Fetterley's "resisting reader."[16] While it is difficult to reconstruct the poet's intentions (if any) for a female audience, much of the terminology developed by these scholars will be useful in discussing Lalage. As I demonstrate below, Lalage's portion of the ode is very much in step with the feminist arguments just summarized.

We must also, however, consider the recent developments in feminist film theory that acknowledge a still more complex network of relationships among women and men, viewers and viewed. Many have noted, for example, that Mulvey's treatment of the gaze excludes the possibilities of both masochistic pleasure on the part of the female viewer and the male viewer's identification with the desired object's position of powerlessness.[17] Sara Mills, writing on feminist reader-response criticism, finds similar difficulties in feminist literary scholarship. She problematizes Fetterley's "resisting reader" by pointing out that the approach offers too few critical options.

> Fetterley is implicitly describing the notion of the dominant reading of a text which is that which presents itself as self-evidently the reading of the text . . . The notion of a dominant reading has been questioned to some extent in recent theorising, especially since this notion of a reader being proffered a position to read from may be seen as reinstituting a view of the reader as passive and as not having to engage in a negotiation with the text. In using the term "dominant reading," it is necessary to ask whether, after all, it is so easily recognised, and whether in fact there may be a number of dominant readings within the text. (emphasis in original)[18]

Mills goes on to argue that, even within a group composed entirely of women readers, one may still find a variety of responses to a particular text (1994.28–29). One should not oversimplify, she observes, when attempting to predict an audience's response.

On this note, therefore, we should be prepared for audience positions in *Carmina* 2.5 that are not just variable but actually unstable. Early versions of feminist film theory would allow us only to conclude that the ideal audience of 2.5 is male and willing to act as voyeurs. We will find, instead, that the ode lacks any straightforward confirmation of male power and male viewing capacity, revealing instead the fundamental instability of the male viewing position. A male audience encountering the text will ultimately find the disruption of the comforting alliance of vision and power that Lalage initially promised; a female audience shifts from having to choose among masochism, immasculation, and resistance to being an outside observer of the male viewer's precarious state.

One is likely, at first, to be an active participant in the dynamic that the ode presents. Here the ode's use of direct address and the omission of a narrative frame are critical. The poet describes to his addressee, and hence to those of us in the external audience, a young animal's fitness for farm work (*nondum subacta . . . comparis aequare*, 1–3). Because the speaker omits important pieces of information in these lines, however (the kind of animal, the setting of the conversation), we must supply such information with our imaginations. In this case, the scene we provide might be, for example, a paddock containing a young ox on which the speaker is commenting. This imaginative process is important for our relationship to the poem: as Wolfgang Iser argues, when the readers of a text must fill in missing pieces of information as they read, they automatically become more involved in that text (1974.71). We become involved in the poem because of our complicity in the visualization of the scene.

The order in which we come upon the different pieces of information in this first stanza is also important for our response to and involvement in the text. Though the first two pieces of information will soon turn out to have sexual connotations, this is emphatically not the case when we first encounter them. As Elaine Fantham observes, we can initially read on a literal level the poet's opening statement that the heifer cannot yet bear a yoke (1–2).[19] This is the case as well with the following phrase, "nondum munia comparis aequare [valet]," "(She) is not yet strong enough to keep up with the duties of a yokemate," 2–3. The Latin cannot even tell us for certain the subject's gender. Because Horace allows a degree of ambiguity here, the first two lines provoke little reaction other than our impulse to provide a picture of the scene.

Lines 3–4 (*tauri ruentis . . . pondus*) disrupt any level of comfort that we might have reached in the opening two clauses. Whereas just a moment ago our subject was genderless and not even definitively bovine, we now learn that she is female and a heifer—at the very moment that we are presented with the image (vivid, albeit retracted in the same breath) of this heifer being mounted by a bull. At the moment of being identified and gendered, she is also sexualized. Some scholars have considered the lines tasteless. Since I am reluctant to question the poet's taste, I believe that the image is intended to be disturbing. Because we in the external audience have readily accepted the poem's opening scenes, we abruptly find that we must accommodate this one as well. The sexual scene (although discarded immediately by *nec*) leaves an impression that will color the rest of our encounter with the ode.[20] The bull rushing toward his chosen mate represents the wish, the potentiality, that is the underpinning of the poet's address. Ronnie Ancona sums up the effect by noting that the lines "[provide] us with a statement about the impossibility of sexual intercourse in the present, along with the image or fantasy of its attainment" (1994.33). Therefore, as Fantham shows with her detailed account of the first two images' sexual coding, we must revise our initial understanding of the stanza's earlier lines as well.

The charged image of the sexualized heifer continues into the second stanza, in which the poet finally identifies her as human. The possessive (*tuae*, 5) has been carefully delayed, and for good reason. Negated or not, the description of a young woman's deflowering might not be rhetorically successful as the opening of a poem, whereas the imaginative transferal of the heifer's sexual initiation to the young woman who replaces it is disturbing but more palatable. Nevertheless, it is at this stage that any audience member inclined to be "resistant" will feel uncomfortable with what the poet describes. Also, as Ancona observes: "*Nondum subacta* suggests that there will be a time when the 'subduing' will have been completed, just as *nondum valet* denies a present state but suggests its future reversal" (1994.32). Temporal markers encourage us to create a series of future events and give the scene additional depth and impact.

With the combination of this vivid imagery and his direct address, the poet places us in the setting he describes, perhaps at the edge of the meadow. From this vantage point, we observe the heifer. She is repeatedly described in language that is ambiguous in tone but that, in the light of lines 3–4, can readily be interpreted sexually. As Colin W. Macleod notes, *aestum* at line 7 implies sexual heat, while *praegestientis* (9) and *ludere* (8) have obvious sexual connotations (1979.99). *Gravem* at line 6 also has a sexual force. The summer heat that weighs on Lalage foreshadows the combined weights of yoke and bull that she could not bear in lines 1–4. We thus consistently see the heifer in a sexual context. Like the first stanza, the ode's second full sentence contains a pretended insistence on innocence and restraint that nevertheless fails to conceal the scene's implications.

If we break down the scene's performative structure, this is what we find: a speaker and addressee (both male) who are watching a young woman (or heifer) while the speaker describes and thus eroticizes the heifer/maiden for the addressee. Happy in her meadow, she appears to be quite unaware of being observed and oblivious to her immediate and proposed eroticization. Lalage's situation develops the archaic Greek topos in which maidens playing in a meadow are flagged as sexually vulnerable.[21] Since meadows are usually some distance from settled areas, they are both liminal and dangerous. Young women who play in them can also be considered liminal, since their ability to move about unsupervised outside the home informs us that they are moving from childhood to marriageability. Lalage's mere presence in this meadow indicates that she is a female in transition, a young woman becoming sexually mature.

To summarize, the concatenation of vision and the eroticization of the object of vision are central to this scene's functioning. In the terminology of film scholars, the pair of men in the poem have "appropriated the gaze." They are empowered both to look and to enjoy the act of looking. As Mulvey says of women in Hollywood movies of the 1930s to 1950s, the "heifer" has been "coded for strong visual and erotic impact," whereas the speaker and addressee have been authorized to extract pleasure from their own act of watching. From a Roman perspective, though, being a viewer meant something more than just power and possession. David Fredrick notes that "extramission" may, for classical philosophers, have been the critical element of what we now call "the gaze." According to this early theory, particles traveling from the viewer's eyes penetrate the body of the object of vision. Vision, therefore, has close links with sexual penetration.[22] The men in *Carmina* 2.5 are all the more definitively gendered as male by their role in this specular interchange, marked as having power that is essentially masculine.

The heifer, on the other hand, seems not only to lack the power of the gaze but even to lack consciousness or what Mary Ann Doane calls "subject-hood."[23] She also continues to lack a name, for which I compensate by prematurely calling her Lalage. Lalage's lack of conscious participation at this stage of the ode challenges any critical claim that the poem is about a reciprocal interaction between her and her lover.[24] Even though she is not yet available to gratify the addressee's desires, it is telling that she has little human presence in the ode; only in lines 15–16 is she not only active but also human. She is most vividly represented as a heifer, a manifestation that deprives her of speech and subjectivity.[25] Her bovine form and her unthinkingly sensual experience of the summer heat locate her closer to the natural than to the civilized world. At the same time though, her dense literary history renders her a cultural artifact, something natural that (like a domestic animal in a pasture) has been tamed by and made safely accessible to men. Created as text, Lalage is handed over by one man to the other, a physical and literary being who exists only to gratify desire.[26]

What part does the external audience play in this equation? I argued above that the audience of a lyric poem is likely to identify with the addressee, who is male. Because the transition from internal audience to external audience is so smooth, we in the external audience are invited to take part in the speaker's visual enjoyment of and fantasizing about Lalage. Mulvey's comments on traditional American cinema are again helpful, as she notes of two exemplary Hollywood movies that "the film opens with the woman as object of the combined gaze of spectator and all the male protagonists in the film . . . as the narrative progresses she falls in love with the main male protagonist and becomes his property . . . By means of identification with him, through participation in his power, the spectator can indirectly possess her too" (Mulvey 1975.13). The poet, by drawing us into the scene, encourages our complicity in its act of voyeurism. If we identify naïvely with the addressee, we hope that we, as well as the addressee, will eventually possess Lalage, whom the poet offers to both us and the addressee as an abstract, mythologized "woman."[27] This identification produces in us a sympathy with the addressee, with his hopes and goals. This fellow feeling has contributed, I believe, to the ode's frequent reception as a description of a real or likely relationship.

Any identification with the addressee, however, also creates a psychological and physical distance between us and Lalage. While the gaze of lines 1–9 does imply male power and subjectivity at the expense of a female capacity for action, this same gaze also maintains a distance between viewer and viewed, extending the restraint that was introduced by *nondum* in line 2. Gertrud Koch, defining concisely film theory's appropriation of the semiological term "suture," reminds us that "the spectator's perception is welded together with the orchestration of looks as prescribed by the camera, making us see a film 'with the eyes' of the camera, the eyes of a male director."[28] Looking both expresses and produces desire at the same time that it requires and maintains distance.

Our visual experience is modified when the poet shifts metaphors in lines 9–10, describing Lalage now as a grape instead of heifer. The transition—abrupt, even awkward—occurs because of the different connotations that each metaphor contains. Both "young female animal" and "ripening fruit" can be applied to a young woman who is desired by a man. Horace most likely uses the heifer to open *Carmina* 2.5 because the heifer offers more extensive narrative possibilities. If she is represented first as an animated being, Lalage can be better displayed in overtly sexual language: because, as heifer, she is an active, mobile being, she can further involve the ode's various audiences. The literary antecedents of the grape, however, make it finally a more complex comparand than the heifer. The grape conspicuously recalls Sappho's apple poem (frag. 105a LP; trans. Carson 1986.26):

οἶον τὸ γλυκύμαλον ἐρεύθεται ἄκρωι ἐπ' ὕσδωι,
ἄκρον ἐπ' ἀκροτάτωι, λελάθοντο δὲ μαλοδρόπηες,
οὐ μὰν ἐκλελάθοντ', ἀλλ' οὐκ ἐδύναντ' ἐπίκεσθαι . . .

As a sweet apple turns red on a high branch,
high on the highest branch and the applepickers
    forgot—
well, no they didn't forget—were not able to reach . . .

Himerius called this fragment an *epithalamium*, saying that Sappho described the bride as an apple.[29] And as Anne Carson points out, even if we do not assume the apple is a metaphor for a woman, Sappho's poem still informs us about the ancient view of desire. "A space must be maintained or desire ends . . . If there is a bride, she stays inaccessible. It is her inaccessibility that is present."[30] The unripe grape of Horace's *Carmina* 2.5 conveys the same inaccessibility, but also a tantalizing promise of imminent juiciness and edibility. Because Lalage's youthfulness is a focus of the ode, her comparison to unripe fruit implies that, if she is not seized at the moment of ripeness, she will no longer be desirable. Horace's deployment of the grape thus hints at the brevity of the period during which Lalage will be sexually mature and also still sexually interesting.[31] As a result, the denial of access to the *uva* continues the process of eroticization that we observed in the ode's first two stanzas. Lalage becomes all the more enticing for her distance, more available as an object of fantasy. In the speaker's injunction that his addressee *tolle cupidinem* (9), we find a denial that is simultaneously self-eroticizing. By claiming that the grape does not yet bring pleasure, the poet tacitly acknowledges the likelihood that the addressee will want to possess it. This form of denial has much the same effect as the opening stanza's admonishment that the heifer cannot yet bear the bull's weight. The image undermines itself, demanding the presence of desire at the same time that desire is deferred.

    The movement toward desire that is implied by the grape finds its temporal analogue in the subsequent lines. In response to the present-tense prohibitions of the opening two stanzas, the rest of the third stanza and the fourth offer promises for the future (*Carmina* 2.5.13–16):

iam te sequetur: currit enim ferox
aetas et illi quos tibi dempserit
    adponet annos; iam proterva
        fronte petet Lalage maritum

> Soon she will follow you: for fierce time
> rushes along and will add to her the years
>   that it takes from you; soon Lalage, with
>   wanton brow, will seek a husband

Soon the grape will ripen (10–12), soon Lalage will pursue a husband (13–16). The patterning of the third and fourth stanzas has great rhetorical impact. Because both internal and external audiences are aware, on some level, of the futurity inherent in the grape image, we are all the more receptive to the promises of *distinguet, sequetur,* and *petet.*[32] These future tenses create the grape's destiny. As Page duBois notes of Sappho's apple poem: "The fruit ripens for the picker, who consumes and thus destroys it" (1995.48). The presence of the grape implies that the addressee will inevitably possess Lalage.[33]

After the grape image, however, the connection between the addressee and Lalage becomes unclear. Nisbet and Hubbard (1978 ad loc.) identify a tricolon in lines 13–16 whose last element, a pronoun, must be supplied (*te . . . tibi . . . [te] maritum*). Those who believe that the addressee will "get the girl" share Nisbet and Hubbard's position; critics on the other side argue that *dempserit* (14) indicates the addressee's own increasing age, which makes it unlikely that he will win Lalage. The latter group tends also to see *maritum* as referring to a man other than the addressee.[34] In this debate, I opt for a more ambiguous reading of *maritum*. Although I agree that *[annos] dempserit* makes the addressee's status problematic, *dilecta quantum* (17) recalls Catullus 8, in which the poet mourns the loss of his onetime *amata*. Horace hints with these lines at the simultaneous possibilities that the addressee will never win Lalage and that he will win her but subsequently lose her.

The ambivalence of our readings of the addressee's amatory success and failure adds a certain piquancy to the ode. I cannot agree here with Macleod, who believes (1979.100) that lines 13–16 indicate only pathos and loss. If this were the case, the transition to the "former beloveds" would be awkward, as the addressee seems (however briefly) to have been partnered with each at some point in the past. Nisbet and Hubbard's suggested tricolon is plausible because it allows at least the possibility of possession, without which the ode would not have the momentum to continue the theme through the final two stanzas. If, however, we choose an entirely optimistic interpretation, we cooperate with the poet by taking on the role of a fantasy-filled lover who is unable to see the reality of his circumstances. The lover believes that he wants and can have an affair, when what is really compelling is the desire prompted by the beloved's absence. "Who ever desires what is not gone?" asks Anne Carson (1986.11); "No one." The text is not about a relationship but simply about the desire—immediate and sexual—of the addressee for Lalage, who is herself a generic, pursuable "woman" rather than a true representation of an individual. Our prophetic poet never shows us a relationship attained, but merely claims that Lalage will reciprocate her lover's pursuit. The poem would not work if an actual relationship were represented for us, any more than if the addressee were assured of his success.

The structure of the poem supports my contention, for Lalage, at the moment that she becomes the pursuer, disappears from the text. She last appears in *dilecta quantum* (17), a phrase that, hinting as it does at passion satisfied, gives us our only vision of Lalage possessed. She slips away in the midst of a comparison with earlier, more evanescent beloveds. We are left with two closing stanzas that are even more explicit about absence and desire than the first four.

Evading their would-be commentators as well as the addressee, the trio of Pholoe, Chloris, and Gyges have frustrated numerous attempts to produce a satisfactory reading of lines 17–24. The prevailing attitude is summed up by Nisbet and Hubbard, who ask: "Horace professes to prefer the animal vitality of Lalage to three more fugitive and enigmatic beauties: why then does he go on about them for the last two stanzas?"[35] Several scholars characterize the stanzas as a "dying fall." This peculiar term manages to be evocative while evading the thorny question of what the passage is actually doing.[36] Thus these eight lines, traditionally discussed en bloc, have been granted little intrinsic purpose other than to serve as a collective foil for Lalage.

Rather than being merely a tripartite foil, the trio is of the greatest importance to a correct understanding of the ode. The former lovers provide us with a dramatic representation of how the lover should read Lalage and of how we in turn should read the poem. We can redeem the "fugitive beauties" both by looking at them individually and by reflecting on how they contribute as a series to the portrayal of Lalage (*Carmina* 2.5.17–24):

> dilecta quantum non Pholoe fugax,
> non Chloris albo sic umero nitens
>   ut pura nocturno renidet
>   luna mari, Cnidiusve Gyges,
>
> quem si puellarum insereres choro,
> mire sagaces falleret hospites

discrimen obscurum solutis
    crinibus ambiguoque vultu.

beloved as skittish Pholoe was not,
nor Chloris, gleaming with her white shoulder
    as the clear moon gleams on the night sea,
        or Cnidian Gyges,

whose imperceptible difference, if you set him
in a chorus of girls, would trick
    even marvelously perceptive guests
        with his loosened hair and androgynous face.

Structurally speaking, the lines of the final two stanzas are controlled not simply by Pholoe, Chloris, and Gyges but also by the quality of elusiveness that each embodies. Since the elusiveness of each successive beloved is described ever more vividly and in greater detail than the last, the stanzas acquire their own peculiar momentum. Each wins a few more words from the poet, with the result that the closing passage, far from being a "dying fall," forms a tricolon crescendo of inaccessibility in which the increasing rhetorical intensity of the lines is disconcertingly at odds with the progressive evanescence of the three beloveds.

The theme is established, ever so briefly, by Pholoe's description as *fugax* (17). We learn nothing else of Pholoe except this one loaded, yet thematically constrained, attribute. The epithet functions much as does the bull's brief appearance in lines 3–4: we can create a scenario in which her lover pursued her (erotically and playfully, one assumes), and she fled (delightfully, perhaps even delightedly). This one erotically charged epithet is powerfully bivalent. By allowing his audience to fill in this first set of connotations, the poet can then use the epithet as a springboard into a set of different images: beauty, desirability, inaccessibility.

Chloris, who resembles Lalage in being a conspicuously artistic product, receives slightly more space in the text than does Pholoe. Her evocative two and a half lines find a likely antecedent in Sappho 96.6–11 LP:

νῦν δὲ Λύδαισιν ἐμπρέπεται γυναί-
κεσσιν ὥς ποτ᾽ ἀελίω
δύντος ἀ βροδοδάκτυλος σελάννα

πάντα περρέχοισ᾽ ἄστρα· φάος δ᾽ ἐπί-
σχει θάλασσαν ἐπ᾽ ἀλμύραν
ἴσως καὶ πολυανθέμοις ἀρούραις.

She is now conspicuous among Lydian women
like the rosy-fingered moon
who, when the sun has set,
surpasses all the stars; and she sends her light
equally toward the salty sea
and fields full of flowers.

Apart from Nisbet and Hubbard, who argue that Horace is referring to the moon itself rather than to its reflection in the water, scholars have generally taken the Horace passage as describing Chloris's elusiveness.[37] The description of Chloris's shoulder contains conflicting, tantalizing images of solidity and immateriality. Because her shoulder's whiteness initially recalls the whiteness of a marble statue, the actual comparand— moonbeams on water—creates confusion. This contrast is intended to provoke a physical response. Her gleaming white shoulder attracts the hands of addressee and audience (is it solid? can it be grasped?), at the same time that the shoulder, like the grape, denies possession.

The final figure of the group moves us into that preeminently cultured gathering, a symposium. Gyges, the most peculiar and striking of the "former beloveds," both explicates and disrupts our text. Brought to our awareness by the phrase *si insereres . . . falleret* (21–22), Gyges exists only in a subordinate clause. The construction within which Gyges appears invites the addressee (*tu*) and the external audience to take charge of introducing him into the ode and its closing symposium. Just as the poet creates Lalage as desired object for the addressee, we and the addressee are invited to offer up Gyges as desired object for the *hospites*. At the same time, our power to do so is heavily qualified, for the lyricist makes Gyges' clause a contrafactual condition. *If* we were setting Gyges in that chorus (which we aren't, as we tell our Latin students), he would have a truly independent existence within the text. As things stand, though, Gyges is twice removed from any reality. Created by a poet, living only in a poem, he and the scene within which he appears are hypothetical even for the world of the ode.

Roman social norms suggest the possibilities inherent in the final stanza of *Carmina* 2.5. This party in miniature, a delicately sketched scene that only *choro* (21) and *hospites* (22) indicate must be a symposium, is a gathering for which dancing girls provide much of the entertainment. Gyges' presence in the chorus indicates that he must not be a Roman citizen. He is probably a slave; because he is fair-skinned, longhaired, and beardless, he is not yet an adult. These factors together make him a legitimate (and likely) object of adult male desire and a subject of ped-erastic verse.[38] As was true of Lalage, Gyges is watched. Being on stage, exposed to the gaze of the *hospites*, further compromises his social sta-tus. He is thus represented—as are the *puellae* in the chorus—as a po-tential passive sexual partner. In short, watching Gyges indicates his pen-etrability and is virtually equivalent to penetrating him.[39]

By introducing the internal audience of *hospites*, Horace complicates the different levels of audience for the ode as a whole. The ode began with an internal audience (the addressee) and implied an external audi-ence. For these two audiences, one could predict similar responses to the text. With the *hospites* of line 22, however, the poet introduces a differ-ent kind of internal audience. In lines 21–24, guests (presumably male) are watching a group of performers that includes young women and Gyges.[40] These watchers, included in the contrafactual that sets Gyges in the chorus, are imaginary for the addressee as well as for the external audience. External audience and addressee therefore watch the *hospites* while they (and we, through their eyes) watch Gyges. Their fascination with Gyges provides a model for our own behavior, advising us to repli-cate the actions and perceived emotions of those in the text. Horace in-structs us in how we, too, might respond to Gyges and the choral scene.

Gyges' seductively fugitive quality is enhanced by specific features of the scenario in which we (almost) encounter him. Gyges, our speaker tells us, is able to blend in with the maidens and thus deceive the ob-servers (*falleret*, 22). He is so feminized that he cannot be distinguished from the surrounding women, even though the undifferentiated *hospites* who watch him are characterized by their perceptive abilities (*mire sagaces*, 22). We can infer that the *hospites* routinely display uncanny proficiency at reading gender. Even these watchers, however, fall short when faced with Gyges. The scene generates a tension between their usual skill at de-tection and Gyges' remarkable opacity in the face of attempted readings.

For Hans Peter Syndikus, Gyges' camouflage in a girls' chorus re-calls Achilles' efforts to avoid the Trojan War by hiding on Skyros among the daughters of King Lycomedes.[41] This theme receives suggestive treatment in Pompeian frescoes, where Achilles is painted the same light color as the maidens' faces rather than the darker color conventionally used for men. Syndikus identifies this feminization of Achilles' com-plexion as symptomatic of the ancient preference for a young man to have "eine mädchenähnliche Anmut," a girlish appearance.[42] Achilles' coloring in this type-scene also has the effect of emphasizing his likeness to the young women around him.

The special piquancy of the Achilles on Skyros theme lies in Achilles' near invisibility and the ensuing challenge he presents for the Greeks who come seeking him. The House of the Dioscuri offers a particularly arresting example of the fresco type.[43] This painting drops us into Achilles' drama at the point when Odysseus and Diomedes, having distinguished Achilles from the young women who are his camouflage, separate him from the group. Here the dark-skinned Odysseus and Diomedes seize the fairer Achilles by the arms while he struggles and his gown slips aside to uncover his legs. The event also has an internal audience, members of Lycomedes' court who watch the seizing of Achilles.[44]

Gyges in the chorus hypostatizes the theme of detection or identification that is central to the Pompeian fresco. He also further develops the scene's eroticism and hints of sexual violence. In general terms, Odysseus and Diomedes model our impulses upon reading lines 21–24. Furthermore, because of the eroticism produced by Achilles' fair skin and exposed body, the fresco enhances the traditional mythical narrative with the suggestion that the feminized Achilles is available to Odysseus, Diomedes, and other viewers as a sexual object. Both internal and external viewers of the chorus want to distinguish Gyges from the choral group and pluck him from it.

For Horace's ode and for the Pompeian fresco, this process of discovery and detection is of the greatest importance. We in the external audience have more information than do the *hospites*. We can therefore compare the ode's audiences to one another not only with respect to their positions inside or outside the text but also with respect to the differing degrees of information they possess. Like the former beloveds' crescendo of inaccessibility, the various audiences' knowledge is inversely proportional to their proximity to the stage. For the *hospites*, the ode's imagined internal audience, Gyges is a woman with loose hair and a beautiful, androgynous face—the female, or at least feminine, object of male desire. But the external audience and the addressee have information that these guests lack. We can surpass the guests in discernment (*sagaces* though they may be), for we know that Gyges is male. He is therefore that most erotically charged of enigmas, an extremely effeminate young man.

Horace produces here a thumbnail representation of the Roman fascination with the identification of gender. In addition to having long hair and an androgynous face, Gyges is dressed like a woman, singing like a woman, and moving in a feminine way. His audience would have considered these elements when evaluating his gender. Clothing, voice, and gesture were, as Maud Gleason and Amy Richlin both demonstrate, critical elements in determining masculinity—or, in Gleason's now much-quoted words, "Masculinity in the ancient world was an achieved state, radically underdetermined by anatomical sex."[45] The Roman concern with maintaining a masculine identity and identifying the gender status of others is reflected in the ode's focus on Gyges' ability to deceive his audience.

For the guests at the imaginary symposium, Gyges' masquerade as a woman is successful enough that he is completely subsumed into the choral group. For those of us who have fuller information about this scene, however, Gyges is an immensely provocative figure. Since we understand the ambiguity and deceit inherent in this symposiastic performance, we project our knowledge onto the guests' view of Gyges. Aware of his sex, we strive nevertheless to pick Gyges out, to define him. We are thus in the odd position of knowing what sex Gyges is at the same time that, because of our partial identification with the watching guests, we are misled by his representation as feminine; his extraordinary appeal comes from our inability to define him completely.

Gyges' perplexing nature is ultimately what makes him desirable. Like Chloris's shoulder or the moonbeam, he lacks definition and boundaries. This indeterminacy insinuates itself into the text, with the result that the poem, like the image, leaves us grasping. Our reading experience thus has important ramifications for our understanding of the rest of the poem. When we encounter Gyges, we share the addressee's experience of Lalage in that we all become observers of a beautiful, eroticized feminine figure whom we can in no sense fully grasp. Since Gyges is never revealed as fully himself, we leave the poem dissatisfied, having never entirely viewed or possessed him. Our experience of Gyges is so disturbing that we can more fully understand the appeal of Lalage: desire requires that one lack the *amatus* or *amata*. The ode is thus, in part, about the compelling nature of what one does not have, a pull that Horace allows us to appreciate more completely by making us experience it ourselves.

The language of the final two stanzas mirrors the intangibility of its subject. Syntax denies the reality of the symposium: within the story line of the ode, the scene of Gyges in the chorus never actually takes place.[46] The image of Gyges among the maidens nevertheless makes a lasting visual impression. Our relationship to the elusive Gyges is thus mirrored in our relationship to the very language of the text, since we are simultaneously given and denied the perplexing image. We recall the bull's rush toward the heifer, negated at the same time that it was described.

Here, however, it becomes apparent how limited the terms of early feminist film theory are for this particular ode. In Laura Mulvey's original formulation, the female object of desire was also the object of the gaze, perpetually subject to the power of the viewer. Gyges, the penetrable *eromenos*, seemed initially to be an ideal feminized object of vision and desire. He was a good fit for Mulvey's 1975 formulation of feminist film theory, since he appeared to reinforce through simple antithesis the masculinity of those who observed him. Gyges' name and its implications, however, make it difficult to map Mulvey's original structure directly onto the dynamics of *Carmina* 2.5. The initial resonance of "Gyges" is not a problem: the name first designates a particular ethnic identity for its bearer. Reinforced by the epithet *Cnidius*, it identifies Gyges as eastern. The name thus carries the same associations of decadence and sensuality that accrue to the (probably) Greek or eastern courtesans with whom Gyges is on display. Falling into either of these groups adds to the likelihood that Gyges is a slave or freedman. So far, so good— as long as we acknowledge only his name's generic significance.

Gyges' lineage is, however, notably richer than this. Involved as he is in a sexually charged scene of visual pleasure, he inevitably recalls Herodotus's story of Gyges and Candaules.[47] Gyges, the retainer of the Lydian king Candaules, is forced by his master to gaze upon the naked queen. The queen, who, in turn, sees Gyges, then gives him the choice of killing Candaules or being himself killed. As Roger Travis argues, in this story, "spectation serves as an indicator of the movement of power," with the result that the name Gyges comes to be associated with confusion over whether or not "looking" actually does equal "power" (2000.333–35). Herodotus's Gyges oscillates between the roles of viewer and viewed. Found out and subjugated by the queen, who herself explodes any stable relationship between seeing and being seen, Gyges responds by killing Candaules. Forced to watch by his king, then forced by his queen to watch and to kill, Herodotus's Gyges implies that a viewer can be powerful, impotent, or each in turn.

Once king, Gyges performs no deeds of note other than to send lavish gifts to Delphi and to conquer Colophon. Herodotus makes it clear that he finds Gyges entirely uninteresting once he has completed his usurpation of power. Gyges' subsequent lack of forcefulness is consistent with Herodotus's representation of him as not acting on his own initiative at any stage of his road to the kingship. He spies on the queen at Candaules' demand, then spies on and kills Candaules at the queen's command. Gyges' relationship to power is thus extremely ambivalent, a problem that Herodotus never directly addresses.

Horace's Gyges encapsulates the internal contradictions of his predecessor. Though he is eroticized in part by his feminine appearance, he is more emphatically feminized by the very fact of being watched, a position that indicates that he is feminine. Like Lalage, he has acquired "to-be-looked-at-ness." At the same time, his name calls into question the masculinity—and the safety—of any man who looks at him. To begin with, his presence in the chorus raises the question of his origin. Are we to wonder if the Herodotean Gyges, either before or after ruling Lydia, existed outside Herodotus's narrative as a beautiful slave boy at Rome? Approached from this perspective, Gyges embodies the Roman male's anxiety about the stability of his social role, becoming living evidence that a man can be watched and that power can be lost. The inverse is also true: Herodotus tells us that the object of vision can unexpectedly reclaim a degree of power, becoming a potential danger to those nominally in authority over him.[48] Perhaps this facet of Gyges reveals Roman anxiety regarding the stability of the relationship between slaveholder and slave. So who, finally, has the power at Horace's symposium? Is it the *hospites*, who (unknowingly) watch a debased version of themselves? The external audience, who knows that the *hospites* are enjoying the embodiment of their own potential downfall? Or is it perhaps Gyges, who, though penetrable with respect to his body, is able to confound his viewers' understanding of who he is and can challenge their confidence in their own status?

An effeminate man, Gyges is accessible to the gaze because he is socially powerless. The converse is true as well, for he loses social standing when he becomes the object of vision. Like Lalage's body, his body is available to the sexually charged look of the elite male. In the second layer of analysis, though, Gyges refuses final confirmation of the watcher's viewing capacity. While at first seeming to reiterate the dynamic that Lalage made possible, he simultaneously inverts it, reminding us and the ode's other viewing audiences that vision carries with it its own risks.[49]

In the end, the text refuses any direct answers. This much is clear, once we have been tantalized and nonplussed by Gyges. In these last two stanzas, the speaker's preoccupation with vision and with disrupting normative power dynamics shows that he does not begin the ode with the intention of describing the course of a relationship. Instead, he mocks the norms of erotic poetry and the normative stance of the erotic poet while portraying vividly the truths of constructed masculinity and erotic desire. The lover may think that he can watch the object of his desire because of his own masculinity, but Gyges successfully oppugns both the lover's claims to masculinity and the normative status of "watching."

While Lalage does not seem to invert the lover's own status as does Gyges, she exposes the conceits that lie behind the creation of amatory verse. She is in no respect a "real" woman, but is, instead, a construct that reveals only the lover's desires. According to the ode's explicit claims, Lalage is watched because she is attractive. In truth, however, she is attractive because she is watched. Without giving any physical description of the young woman who leads off the ode, Horace convinces us that she is beautiful, desirable, and worth pursuing simply because she is observed and commented upon. As the ode's speaker eroticizes Lalage for his friend, so Horace performs the same function for those of us who read the poem now. Reading or listening to the ode will be, if we allow it, an erotic experience in and of itself.

Keeping in mind the self-consciousness of the poet's manipulations will allow us to distance ourselves from them. Although a female interpreter may be more successful at doing this, I do not believe that is necessary to "read as (or like) a woman." Let us therefore note that *Carmina* 2.5 offers a range of audience positions and that these may shift in the course of the poem. While Lalage is not represented clearly enough to allow the external audience to identify with her, the external audience risks identifying with the ode's addressee. If this occurs, then an interpreter will view the addressee as successful in winning Lalage. If one avoids such an identification, one is more likely to provide the addressee with an ambivalent degree of success.

Finally, approaching Gyges with an eye to the constructions of gender and desire allows us to see that the primary concern of *Carmina* 2.5 is not, as critics usually assume, the success or failure of a courtship. Horace's *ego* initially offers a scenario in which the men are entirely dominant and the woman purely objectified. He does so, however, in a very self-conscious way, ultimately interrupting and making ironic the ode's scopophilia and its apparent dynamic of exchange between men. Our poet comments ironically on the conventional dynamic of erotic poetry even while implicating his audience in that dynamic. In the process, he shows that the relationship between lover and beloved is entirely a literary construction.[50]

Notes

1. All translations are my own unless otherwise noted.

2. Such a description is, of course, entirely self-serving on the part of the lover. Use of elements from nature is common in erotic verse to persuade the beloved; see Ancona 1994.70. This topos is the mirror image of erotic poetry's "aging woman" topos, in which a rejected lover warns his beloved that soon she will be too old and ugly to attract a man. Cairns 1972.86 gives a more detailed discussion of the latter type. *C.* 1.25 and 4.13 are the preeminent Horatian examples.

3. Scholars assume that Horace was familiar with, among other early texts, Anacreon 417 PMG:

πῶλε Θρηικίη, τί δή με
  λοξὸν ὄμμασι βλέπουσα
νηλέως φεύγεις, δοκεῖς δέ
  μ᾽ οὐδὲν εἰδέναι σοφόν;
ἴσθι τοι, καλῶς μὲν ἄν τοι
  τὸν χαλινὸν ἐμβάλοιμι,
ἡνίας δ᾽ ἔχων στρέφοιμί
  σ᾽ ἀμφὶ τέρματα δρόμου·
νῦν δὲ λειμῶνάς τε βόσκεαι
  κοῦφά τε σκιρτῶσα παίζεις,
δεξιὸν γὰρ ἱπποπείρην
  οὐκ ἔχεις ἐπεμβάτην.

Thracian filly, why, looking
  slant-wise at me with your eyes,
do you flee stubbornly, and think
  that I know nothing useful?
Let me tell you, I could easily
  throw a bridle on you,
and, holding the reins, could steer you
  around the goalposts of the race course;
but now you graze in grassy meadows
  and play, skipping lightly,
for you do not have a skilled rider
  who is experienced in horses.

See also Horace's use of the theme at *C.* 3.11.7–12. Macleod 1979.97–101 treats the motif of the ripening fruit. Cf. Syndikus 2001.364 and Nisbet and Hubbard 1978.84–85.

4. Some critics believe that the lover and Lalage will marry (Fantham 1979.48 and Quinn 1980.205–08); others consider it unlikely that the addressee will actually possess her (Reckford 1969.104–05, Boyle 1973.180, Jones 1983, and

Ancona 1994.34–35). Still others believe that the text focuses on what changes will come with time: Nisbet and Hubbard 1978.79 consider the poem a soliloquy in which the poet predicts the favorable developments that time will bring him. Jocelyn 1980.199 believes the poet is warning that Lalage will become a *mulier secutuleia*, a nymphomaniacal "woman who pursues" and is unattractive because of her sexual aggressiveness.

5. In their claim that *C.* 2.5 is a soliloquy, Nisbet and Hubbard 1978 ad loc. rely on Housman's reading of *amici* in Epode 13 as a vocative of Amicius. See also Boyle 1973.179 and Porter 1987.117. Syndikus 2001.361 and n. 2 and Fantham 1979.47–48, 52 both argue for a nonspecific addressee, the former for reasons of decorum and the latter because the poem describes a fictional scenario. Ps.-Acro further encourages critics to envision a concrete recipient of the text by hinting that the poem is moral or didactic in character: "agit . . . ut revocet intemperatam mentem a cupiditate et desiderio virginis immaturae" ("He does this . . . in order to call back the immoderate mind from lust and desire for the young maiden").

6. Wolfgang Iser and Hans Robert Jauss are considered the originators of this approach. Gold 1992 is an example of the interest in this approach among classicists. See also Pedrick 1986, Pomeroy 1980, and Rabinowitz 1986.

7. Johnson 1982.3; Dunn 1995 discusses direct address in the *Carmina*. Frye 1957.249–50 seems to be the earliest treatment of the subject.

8. Discussing *C.* 1.23, Ancona 1994.70–71 notes that "the beloved's readiness for sexual activity is implied through her identification with spring, thus making the lover's claim of her timeliness seem natural . . . Implicitly, the poet/lover's argument is that the flowering of desire should be a natural phenomenon of human experience, just as the coming of spring is part of the natural order of the seasons." Cf. Davis 1991.52 and passim.

9. Walker 1993 describes Thucydides' use of *enargeia* in addition to giving a lucid review of both ancient and modern theoretical discussions of the phenomenon. Zanker 1981 covers the development of the term in ancient criticism.

10. See also Quintilian 6.2.32.

11. Pedrick 1986.194–95, calling this approach "eavesdropper theory," applies it effectively to Horace *C.* 3.9.

12. Fetterley 1978.xx. See also Schweickart 1986.39–44.

13. In this article, Mulvey assumes without discussion a male spectator, but she addresses in a later paper the question of the spectator's gender; see Mulvey 1975.11 and 1981.12–15. Cf. Doane 1987 on the inadequacy of the female gaze. Much recent feminist film criticism has moved on to the production and evaluation of films that not only are produced by women but speak to a female audience. On this topic, see, especially, de Lauretis 1987.127–48. Clover 1992 identifies the masochistic processes of viewing. Fredrick 2002b.13–16, Benton 2002.32–33, and Eldred 2002.63–65 provide recent evaluations of film theory in the context of classical literary scholarship.

14. Doane 1987.5. Kaplan 1983a.1–2 describes the male gaze in classical film as "dominating and repressing women through its controlling power over female discourse and female desire." Mulvey 1975.17 originally argued that "there are three different looks associated with cinema: that of the camera as it records the pro-filmic event, that of the audience as it watches the final product, and that of the characters at each other within the screen illusion."

15. The general trend has been for scholars to present progressively more complicated evaluations of the process through which a female viewer must go. Rich et al. 1978.87 suggest that feminist film criticism has hitherto taken too monolithic a view of male culture: "As a woman going into the movie theater, you are faced with a context that is coded wholly for your invisibility, and yet, obviously, you are sitting there and bringing along a certain coding from life outside the theater . . . How does one formulate an understanding of a structure that insists on our absence even in the face of our presence? What is there in a film with which a women viewer identifies? How can the contradictions be used as a critique?" The criticism is a valid one. However, I believe that the "ideal audience" of any of Horace's odes is male: Horace does not, to my mind, give the impression of being very interested in women or in women's reception of his work.

16. For Mulvey, at least, cinematic resistance involves critiquing the roles offered by classic films before abandoning them for radical filmmaking, hardly a viable option for classicists.

17. See Fredrick 2002b.14–16 for the most recent summary of this debate.

18. Mills 1994.27–28. See also Sharrock 2002c.271–72.

19. Fantham 1979.49. See, contra, the observation of Syndikus 2001.362–63 that the association of girl with heifer was so common as to render the metaphor immediately transparent.

20. Commager 1962.253 notes that the stanza's heavy, repeated *nondum* (1, 2) is in conflict with the sexual scene, where the bull's motion is negated only by a single, lighter *nec* in the third line. Syndikus 2001.362 sees *nondum*, as well as *tolle* (9), as producing a tension that will finally be released by *iam* (10, 13).

21. The earliest extant representation of this theme is Persephone's kidnapping by Hades in the *Hymn to Demeter*; see Fowler 1984.141–42. See also Arthur 1977.12–13, Burnett 1983.266–76, and duBois 1995.49.

22. Fredrick 2002b.2–3. The theory of extramission, which appears to have originated with Democritus and been embraced by Plato and others, held that the eye saw by projecting a ray that bounced off objects and re-entered the eye through the pupil. By this theory, seeing an object meant virtually having contact with that object. See Lindberg 1976.1–17 and cf. Park 1997.35, 39. Park holds that the theory originated with Empedocles rather than Democritus, but, on this issue, see Lindberg 1976.4.

23. Mulvey 1975.11–12, Doane 1987.5.

24. We can apply to the poet's control over Lalage in *C.* 2.5 the comments of Gold 1993.88, who observes that "Propertius can manipulate [Cynthia's] time,

her space, and her attributes . . . She is endlessly adaptable by the poet because she is a projection of his desires and anxieties, as unstable and slippery as his thoughts." While it can be argued that a conventional Roman marriage did not require reciprocated affection, a claim of concern with the beloved's response is standard in amatory verse.

25. The semantics of Lalage, "Babble," have, of course, been much discussed in scholarly treatments of *C.* 1.22. Its application in the present text is profoundly ironic.

26. See Gayle Rubin's feminist reading of Lévi-Strauss on women as objects of exchange in male kinship systems (Rubin 1975.173–77, 204–10). Richlin 1992c.165 notes that women in the *Metamorphoses* often take forms that deprive them of human speech; Greene 1999.415 treats the ability of the poet-lover to make his beloved part of the natural landscape.

27. For a lucid explanation of the distinction between "women" (a class of individual subjects) and "woman" (an idealized political and economic category), see Wittig 1992.12–17.

28. Koch 1985.141–42. See also Metz 1982.49–51. We can compare Koch's observation to Davidson's re-evaluation of Polybius's narrative technique, about which he argues that "we are presented in the *Histories* with a complex network of appearances and perceptions, where events are always mediated through the gaze of the inhabitants of his history and that of the supposed readers" (Davidson 1991.10).

29. Himerius *Or.* 1.16. On fruit as an erotic metaphor in archaic lyric, see Burnett 1983.267–68 and n. 102, Carson 1990.145–48, and duBois 1995.49–50. Syndikus 2001.364 touches on the metaphorical use of grapes.

30. Carson 1986.26–27. See Leach 1993 for a discussion of the same concern in Cicero.

31. Both Greek and Roman erotic epigrams addressed to boys demonstrate most explicitly the lover's simultaneous impatience for the beloved's maturity and his fear of the beloved's reaching adulthood (and hence losing his attractiveness). See Richlin 1992a.34–37, 42–43. Cf., e.g., *C.* 3.15 and 4.13 for Horace's attention to the other end of women's life cycle.

32. I choose the ms. variant *petet* over *petit*, as the ode shows, until line 17, a consistent movement toward the future.

33. In response to the grape's effect in *C.* 2.5, Jones 1983.36 aptly terms the ode "a mimetic expression of hope."

34. Macleod 1979.100 and Jones 1983.34–35.

35. Nisbet and Hubbard 1978.79. Others treat the lines primarily in terms of form and imagery: Jocelyn 1980.199 believes that the trio serve as a positive foil to Lalage's inappropriate behavior. Fantham 1979.48 and Macleod 1979.100–01 think they enhance Lalage's superiority, while Syndikus, who takes an aesthetic approach to the ode as a whole, believes that the ode's final lines reflect the beauty of the world of love (Syndikus 2001.365).

36. See Syndikus 2001.372, Nisbet and Hubbard 1978.79, Macleod 1979.100–01, Jocelyn 1980.199–200.

37. Nisbet and Hubbard 1978 ad loc., who argue for a closer similarity between Horace's ode and the possible Sapphic antecedent. See, contra, Macleod 1979.100 and Jocelyn 1980.199–200.

38. See Richlin 1993.532–38 and passim. Male slaves had their hair cut when they reached adulthood; Juvenal refers to this practice and the accompanying festivities at *Sat.* 3.186–87.

39. Edwards 1993.68–81 discusses the ancient assumption of sexual passivity (*mollitia*) in those who were perceived as effeminate, as well as the association of effeminacy and easternness (92–97). Cf. Balsdon 1979.226, who notes that "at slave-sales, the prettier a boy . . . the higher his price." See also Edwards 1997 and Walters 1998 on the *infamia* accruing to men who exposed themselves to the public gaze. On dancing, see Corbeill 1996.135–39 and Corbeill 2002.194–96.

40. See Murray 1993.90–91, 101 for a discussion of the position of women vis-à-vis the Horatian symposium. While the only women at Greek symposia were *hetairai*, apparently even *matronae* could attend a Roman *cena*; still, some ancient authors hint that any woman's presence at the symposium violated Roman norms. Murray 1993.99 and 101–02 (on *C.* 3.14) believes that Horace was uncomfortable with the idea of women at symposia. I do not detect such discomfort, but I agree that the Horatian symposium seems quite male dominated, perhaps contrary to the social norms of his time.

41. Horace may well eroticize the same mythological episode in *C.* 1.8.13–16: "quid latet, ut marinae/filium dicunt Thetidis sub lacrimosa Troiae/funera, ne virilis/cultus in caedem et Lycias proriperet catervas?" "Why is he hiding, as they say the son of ocean Thetis hid just before the mournful destruction of Troy, lest men's clothing drag him to death and Lycian hordes?" See Nisbet and Hubbard 1970 ad loc. for their identification of this passage's mythological content. Jaeger 1995 discusses at greater length *C.* 1.8 and Sybaris's association with Achilles; see Leach 1994 on gender roles in the same poem.

42. Syndikus 2001.366. For further discussions of this fresco type, see Schefold 1952.127–28 and plate 39 and Leach 1994.339–41. Cf. Anacreon 15, Horace *C.* 4.10, Ovid *Met.* 9.712–13.

43. Although the painting from the House of the Dioscuri postdates our text, this was a popular and prevalent theme. Ling 1991.134 identifies a lost Greek original of the fourth century as the archetype for both the painting from the House of the Dioscuri and a poorer-quality version from Pompeii IX 5, 2; there may have been countless intermediaries.

44. Ling 1991.130–34 argues that the onlookers in this fresco derived from the archetype and hence were integral to the scene. Sharrock 2002c.265–66 notes that the observers have a "directive function" in relation to those of us outside the painting. We are supposed to watch, too.

45. Gleason 1995.59 and passim, Richlin 1993.541–42, 544–48. This was es-

pecially true of the orators; see Gleason 1995.58–59. While her focus is on the second century C.E., Gleason argues convincingly that the same patterns held true from at least the late republic on.

46. Cf. Reckford 1969.105, who says that "Odes II, 5 does not end . . . with the acceptance of present reality. Instead, the final action takes place in the imperfect subjunctive, in dream and idea."

47. Might Gyges' epithet *Cnidius* likewise direct us to Praxiteles' Aphrodite? While we cannot be sure that the story told by Pliny and Lucian was in circulation by Horace's time, it is tempting to see in the adjective some resonance with that story in which visual desire leads to rape—with inversion of both gender and ontological status, no less.

48. See, though, the suggestion of Olinesis 2002.98 that "Gyges' tresses pose no . . . threat, perhaps because the beloved boy is consistently envisioned as the passive object of male admiration."

49. Fredrick 2002b.3 notes that Actaeon embodies the fragility of the male gaze.

50. I would like to thank Ronnie Ancona and Ellen Greene for including this paper in their collection. An earlier version appeared as Sutherland 1997. I am grateful to Steven Oberhelman, the editor of *Helios*, for permission to reprint. Ronnie Ancona, William S. Anderson, Helen Cademartori, Mark Calkins, Steven Oberhelman, Andrew Riggsby, Patrick Sinclair, and Victoria Wohl gave much-appreciated feedback on the 1997 version. The anonymous referees for the current project and Martha Malamud, series editor for Arethusa Books, have made further significant improvements. Any remaining errors or infelicities are my own responsibility.

Ovid's Satirical Remedies

Christopher Brunelle

Does Ovid praise or condemn the society that he so vividly describes? The variety of answers to this old question continues to grow. But there is a certain impetus in recent scholarship to paint Ovid in the colors of a moralist: a poet whose descriptions of Roman life implicitly critique the then current standards of Roman behavior. Ovid was once known as the poet of elegiac love, but this newly discovered penchant for social criticism begins to turn him into a writer of satire. Perhaps the old question should be replaced by a new one: if Ovid is the elegiac scourge of imperial Rome, does he have other thematic connections to the Roman satirists?

Earlier scholarship rarely cast Ovid in such a critical role. His love elegies used to be taken as the poetic elaboration of the sentiment expressed in the third book of the *Ars* (3.121–28): Ovid is delighted to be a citizen of modern Rome because it offers the proper sort of refined *cultus*. Immorality is trivial compared to inelegance.[1] But a number of recent studies have refashioned Ovid into a poet whose humor, instead of glorifying the erotic world of Rome, condemns it. According to Ellen Greene, Ovid's misogynistic humor criticizes rather than celebrates Roman social structures; if war is inhumane and cruel, and love is a form of war (*militia amoris*), then love, as practiced in Rome, is inhumane and cruel.[2] Sharon James praises Ovid for his powerful images of men's abuse of female slaves, but reminds us that "the picture Ovid draws is not one he endorses."[3] In his work on Ovid's *Ibis*, Gareth Williams argues that what the reader may suspect to be a delight in the macabre on the part of Ovid is simply an outgrowth of the poet's main task, to observe the fundamentally jaded mores of Roman life. Ovid replicates Rome's sensationalism without necessarily claiming it as his own; his "relish in the grotesque reflects his own acute observation of entrenched Roman attitudes."[4] In a similar vein, the question of Ovid's stance towards the rape victims in the *Metamorphoses* was raised decades ago and a provisional answer was offered: the poet is sympathetic to the characters who suffer sexual violence.[5] Ovid no longer writes encomia, he writes exposés.

The new *Ovide moralisé* is connected to the equally long-standing question of whether his readers can separate the pleasure of wit from the discomfort of misogyny. One way to achieve this separation is to ascribe it to Ovid himself. Modern critics like Williams and Leo Curran credit him with the ability to distinguish literary fun from social commentary, and if we, too, want to enjoy his poetry without condoning the actions it depicts, we can take comfort in the idea that Ovid was just like us. The modern Ovid is still as witty as ever, but now he unveils misogyny without endorsing it. On the other hand, this modern strategy may not be necessary; we could more easily agree with Alison Sharrock that one can enjoy and study Ovid's poetry without approving of all that it represents (1998.184).

But if his new role is that of a social critic, it may be useful to imagine Ovid as a writer of elegiac satire. Ovidian elegy is, after all, an almost infinitely flexible genre—or "supergenre," to use Stephen Harrison's attractive term—and the inclusion of satire within the bounds of elegy would simply mark one more point on the map of Ovidian *Kreuzung der Gattungen* (Harrison 2002.79). The connection between Ovid and satire has been made before. Even in the nineteenth century, Ovid's generally "tender and good-hearted nature" occasionally turned his poetic irony into "true and proper satire," and medieval poets have been said to write Ovidian satire on the subject of amorous clerks.[6] These connections are possible, in part, because of the amorphous nature of satire, which even the Romans refrained from defining.[7] Modern scholars can be equally free in their use of the term; if elegy is a "supergenre," then satire is an "anti-genre" whose defining quality is its inability to define itself (Freudenburg 2001.1). Those who connect Ovid and satire can do so on the simple basis of the poet's criticism of society and its rules, irrespective of the elegant and elegiac style in which Ovid's criticism is couched. To borrow a modern definition from the philosophers, satire is what satirists write, and everyone, even Lucretius, is a satirist at some point.[8]

Nonetheless, to the extent that satire engages itself in the description and criticism of social standards, our modern Ovid seems to be working towards some of the same goals as his satirical brethren. The use of the didactic mode in the *Ars Amatoria* and *Remedia Amoris* brings him even closer to the Horace of the *Satires*, since the eroto-didactic poems, unlike their strictly elegiac predecessors in the *Amores*, include not just descriptions of society but prescriptions for society. Though it may not always offer a cure, satire likewise focuses on the ills of society. The narrator of Ovid's *Remedia*, then, is related to the narrator of Horace's *Satires* in his use of curative imagery and his interest, no matter how ironic, in improving the lives of his readers.

A passage in the *Remedia Amoris* offers a test case for the new definition of Ovid as satirist. The discussion of ugly sex (*Remedia* 399–440) encourages the reader of the poem to focus on the disgusting aspects of the female body: it leaks, it stinks, and it shocks. These unpleasant bodily qualities connect the body of the elegiac *puella* to a recent area of critical discussion in Roman satire, namely, the role of the body (Braund and Gold 1998). Here Ovid is like other Roman satirists in his treatment of the female body: its imperfect and revoltingly moist nature both horrifies and titillates the male viewer. But Ovid goes one step further than the satirists in that he forces his audience to respond to his unpleasant images by repeatedly demanding their opinion of these images before he gives his own. This section of the *Remedia*, by focusing on elegy's and satire's misogynistic material and implicating the reader in the process of delight and disgust, emphasizes the reader's responsibility in producing a misogynistic reading. So scholars who want to credit Ovid with a satirically critical approach to the world should consider the ways in which his depictions of misogyny require the audience's reaction.

Ovid's discussion of ugly sex comes just after the midpoint of the *Remedia Amoris*. The poem begins with a speech to Cupid, who is rightly concerned about the harm he might suffer from a poem that claims to cure lovers; in direct contrast to the beginning of the *Amores*, here Ovid gains Cupid's approval. Turning to his amatory audience, the poet then advertises his services to men and women who have fallen in love and want to get out, and after a brief invocation of Apollo, god of healing and poetry, he launches into his long list of cures for love. This list contains two major sets of strategies. The first set suggests methods of keeping oneself busy with work or travel, on the principle that erotic attachment will wither in the absence of *otium* (*Remedia* 139: "otia si tollas, periere Cupidinis arcus"). The second and longer set of strategies is designed to help those who cannot escape Rome and love's proximity. These students must rely on a course of aversion therapy, a repeated emphasis on the disgusting reality behind the façade of love. After a series of tips on the correct way to loathe one's lover in public and a digression on the suitability of elegy to handle such themes, Ovid turns to the private realm of ugly sex and lingers there for several dozen lines. These couplets conclude what Hermann Fränkel once labeled a "hideous passage";[9] we will see that its hideous nature may lie not only in its misogynistic content but also in its interactive demands on the reader. Ovid's satirical impulses involve more than unpleasant images of the body, they involve the audience as well (399–440):

ergo, ubi concubitus et opus iuvenale petetur   399
    et prope promissae tempora noctis erunt,   400
gaudia ne dominae, pleno si corpore sumes,
    te capiant, ineas quamlibet ante velim.
quamlibet invenias, in qua tua prima voluptas
    desinat: a prima proxima segnis erit.[10]   404
et pudet, et dicam: Venerem quoque iunge figura,   407
    qua minime iungi quamque decere putas.
nec labor efficere est: rarae sibi vera fatentur,
    et nihil est, quod se dedecuisse putent.   410
tunc etiam iubeo totas aperire fenestras
    turpiaque admisso membra notare die.
at simul ad metas venit finita voluptas
    lassaque cum tota corpora mente iacent,
dum piget, ut malles nullam tetigisse puellam
    tacturusque tibi non videare diu,
tunc animo signa, quaecumque in corpore menda est,
    luminaque in vitiis illius usque tene.
forsitan haec aliquis (nam sunt quoque) parva vocabit,
    sed, quae non prosunt singula, multa iuvant.   420
parva necat morsu spatiosum vipera taurum;
    a cane non magno saepe tenetur aper.
tu tantum numero pugna praeceptaque in unum
    contrahe: de multis grandis acervus erit.
sed quoniam totidem mores totidemque figurae,
    non sunt iudiciis omnia danda meis.
quo tua non possunt offendi pectora facto,
    forsitan hoc alio iudice crimen erit.
ille quod obscenas in aperto corpore partes
    viderat, in cursu qui fuit, haesit amor,   430

ille quod a Veneris rebus surgente puella
    vidit in immundo signa pudenda toro.
luditis, o si quos potuerunt ista movere:
    afflarant tepidae pectora vestra faces.
attrahat ille puer contentos fortius arcus,
    saucia maiorem turba petetis opem.
quid, qui clam latuit reddente obscena puella
    et vidit quae mos ipse videre vetat?
di melius, quam nos moneamus talia quemquam!
    ut prosint, non sunt expedienda tamen.   440

As I was saying, when you're eager for sleeping together and doing a young man's work, and it's almost time for the night she promised you, make sure your mistress's charms don't take you in while you're still hot—so I recommend mounting someone else beforehand. Just find some girl, and let your freshest pleasure stop with her; round number two will be slow going. I blush and I rush to admit: make sure you have sex in the posture that makes each woman look her worst. This is very easy to do; it's the rare woman who tells herself the truth, and they all think everything makes them pretty. There's more: make sure to open the windows wide and let the sunlight reveal her ugly limbs. But as soon as your pleasure has reached its goal, and you're just lying there, exhausted in body and mind, while you're disgusted, and wishing that you'd never touched any girl, and can't imagine touching any for a long time to come, then memorize all her bodily faults, and keep your eyes fixed on her blemishes. Now, someone will probably call this advice trifling—and it is, but individual points can have great collective force. A tiny snake can kill a massive ox with one bite, and wild boars are often brought down by terriers. You just collect all my points and use their overwhelming number; little safeguards will soon add up. But since there are no fewer styles than postures, I don't think I have to describe every single one. Something that doesn't upset you may well be entirely wrong in someone else's eyes. One guy looked at his naked girl down there, and his performance stopped in midact. Another guy felt the same thing, but his girl got up after they were done, and he saw the stains on the sheets. You're just playing, if things like that can move you; your heart was only stirred, not shaken, by love. If Cupid comes back and hits you harder, it'll hurt, and you'll need real help. What about the guy who secretly hid while his girl relieved herself and saw what our very customs forbid us to see? God forbid I should offer that kind of advice to anyone! It may help—but I can't talk about that in class.

An accepted facet of the Ovidian narrator is his constant attention to the poetic act, his interest in the status of his own poetic performance and the response of his audience. Such narrative attention is uniquely strong in this passage. First, Ovid anticipates objections to the utility of his advice by agreeing with those objections and admitting that none of his points is very strong on its own. But he also claims that each of them has some small use, and he encourages his reader to remember them all (419–24). It is standard dialectical procedure to build up a pile of circumstantial evidence, but few dialecticians would make this procedure so explicit, and no one but Ovid would admit that the objections are justified. It can also be a dangerous procedure for the orator. Quintilian, in his handbook of oratorical education, explicitly warns his students about the dangers of raising hypothetical objections, even if those objections can be answered (5.13.44–50). Ovid, however, is not simply ready to make a joke at his own expense; with the references to *aliquis* and *tu*, his joke also reinforces the interactive role of the reader. Moreover, his image of a pile or heap (*acervus*) of arguments reflects a way of thinking about Roman satire. As Kirk Freudenburg has recently argued, Horace's first satire tries to disassociate his own brand of satirical diatribe from the "piling up" of arguments in the style of Chrysippus. Even if Horace's attempt is successful, it nonetheless assumes a prior definition of satirical diatribe as a pile of arguments, and his victory is only temporary; Persius ends his collection of poems (and reproblematizes the definition of satire) with the word *acervus* (6.80) (Freudenburg 2001.28–32, 207–08). Ovid's elegiac heap, then, spills over into the field of satire.

Ovid next acknowledges that people read and behave in different ways and thus that his own advice can be read in different ways (425–28). The variety of reader experience encourages Ovid's reader to read in more than one way. By introducing a hypothetical critic, an *alius iudex*, who may take offense at details that his readers do not find disturbing, Ovid encourages his readers to read as if they were that *alius iudex*. It is important to note that Ovid does not immediately denigrate this *alius iudex*; he implies that this other way of reading is neither better nor worse, merely different. Ovid then suggests that one man fell out of love upon seeing his lover's *obscenae partes;* another was cured at the sight of the bed's post-coital *signa pudenda*.

Not until he has made these suggestions does Ovid declare that they work only for lighthearted lovers (433). Ovid trips his reader up by denying any real utility to his advice after asking the reader to evaluate it. Nowhere else in the *Ars* or the *Remedia* does Ovid lampoon the reader;

he frequently ridicules his own advice, but only here does he explicitly ridicule the reactions of his audience. Nor is this a standard attack on the didactic student in the style of Hesiod's μέγα νήπιε, "you big fool" (*Works and Days* 286) or Lucretius's *puerorum aetas inprovida*, "the thoughtless time of youth" (1.939), since none of Ovid's didactic predecessors laugh at their readers for foolishly heeding the poet's deceptive advice. Teachers commonly pull rank on their students, but only Ovid pulls the rug out from under them. This is, therefore, not a didactic but a satirical salvo. Horace plays a similar trick in the *Satires* in a situation that also deals with the problems of erotic attachment; he quotes a bit of hypothetically useful advice and then scornfully asks his audience whether they could possibly expect emotional help from such weak argumentation (*Satire* 1.2.105–10). Ovid's brief inclusion and derision of another man's erotic experience links him to the aggressive rhetorical world of satire.

Moreover, the rhetorical attribution of disgust to others may itself be a sign of superiority. Roman moralists like Seneca take the upper hand in their diatribes by harping on the excessive *fastidium* that excessive wealth causes in some individuals; anyone who won't eat a fish that hasn't expired in front of his own eyes is unwilling to accept the natural ways of the world (including the fact that most fish die before they reach the dinner table). By pointing out that person's artificially inflated sense of disgust, one can imply that one's own ethics are superior.[11] Ovid likewise takes the upper hand by forcing his readers to acknowledge their sense of disgust. The narrator infers the readers' *fastidium* and thereby supports his own superiority. True, he admits that he reacts in a similarly visceral way (*di melius!* 439) to the next piece of advice (and thus undercuts yet again the supposed authority of the teacher's *persona*); still the introduction of unpleasant material into the curriculum and his assumption of the readers' adverse reaction to that material is another way for the Ovidian narrator to maintain hierarchical control of the reading process.

Ovid ends the passage by introducing another hypothetical example, the man who watches his *puella* relieve herself.[12] For the second time, Ovid asks us to evaluate this example before telling us what he himself thinks, but now Ovid responds with revulsion, rather than derision, and claims that such things simply can't be talked about—even though he just has. Ovid engages in an amusing version of didactic *praeteritio*, and the humorously outlandish nature of the advice shows that a proper set of instructions for falling out of love is not easy to write. But again, he also focuses on the reader's response to this advice. The rhetorical question (*quid, qui* . . ., 437) demands a reaction from the reader, and for the purpose of creating an interactive dialogue, any reaction will do. Ovid's point is not to determine whether hiding in the bathroom is useful for falling out of love; the point is to provoke an answer, any answer, from the audience.

To provoke an answer, Ovid repeatedly addresses his audience. Within the space of eleven couplets he refers to eight different hypothetical audiences in different grammatical ways, and he refers to several of those audiences repeatedly.[13] It is not simply an issue of second-person verb forms and pronouns, although Ovid uses them in this passage at least as often (seventeen times) as he does elsewhere in his didactic works. The reader is also drawn into the action of the poem by the variety of second- and third-person audiences, by the range of possible reader responses that the narrator creates. Here, then, more than anywhere else in the *Ars* or *Remedia*, Ovid highlights the active role of the reader in responding to the content of the poem and the active role of the narrator in framing that response.

The verb *luditis* (433) plays a crucial role in the narrator's game. Play is a central concept in the *Amores* and the *Ars Amatoria*, but it occurs nowhere else in the main body of the *Remedia*. Only here in the advice of the *Remedia* is love thought of as a game; everywhere else in the poem love is a serious disease.[14] The metaphor of love as disease separates the *Remedia* from the *Ars*; thus the *Remedia* most clearly recalls the playful world of the *Ars Amatoria* at the point of its greatest narrative complexity and its most graphically misogynous advice.

As many readers have admitted, the physical imagery in this passage is more explicitly unpleasant than anywhere else in the Latin elegiac corpus. Ovid not only includes a number of disquieting details but repeatedly asks his student to stare at them; the feeling of disgust relies most commonly on the sense of sight.[15] The description of women's genitalia, always vague in Ovid (*partibus illis*, "those parts," *Ars* 2.707; *loca*, "places," *Ars* 2.719; *locus ille*, "that place," *Ars* 3.799), now includes condemnatory adjectives (*turpia membra*, "ugly limbs," 412; *obscenas partes*, "disgusting parts," 429).[16] Rumpled bedsheets are a standard and equally vague part of the erotic scenery (Prop. 2.29b.35–36, Tib. 1.9.56, Ov. *Amores* 1.8.97), but stained bedsheets are mentioned only here ("in immundo signa pudenda toro," 432). Bodily waste (*reddente obscena puella*, 437) has no place in the elegiac world. Admittedly, the *Amores* have their share of disagreeable imagery, particularly in Ovid's discussions of abortion (*Amores* 2.13 and 2.14) and impotence (*Amores* 3.7). But beyond a pair of somewhat strongly worded couplets, none of these three poems, nor anything in Propertius or Tibullus, matches the *Remedia* in its concentration of upsetting images.[17]

To spy on the *puella* as she relieves herself is an appropriately egregious suggestion with which to conclude this section, but the attentive reader will recall two similar images. First, we should remember that Ovid has spied on women before. In the *Amores* (1.8), Ovid describes the horror of listening, while hidden behind a door, to an aged courtesan engaged in educating a young *puella* how to deceive her male admirers. Ovid's horror comes from hearing his rival at work, a female rival who shows that she is equal to him in the task of providing an education in the rules of love. The figures of the *lena* and the elegiac *poeta* are not as dissimilar as they may seem; though the *lena* may be stereotypically old, ugly, greedy, and drunken, she is also a self-professed erotic expert with a didactic mission, and she therefore "shares more with the poet than she is contrasted with him."[18] More importantly, the description of the hidden lover in the *Remedia* contains several verbal echoes of the scene in *Amores* 1.8. In addition to the image of the man secretly watching women at work, Ovid also includes the phrase *moneamus talia* (439), and the only other figure in all of Ovid's elegies to "give such advice" is the *lena* herself.[19] The phrase *reddente obscena* (437), likewise, has not just a literal but a literary interpretation; *reddere* is a standard poetic term for speaking or writing (*Amores* 3.2.84, *Ars* 1.205, 3.295), and *obscena* can refer to bawdy poetry as well as to bodily products (*Fasti* 3.675–76, *Tristia* 2.497), so we might not just imagine a man who watches his girl relieve herself but also a man who watches her utter dirty words, just as the *lena* did in *Amores* 1.8 and just as Ovid himself is doing here in the *Remedia*. Not only are Ovid and his student remarkably similar to the female characters of *Amores* 1.8 but the process of relieving oneself sounds very much like the process of writing the sort of poetry we find here in the *Remedia*.

The humor of the *Remedia*'s suggestion, however, relies on a different and more misogynistic set of circumstances. The *lena*'s voice is replaced by Ovid's, of course, but the emphasis on her voice is replaced in the *Remedia* by an emphasis on vision, the role of chance is replaced by premeditated secrecy, and the rupture in midsentence of the *lena*'s dialogue is replaced by the impression that the man in hiding was not discovered by the *puella*.[20] In *Amores* 1.8, the didactic tables are turned on Ovid; the poem's self-deprecating humor relies on the same display of erotic loss of control as do the poems on abortion and impotence. In the *Remedia*, Ovid pretends to lose control of the lesson (*di melius!*), but maintains control of the gendered material; the humor of the advice is entirely at the woman's expense. The abject male narrator is replaced by the narrated female object.

The second image recalled by the *Remedia* comes not from *Amores* 1.8 but from *Satire* 1.8, Horace's scatological exposé of ugly witches. Priapus, the phallic god of fertility, describes how his garden was visited one night by the witch Canidia and her equally vile companions. Their magic rites are interrupted by a fart from Priapus, who says you'd really have laughed to see those witches run away, dropping their dentures and wigs. Priapus, the only farting statue in the world, is a figure of fun, but the last laugh comes at the expense of the witches; the male narrator (Priapus, or Horace) tells jokes at his own expense, but the women bear the brunt of his comic abuse.[21] Likewise, Ovid makes fun of himself and of his hypothetical student, but it is the attack on the woman's body that allows his satirical humor to create a sense of male bonding. It is not simply that the evacuation of bodily waste connects the *Remedia* to the cloacal obsessions of the Roman satirists (Gowers 1995.30–32); Ovid joins Horace (and Juvenal) in making women's behavior in the bathroom a source of man-to-man camaraderie.

Likewise, only here in his elegiac corpus does Ovid refer to bodily fluids other than blood and tears. Even the amorous bedroom scenes in the *Ars* and the *Amores* make no reference to moist bodies.[22] Erotic activity naturally and normally creates moisture, and Ovid laments its absence during a night of impotence and sexual frustration (*Amores* 3.7). His anonymous *puella* avoids the domestic disgrace of spending the night with an impotent man by splashing herself with water; she thus pretends to clean herself, despite the fact that there is nothing to clean.[23] Ovid underlines the erotic significance of bodily fluids by their conspicuous absence.

Blood and tears do flow through the *Amores* and the *Ars*, but only in order to support the description of emotion: the blush of embarrassment (*Amores* 2.5.34), or the tears of pain and sorrow (*Amores* 1.7.57, 3.9.11), or the scratched face of misery (*Amores* 3.6.48). Because Ovid's erotic world requires the control of one's emotions, these bodily fluids can also be found in the list of controlled substances. Ovid teaches his women to cry on command (*Ars* 3.291, 3.432, 3.677; cf. *Amores* 1.8.83–84), to stop blood from rushing to their face in anger (*Ars* 3.503) or to feign the opposite (*Ars* 3.200), and to tear their cheeks in mock misery (*Ars* 3.678). The two common bodily fluids of Ovid's world are a valuable and controllable commodity. Here in the *Remedia*, other bodily fluids are not so easily contained. Food and sex naturally produce the sort of moisture that, on account of its uncontrollable nature, is removed from public scrutiny. The unregulated qualities of the woman's body allow Ovid to make good poetic use of her liquid assets.

Ovid has prepared the way for these unpleasant fluids with another image of liquid disgust. The male student has recently been encouraged to visit his *puella* in the course of putting on her morning makeup (351–56) in order to be revolted at the slimy, greasy, and smelly aspect of the cosmetics:

> tum quoque, compositis sua cum linit ora venenis,
> > ad dominae vultus, nec pudor obstet, eas:
> pyxidas invenies et rerum mille colores
> > et fluere in tepidos oesypa lapsa sinus.
> illa tuas redolent, Phineu, medicamina mensas;
> > non semel hinc stomacho nausea facta meo est.

> Then too, when she's smearing her face with synthetic poisons, you should go to see her; don't be embarrassed! You'll find little boxes and countless colors, and her skin cream will be slipping and sliding down into her warm lap. Those prescriptions smell like your dinners, Phineus; more than once they've upset my stomach.

The process of creating beauty is itself ugly. The student's passion, says Ovid, will certainly be cooled at the sight of the mechanics of female beauty, the lanolin (*oesypa*) running down her face into her bosom or her lap and the revolting smell of it all. This female's fluids are once again out of her control.

Ovid has, of course, adapted this section from *Ars* 3.209–18, where he warns his women to keep men away from their daily cosmetic rituals. The parallels are particularly clear in his description of the makeup itself (3.211–14):

> quem non offendat toto faex illita vultu,
> > cum fluit in tepidos pondere lapsa sinus?
> oesypa quid redolent, quamvis mittatur Athenis
> > demptus ab inmundo vellere sucus ovis?

> Who isn't put off by the scum smeared all over her face, when its weight makes it slip down into her warm lap? What does skin cream smell like, even when it's imported from Athens? It's just the oil removed from the dirty fleece of a sheep.

The *Remedia*'s standard reversal of advice from the *Ars* is strengthened by a considerably more hostile tone; Ovid paints an image of the same process in a much less pleasant light.[24]

The term *faex* (the sediment normally suspended in any liquid) creates an unflattering description of cosmetics. It implies that scum and dross are the primary ingredients of these unguents, although there is no ancient evidence for their use in cosmetics. But this dross was a natural part of everyday life; one would find *faex* at the bottom of any barrel of oil or wine. It even had a positive use in agriculture, according to Pliny (*Nat. Hist.* 17.259): sick trees could be revived by pouring wine lees upon their roots, just as the related *faecula* had many medicinal uses. The use of *venena* (*Remedia* 351), on the other hand, implies that the woman is just as skilled in poisons as Medea or Circe, whose strategies have been denounced on several occasions (*Ars* 2.99–106, *Remedia* 249–90).

The form of the sentences also alters the tone. In the *Ars*, Ovid asks a rhetorical question (*oesypa quid redolent?*) without actually stating how bad it smells. In the *Remedia*, Ovid uses indicatives (*invenies, redolent, facta est*) to answer the question: *oesypum* smells like excrement or vomit. Unsurprisingly, lanolin does not really smell as bad as Ovid claims: Pliny (*Nat. Hist.* 29.36) vouches for its strong odor, but to compare it to Phineus's meals, befouled by the Harpies, and to claim that one's stomach has been repeatedly upset by the smell borders on the ridiculous.[25]

The emphasis, then, on slime, grease, and odor intensify the amusingly negative tone of the *Remedia*'s picture: the woman's cosmetics slide down her face into her bosom, or farther, and their viscous journey prepares us for the next trip farther down the moist female body. Ovid's painted lady becomes an unpleasantly wet woman. A woman who is so unpleasantly and uncontrollably wet looks less like the typical elegiac *puella* and more like the typical target of Roman satire, a genre that derives much of its invective from a focus on the leaky and imperfect body and a condemnation of female bodily fluidity.[26] Ovid begins his discussion with sex and ends it with the toilet; both involve unpleasant liquids, and both liquids are described as *obscena*. But the obscenity and the unpleasantness are connected only to the woman's body, not the man's. Once the man relieves his urges, the narrator's focus shifts to the horror and the humor of the woman's unpleasantly moist body. Both man and woman will have contributed to the *signa pudenda* that defile the bed, but the shame and revulsion operate on the man through the woman.[27]

The *Remedia* does not pretend that a man's body is perfectly dehydrated. But a gendered disparity nonetheless allows the male student to stay comfortably dry. Those who find abstinence too difficult are advised to have sex beyond the point of pleasure to the point of revulsion (533–42), as if someone were to drink too much water from a stream (535–36):

> sed bibe plus etiam quam quod praecordia poscunt;
> gutture fac pleno sumpta redundet aqua.

> But drink even more than your chest demands; fill up your throat, and let
> the water you've taken in spill back out.

Ovid reestablishes the connections between sex, fluids, and excess, and he creates the image of a man's body unable to control its liquids. But the fluid in this image is innocuously and explicitly limited to water, and even this uncontrollable excess is confined to the upper body, the mouth and the throat. Aversion therapy is never beautiful, but it can be much uglier than this; Ovid uses no condemnatory adjectives, and *aqua, praecordia,* and *gutture,* by cordoning off the man's lower body and its more disquieting fluids, prevent this image from raising the Petronian or Juvenalian implications of the earlier bedroom scene. Likewise, Ovid's final piece of advice in the *Remedia* concerns the proper use of wine: a man should drink either none at all or too much (803–10). Again, an excess of fluids can help prevent a recurrence of love, but only by drowning the senses (*corda sepulta,* 806), not by creating a feeling of revulsion.[28]

The content of this section of the *Remedia* is misogynistic in its emphasis on the capacity of the woman's body to produce disgust, shame, and humor. Moreover, this content cannot easily be inverted to produce a reading for female students of the *Remedia.* That there can be female students of the poem is clear from the introduction, in which Ovid advertises his services to both sexes, though he admits that women may not always be able to apply his examples to their own situations (49–52). His caveat holds true in this passage. Its advice is focused not so much on social interaction as on bodily action, and the irreducible physical differences between men and women prevent the *puellae* from putting their *viri* into many of these didactic roles. In Ovid's world, men cannot be surprised while putting on their morning makeup, nor can men, in the normative heterosexual situations that Ovid envisages, be the direct object of a verb like *ineas* (402). The images of sexual disgust over which Ovid lingers recall the many times in the *Ars* when the woman's body, and not the man's, was brought up for inspection (Myerowitz 1985. 127–28). The frequent examples from mythology are equally slanted in men's favor, since Ovid offers almost nothing from Greek myth to show a woman's successful escape from love (Davisson 1996). This mythological imbalance in Ovid's advice is complemented by what we may call a social imbalance: Ovid's fictive *puellae* would have just as much trouble in finding social equivalences for his masculine advice as they would in finding mythological heroines to embody the precepts of his male heroes.

Like Horace at the beginning of the *Ars Poetica*, here Ovid displays an ugly female body to an audience of men and suggests the appropriate response: revulsion and laughter.[29] And like the figwood Priapus of Horace's satire, Ovid's student spies on a woman's secret activities. But Ovid outdoes Horace in asking for the student's response before offering his own. Both poets tell their readers what they think of the female body, but only Ovid requires his readers to tell him what they think first. Whatever delight or disgust may result from this passage, Ovid implicates the reader in the production of that response. When Fränkel referred to this text as a "hideous passage," perhaps he was dismayed not so much by its content as by its insistent demands on the reader. Ovid may revel in the horrors of the female body, but he revels even more in the reactions of his audience. Moreover, his revelry is directed at a particularly masculine audience, one that can more easily play along with him as he inverts the world of the *Ars* without inverting its gendered roles.

Scholars, then, who want to reposition Ovid on the moral map, who want to see his wittily disturbing images not as a sign of his turpitude but as proof of the poet's investigative acumen, ought to consider those points where Ovid most closely resembles the writers of Roman satire. He is not a Roman satirist, of course, but an elegist, and the boundaries of the two genres are not so poorly defined that we should abolish their useful terminology. Generically speaking, Ovid is not a citizen of the world; he simply runs a lucrative import business. So our passage from the *Remedia* is not enough to turn Ovid into Juvenal, but it provides more than one link between the genres. Satire requires more than the description of unpleasant details, otherwise we might label Valerius Maximus as a satirist for his anecdote about the disgraceful death of Gnaeus Carbo.[30] In particular, Ovidian scholars ought to consider the interactive nature of his occasionally satirical humor. These lines from the *Remedia* are certainly misogynistic in their abuse of the female body, but Ovid's misogyny demands the reader's participation. Ovid puts his reader in the interpretive role of Goldilocks, for whom some advice is too hot, some advice is too cool, and some advice is just right. In other words, Ovid asks his reader: what's right for you? What kind of advice do you respond to? The analysis of an author often reveals as much about the analyst as it does about the author; Ovid, in this satirical section of the *Remedia*, is well aware of his reader's active and self-revealing role.

One more comparison with Horace may help to solidify the relevance of Ovid's interest in reader response. As Dan Hooley argues, the point of Horace's diatribe on adultery (*Satire* 1.2), with its incessantly authoritative analysis of proper and improper modes of sex, may be that "scripts authorize certain dynamics of response—that we readers are both involved with and responsible for what goes up (or down) on the page." More explicitly, the point of the poem's uproarious conclusion, in which Horace imagines himself in the nude and on the run from his mistress's husband, may simply be to force its readers to say what they think: "The comic scene, the big joke, most explicitly of all generic tricks, calls for response: do you think this funny, and why?" (Hooley 1999). So then with our didactic poet. We want to know whether Ovid is a social critic, but Ovid is asking a similar question of us.

In the end, Ovid out-satirizes Horace. The elegiac poet had unveiled his ideal *puella* as a nude sculpture (*Amores* 1.5), the forerunner of Pygmalion's art project in the *Metamorphoses* and the poetic equivalent of Praxiteles' famous statue of Aphrodite in Cnidos. Now Ovid the satirist turns the ideal *puella* into an ordeal. He adds a hint of Horace's witch and asks us what we think of his new piece of art: Ovid's *Canidian* Aphrodite. How do you like that?[31]

Notes

1. In the *Ars*, "we move in a totally non-moral world, but not an unrefined one nor a stranger to good manners or to artistic and literary culture" (Rose 1966.330). "Nothing is more sincere in Ovid's love poetry than its joyful approval of contemporary reality, than the contented celebration that a society makes of its own existence—and often that is the occasion for poetry that appreciates the results" (Labate 1977.335–36). Ovid reflects contemporary Rome's "spirit, grateful subserviency to the ruler who had established peace, and enthusiastic appreciation of its blessings" (Owen 1949.632).

2. "In refusing to perpetuate the illusions and self-deceptions that he believed were so much a part of love and love poetry, Ovid's poems reflect a deep commitment to the moral responsibility of the poet to show the cruelty and inhumanity perpetrated in the name of culture, in the name of *amor*" (Greene 1998.113).

3. James 1997.74, with further bibliography on the "sympathetic Ovid" at 60 n. 1.

4. Furthermore, "The way in which he captures and wittily plays on erotic sensibilities in the *Ars Amatoria* and *Remedia Amoris* is not dissimilar; the need to squeeze the last frisson of discomfort from every embarrassing scene, to hide nothing in the way of sensual, disturbing detail, to present human behaviour as

operating independently of a moral code, all this is familiar enough in the love-poems" (Williams 1996.84).

5. Curran 1978.237. For a response to Curran, see Richlin 1992c; for a response to Richlin, see Johnson 1996.

6. "Il carattere mite e buono di Ovidio" makes him unsuited for satire, but "Spesso ciò non di meno l'ironia del poeta, allargandosi dal mondo interiore di lui al mondo esteriore, diventa una vera e propria satira" (Sappa 1883.360–61); Haller 1968.133.

7. Classen 1988. Haller 1968.128 adds a caveat: "Ovid himself, of course, is never satiric in the same sense that this poet [of the *Altercatio Phyllidis et Florae*] is satiric."

8. His diatribe against passion (4.1058–1287) "partakes in and extends a recognizably satiric tradition" (Hooley 1999, with further scholarship listed in n. 2). Henderson briefly connects the second half of the *Remedia* with "the satirical passages of illustration in Lucretius' study of sexuality and sexual *mores*" (Henderson 1979.79). D'Elia 1959.223 refers to this part of the *Remedia* as a failed satire.

9. Fränkel 1945.68, in reference to *Rem.* 299–440.

10. I follow Kenney's 1995 OCT in omitting 405–06: "sustentata Venus gratissima: frigore soles, / sole iuvant umbrae, grata fit unda siti" ("Sex is most delightful when delayed. When it is cold, sunshine is pleasant; when it is sunny, shade is pleasant; when you're thirsty, water is delicious").

11. Seneca *Nat.* 3.18.2–3. See Kaster 2001.188, with further material from Horace and Juvenal at 163–64.

12. Evidence from Pompeii suggests that this form of spying may have been rather easy, since total privacy was not possible (Jansen 1997).

13. *aliquis* (419), *tu* (423), *alio iudice* (428), *ille* (429), *ille* (431), *luditis* (433), *qui* (437), *quemquam* (439).

14. In his opening speech, Ovid tells Cupid to go away and play (*ludere* 23, *lude* 24), i.e., to keep himself out of the serious business of the *Remedia*.

15. Kaster 2001.155. References to vision: *die* (412), *lumina* (418), *viderat* (430), *vidit* (432), *vidit* (438), *videre* (438).

16. Genitalia and buttocks "are simply not described" in Roman elegy (Richlin 1992a.47). Elegy constructs its ideal *puella* without *pudenda* (Fredrick 1997.174).

17. Ovid describes abortion with a brutally agricultural verb ("vestra quid effoditis subiectis viscera telis?" "Why do you shove weapons into your own guts and uproot them?" *Am.* 2.14.27) and his own genitals with a military metaphor ("nunc ecce vigent intempestiva valentque, / nunc opus exposcunt militiamque suam," "Look at that! It's not the right time, but now they're healthy and lusty, now they clamor for work and battle," *Am.* 3.7.67–68). But neither of these two poems sustains the *Remedia*'s level of raw imagery, and Sharrock brings out the lighter and more literary side of *Amores* 3.7; see Sharrock 1995.

18. Myers 1996.20; Sharrock 1994b.84–86 and Labate 1977.298–309, especially 305–06.

19. "Fors me sermoni testem dedit; illa monebat / talia (me duplices occuluere fores)," "Chance let me witness the conversation. This is the advice she gave (I hid behind the double doors)," (*Am*. 1.8.21–22. The only other conjunction of *monere* and *talia* in Ovid occurs at *Met*. 3.732: *talibus exemplis monitae*. Ovid's phrase *grandis acervus erit*, "The heap will be huge" (*Rem*. 424) first appeared in the mouth of the *lena* (1.8.90); these are the only two instances of *acervus* in Ovid's elegiac poetry.

20. Voice in *Am*. 1.8.20–21 and 119; vision in *Rem*. 412, 417–18, 430, 432, 438—and images are much better than sounds at creating a sense of disgust; see Kaster 2001.155. Chance in *Am*. 1.8.21 ("fors me sermoni testem dedit," "Chance let me witness the conversation"); premeditation in *Rem*. 437 (*clam latuit*, "He hid in secret"). Interrupted activity in *Am*. 1.8.109 ("vox erat in cursu, cum me mea prodidit umbra," "Her speech was still going when my shadow betrayed me"); there are no such indications in *Rem*. 437–40.

21. Habash 1999.285–97, Henderson 1989.60–62.

22. There are two minor exceptions. Ovid once compares the eyes of an aroused woman to sunlight shining on a pool of water (*Ars* 2.721–22: "aspicies oculos tremulo fulgore micantes, / ut sol a liquida saepe refulget aqua," "You'll see her eyes glittering with a shimmering glow, like the sun's usual reflection from a pool of water"). But the moisture is only in her eyes and only in a simile. Ovid briefly considers the moist lips of his *puella* (*Am*. 2.15.17: "umida formosae tangam prius ora puellae," "Let me first touch my lovely girl's moist lips"), but only in the middle of a fantasy in which he pretends to be her ring; we may agree with McKeown 1989.323 that *umida* is a "nicely sensual detail," but the sensuality is immediately undercut by the joke in the next line ("tantum ne signem scripta dolenda mihi," "Only don't make me sign documents that I'll regret!" 18).

23. "Dedecus hoc sumpta dissimulavit aqua," "She disguised this disgrace with the water that she drew" (*Am*. 3.7.84). The motif of arid impotence occurs elsewhere in the poem (31–32, 51).

24. The correspondences between the two sections are tabulated by Geisler 1969.333. Richlin notes that Ovid takes the repellence of these ingredients for granted, whereas the recipes for cosmetics in the *Medicamina Faciei Femineae* are not nearly so unpleasant: "The ingredients [listed in the *Medicamina*], largely vegetable and pleasant-smelling, contrast with the invective picture of makeup [in the *Rem*. and *Ars*] as disgusting" (Richlin 1995.197).

25. "In itself [the smell of *oesypa*] would hardly occasion nausea" (Henderson 1979.86). Phineus's difficulties with the Harpies are a "set motif, from Apollonius Rhodius onwards" (Lilja 1972.226). See Ap. Rh. 2.191–93, 229–30, also Vergil *Aen*. 3.227, Petronius *Sat*. 136.6 (where the Harpies' contagion is a *venenum*), Apollod. 1.9.21. None of our sources explicitly describes what it is that

the Harpies do to the food, but for the most colorful picture of their poor table manners, cf. Val. Fl. 4.454–58 and 493–98, esp. 497–98: "tum sola conluvie atque illusis stramina mensis / foeda rigant" ("Then they drench the ground and the rugs with gross sewage, making a mockery of the meal"). The terms *conluvie* and *rigant* imply effluvium; Harpies have more than simply bad breath. Hence the Harpies' lack of control over their bodily fluids corresponds to the cosmetics that flow down the torso of the *puella*.

26. Braund and Gold 1998, with analyses of bodily fluids by Miller 1998, Reckford 1998.341–44, and Gold 1998.374–76.

27. "I am of the view that semen is of all sex-linked disgust substances the most revolting to *men*: not because it shares a pathway with urine, not even because it has other primary disgust features (it is slimy, sticky, and viscous), but because it appears under conditions that are dignity-destroying, a prelude to the mini-shames attendant on post-ejaculatory tristesse" (Miller 1997.103–04).

28. Watery discharge regains some of its unsavory feminine connotations near the end of the poem. Ovid asks his student to avoid places that conjure up happy erotic memories, and he compares them to the female monster Charybdis, who regurgitates the water that she has swallowed (740): "hic vomit epotas dira Charybdis aquas."

29. For a gendered analysis of the opening scene of the *Ars Poetica*, see Oliensis 1998.198–202.

30. Val. Max. 9.13.2; Kaster 2001.159–60.

31. Many colleagues and friends asked good questions of me, too. For their generous gifts of assistance, advice, and acumen, thanks to Ronnie Ancona, Ellen Greene, Paul Allen Miller, Bob Kaster, Jon Bruss, and Serena Zabin. Any translations or errors are my own.

The Fixing Gaze

Movement, Image, and Gender in Ovid's *Metamorphoses*

Patricia Salzman-Mitchell

"Set-piece description is regularly seen by narratologists as the paradigm example of narrative pause." This is how Don Fowler begins his discussion of narration and description as problems raised by ekphrasis (1991.25–26). This detention of the story, where "the plot does not advance, but something is described"—this, in itself, a questionable statement—has been discussed principally by Mieke Bal.[1] However, the meanings of narrative detention for gender have been less often explored. Laura Mulvey observes that "the presence of woman is an indispensable element of spectacle in normal narrative film, yet her visual presence tends to work against the development of a story line, to freeze the flow of action in moments of erotic contemplation" (1975.11). If we think in terms of the traditional gender paradigm that associates the male with activity and the female with passivity, one imagines a certain identification of narrative with the active and advancing masculine (or at least with masculine traits), and description with the passive and static female.[2] When Leonard Shlain relates the female to image and the masculine to literacy, he suggests that the female is metaphorically connected with space, while the male is envisioned as time.[3] The poet William Blake seems to have seen male and female in a similar way when he says: "Time and Space are Real Beings, a Male & a Female. Time is a Man and Space is a Woman."[4] This dichotomy can be applied to narratological issues, for descriptions are commonly of spaces and narrations tell us about actions in time, thus in a broad way, descriptions in a text may be seen as more feminine moments and narrations as more masculine ones, though as I will show in the next pages, there is much room for discussion on this question.

Visual imagery is an essential part of description; in the play and interaction between narrative and description, the act of looking becomes significant, for both characters and readers construct *phantasiae*, or mental pictures, from a work's images. The most appropriate set of ideas with which to approach questions of looking, visual imagery, and gender is found in gaze theory, developed initially in film studies. As has been shown principally by feminist film critics, gender is deeply entrenched in the act of looking. Mulvey's seminal idea that "the gaze is male" because Man is the bearer of the look and Woman is a visual object still has enormous influence, despite the many criticisms of later scholars.[5] For Mulvey, the viewer identifies with the male protagonist whose look controls erotic events. Yet Mulvey's views have been contested and deemed rather monolithic by many. Other critics value her ideas and build on them. For instance, using the polar categories male versus female can be misleading, for it excludes the question of what happens with the gaze of a gay, trans-sexual, or bisexual viewer. Some critics suggest that categories like race, ethnicity, age, and social background affect the character and implications of the gaze (Devereaux 1990). Others object that Mulvey does not consider what happens when the viewer, filmmaker, or main characters are women. Mulvey did respond to these criticisms, yet she implies (1989b) not that women may "own a gaze" but that they can "borrow" it by identifying with the gaze of the male viewer and thus acquiring some power. This is a sort of gender inversion that she calls "trans-sex" identification. She is not questioning the "male gaze" per se but suggesting that female spectators can also adopt it by identification with the male viewer. What is important in this contention is the idea that, while the eyes may be female, the gaze may still be seen as male.

Edward Snow's arguments are particularly insightful, for he wonders whether simply defining the gaze as male may be counterproductive and solidify the male position of power that feminism is trying to unmask: "Nothing could better serve the paternal superego than to reduce masculine vision to the terms of power, violence, and control, to make disappear whatever in the male gaze remains outside the patriarchal" (Snow 1989.31). Yet questions of whether women can own a gaze, and what kind of gaze (or gazes), are still at the center of the debate. E. Ann Kaplan suggests, for example, that reducing the nature of the gaze to the issue of power is flawed, and she proposes to explore alternatives like the gazes of mother and child, which are reciprocal and not conceived strictly in terms of power (1983b). The problem, according to Kaplan, is that women can receive and return the gaze, but cannot act on it. Yet although critics have argued against a monolithic view of the gaze as male, Mulvey's idea is still seminal, and it generates, together with its successors, productive readings of ancient literature. We recognize, at least in Ovid and in many other Greek and Roman authors, that men who look have more power over what they see and are able to "act on" it, as Kaplan suggests. Women, on the contrary, tend to be passive. Still this cannot be taken as an infallible norm; in the *Metamorphoses*, the power balance is often destabilized and the boundaries between male and female, active and passive, human and animal, and human and divine are constantly questioned.

The present paper explores the erotic and gender(ed) implications of the interactions between gaze and movement in Ovid's *Metamorphoses*. It deals specifically with the effects of the gaze on characters (who literally stop or advance their actions) and on the pace of the narrative. The essay is a feminist reading of the episodes of Perseus and Andromeda and Atalanta and Hippomenes and argues that the eyes of males usually have the power to fix visual objects, namely women, while at the same time, they delay the narrative. Yet Ovid also plays with the constant destabilization of this model, and we often see that the object of visual contemplation itself has some power to paralyze the viewer; there is some two-way movement.

Perseus's Stupefaction

I move now to the story of Andromeda and Perseus, which has many points of contact with the tale of Pygmalion and his ivory maiden in Book 10. We do not find a male artist here, instead a hero. Perseus visits the land of the Ethiopians and finds Andromeda chained to a rock, Ammon's punishment for her mother's crime. The affair begins with the gaze of Perseus (*Met.* 4.672–77):

> quam simul ad duras religatam bracchia cautes
> vidit Abantiades, nisi quod levis aura capillos
> moverat et tepido manabant lumina fletu,
> marmoreum ratus esset opus; trahit inscius ignes
> et stupet et visae correptus imagine formae
> paene suas quatere est oblitus in aere pennas.

As soon as Perseus saw her chained by her arms to a rough rock, save for the fact that a light breeze would stir her hair and tears were trickling from her eyes, he would have thought she was a marble statue; unknowingly, he burns with the fire of love. He is stupefied and, seized by the sight of the beauty he has seen, he almost forgot to flap his wings in the air.[6]

Perseus sees Andromeda immobile and believes her a marble statue—except for her wind-blown hair, which can be understood as a sign that she is still alive (see Barkan 1986.53). This scene accords well with others in the poem, for example, Pygmalion's sculpted maiden (who is herself an *opus marmoreum)*, where women looked at are depicted as inactive, and thus their description as "pictures" provides a moment of narrative pause for erotic contemplation. Beauty is equated with immobility, and the male gaze fixes the figure of the girl and slows down the narrative. The reader, focalizing with Perseus, also stops "his" (or "her," if the female reader identifies with Perseus trans-sexually) gaze in the contemplation of the statue-like Andromeda. Perseus falls in love with the frozen image. The stirring of her hair gives reality to the picture and anticipates the possibility of movement and pleasure.

Perseus constitutes an odd case: though a human, he can fly like the gods, and this endows him with a gaze directed downward, a gaze characteristic of deities (*despectat*, 624; *conspicit*, 669).[7] Perseus's mobility, also seen here in the fact that he is a traveling hero, emblematizes masculine movement against feminine fixity—not only with reference to Andromeda but in relation to all the other female places that Perseus travels through: the dwelling of the Graeae (773–75), the house of Gorgons (778–79), and the garden of the Hesperides (628).[8] Perseus views Andromeda, but the passage insists on her "not seeing." First, her eyes are covered with tears (*manabant lumina fletu*, 674), and then it is said that, if she were not tied up, she would modestly cover her face with her hands.[9] Instead, her tears do the job: "manibusque modestos /celasset vultus, si non religata fuisset; /lumina, quod potuit, lacrimis inplevit obortis," "If she had not been in chains, she would have covered her modest face with her hands; she did what she could and filled her eyes with rising tears" (*Met.* 4.682–84). Andromeda's eyes acquire an alternative function, which is to not see. Although she does not look, it cannot be said that her eyes are completely inactive, for they "do what they can" to cover her face. It is a frustrating and frustrated attempt, but an attempt still at some kind of activity. We can think that Andromeda, the "picture-statue," is still trying to act and, in a way, rejecting a completely immobile role for herself in the narrative.

It is peculiar, however, that Ovid never says that she would cover her nudity if she could. While not looking at a man's eyes before having been formally introduced to him is what a virgin should do, her embarrassment is surely also due to the fact that she is naked. The issues to be borne in mind here are, as with Pygmalion's statue, modesty and marriageability. Andromeda cannot "look back" because modest women should not do so. Andromeda is, then, for the most part, the fixed, immobile, statue-like beauty that the male gaze freezes for his pleasure. The viewer delights in the prospects of making her mobile. And it is the unbinding of Andromeda that Perseus sees as a passport to marriage (*praeferrer cunctis certe gener*, "Surely, I should be preferred as son-in-law over all the suitors," *Met.* 4.701). One supposes that it is not only the statuelike condition of Andromeda that seduces Perseus, but the fact that she appears as a "blind" woman. Just as silence was praised in women in the ancient world, the man here desires a woman who cannot or does not want to see. Andromeda, covering her face in shame, conveys the idea that she does not possess powerful, threatening, and castrating eyes, which is precisely what Perseus has been fighting to eradicate in Medusa and the daughters of Phorcys by robbing them of their gaze.

The obvious fact that Perseus actively sees while Andromeda is clearly the passive object has led to the straightforward application of Mulvey's monolithic male gaze to the episode. Charles Segal, for instance, shows the link between the stories of Pygmalion and Andromeda by affirming that "Andromeda is the inverse of Pygmalion's beloved, a living body made into a statue-like spectacle for a male viewer"; he insists that Andromeda is only an erotic object and that her "statuesque role is Andromeda's only function in the episode." For Segal, Andromeda's body as a statue somehow legitimizes "male erotic viewing under the rubric of art."[10] I, however, am not completely satisfied with assigning no agency to Andromeda (she is at least capable of talking and expressing herself—which Pygmalion's girl is not) and less inclined to assign to Perseus absolute control, for he suffers some destabilization from the very act of looking and almost loses control.

While Perseus is as mobile as one can be—he flies around in every direction—he needs to constantly flap his wings in midair, which flapping is curiously endangered by the paralyzing effects of love (note, in particular, *stupet* in line 676).[11] In this he is like the feminized lover of Latin love elegy. Love makes a man weaker, it paralyzes him, and, like a woman, he becomes immobile and passive. The reference to the chains of love in line 679 is interesting in this respect (*Met.* 4.678–79):

> ut stetit, "o" dixit "non istis digna catenis,
> sed quibus inter se cupidi iunguntur amantes,"

> As he stood he said: "Oh, you do not deserve these chains, but those that bind fond lovers to each other."

While some see them as one more element of male domination and power (entrapment and enclosure are common features of rape), the "chains of love" also provide a different dimension to the power relations in this story.[12] The reference unavoidably recalls the *servitium amoris* of Latin elegy, where it is normally the male lover who finds himself a slave to love and to a cruel mistress. Perseus's allusion to erotic chains precisely at the moment when he *stetit* and *stupet*, losing control (though briefly) of himself, evokes the feelings of domination experienced by the elegiac lover and hints at the fact that Perseus is feeling trapped and powerless like a slave. He could be using elegiac language to express his own feelings. It is, then, the female object of the gaze and desire, who, by her very immobility, controls, even disturbs and overmasters, the viewer. In a more recuperative reading, we can think that the very fixed image of Andromeda as statue affects both the male gaze and the narration, which stops and centers on her image. A double-edged play is at work. Not only does Man's gaze freeze Woman's image, detaining the story, but Woman's image affects the masculine narrative progression, paralyzing Man and, with him, the eyes of the external viewer-reader (I am assuming a trans-sex identification for women readers here). The reader is not immune or detached, but is affected by what he sees and reads.

So one way of reading the episode is to identify with Perseus's gaze, whether we are male readers or female. But there are other options. I propose here that one way of resisting Perseus's and Ovid's gaze is to put into question their reliability and to expose the mechanisms whereby Andromeda is constructed by the narrator and focalizer as a fantasy for and by the male gaze. First, let me disagree with Segal's idea that Andromeda is simply the inverse of Pygmalion's maiden, for Andromeda seems to display the same changes observed in the Pygmalion episode (a statue is loosened up by love and comes to life). As we saw before, Andromeda is constructed as a *marmoreum opus*. The word *opus* cannot but have meta-critical overtones, and we even can recognize a sound-play between *marmor* and the very elegiac word *amor*.

In the construction of Andromeda as a marble statue, Ovid plays a trick on us (perhaps his preconceptions play a trick on him): he shows himself to be an unreliable and subjective viewer whose gaze the female reader-viewer can resist. When Ovid admonishes the male lover to avoid reproaching a woman with her "faults" (*vitia*) in the *Ars Amatoria*, he brings forward the example of Andromeda: "Nec suus Andromedae color est obiectus ab illo," "And her color was not made a reproach to Andromeda by him" (*Ars* 2.643). Her *color* is here, by implication, considered a *vitium*. Andromeda's example is again mentioned in *Heroides* 15, where Sappho writes (35–38):

> candida si non sum, placuit Cepheia Perseo
>   Andromede, patriae fusca colore suae.
> et variis albae iunguntur saepe columbae,
>   et niger a viridi turtur amatur ave.

> If I am not dazzling white, Cepheus's Andromeda, dark with the color of her country, did please Perseus, and white doves are often joined with those of varied hue, and the black turtledove is loved by the green bird [the parrot].

The color of Andromeda's skin varies, and there is much discussion about this issue.[13] In the Asian account, she is white, and in the African account, she is black.[14] Ovid appropriates the African version in the *Heroides* and three times in the *Ars Amatoria*; in Latin elegy, she becomes a paradigm of the black woman who was loved despite her color. In the version in the *Metamorphoses*, the home of Andromeda, daughter of Cepheus, is Ethiopia. Her representation as a marble statue is then curious. Since the story takes place in Ethiopia, we are led at first to believe that Andromeda is black, but the imagery of a marble statue is normally associated with pure whiteness of body.[15] It is surprising that W. S. Anderson, a critic with a very deep knowledge of Ovid, does not notice this problem. Anderson comments on the line: "Andromeda had a beautiful body, white like marble, nude like most statues" (1997 on 4.675). It seems to me that Anderson does not register the incongruity of the myth and her description because he falls into the trap of aligning himself with the gaze of the desiring male subject in the tale: "Throughout the history of western art, figures of female beauty, whether virginal or provocative, sacred or secular, are regularly assimilated to an ideal of European whiteness, even where ethnic origin might suggest they should be represented otherwise" (McGrath 1992.7). The version of the story that Ovid had in mind, on the evidence of Sappho's letter and the setting of the tale in the *Metamorphoses*, was the African version, which makes Andromeda black. But when Ovid tries to describe her beauty, he still does it with images of whiteness. Like Apollo wishing that Daphne would comb her hair (*quid, si comantur?* "What if her hair was combed?" *Met.* 1.498), the viewer is here changing the nature of the image. Andromeda is not considered beautiful in her blackness, but Ovid seems to be saying that "she was so beautiful, she even seemed white (*marmorea*)." Perseus's male gaze annihilates what Andromeda *is* and constructs her as a perfect fabrication of a man's mind that suits his taste and desire, just as Pygmalion will do in Book 10.

One wonders, however, why Ovid varies his presentation of Andromeda. In the other Ovidian passages where the heroine appears, she is not the direct object of the erotic gaze, but her color is referred to in a somewhat oblique way. In Ovid's *Heroides* 15, the first-person speaker is a woman, Sappho. On the other hand, in the *Metamorphoses* scene, she is the object of the gaze who entraps the onlooker, and this effect could be lost if her blackness were emphasized. Perseus/"Ovid" silences and distorts Andromeda's image, and, I believe, despite all the assumptions that color prejudice was almost non-existent in the ancient world, that this is a judgment on race.[16] When something negative is said, texts mention "black Andromeda," when something positive is meant, she is metamorphosed into a "white statue." We can here observe how, as Mary Devereaux and others point out, it is not just a question of whether the viewer is male or female that affects the gaze, race and ethnicity are also at play. Ovid, as a white Roman male, must construct his "picture perfect" heroine as a shining white marble statue.

I cannot leave this episode without saying a few words about Medusa.[17] If Andromeda had returned his gaze, Perseus would have been completely petrified. This possible petrification by a woman is what Perseus manages to avoid in his encounter with Medusa, his fierce female enemy who has the power to turn brave men into stone. Perseus had defeated her with her own lethal gaze. As Leonard Barkan suggests, Perseus is a master of mirror and reflection, and that is why he can manipulate the girl's image and even produce a reflection of Andromeda that is sieved through his own subjectivity. Interestingly, while most mirrors in the *Metamorphoses* only serve the purposes of feminine toilette or self-contemplation (e.g., Narcissus), Perseus put the force of the mirror to a very masculine and epic task: killing the monster. What is remarkable is that, while Ulysses hears the song of the Sirens and is enriched by the experience, Perseus gets to see the monster and thus acquire the knowledge of the unknown and the "other" needed to defeat it. While looking at the horrific Medusa provokes petrifaction in the viewer, the text also suggests that she has a powerful gaze (cf. *Met.* 5.240–41: "sed nec ope armorum nec, quam male ceperat, arce/torva colubriferi superavit lumina monstri," "But neither by the power of arms nor by the stronghold he had wrongly taken did he overcome the fierce eyes of the serpent-bearing monster"). Perseus uses his shield as a mirror, looks at Medusa reflected in it, and decapitates her when she is asleep. This episode resembles that of Argus, who is also doomed when he falls asleep and whose eyes are also meaningful.[18] The story deals with the loss of sight through decapitation of a female monster, who thereby loses her sight and her phallic gaze. It is worth remembering that Perseus was already a robber of female eyes, as he had stolen the only eye that the two daughters of Phorcys shared.

Perseus tells the story of why Medusa had snakes in lieu of locks: once she was a beautiful girl whose best feature was her hair. Neptune raped her in a temple of Minerva, and the goddess punished her by turning her hair into snakes. This is, in itself, remarkable, for the victim is punished instead of the rapist. Goddesses are powerless before gods, and thus they need to perpetrate their vengeance on the victim. The text stresses that Medusa, the girl, was an object of amazement and visual enchantment (*Met.* 4.794–97):

> clarissima forma
> multorum fuit spes invidiosa procorum
> illa, nec in tota conspectior ulla capillis,
> pars fuit.

> She was most famous for her beauty and the envious hope of many suitors, and no part of all her beauty was more striking than her hair.

From beautiful spectacle, she is transformed into a horrifying sight that cannot be gazed upon. We have a girl object of the gaze who is turned into a most powerful viewer. This is precisely what makes Medusa intolerable and deeply threatening: a female may possess a gaze and turn men (literally) into objects (of the gaze).[19] The petrifying power of Medusa's eyes is a hyperbolic metaphor for any woman who wishes to see and to have an impact on the world with her eyes.[20]

Perseus uses the head of Medusa to destroy his enemies and to vanquish his opponent in the contest for his bride. Andromeda and Medusa are thus opposites: Medusa is the bad, monstrous, and powerful woman, who can fix, control, and petrify with her eyes, the one who cannot be looked at, but she does not have the power to petrify *until* she is beheaded. Andromeda is the powerless, bound, marriageable woman, fixed (turned into stone) by the male gaze who cannot, in her modesty, look back at the gaze of Man, thus embodying the fantasy of a blind woman. Very well, but are these two women really so different? Like a ball, Andromeda's image bounces back and almost petrifies her viewer, although Perseus resists. There is something of Medusa in Andromeda: a domesticated Gorgon who can still be controlled and loved, although she can nonetheless surprise you.

The episode clearly displays the power of the male gaze, yet it invites an exploration of "the risks entailed by the male in his control of the gaze" (Keith 1999.222). At first glance, we can see the monolithic male gaze working fairly well, but soon we realize that Perseus's control actually hangs by a thin thread and that his gaze and masculine supremacy are often in danger of destabilization. Likewise, while the male reader (and female reader in trans-sex identification) can focalize with Perseus and enjoy the pleasure of looking, the resisting reader can disarticulate the viewer's fantasy and expose the strategies whereby Andromeda is constructed as a work of art and deprived of her own identity. We can be fooled by Perseus's gaze and Ovid's narrative, or we can decompose the layers of reflections that the master of the mirror imposes on us. The first road, just as with Perseus, paralyzes us and leaves us stupefied before Andromeda's image. The second will surely give us more critical mobility.

Slowing Down Atalanta

The second part of my paper deals with issues of gaze and movement in the episode of Atalanta and Hippomenes. Running is a characteristic of some virgins in the *Metamorphoses*, and various characters run away from their suitors until they become fixed in one way or another: Daphne, Syrinx, and Lotis. That that fixation is a common aspect of marriage imagery is well known, but I wish here to connect it with the function of the gaze. Venus narrates the tale of Atalanta and Hippomenes in Book 10, within the song of the Thracian bard Orpheus. An oracle has told this girl of swift feet that marriage will be her bane (*Met.* 10.564–66):

> coniuge . . .
> nil opus est, Atalanta, tibi: fuge coniugis usum.
> nec tamen effugies teque ipsa viva carebis.

> There's no benefit for you in a husband, Atalanta, flee the contact of a husband. And yet you will not flee, and though alive, you will lose yourself.

So Atalanta turns herself into the stereotype of the "running virgin" who lives in the woods ("per opacas innuba silvas / vivit," "Unmarried, she lives in the shady woods," *Met.* 10.567–68), just like Daphne, Callisto, and Diana. The insistence of the oracle on the idea of fleeing (*fuge, ef-*

fugies, and later *fugat*, 569) recalls Daphne's flight in Book 1. Again, as in Daphne's episode, the emphasis on the feet (563, 570, 653) can be taken as metapoetic and assimilates Atalanta to the elusive elegiac *puella*, who is often seen as a metaphor for an erotic poem.[21]

Atalanta's identification with the *dura puella* is also to be observed in the affirmation that *illa quidem inmitis*, "She, in truth, was harsh" (573). In Ovid's presentation of the girl, there are obvious intertextualities with Propertius, who mentions that Milanion conquered harsh Atalanta ("Milanion nullos fugiendo, Tulle, labores/saevitiam durae contudit Iasidos," "Milanion conquered the cruelty of harsh Atalanta, Tullus, by fleeing from no toil," Prop.1.1.9–10) and refers to her speed ("ergo velocem potuit domuisse puellam," "Thus he could subdue the fast-footed girl," Prop.1.1.15). But what is rather un-elegiac is Ovid's insistence on the idea of marriage (10.564, 567, 571, 576, 613, 618, 620, 621, 634, 635), which is a central issue in the *Metamorphoses* heroine's life.

Atalanta's virginity is signaled by mobility and running, but at the same time, her speed is described with images of flying, especially in *passu volat alite virgo*, "The maiden flies by with winged foot" (10.587) and in the simile of the Scythian arrow in 588. Another obvious image of flying is the reference to the *talaria*, "wings on her feet," flowing with the wind as she runs, which has given much trouble to translators and commentators ("aura refert ablata citis talaria plantis," "The breeze bears back the streaming wings on her swift feet," *Met.* 10.591).[22] The word *talaria* links Atalanta to two important characters who have winged ankles or sandals, namely, Mercury and Perseus. From a gender viewpoint, we can thus align Atalanta with two mobile males whom we have seen flying around, surveying the world, and spotting immobile women in the *Metamorphoses*.

Atalanta engages in running contests, with the promise of wedlock for the suitor who can outdo her in the race. Many young men pay the penalty for losing with their lives. One day, Hippomenes, wondering who would be so silly as to look for a bride at such a high price, sits as a spectator of the unfair race: "sederat Hippomenes cursus spectator iniqui" (*Met.* 10.575). This line is quite remarkable in regard to issues of gazing and mobility. In contrast with Atalanta's running, the text shows us a man who is immobile. He is an almost detached spectator who looks down on the whole event as ridiculous, yet who, at the same time, comes to observe the race in search of scopophilic pleasure. But Hippomenes' gaze changes; Venus describes what happens to him when he first sees the girl (*Met.* 10.578–80):

ut faciem et posito corpus velamine vidit,
quale meum, vel quale tuum, si femina fias,
obstipuit

When he saw her face and her body without clothing, like mine, or like
yours—if you were a woman—he was stupefied.

Posito velamine recalls Diana *sine veste* in Book 3 (*visae sine veste Di-
anae*, *Met.* 3.185) and thus turns Hippomenes into a sort of voyeuristic
Actaeon. The naked body of Atalanta is then assimilated to the body of
a goddess. The phrase *quale meum* compares her to the speaker, Venus,
and her body without clothes makes us think of Diana in her bath, who,
in the ekphrasis of Book 3, is presented very much like a picture to be
looked at. Statues of the naked Aphrodite are pervasive in antiquity and,
according to some, may have inspired Pygmalion's ivory maiden.[23] Their
erotic appeal through the eyes is brilliantly conveyed in the story in Lucian *Amores* 13–16 of a man who fell in love with the statue of Cnidian
Aphrodite made by Praxiteles. Likewise, Hippomenes' paralysis, denoted
by the verb *obstipuit*, aligns the boy with Perseus, who almost loses control at the sight of Andromeda, and with Pygmalion contemplating the
ivory statue coming to life (*stupet* at *Met.* 10.287). Here again, it is not
only the viewer who fixes the image, the image can also affect the viewer.

There is another relevant point in Venus's intrusive comparisons.
The parallels with her own naked body obviously point at Atalanta's
beauty, but the comparison with Adonis—if he were a woman—is problematic, for it conveys gender ambivalences in Atalanta. She is a girl, but
a girl who cannot be fixed in marriage, a mobile girl who possesses, at
some level, more power than her male suitors. The situation is complex,
because Hippomenes, the *iuvenis*, is here viewed as a sort of Adonis, a
boy under the influence of a powerful female.

Soon, however, the narrative presents the figure of Atalanta in more
detail, and we readers focalize with Hippomenes, and with his gaze. The
narration is detained (*Met.* 10.588–96):

quae quamquam Scythica non setius ire sagitta
Aonio visa est iuveni, tamen ille decorem
miratur magis: et cursus facit ipse decorem.
aura refert ablata citis talaria plantis,
tergaque iactantur crines per eburnea, quaeque
poplitibus suberant picto genualia limbo;
inque puellari corpus candore ruborem

traxerat, haud aliter, quam cum super atria velum
candida purpureum simulatas inficit umbras.

Though she seemed to the Aonian youth to go no less swiftly than a
Scythian arrow, yet he admired her beauty more; the race itself gave her
beauty. The breeze bears back the streaming wings on her swift feet, and her
hair is thrown back over her ivory back, and the ribbons with decorated borders were placed at her knees. Her body had acquired a blush of girlish brilliance, no different than when a purple awning drawn over a gleaming white
atrium stains it with borrowed shades.

While reading this episode, the reader wonders when the metamorphosis will come. While the physical transformation only occurs at
the end when the lovers are turned to lions by Cybele, I suggest that
these lines present a gradual transformation of Atalanta into a wife by
first transforming her into object of the gaze and then by gradually slowing her down and fixing her image. The *visa est* of line 589 shows Hippomenes as viewer of Atalanta, who, with the reference to her *terga
eburnea* in line 892, is assimilated to a work of art (previous lines seem
to focus more on the effects of the image on Hippomenes). Such phrases
are narratological and visual markers that focus our eyes and frame the
description to come. They act like the cinematographic camera when
framing the image for the gaze of the viewer. *Miratur* again points at the
boy's amazement and erotic paralysis. Likewise, visual infatuation is expressed later in the fixation of Hippomenes' eyes on her ("constitit in
medio vultuque in virgine fixo . . ." "He stood in the middle, and with his
eyes fixed on the girl . . . ," *Met.* 10.601). But there is here a reciprocal
play of power and fixation in which the gazer is fixed by the image he
sees, for the passive *fixo* referring to Hippomenes' *vultus* implies that,
while he fixes the image with his eyes, he is also fixed by it.

The connections with art are relevant here. The reference to *terga
eburnea* in line 592, in a book where we have just read about Pygmalion's
eburnea virgo, cannot be taken, following our previous discussion of *Metamorphoses* 10.578–80, as anything but a reference to a statue. What is interesting is that the erotic and marriageable girl is again described as an
immobile image. A wife who is swift-footed seems inconceivable to
Ovid/Hippomenes, so he needs to turn her image into something that is
static. The reference to the atrium in the simile of lines 95–96 also hints
at a desire for domesticity for Atalanta, as the atrium is a space where the
Roman *matrona* would weave and rule over the household. Thus right
from his first glance, Hippomenes is trying to fix Atalanta and detain her

running. The story will become, then, the effort of the lover to stop her movement and convert her into a "proper," immobile, erotic object. The same effort of the lover to detain the free movement of his prospective wife is seen in the episode of Thetis and Peleus in Book 11, where Thetis remains a virgin only so long as she can move and change form but becomes a fixed and immobile bride when Peleus keeps firm hold of her.

The next indicator of Atalanta's transformation is seen in the way she returns Hippomenes' gaze (*Met.* 10.609–10):

talia dicentem molli Schoeneia vultu
aspicit et dubitat, superari an vincere malit

With soft expression, the daughter of Schoeneus looks at him while he says this and wonders whether she prefers to win or to be overcome.

This is the first time that she looks at him, yet her gaze does not seem to objectify the young man; although later on the text insists on his being beautiful, there is no detailed description of the body of Hippomenes as there is of the body of Atalanta. While once hard (*inmitis*), Atalanta's face (and eyes) are now *mollis*. Next we read a monologue where, as often in female characters, the girl expresses her doubts and battles with her soul. It is noteworthy, though, that she begins to think of herself in the passive. Atalanta recognizes that what has ensnared Hippomenes is her image: "a! miser Hippomene, nollem tibi visa fuissem!" "Ah, miserable Hippomenes, I wish I hadn't been seen by you" (*Met.* 10.632).

Soon Hippomenes competes with her in running and finally vanquishes her with the help of Venus's golden apples.[24] But the race is a constant effort of the male to stop and delay the female. In this sense, the repetition of the word *mora* is relevant. Venus is the first to use the concept when she recognizes that there was little time to give Hippomenes help ("nec opis mora longa dabatur," 643).[25] Further, the crowd cheers on Hippomenes and tells him not to tarry: *pelle moram: vinces!* "Do not delay: you will win!" (659). And, in part, it is his image that delays Atalanta in her running: "o quotiens, cum iam posset transire, morata est / spectatosque diu vultus invita reliquit!" "Oh, how often, when she could have passed him, did she tarry, unwilling to leave behind the face that she had contemplated for a long time" (*Met.* 10.661–62). In this case, Atalanta assumes the position of a viewer, who, like Perseus, is stopped by the image. But she is still mobile like a man. Soon, however, Hippomenes throws one of the golden apples on the side of the path, and avid Atalanta stops to pick it up: "obstipuit virgo nitidique cupidine pomi /dec-linat cursus," "The maiden was stupefied, and the desire for the brilliant apple made her turn away from her course" (666–67). The yearning for a fruit, as we see in the episode of Proserpina, who eats a crimson fruit (*puniceum pomum*, *Met.* 5.536), is a frequent theme in the Western tra-dition, with its most paradigmatic example in the Bible. The deep pur-ple fruit is the color of love, passion, and sexual maturity; it is a com-mon symbol of sexual desire and even presages the loss of virginity. It is, after all, the fruit of Venus. But Atalanta leaves the fruit behind and, with a new burst of speed, makes up for her *mora* (669) and races ahead. The same trick is played again: "et rursus pomi iactu remorata secundi / consequitur transitque virum," "And after being newly delayed at the tossing of a second apple, she followed on and passed the man," *Met.* 10.671–72. The conclusion of the race and the story are piquant (*Met.* 10.676–80):

> an peteret, virgo visa est dubitare: coegi
> tollere et adieci sublato pondera malo
> inpediique oneris pariter gravitate moraque,
> neve meus sermo cursu sit tardior ipso,
> praeterita est virgo: duxit sua praemia victor.

> The maiden seemed to hesitate as to whether she should go after the apple or not: I forced her to pick it up and added weight to the apple she held. Equally with the weight of the burden and with the delay I impeded her, and lest my speech be slower than the race itself, the maiden was overtaken, and the winner took his prize.

Atalanta is now referred to in the passive voice (*visa*), she "seems / is seen" and "she was overtaken" (*praeterita est*). Further, *duxit* is inter-esting in light of the use of this verb in an expression that refers to a male "taking a wife" (*uxorem ducere*), and one even wonders if the weight im-plied in *gravitate* may hint at a future pregnancy for Atalanta: the essen-tial role of a wife in ancient times.[26] The verb *impedio* creates an witty pun, for it is precisely her feet that the weight of the apples hinders. And so Atalanta is newly detained (*moraque*), but this time her transformation is complete. With the loss of the race, she has become a "delayed" girl, and thus marriageable. She has now left behind the characteristic that most marked her individuality, her excellence in running. Anderson is right when he observes that by desiring Hippomenes' victory, Atalanta is, in a way, accepting a form of death. "We might be tempted to read this dilemma as Ovid's poetic representation of the universal dilemma of the woman (or man) in love: she must 'die' as an independent *puella* in order to become a wife" (Anderson 1972 on 10.629–30).

To conclude the story, Venus draws attention to herself as narrator and to Adonis as audience. The same *mora* with which Atalanta was affected is what Venus fears might affect her narrative. This coincidence is also piquant from a reader-response viewpoint, for Venus is aware that, when we see Atalanta delayed, the gaze of the reader-viewer is delayed with her and, in this sense, it is noteworthy that, as Anderson shows, lines 669–70 are largely dactylic when Atalanta speeds up, but then the spondees prevail in 671 as she slows down (Anderson 1997.669–72).

As Laura Mulvey suggests, images of women in narrative tend to detain the action in moments of erotic contemplation, and both reader and internal male viewer often have the power to paralyze, control, and fix the images they see. In this sense, we can think of description in narrative texts as the more feminine, "less active" moments in the progression of the story line. Yet as we have observed, this is not an absolute rule, and, in a more recuperative reading, we can see how static images of women affect the viewer by detaining his actions and by provoking stupefaction in him. Yet this capacity of female characters is usually finally overcome by the power of males to fix women in matrimony and control their visual image. Although Ovid's *Metamorphoses* is a male-biased text, and this final triumph of the male in the episodes that I have surveyed ultimately preserves traditional gender values, the poem presents many destabilizations and deconstructions of gender hierarchies, even if only momentarily. The power of Andromeda's and Atalanta's images to stupefy Perseus and Hippomenes and Medusa's capacity to petrify her viewers offer moments where alternative roles for women are adumbrated, even when the final outcome responds to a patriarchal Roman outlook. A feminist reading of the text can help us not only unmask male-oriented perceptions, as with the color of Andromeda, it also aims at bringing those moments of female agency into the spotlight. This possibility of finding female agency and unmasking gender stereotypes makes the *Metamorphoses* uniquely open to feminist readings and shows that, in the end, the male is not completely infallible.

Notes

1. Bal 1997.36–43. On narrative and description, see also Genette 1982. 127–44.

2. On activity and passivity in relation to gender in the ancient world, see, especially, Halperin 1990.29–38, Veyne 1985, and Skinner 1997.

3. Shlain 1998.23. Shlain suggests that the invention of writing, which involves a more sequential, *one-at-a-time* perception of the world, brought a more masculine outlook to humankind and replaced the more female-oriented world of the image, which involved a more holistic, *all-at-once* type of perception.

4. William Blake, *A Vision of the Last Judgement*, p. 91. See Keynes' edition, 1966.614. It is particularly interesting that Blake was both a poet and a visual artist who often combined image and text in his work.

5. Mulvey 1975. For criticism of Mulvey, see Kaplan 1983b, Devereaux 1990, Snow 1989, and other important studies such as Doane 1987, Penley 1989, De Lauretis 1984, Studlar 1988, and Armstrong 1989.

6. Translations of the text of the *Metamorphoses* are mine, based on the Loeb edition (1984) by G. P. Goold.

7. See, for instance, Juno in *Met.* 1.601 and 605–07 and Mercury in *Met.* 2.708–10.

8. See Keith 1999.221. On Perseus as "master of motion," see Barkan 1986.53.

9. The lowering of the eyes can be equated with the blush. The whole episode of Perseus and Andromeda is parallel to Aeneas's quest for Lavinia; see Otis 1970.159–65. In this sense, Lavinia's blush corresponds to Andromeda's lowering of the eyes.

10. Segal 1998.19, 20, and quote on 21.

11. Cf. Pygmalion's reaction when the ivory maiden comes alive: "dum stupet et dubie gaudet fallique veretur," "While he is stupefied, he rejoices doubtfully and fears he is being deceived" (*Met.* 10.287). The text hints at a similar effect on the lover in the episode of Herse and Mercury in Book 2, where Mercury sees her from above when he is flying through the Munychian fields: "obstipuit forma Iove natus et aethere pendens / non secus exarsit," "The son of Jove was stupefied at her beauty and, hanging in midair, caught the fire of love" (*Met.* 2.726–27). See also how Circe is paralyzed at the sight of Picus: "qua simul ac iuvenem virgultis abdita vidit, / obstipuit," "As soon as, hidden in the bushes, she saw the youth, she was stupefied" (*Met.* 14.349–50).

12. For rape and entrapment, see Segal 1998.21.

13. For a detailed discussion, see McGrath 1992.

14. In an obscure version, the setting is Joppa in Phoenicia. Pliny (*Nat. Hist.* 9.4.11) comments that the skeleton of the monster that terrorized Andromeda was brought to Rome from Joppa. Note that, in many ancient pictures, Andromeda is seen as white; see McGrath 1992. In Heliodorus's *Aethiopica* 4.8, a later text, it is said that queen Persinna had sex with her husband while looking at a picture of a "white" Andromeda, and thus she had a white baby girl, whom she felt obliged to abandon lest someone accuse her of adultery, given that the Ethiopian queen was herself black.

15. Cf. *OLD* 1997 s.v. *marmoreus* 2: "resembling marble, esp. whiteness (*of the human body*)."

16. For the absence of racial prejudice in the ancient world, see Snowden 1970 and 1983.

17. For a good study of Medusa, see Wilk 2000.

18. On the episode of Argus and its metacritical implications for the whole poem, see Konstan 1991.

19. It is interesting that there seems to be no evidence of Medusa petrifying women in classical versions; see Zeitlin's discussion in Vernant 1991.138 n. 48.

20. On beheading and the suppression of women's identity, see Eilberg-Schwartz and Doniger 1995.

21. The fact that Elegy "limps" rather than "runs" could be seen as a problem here. However, in Propertius's implicit comparison of the elegiac mistress with Atalanta in 1.1, we have a connection between the running virgin and the elegiac *puella*. The problem of limping could be solved by thinking that Atalanta and other running virgins are "written girls"/erotic poems, but with no strict reference to elegiac meter.

22. See the discussion in Anderson 1966.

23. For Diana as a picture, see Salzman 2001.ch. 2. Other versions of the Pygmalion myth suggest that the artist was actually in love with the goddess Aphrodite. Cf. Clemens Alexandrinus *Protrepticus* 4.57.3. See the discussion in Bauer 1962.15.

24. For the erotic connotations of apples, see Segal 1969.46 and Gentilcore 1995.

25. On *mora*, its wordplays with *amor* and their erotic implications, especially in elegy, see Pucci 1978, especially 52–54 with notes 1–3.

26. Cf. *Met.* 9.287–89 of Alcmene's pregnancy: "tendebat gravitas uterum mihi, quodque ferebam/tantum erat, ut posses auctorem dicere tecti/ponderis esse Jovem," "The weight distended my womb, and the burden I was carrying was so great that you could tell that Jove was the father of the hidden weight."

8 Facing Facts

Ovid's *Medicamina* through the Looking Glass

Victoria Rimell

> Medusa, sit down. Take
> the weight off your snakes. We have
> a lot in common. Snakes, I mean.
>
> Tell me, can you really turn men
> to stone with a look? do you
> think, if I had a perm—
> maybe not.
>
> Don't you think
> Perseus was
> a bit of a coward? not even
> to look you in the face.
>
> you were beautiful, when you
> were a moon goddess, before
> Athene changed your looks
> through jealousy
>
> I can't see what's wrong
> with making love
> in a temple, even
> if it was her temple
>
> it's a good mask; you must
> feel safe and loving
> behind it,
> you must feel very powerful.
> tell me, what conditioner do you use?
> —M. Wandor, "Eve meets Medusa"[1]

Ovid's *Medicamina* is not much to look at, it seems. Very little has been written about this fragmented poem, of which the final one hundred lines or so are missing,[2] and until quite recently (with the arrival of Rosati's commentary in 1985), it was mostly tagged as a pedantic, plodding, grocery list that made very little effort to sweeten its didactic pill. In one of the few brief discussions of Ovid's thesis on cosmetics, L. P. Wilkinson synopsized: "After fifty or so spirited lines of introduction, he plunges into a series of versified recipes, presumably taken from some prose treatise by a professional pharmacologist. It is hardly a matter of regret that after a further fifty lines our manuscripts break off. One would like to think that Ovid broke off too" (1955.188). When it has been read at all (and it's worth noting that Ovidian critics in the last twenty years have left it well alone), the *Medicamina* has been packaged as self-evidently frivolous, superficial, and pragmatic. Thus for Peter Green (1979), as for Wilkinson, when Ovid does his "science bit"[3] and dismisses the hocus-pocus of beautifying spells, he seriously intends to inform and instruct. While few critics today would take Ovidian didacticism or claims of authenticity at face value, it is not clear what *else* we might make of the *Medicamina*, a poem that instructs on perfecting facades. This essay considers the role this text might play within Ovidian poetics and within Ovidian landscapes of desire. I will be discussing how the *Medicamina* fuels and abridges the ways in which Ovid wields the arts of mirroring and making up in his mapping of subject-object relations. In particular, I want to suggest, antiquity's central (and related) myths of catoptric thanatosis, Perseus's killing of Medusa and the tragedy of Narcissus, become animating subtexts in the *Medicamina* both for Ovid's imagining of the self-indulgent *puella* at her toilette and for the poet's and readers' experience of spying on her cosmetic routine.

In purporting to address a female audience of aging beauties, past-it Venuses who will soon be forced to discard narcissism's most vital accessory ("tempus erit, quo vos speculum vidisse pigebit," "The time will come when you'll hate looking in the mirror," 47), the *Medicamina* does the charitable deed of performing for them the function of a looking glass: this is how they *really* look. What we see in the *Medicamina* might be construed as a mirror image; yet despite its claims to genuineness and objectivity, this reflection or representation must remain (necessarily, and self-consciously) a virtual reality, one fantasized by a wannabe voyeur or by a Perseus-poet unable to look (and cunning enough to avoid looking) his vile Medusa in the eye. Ovid's didactic poem is all done with mirrors, those dubious and perilous tools for presenting truth—especially in the

hands of a writer who has made Narcissus the primal incarnation of delu-
sory desire and of self-reflexive, duplicitous poetics. In this polished,
specular poem that (in a gesture vindicated by the ubiquity of *cultus*) employs and embodies women's instrument of self-formation, Ovid con-
jures up and re-presents the female face, imagining the lumpy, malodorous pastes and potions applied in the reflective surface of his text
that, once removed, will reveal a complexion that shines "more radiant"
than her own mirror ("quaecumque afficiet tali medicamine vultum /
fulgebit speculo levior illa suo," 67–68).

By the end of the poem, Ovid predicts, and by the time those
crushed narcissus bulbs have taken effect (64–65), the subject who has
been "brought into being" alongside the composition of the poem itself
(and alongside the brewing and blending of ingredients to constitute the
final *medicamina*), will be able to rival, even usurp, the poet's command
and incarnation of the *speculum*. Re-armed with a mirror-like countenance, the born-again *puella* is more than a match for her maker, fulfilling Ovid's fantasies of agonistic "equality" in *Ars Amatoria* 3 (*ite in bella
pares*, "Go into battle on equal terms," 3.3). As we read, the ingredients
for this ritual, Gorgon-like face mask become less and less mundane,
until at lines 81ff., the subject is to smear herself with the golden honey,
myrrh, frankincense, and incense that might otherwise have been offered
to a goddess (83–84). Ovid's poem is a (potentially inverted) version of
the Pygmalion myth that narrates the making up and metamorphosis of
an elegiac *puella*, the Narcissus-Medusa hybrid who, since Propertius,
has been hellbent on capturing her master's and her readers' eyes as soon
as they so much as set eyes on *her*. With its didactic, realist looks, the
Medicamina toys with the illusion of exposing the mechanics of writing
elegy (along with the Medusan "other face" of sister Venus glimpsed behind closed doors)—that is, with revealing the potentially unsightly
process of conjuring up an object of desire. This is precisely the trick
Ovid pulled off in the opening poems of the *Amores* and in *Ars Amatoria*
1, which began *without* a beloved. Yet in the *Medicamina*, the project is
one of (comic) palingenesis, as the challenge is to recycle, or make over,
the same old girl. This is one he prepared earlier.

Making It Up

The *Medicamina* has an axe to (re)grind about the wonders of
imperialist cultivation (the message is banged out, aggressively, in the
opening lines: *cultus*, 3; *cultus*, 5; *culta*, 7). And in terms of its in-her-face
celebration of *cultus*, in which *medicamina* and cosmetics play a funda-

mental role, the poem could be said to read like a micro-manifesto of Ovidian poetics. Just like the small, often convex mirrors found on the Roman woman's dressing table, this short, frivolous poem has a miniaturizing, epitomizing effect:[4] the spotlight is on the *puella*'s face (no full-length mirrors in these boudoirs), and we home in on some defining features of Ovidian poetry. Philip Hardie opens his recent book on Ovid by reminding us of the centrality of *cultus* (as well as of spectacularity) to both Ovid's lifestyle and poetics.[5] In dealing solely with cosmetics, an arena synonymous with *cultus* or *ars*, the *Medicamina* offers up a prime showcase for authorial self-positioning (as well as for the molding of the Ovidian reader as viewer). The long-suffering *puella* is patched up to serve another stint as mannequin for Ovid's poetics of artifice, making his predecessors Propertius and Tibullus (for whom the natural look is always in) seem drab and passé by comparison. This is where we are shown (alongside *Ars* 3.155–92) Ovid's most explicit and concentrated packaging of a twisted moral code, which not only privileges contrivance and novelty over primitiveness and tradition, but also markets *cultus* as a means to *improve* and emancipate nature.[6] The *Medicamina*, which revels beyond even the *Ars Amatoria* in simulation and self-pleasuring (for *both* sexes), rubs up against the ethos of Tibullus 1.8 and Propertius 1.2 in particular. In 1.8.9–16, Tibullus tells Delia:

> quid tibi nunc molles prodest coluisse capillos
>   saepeque mutatas disposuisse comas,
> quod fuco splendente genas ornare, quid ungues
>   artificis docta subsecuisse manu?
> frustra iam vestes, frustra mutantur amictus;
>   ansaque compressos colligat arta pedes.
> illa placet, quamvis inculto venerit ore;
>   nec nitidum tarda compserit arte caput.

> What good does it do to style those silky curls,
> and try out different hairstyles?
> Why paint your cheeks with bright red rouge, why
> get your nails professionally trimmed?
> To keep changing your tunic and your cloak is daft,
> and so is cramping dainty feet in tight-laced shoes.
> That girl's attractive, though she's free of makeup,
> and takes no pains to sleek her hair.[7]

Propertius, likewise, fixates on unadorned beauty: see 1.2.1–8 (cf. Prop 2.18):

quid iuvat ornato procedere, vita, capillo
    et tenuis Coa veste movere sinus,
aut quid Orontea crines perfundere murra,
    teque peregrinis vendere muneribus,
naturaeque decus mercato perdere cultu,
    nec sinere in propriis membra nitere bonis?
crede mihi, non ulla tuaest medicina figurae:
    nudus Amor formam non amat artificiem.

What use is it, my love, going out with the latest 'do,
or swinging floaty skirts of Coan silk?
What's the point of drenching locks in Syrian myrrh,
or selling yourself in foreign finery?
Why wreck all nature's charm with purchased ornament,
and stop your figure showing off its own appeal?
Trust me, no medicine can improve your beauty:
for naked love despises artificial looks.

In purporting to empathize with the requirements and desires of his female audience, Ovid smashes all Propertius's rules. There is no shame,
he tells us, in distending earlobes with precious gems, donning gold-embroidered gowns, or sporting elaborate perfumed hairdos, especially as
men are equally vain: "nec tamen indignum: sit vobis cura placendi, /
cum comptos habeant saecula vestra viros" (23–24). Whereas in *Ars*
1.505ff., Ovid advised his male readers not to take the business of grooming to an extreme but simply to be "well-presented" (just as women in
Ars 3 are tipped to avoid *viros cultum formamque professos*, "Men who pro-
fess elegance and good looks," 3.433), here they are given license to dress
up to the nines, and the implication is even that it is men, not women,
who have the prerogative on *cultus* (the bride struggles to know what to
add to compete with her groom: "feminea vestri poliuntur lege mariti, /
et vix ad cultus nupta, quod addat, habet," "Your husbands are preened
to female standards, and the bride hardly knows what to add to his chic-
ness," 25–26). Authenticity in Ovid is *always* an act: hence the "bare" face
of any woman treated with these *medicamina* will not glow naturally
(*nitere in propriis bonis*, Prop 1.2.6), but on account of the wondrous mask
that has seeped into the skin and still clings, as if by magic, to the pores
("dic age . . . candida quo possint ora nitere modo," "Tell now . . . how
your faces can shine bright and fair," 51–52; "tempore sint parvo molli
licet illita vultu, /haerebit toto nullus in ore color," "You only need smear
it on your soft face for a short time, and not a hint of redness will re-

main," 97–98). If "natural" is fake, so is nature itself, which can provide examples of just the kind of narcissistic vanity that defines Ovid's Rome: the peacock, Juno's bird, takes pleasure in self-display, just as other birds exult in their own beauty (33–34); and as line 29 hints, the Narcissus myth is an eternal reminder of the way in which natural, wild landscapes offer up more (watery) mirrors than Venus's bed chamber (*rure latent fin-guntque comas*, "They hide out in the country, but still they're all coif-fured": how else is one to avoid a bad hair day when out of town?). Tra-ditionally, the elegist claims to want to situate himself in opposition to everything that the art of making up represents: luxury, hedonism, fri-volity, wealth. Yet in Ovid, and in the *Medicamina* in particular, age-old anxieties about women as consumers are sidelined in favor of a celebra-tion of the imperial cornucopia (see Habinek 2002.50). Cosmetics play a vital role in what Duncan Kennedy (1993) has termed Ovid's "theatri-calisation of eros."

For Ovid, then, making up is the ultimate *ars*, standing for experi-mentation, mutability, masquerade.[8] Just as the *puella* puts on a face mask to become a new woman, so the made-up poet deceives and dazzles his audience with a succession of guises peeled off and reapplied. Ovid tri-fles with a wardrobe of looks, is seduced (or inspired) by dozens upon dozens of women, all of a different "type" (see *Amores* 2.4), and can pro-duce a new poem for each day's new style ("nec genus ornatus unum est," "Nor is there just one form of adornment," *Ars* 3.135; "nec mihi tot posi-tus numero conprendere fas est: / adicit ornatus proxima quaeque dies," "Nor can I count up all the fashions there are these days—every day adds more adornments," 3.151–52). The *Medicamina's* systematic denuding of the elegiac *puella*, its voyeuristic glee at uncovering the unfinished opus of her face, is also an exercise in Ovidian self-exposure: it is all too apt that the poet breaks off mid-glance ("vidi quae gelida madefacta papavera lympha / contereret, teneris illineretque genis," "I saw one woman pounding poppies moistened with cold water, and rubbing them onto her tender cheek," 100–01), allowing his audience, whether intentionally or not, to catch him in as compromising a position as his self-cultivating subject. At *Ars* 3.210, Ovid spells out the notion that *ars* (with a lower-case or capital a) is synonymous with cosmetics, when he advises women that *ars faciem dissimulata iuvat*: don't forget, girls, load on that mascara and read my *Ars*. We might imagine that the dressing table, stacked with pots and paints, looks rather like the poet's desk in the middle of a writ-ing session, and that spying on a girl while she is making herself up is un-cannily like discovering the poem you're reading is unfinished, a *rude opus*

(*Ars* 3.228). The idea that the success of the completed, made-up face depends on disguising the exhaustive, dirty work of creating it recalls Horace's famous portrait of creative genius in *Epistle* 2.2.122–25, in which the poet in full flow looks playful and casual, while, beneath the mask, he strains with the sheer effort of the role.[9] Ovid's fly-on-the-wall documentary of his *puella* staggering under the weight of her jewelry, or wearing a stinking face pack, is similarly tortuous.[10]

Likewise, in *Ars* 3.205–08, when Ovid recommends his *Medicamina* as further reading, the poet's perfectionism is implicitly twinned with the pains women should take over their own beauty: the poem is "parvus, sed *cura* grande, libellus, opus" ("I have a book, a small work, but great in terms of the effort it cost," *Ars* 3.206), echoing the first line of the *Medicamina* ("discite quae faciem commendit *cura*, puellae," "Learn what pains can enhance your looks, girls"). Ovid's *ars* is not *iners* on women's behalf (*Ars* 3.208), in the same way as its inspiration will transform an unkempt woman (compared to an unhewn, *iners* lump of rock) into a million-dollar gem. The beginning of the *Medicamina* traces, through the muse of the self-cultivating *puella*, a crude aetiology of Roman elegy—from the rustic Sabines, *Tatio sub rege* (11), who cared for the *rura paterna* rather than themselves and spun an altogether different *opus* ("assiduo durum pollice nebat opus," "With tireless thumb she spun, a harsh labor," 14), to their descendants, the *tenerae puellae* who lust after flashier, more contemporary, Ovidian texts ("vultis inaurata corpora veste tegi," "You want your bodies clothed in gold-embroidered gowns," 18). Writing a poem and creating a look are analogous, corresponding, *mirroring* projects.

In composing a poem about the activity of measuring out raw materials for recipes that also amount to *this Medicamina*, Ovid rubs our faces in the poetic unsuitability of these ingredients, exposing the crafted patternings, blendings, and juxtapositions of his poetic process. Thus the weighing scales, used to measure and balance out the vetch and barley, gum and Tuscan seeds, roasted lupins and bloating beans, double as technology to churn out distichs with textbook precision, again and again. Ovid's model Augustan *puella* is already a paragon of imperfect poise (a takeoff on limping Elegia): she wears earrings so huge that two are an excessive burden (21–22):

> induitis collo lapides oriente petitos
> > et quantos onus est aure tulisse *duos*.

> You decorate necks with stones sought from eastern lands
> so large the ear finds more than one too much to bear.

Doubleness marred by lopsidedness is, likewise, the recipe required in lines 55–56, where two pounds of vetch, bulked up by ten eggs in the hexameter, now outweighs the same, unadulterated portion of barley in the pentameter:

> par ervi mensura decem madefiat ab ovis:
>   sed cumulent libras hordea nuda *duas*

> Take the same amount of vetch, add ten eggs to moisten:
> but let the skinned barley weigh two pounds.

By lines 79–80, we are well accustomed to the measuring rhythm (Ovid's lesson in metrics is sinking in), and the schoolmaster poet predicts our interrogation (*si quaeris*). We both know what's coming next: an instruction on calibration that doubles as a visualization of the crafting and splitting of prose (and prosaic stuff) into two elegant couplets. Like the sizing-up of elegy's fleshy clone at lines 21–22, the pentameter in this couplet is labeled (for beginners, ladies), as number 2:

> pondere, si quaeris, quo sim contentus in illis,
>   quod trahit in partes uncia secta *duas*.

> If you ask what measure of this I'm happy with,
> I'd say one ounce, divided into two.

Along the way, our practical lessons in learning "right weights" (*pondus iustum*, 76) are accompanied by frequent, varied exemplifications of the symmetry and counterpoise required, all appealing to the visual imagination of the reader keen to perfect *appearance*. Lines 71–72 mark the equilibrium of roasted lupins and fried beans on either pan of the scale (*utraque . . . aequo discrimine . . . utraque*), the shrinking of six into five feet drawn out by *comminuenda* ("to be pounded up small," 72). Similarly, *pariter* at the center of line 75 is the fulcrum of a scale that will measure out one ounce, a *iustum pondus*, in line 76. If we join the dots in the perfectly proportioned couplet at lines 91–92, we get an artist's impression of the pharmacist's scales (as well as the vain woman's smile), with fennel balancing myrrh (five and nine scruples respectively) in both hexameter and pentameter:

> profuit et *marathos* bene olentibus addere *myrrhis*,
>   (quinque parent *marathi* scripula, *myrrha* novem)

> I'd recommend you add fennel to the fragrant myrrh,
> (you want five scruples of fennel, nine of myrrh).

Lines 93–96 establish a more complex pattern: a handful of rose leaves mixed with salt of Ammon is to equal the amount of incense, a tricky balancing act that demands rereading the initial instruction on measuring incense in lines 83ff.: the combination of roses and salt in line 96 is somewhat confused by the twinning of salt with incense in line 94, especially as the formula is repeated, visually, in 96 (with *sal* and *tus* inverted):

> arentisque rosae quantum manus una prehendat,
>> cumque Ammoniaco mascula *tura sale*.
> hordea quem faciunt, illis affunde cremorem:
>> aequent expensas cum *sale tura* rosas.

> Add dry rose leaves, as much as a hand can grasp,
> and frankincense with salt of Ammon.
> Then, to the mixture, pour in the juice that barley makes;
> weigh leaves and salt together to match the incense.

The ingredients for Ovid's *medicamina* are spooned out in bullet-point distichs, leading readers by the hand through behind-the-scenes elementaries in putting together the *face* of an aesthetically enticing opus. For women, Ovidian self-fashioning, as Eric Downing phrases it in his discussion of *Ars* 3 (1999), is explicitly a kind of artification: learning about cosmetics, here as in *Ars* 3, is not only facilitated by, but also implicitly equivalent to, an acquaintance with (even, an "imitative incorporation" into)[11] Ovid's *libellus*. Yet the *Medicamina* also foresees the possibility (and the erotic thrill) of metamorphosing the *puella* into a rival makeup artist, as well as—or instead of—the raw material for elegiac sculpting. Ovidian narcissism, which tutors all boys and girls in the art of making up themselves, threatens ultimately to put the poet out of business. Whichever way we look, the art of wielding mirrors seems destined never to have a happy ending.

And Now for Your Close-up

The *Medicamina* raises the veil on what women do behind closed doors, breaks the spell of female masquerade. Ovid's spiteful eavesdropping on the secret ceremonies of making up plugs straight into the kinds of misogynistic sketches of aging women, or of perfectly powdered beauties caught just when their deceptive mask is slipping, that we encounter in Plautus, Horace, Martial, and Juvenal.[12] For (male) fans of Ovid's seduction campaigns, the poem is potentially a gross turnoff, a spoof tutorial caricaturing the reader as a reluctant pupil who has to be force-fed facts he'd really rather *not* know. In the *Remedia Amoris*, Ovid recommends that one of the fastest ways to become repulsed by your lover is to interrupt her unexpectedly in the middle of her beauty routine (*Rem.* 351–56):

> tum quoque, compositis cum collinet ora venenis,
>   ad dominae vultus (nec pudor obstet) eas.
> pyxidas invenies et rerum mille colores,
>   et fluere in tepidos oesypa lapsa sinus.
> illa tuas redolent, Phineu, *medicamina* mensas:
>   non semel hinc stomacho nausea facta meo est.

> Then when your mistress is painting her cheeks with concoctions of dyes,
> don't be ashamed to go look at her face.
> Boxes you'll find, one thousand different hues, and
> juices that melt and drip onto sticky breasts.
> Such drugs smell of your table, Phineus: one whiff of them
> has turned my stomach more than once.

Medicamina stink: women making up are foul harpies and, at the same time, as blind as Phineus (if they think their complexions look good midfacial). We might also read the *Medicamina* alongside Ovid's heartfelt advice in *Ars* 3, following his recommendation of this *libellus* (209–18, 225–30):

> non tamen expositas mensa deprendat amator
>   pyxidas: ars faciem dissimulata iuvat.
> quem non offendat toto faex inlita vultu,
>   cum fluit in tepidos pondere lapsa sinus?
> oesypa quid redolent? quamvis mittatur Athenis
>   demptus ab inmundo vellere sucus ovis.
> nec coram mixtas cervae sumpsisse medullas,
>   nec coram dentes defricuisse probem;
> ista dabunt formam, sed erunt deformia visu:
>   multaque, dum fiunt, turpia, facta placent;
>
> . . . .
>
> tu quoque dum coleris, nos te dormire putemus;
>   aptius a summa conspiciere manu.
> cur mihi nota tuo causa est candoris in ore?
>   claude forem thalami! quid rude prodis opus?
> multa viros nescire decet; pars maxima rerum
>   offendat, si non interiora tegas.

Let no lover spy boxes arranged on your dressing table;
faking it's the best beauty aid you have.
Who wouldn't be appalled at a face smeared in paint so thick
it slipped and dripped onto sweaty breasts?
What does that wool-oil smell like! Just because those juices
from a dirty fleece are sent from Athens,
I don't approve of getting out a stag's mixed marrow, not in public,
nor should you clean your teeth for everyone to see.
Such things may make you gorgeous, but they're grim to watch:
there's lots that's gross to do but lovely when it's finished.

. . . .

So while you're making up, let us think you're sleeping;
much better to be seen when the canvas is complete.
Why must I know the tricks behind the whiteness of your face?
Shut that bedroom door! Why offer up a work half done?
There's lots men are better off not knowing; in fact, most things
you do would cause offense, if you didn't keep them veiled.

Similarly, when Ovid in *Amores* 2.17 marvels at Corinna's drop-dead looks, which rival those of Propertius's Cynthia, he is careful to point out that she will use a mirror to appreciate her reflection only once it has been perfected ("cur est tam bene nota sibi? / scilicet a speculi sumuntur imagine fastus, / nec nisi conpositam se prius illa videt!" "How come she knows herself so well? I'd bet she gets her arrogance from her mirror image—and she never sees that before she's fully made-up!" 8–10). When we read between the lines (and peep through the crack in the bedroom door), Ovid's amazement at Corinna's superior self-knowledge is spiked with sarcasm, and his own beguilement ("o facies oculos nata tenere meos," "O face, born to capture my eyes," 2.17.12) is safely formulaic (mirroring Propertius's opening line: "Cynthia prima suis miserum me cepit ocellis," "Cynthia was the first to capture me, her victim, with her eyes," 1.1, and coming a little too close to parroting his disinfatuation of *Amores* 1.10.10: "nec facies oculos iam capit ista meos," "Those looks of yours no longer capture my eyes"). We might compare lines 33–34 of the *Medicamina* ("laudatas homini volucris Iunonia pennas / explicat," "The bird of Juno spreads out feathers praised by man"), laced with the echo of *Ars* 1.627 ("laudatas ostendit avis Iunonia pinnas," "The bird of Juno shows off her much-admired wings"), which makes Juno, as mere runner-up in the beauty contest judged by Paris, a prime example of the deluded woman who *thinks* she's Venus.[13] In both texts,

Ovid lets his readers play the hero and see the *real* her, warts and all (you can't miss those *maculae* and *tubera*, subtly erased and scraped off in lines 78 and 85). Dismorphophobia gets provoked in Ovid by the uncanny and frequently mythologized realization that the mirror is always a flawed instrument by which to obtain self-knowledge, and that another person will always be able to see you more clearly, and more truthfully, than you can see yourself. Mirrors lend women the power to know and control appearances, yet in so doing, we are reminded, they expose the limits of female individuation: they are the snare she has set herself.[14] Similarly, Ovid's recipe in the *Medicamina* for reviving the femme fatale consists of applying a miraculous mask that recalls the Gorgon's vizard-like ugliness, a lethal catoptric power that will always potentially be the death of her.[15]

Yet like the *Remedia*, the *Medicamina* functions as the *Ars Amatoria*'s mirror text,[16] performing an anti-seduction that cannot but seduce.[17] The more we are told that the "unfinished," Medusan *puella* is better left unseen, the more we long to set eyes on her, just as in the *Remedia*, the man who declares "I'm not in love" is inevitably head-over-heels. In direct contrast to the *Medicamina*, which casts an unforgiving spotlight on the female visage, magnifying those wrinkles, close-up, till they resemble gouged-out furrows (45–46), *Ars* 2 instructs men never to highlight or reproach a woman for her faults, particularly if she is past her prime or has a blemished complexion. (Ovidian rhetoric has a cosmetic effect— he airbrushes flaws with inventive language alone: *nominibus mollire licet mala*, 657.) In *Ars* 2, Ovid also goes out of his way to recommend the older woman ("utilis, o iuvenes, aut haec, aut senior aetas," "This age, or even older, is a profitable one, lads," 667): his readers are to keep on plowing away at this field (668) that bears many unforeseen advantages (experience, elegance, imagination, uninhibitedness). Yet although we subtly avoid seeing the mature *puella* face-on in *Ars* 2, her superficially veiled *vitia* infect the imagination all the more and become comically grotesque once aligned with their politically correct surrogates ("fusca vocetur, / nigrior Illyrica cui pice sanguis erit; / si paeta est, Veneri similis, si rava, Minervae," "If her blood is blacker than Illyrian pitch, then call her darky; if she's got a squint, compare her to Venus, if grey haired, to Minerva," 657–59). Despite (and because of) Ovid's rhetoric, this woman is both seductive and repugnant, both full of initiative and ultimately passive, both an easy lay and the girlfriend from hell.

The misogyny that surrounds the sexually mature woman and invests her with castrating, paralyzing (stiffening) powers has its mythical incarnation in the figure of the Gorgon,[18] and she is the trump card Ovid plays in *Ars* 2 as he concludes his defense of the older woman with one final, dazzling exemplum (699–702):

> scilicet Hermionen Helenae praeponere posses,
> et melior Gorge, quam sua mater, erat?
> et venerem quicumque voles adtingere seram,
> si modo duraris, praemia digna feres.

> Could you honestly rank Hermione over Helen,
> and was the Gorgon better looking than her mother?
> Whoever you are, if you fancy trying older women,
> just stick it out, you won't be disappointed.

The Gorgon's mother may be a pushover for a Perseus accustomed to younger, deadlier women like her daughter (crucially, he'll see her *eyes* confessing defeat: "aspiciam dominae victos amentis ocellos," 691), yet the hint at her continued fertility in line 668 ("iste feret segetes, iste serendus ager," "That field will bear crops, that field must be sown") harbors the threat of Medusa's (re)birth. This anti-Venus, at once irresistible and (or, because) repulsive, is more trouble than she looks: Ovid's appeal, far from reassuring his male readers, whips up the paranoid fear of Medusa's gaze that runs throughout his instruction in *Ars* 1 and 2, books primarily geared, of course, toward hooking the daughters, not the mothers.

The possibility (or the promise) of encountering a Medusa is both scary and tantalizing, and the Ovidian lover is schooled to tread a fine line between exciting competition and emasculating threat. The trick, Ovid tells his readers in *Ars* 2.287ff., is to let *her* play the queen, to let her *think* she is in control of the acts of seeing and being seen ("perde nihil, partes illa potentis agat," "Waste nothing, let her play the powerful role," 294). Let her believe you are spellbound by her beauty, a victim of her Gorgon's gaze ("attonitum forma fac putet esse sua," 296).[19] In reality, he goes on to reveal, she is probably more violent than Medusa, but she, too, will play down her powers and be mild and gentle to her lover ("ut fuerit torva violentior illa Medusa,/fiet amatori lenis et aequa suo," 309–10). The idea that the lover *pretends* to be *attonitus* by his girl's face is undermined by the ensuing revelation that she *really is* a Medusa. To claim that your paralysis is a put-on is one way of defending yourself (or at least your reputation) against a woman's Gorgon-like powers. The lover with a black belt in amatory arts must always wield a mask-like face that is as impenetrable as Perseus's shield ("effice, nec vultu destrue dicta tuo," "Ensure that your looks don't undo your words," *Ars* 2.312): thus petrification can always be passed off as the ultimate self-control. Yet the risk is that a lover grows into the pose that, at first, is so artificially worn; when in *Ars* 1, Ovid advises his students to play the heartstruck beau (just as he did in the opening poems of *Amores* 1), he warns: "saepe tamen vere coepit simulator amare,/saepe, quod incipiens finxerat esse, fuit," "Yet often he who fakes it begins to love truly after all, and becomes what he has pretended to be" (615–16).

Both male and female lovers in Ovid are (to a greater or lesser degree) advised to attempt to manipulate the Gorgon's powers, to discipline their surface appearance:[20] the male reader uses her stony stare to his advantage by predicting and (apotropaically) faking it himself (or so he claims), whereas the *puella* enhances the power of her gaze by assuming a passive, kindly look, thus foiling attempts by her opponent to forearm himself against her withering glance. Ovid's fantasy of erotic interaction is a duel of (potential) equals in which mirroring male and female contestants battle it out for control of the look. The Perseus-Medusa confrontation is repeatedly staged as a drawn out or ongoing collision, in which flashing stares boomerang between lustrous surfaces, human and artificial. And Ovid makes the elegiac couplet, which replays *ad infinitum* an (imperfect) mirroring of the hexameter line,[21] operate as a system to enact and configure every specular patterning. In a tit-for-tat game that plays on elegiac doubleness, men are advised to "deceive the deceivers" (*fallite fallentes*, *Ars* 1.645). In *Ars* 2.197–202, the way to woo women is to ape their every move, advice told in lines that replay Echo's passive-aggressive imitation of Narcissus:

> cede repugnanti: cedendo victor abibis:
> > fac modo, quas partes illa iubebit, agas.
> arguet, arguito; quicquid probat illa, probato;
> > quod dicet, dicas; quod negat illa, neges.
> riserit, adride; si flebit, flere memento;
> > imponat leges vultibus illa tuis.

> Give in if she resists: if you yield you'll come out the winner:
> just play the part that she has written for you.
> If she blames, you blame too; approve what she approves;
> affirm what she affirms; deny what she denies.
> If she laughs, laugh with her; if she weeps, mind you weep, too;
> let her dictate your every expression.

In *Ars* 3, the same instructions are given to women (513–14):

spectantem specta; ridenti mollia ride;
    innuet, acceptas tu quoque redde notas.

Look at him who looks at you; send back his charming smile;
if he beckons, acknowledge and return his nod.

She must look at the object of her desire with gentle eyes (*comibus oculis*, 510), yet although she is actively looking, her gaze is secondary, for she is the mirror image of the man looking at her (*spectantem*). In *Ars* 3.419–21, similarly, the beautiful woman who offers herself to be seen is like a wolf on the *attack*.[22] Thus while the blueprint of *Ars* 3.513–14 (one already stolen, or faked, by men in *Ars* 2) might enact what Luce Irigaray famously dubbed patriarchy's "specular logic," in which women are denied the pleasure of self-representation and permitted only the hysteria of mimicry,[23] the syntax here renders woman *both* object *and* subject: paradoxically, being looked at can itself be combative, as the figure of Medusa proves. Moreover, *both* sexes in Ovid have sanctioned access to the magic of the mirror, the device that notoriously confounds the distinction between self and other.[24]

Mirror, Myrhha . . . Who's the Fairest Now?

Traditionally, of course, mirrors were exclusively female accessories. They lay, literally and symbolically, at the center of the *mundus muliebris* and were frequently associated with effeminacy and general moral decay.[25] As Willard McCarty notes, Aristophanes' *Thesmophoriazusae* (140) uses a mirror to represent woman (alongside a male sword), and there is some evidence that mirrors were thought to be essentially female because of their connection to the moon (which is consistently a goddess) and hence also to monthly rhythms (see McCarty 1989.178). In Ovid, too, all women are narcissists[26] whose self-appreciation is fully contingent on the use of a mirror. When giving out style advice to women in *Ars* 3, Ovid reminds his readers that a looking glass is essential: "nec genus ornatus unum est: quod quamque decebit / elegat, et speculum consulat ante suum," "There's not one form of adornment; each woman should choose what suits her and check her appearance in her own mirror" (3.135–36). Yet at the same time, as we have seen, Ovidian men are given carte blanche to *steal* women's mirrors. In *Ars* 2.215–16, just when Ovid has instructed his *iuvenes* to reflect their girl's every move, he reassures them "nec tibi turpe puta (quamvis sit turpe, placebit) / ingenua speculum sustinuisse manu," "And don't think it shameful (it may be shameful, but it's so much fun), to hold a mirror in your freeborn hand." Just as in the *Medicamina*, women are told that there is no shame in taking pleasure in the self (an indulgence that naturally demands looking in mirrors), since these days men are equally obsessed with their looks ("nec tamen indignum: sit vobis cura placendi, / cum comptos habeant saecula vestra viros," "But there's no shame in it: you should be anxious to please, since men these days are so well groomed," 23–24). The *Medicamina* lampoons the cultural "progress" of Augustus's gold-plated Rome as a self-interested scrabbling for control of the mirror (as ultimate, effeminate luxury as well as a device to display the goodies of empire). This internalization of an imperialist project that has nowhere left to go is read in Ovid as an eroticized battle for the subject position, a civil war for which the Medusa-Perseus conflict, as well as Narcissus's death-by-self, become the core mythic subtexts.

A Perseus-inspired exploitation of the mirror as a weapon to deflect and destroy the specular female look is endemic in Ovidian poetry. In *Amores* 1.14, for example, when Corinna wrecks her tresses with curling tongs, she is pictured agonizing over her reflection in her mirror, which she then surrenders (35–38):

quid male dispositos quereris periisse capillos?
quid speculum maesta ponis, inepta, manu?
non bene consuetis a te spectaris ocellis
    ut placeas, debes inmemor esse tui

Why lament the ruin of your messed-up hair?
Why lay aside your mirror, silly girl, with hand so sad?
You're gazed upon by eyes not used to such a sight—
in order to find pleasure there, forget who you once were.

In *Ars* 3.507–08, the poet holds up a looking glass to expose his reader's face mid-temper tantrum:

vos quoque si media speculum spectetis in ira,
    cognoscat faciem vix satis ulla suam.

If only you could see yourselves mid-passion,
you'd hardly recognize the mirror image of your face.

Here, the control-freak moralist applies precepts very similar to Seneca's in *de Ira*, a text that advises the angry man to look at himself in a mirror so as to face a shocking, unexpected, inner reality ("velut in praesentem adducti non agnoverunt se," "Brought, as it were, face-to-face with reality, they did not recognize themselves," 2.36.1–3). A parallel passage in *Ars* 2 recommends that a frenzied woman be treated with *medicamina* (489, 491).[27] Typically, Ovid has to create a monster before he heroically hacks off her head: passion transforms the average girl into a demon, her veins bulging black with bile, her eyes flashing fire "more savagely than the Gorgon" ("lumina Gorgoneo saevius igne micant," 3.504). Even (or especially) a stunningly attractive woman can be struck dumb by her own look: in *Metamorphoses* 15.232–33, during Pythagoras's speech about bodily change, Helen (who, in the example at *Ars* 2.699–700, is placed in parallel with the Gorgon's mother) weeps when she sees her wrinkles in the mirror ("flet quoque, ut in speculo rugas adspexit aniles, / Tyndaris et secum, cur sit bis rapta, requirit," "Helen also weeps when she sees the wrinkles of old age in her looking glass, and tearfully asks herself why she should twice have been a lover's prey"). Legendary stunner Lais also laid down her mirror when faced with the prospect of decaying looks (*Greek Anthology* 6.1.18; cf. 11.54, 266). Medusa herself, once a beautiful young woman, dies when she sees her gruesome reflection in Perseus's shield.[28]

The *Medicamina*, meanwhile, which begins by showing the mature woman what she *really* looks like in the mirror, replays Perseus's trick of stealing Medusa's petrifying gaze and turning it against her. Ovid has transformed his subject into stone, tacitly associating her with Augustus's marble Rome: just as women need to whiten their swarthy complexions, to slap on a mask to hide and improve what lies beneath, so the cosmetic facades of Rome's public buildings disguise rough, black, earthenware bricks (7–8).[29] Romanization is specifically a *white* man's project:[30] Ovid's preparations cleanse and mask darker skins, and the poem strives towards the racial ideal of the *candida ora* (52).[31]

In this visually epitomizing poem, Ovid's Medusan gaze both represents and stages the process of artistic creation. As Hazel E. Barnes points out, the link often made in Western literature between Medusa and art is reinforced by, if it does not directly derive from, the fact that her son by Poseidon is Pegasus, symbol of poetry.[32] The Gorgon's petrifying skill models artistic reproduction, and her finished statues are perfect realist artworks. In *Metamorphoses* 5.200ff., for example, Astyages thinks his metamorphosed enemy Aconteus is alive and attempts to stab him with his sword; when it bounces off the stone, he is amazed (*stupet*) and paralyzed, as if merely looking at Medusa's work is as risky an act as meeting her eyes ("marmoreoque manet vultus mirantis in ore," "He stood there with a look of wonder on his marble face," 206).[33] The successful artist commands Medusa's gaze not only in the act of creation (petrification) but also in his power to stun an audience. Elegiac portraits of marble-skinned *puellae* typically recast a parallel—or reverse—Pygmalion fantasy that literalizes artistic representation: line 10 of the *Medicamina* ("sectile deliciis India praebet ebur," "India offers ivory to be cut into dainty figures") suggestively fancies the uncultivated female body as an unhewn chunk of ivory (like *Ars* 3.219–20),[34] hinting at a Pygmalionesque project (Pygmalion's dream woman is sculpted from ivory).[35] Looking in mirrors generally is often petrifying (this is especially true of the imperfect ancient mirror, natural or artificial, that worked best when the subject stood very still). Thus Medusa's mythic "cousin" Narcissus is also implicitly turned into stone by his own gaze ("adstupet ipse sibi cultuque inmotus eodem / haeret, ut e Pario formatum marmore signum," "He looks in speechless wonder at himself and stays there motionless in the same pose, like a statue carved from Parian marble," *Met.* 3.418–19). In his grief at losing his beloved reflection in the disturbed surface of the pool, he beats his breast *marmoreis palmis* ("with marble hands"), just as Hermaphroditus, struck by the mirror-like power of Salmacis's eyes, is likened to painted ivory (*Met.* 4.332).[36]

Ovid uses his mirror-text apotropaically in the *Medicamina*, predicting the threat of castration embodied in the wild woman, his untamed, Medusan subject. In his hands, the mirror becomes an instrument of objectification, and the male artist's gaze, with its Medusan ambitions, is overtly aligned with imperialist aggression. Cultivation is empire's project, and in Ovid's opening lines, woman represents a colonized barbarian territory or one of many exotic imports to be processed by civilizing artistry: the didactic *discite* (line 1) soon slips into steely-sounding reporting ("cultus humum sterilem Cerealia pendere iussit / munera," "Cultivation ordered the sterile earth to yield the gifts of wheat," 3–4).[37] We don't need to put a great deal of pressure on these lines to imagine that it is *she* that is to be plowed into shape,[38] then dipped and dyed like a raw fleece ("vellera saepe eadem Tyrio medicantur aeno," 9); that *her* sterile "field" is to be violently weeded of "devouring briers" (*mordaces interiere rubi,* 4); and that the bitter juices of *her* fruit are destined to be sweetened by intensive farming.[39] Her pulchritude, we are later told, will be violently despoiled by age (*formam populabitur aetas,* 45), calling for surgery at the hands of Rome's craftsmen, who will carve her up into bite-sized titillations (*sectile deliciis . . . ebur,* 10). After this pugnacious opening, the comparison of Sabine dames of old ("They would have wished to cultivate their paternal acres rather than themselves") with their "daughters," the delicate it-girls of Augustan Rome (11–17) recalls how the rape of the Sabine women in Romulus's theater in *Ars* 1 marks the initiation of this process of imperial *cultus*, marking the beginning of Ovid's strategies of seduction in a text that commands the theater as an exemplary arena for the performance of spectacular erotics. Throughout the *Medicamina*, the woman who has read *Ars* 3 is reminded of how much work there is to do: after *Ars* 3.281ff., where women are warned about making asses of themselves when their faces get distorted by braying laughter ("ut rudit a scabra turpis asella mola," "As when the mean she-ass brays by the rough millstone," 290), the scene at *Medicamina* 58 hints at her continued bestialization ("lenta iube scabra frangat asella mola," "Bid the slow ass break it on the rough millstone")—the "joke" for voyeuristic readers is always that the broad we catch brewing Ovid's potions needs all the help she can get.

Ovid's program for the cultivation of woman seeks to sanitize and invade her sexual body, visualized as a thorny landscape ready to be pruned (or literally, to be slain: *interiere*, 4), a trunk to be split open (*fissa*, 6), or a fleshy rot seeping nasty juices.[40] Lines 3–4, in particular, predict the feral woman's specifically *castrating* power: those *mordaces rubi*, Ovid warns his male voyeurs, are bound to eat you alive—so be sure to get your retaliation in first. The simultaneous focus in the opening lines of the *Medicamina* on the taming of the *puella*'s face and of her reproductive organs evokes Freud's reading of Medusa's head as female genitalia and the serpents of her (pubic) hair as a writhing mass of castrating and castrated penises.[41] For Freud, the terror of Medusa is a terror of castration that is linked to the sight of something (specifically, he imagines, "the female genitals, probably those of an adult, surrounded by hair, and essentially those of his mother," 1955.273), and her decapitation is thus a retaliatory or self-defensive neutering. Camille Paglia, whose analysis of the Gorgon in Western art frequently echoes the *Medicamina*'s opening metaphor, stresses that "Medusa's hair is also the writhing vegetable growth of nature."[42]

In line 39, Ovid denies the implication that the *Medicamina* are a miracle cure for fading beauty or that there is any such thing as snake-splitting sorcery ("nec mediae Marsis finduntur cantibus angues," "Snakes are not split in two by Marsian spells"). Yet as Alison Sharrock discusses (1994.56 and 50–86), Ovid's opposition between magic and love, and between magic and poetry, is always already collapsed into an identification: under the duplicitous sign of the *pharmakon* (or here, *medicamen*), the discourses of love, poetry, and magic blend into one.

Ovid's Lucretian tirade against *religio*, here as in *Ars* 1.62–79, 2.99–108, and *Remedia Amoris* 249–90, is complicated and undercut by the barely disguised interconnectedness of ancient science and magic, poetry and spells.[43] Indeed *medicamen*, as it is used elsewhere in Ovid, is linked both with specular magic and with the power to castrate (that is, to sever Medusan snakes). The waters that androgynize Hermaphroditus, for example, are charged with a *medicamen* in *Metamorphoses* 4.388.[44] The same term is also used of Medea's anti-aging drugs at *Metamorphoses* 7.262 ("interea validum posito medicamen aeno / fervet," "Meanwhile, the strong potion is boiling in the bronze pot") and of the remedy used by Apollo's son to resuscitate the torn body of Hippolytus (*Met.* 15.533). And at *Metamorphoses* 14.285, Circe uses magic *medicamina* to turn Odysseus's men into pigs.[45] Ovid appropriates witch-like powers in the *Medicamina* to conduct parallel experiments on his *puella*, who may end up with a teenage glow or a face like a hog: his concoctions of barley, seeds, and other crops (themselves products, we might imagine, of his cruel weeding to increase the productivity of woman's soil and to butcher her Medusan looks in lines 2–3) are endowed with a specular magic of their own.[46]

Just as Ovid's *medicamen* can mean both curative potion and noisome drug, so the snake-like powers of his female subject in *Ars* 3 and the *Medicamina* are both unnerved and boosted by his instruction. A predictable objection to *Ars Amatoria* 3, Ovid claims, might be: "quid virus in angues / adicis, et rabidae tradis ovile lupae?" "Why do you add venom to snakes, betray the sheep to the mad she-wolf?" (7–8). His first piece of advice to girls in this book is to make the most of youth and be mindful of encroaching old age; in a passage exploited to reinforce the necessity of reading the *Medicamina*, Ovid exclaims: "quam cito (me miserum!) laxantur corpora rugis, / et perit in nitido qui fuit ante color," "How quickly (ah, what agony!) is the body furrowed by wrinkles, how quickly the color fades, that once blossomed on that lovely face," *Ars* 3.73–74 (compare *Med.* 51–52: "dic age . . . candida quo possint ora nitere modo," "Tell now, how your face can shine bright and fair," and 97–98: "tempore sint parvo molli licet illita vultu, / haerebit toto nullus in ore color," "You only need smear it on your soft face for a short time and not a hint of redness will remain"). Whereas *snakes* can slough off their age with their skins, and stags are not aged by casting off their horns, women have no way of halting the decline.[47] Those crinkly white hairs (75–76) bear no relation to serpents; yet *Ars* 3 and the *Medicamina* both focus on how time can, after all, be tricked with makeup, hair dye, and face masks blended with stag horn (*Med.* 59), peeled off like a thin, dry snakeskin to reveal a brand new her. Creating a Venus-Medusa (an enemy: *portas reseravimus hosti*, "We have thrown open our gates to the enemy," *Ars* 3.577) is a seductive project, as I've stressed, and the price to pay for a good fight, a drama worth *watching*. The masochistic elegiac lover cannot *bear* sweetness, in fact: *suco renovemur amaro*, "Let us be refreshed by bitter juices" (*Ars* 3.583). The opening lines of the *Medicamina*, which shave off her brambles and sugar her tart juices, risk producing a bland, unrealistic artwork that looks more dead than alive and is certainly no turn-on (again, the narcissism of *cultus* may well backfire). In theory, the ideal (voiced at *Ars* 3.609–10) is to mingle fear with "secure enjoyment" ("admiscenda tamen venus est secura timori"); yet in practice, Ovidian elegy continually performs an unstable balancing act in which each half of a coupling (and couplet) is alternately epicized and elegized, fortified and castrated.[48]

Moreover, just as Ovid's refutation of magic serves precisely to highlight his poetic wizardry, so the opening claim in the *Medicamina* that he will teach women how their looks might be preserved, not changed ("et quo sit vobis forma tuenda modo," 2) is undermined by various hints in his recipes of the (painful) process of metamorphosis. As well as the narcissus bulbs threatening to take root in her soil at line 63, Halcyon cream anticipates the fate of Alcyone in Book 11 of the *Metamorphoses*, who loses her beloved Ceyx and becomes a bird doomed to a life of eternal (elegiac) mourning ("addita de querulo volucrum medicamina nido / ore fugant maculas: alcyonea vocant," *Med.* 77–78). The addition of myrrh to the heady mix in line 91 ("profuit et marathos bene olentibus addere myrrhis") is similarly ominous: in *Metamorphoses* 10, this fragrant substance is made from Myrrha's tears when she has been transformed into a tree after committing incest with her father. At the start of her tale, Myrrha is not scared enough of the Furies' gaze ("nec metues atro crinitas angue sorores / quas facibus saevis oculos atque ora petentes / noxia corda vident," "Have you no fear of the sisters with the black snakes in their hair, whom guilty souls see brandishing torches before their eyes and faces?" 349–51), and revels in the power of her beauty. That same youthful, beautiful face is covered by dry, wrinkled bark in line 498 ("mersitque suos in cortice vultus," "She plunged her face into the bark"), and when she gives birth to baby Adonis, she becomes precisely the kind of ugly, aging woman whose tree must be split open at the beginning of the *Medicamina* ("arbor agit rimas et fissa cortice vivum / reddit onus, vagitque puer," "Then the tree cracked open, the bark was split asunder, and it gave forth its living burden, a wailing baby boy," *Met.*

10.512–13; cf. "fissaque adoptivas accipit arbor opes," "A cleft tree gains adopted riches," *Med.* 6), a fate already predicted in the simile at lines 372–77, when she is as indecisive as a great tree struck by an axe that creaks from side to side before falling. Myrrha's myth, which takes a dangerously seductive, Medusan woman (or Medusa-Narcissus) and makes of her disarmed body a picture book Adonis, every narcissist's fantasy lover, might be said to mirror Ovid's manufacture of an aestheticized, marble-skinned *puella* in the *Medicamina.* Yet it also harbors a warning for the narcissistic, mirror-wielding beauty queen whom this poem wants, ostensibly, to honor and (re-)create: all beauty, in Ovid, ends in (Myrrha's) tears, since Venus and Medusa are two sides of one and the same coin.

For the *puella* herself, the presence in the *Medicamina* of changed faces from Ovid's *Metamorphoses* suggests that she risks *becoming* her ingredients. We might note that the constituents of these *medicamina* often look like substitutes for the face or body we *really* want to see. Lines 53ff., for example, play out a transferred striptease: barley is to be stripped from its chaff and only crushed when it is *nuda* (56); the narcissus bulbs must be skinless, *sine cortice* (63), before they are pounded *puro marmore* (64) (a line reminiscent of Narcissus's bare, marble-like skin); and the bark is removed from the gum at 87 ("parte minus quarta dereptum cortice cummi"). The subject is to be sliced up, implicitly, in line 10 ("sectile deliciis India praebet ebur"), just as *alcyonea* is split (*secta*) in line 80. Qualities belonging to ingredients are to be transferred to the female face: thus lupin seeds (69) are pale, like the girl's desired complexion, just like the white lead combined with the blush of red nitre in line 73. The idea that the contents will be internalized and identified with the woman's body is perhaps suggested in line 70: she is to add beans that bloat the body, presumably if *ingested* ("et simul inflantes corpora frige fabas," "At the same time, fry beans that will puff out the body"). Ovid's kitchen table chemistry lets us spy on her spotty, warty, greased up face (as well as visualize the goal of the perfect canvas) *through* the mask he has her apply, just as the voyeur peeps through the chink in the door and pieces together a complete image from a series of titillating flashes of skin and color. In fact, the recipes themselves seem to hint at just such a scenario: line 89 (*per densa foramina cerne,* "Sift them in close-set meshes") could equally translate as "see (these things) through holes, placed close together." Looking is neither safe nor guilt free, however: the ground stag antlers mixed with dusty grain at 59–60 recall the horns grown from the head of Actaeon, who is changed into a stag and then torn apart by hounds as a punishment for spying Diana bathing naked in the woods ("et quae prima cadent vivaci cornua cervo," "and the first horns that fall from a long-lived stag"; cf. "dat sparso capiti vivacis cornua cervi," "On the head she had sprinkled with water, she made the horns of a long-lived stag grow," *Met.* 3.194).[49]

Here's Looking at You

In many ways, then, Ovid's *Medicamina* (especially when set against the other amatory poems) aggressively asserts Irigaray's mirror tyranny, positing woman as object and symbolically sealing off her access to subjectivity by imagining the point at which her relationship with the mirror cracks. The Narcissus myth, churned up in her face pack ("adice narcissi bis sex sine cortice bulbos," "Add twelve narcissus bulbs without their skins," 63) shadows her metamorphosis, as the didactic poet in Lucretian mode reveals the heartbreaking truth of her reflection, the ultimate destructiveness of self-love: while his act of looking (at her) is overdetermined as an act of knowing, the (self-)knowledge *she* acquires through the act of seeing is disempowering, depressing, even deadly. Yet at the same time, Ovid makes it difficult, even impossible, for his (male) audience to relish their appropriation of the mirror and of the Medusan gaze: while *cultus* reigns, *everyone* is caught in the Narcissus trap of dressing to please themselves and no one can be said to escape the mirror's pernicious, talismanic glare. The moral of Medusa's tale is that here is no way to use the looking glass without also being vulnerable to its powers.

Lines 21ff. undercut the imperialist objectification of *puellae* in the opening section of the poem: *cultus* erodes the separation of genders, and in line 21, far from embodying the imported product or a landscape to be colonized and farmed, Roman ladies have become imperialists on a domestic scale who seek out and exhibit the trappings of empire ("induitis collo lapides oriente petitos"). Freud's account of the development of sexual difference based on the fearful perception of lack (of a penis), hinted at in the anxious slashing of her *mordaces rubi* in line 4, is no longer applicable—or rather, what Irigaray characterizes as the narcissistic motivations of Freud's Medusa complex ("to castrate the woman is to inscribe her in the law of the same desire, of desire for the same," 1977.46) are given free rein: men are to view the new, made-up Augustan girl as same, not other, as a rival in the pursuit of cultivated elegance.[50] It is not clear who sets the trends and who copies whom: in lines 23–24, women must keep up with male grooming ("sit vobis cura placendi, / cum comptos habeant saecula vestra viros"); in line 25, the husbands are spruced up according to *feminea lex*, yet these days there is little for the bride to add to the *cultus* displayed (first) by men ("et vix ad cultus nupta, quod addat, habet"). In 27 (unfortunately corrupt), there's no distinguishing subject or lover on the basis of gender († "pro se quaeque parent, nec quos venerentur amores / refert" †, "They all dress up to please themselves, no matter what kind of love they worship"), and although 29–30 are gender specific (*illas . . . cultas*), 31 opens the field once more ("est etiam placuisse sibi quaecumque voluptas," "There is some pleasure, too, in self-satisfaction"). These tips on beautification are for men, too, who are now voyeurs eager to watch and *learn*. When it comes to cooking up *medicamina*, girls need a male accomplice or two (here's a handy opportunity to steal her recipe): at 64, she's to let a *strenua dextra* ("strong right arm") pound up the narcissus bulbs on pure marble (in an image that comes close to suggesting masturbation),[51] and at 75, she is to hand over the second mixture to the strong arms of young men ("da validis iuvenum pariter subigenda lacertis").

Both male and female readers look at their mirror image in the *Medicamina*, an experience that threatens as well as bolsters self-identity. Men, like Narcissus, spy a (seductively repulsive) other who, by a process of metamorphosis that itself parallels the transformation of Narcissus, becomes and is revealed as same, as a version or reflection of himself. This is a poem that flaunts its own success as a didactic work by forcing all its readers, in different ways, to experience an epistemological revelation modelled on the tragedy of Narcissus, the icon of self-love who comes to know that his beloved other is, in fact, himself. Lines 67–68 ("quaecumque afficiet tali medicamine vultum / fulgebit speculo levior illa suo," "Whoever shall treat her face with this prescription will shine smoother than her own mirror") hint at a finale to match the Medusa and Perseus encounter and Narcissus's parallel flash of realization: the woman who, at the beginning of the poem, was a Medusa viewed in a mirror and stripped of her weapons will now (be seen to) embody the shining mirror. Mirrored gazes meet, producing a baffling symmetry that reveals, in a moment, the specular modalities of Ovidian erotics.[52]

Notes

1. In Linthwaite 1987.115–16.

2. Exactly how much of the poem is lost remains a mystery, but it seems likely that we have the first half (concerned with skin treatments) and that a section of similar length about cosmetics (introduced by lines 99–100) followed.

3. Intuiting the best traditions of late twentieth-century cosmetics advertising.

4. As McCarty notes (1989.170), the metals and working methods of antiquity prohibited large mirrors. To get around this problem, artisans often used a convex surface, so that a large scene could be made to fit into a small space. Also see Grabes 1982.43 and de Grummond and Hoff 1982.52.

5. Hardie 2002a.1. See, especially, *Ars* 3.113ff.: *simplicitas rudis ante fuit* ("in the old days, there was crude simplicity") . . . *sed quia cultus adest* . . . ("yet because we live in the era of culture . . .").

6. See Watson 1982 on how, in refusing to accept in a straightforward way the moral idealism that condemns wealth, Ovid appears to stand Augustan moralizing on its head, or rather to draw out its apparent inconsistencies.

7. All translations are my own.

8. In *Epistulae Morales* 114, Seneca connects the cultivation of appearance in Imperial Rome with an interest in experimenting with language: "When prosperity has spread luxury far and wide, men began paying closer attention to their physical appearance . . . and once the mind has acquired the habit of scorning the usual things in life, regarding as mean that which was once customary, it begins to hunt for novelties in speech also: now it summons and displays obsolete and old-fashioned words, now it coins neologisms or misshapes words, now a bold and frequent metaphorical usage is made a special feature of style, according to the fashion that has just become prevalent" (114.9–11).

9. "luxuriantia compescet, nimis aspera sano / levabit cultu, virtute carentia tollet, / ludentis speciem dabit et torquebitur, ut qui / nunc Satyrum, nunc agrestem Cyclopa movetur," "He will prune away excess, smooth roughness with wholesome refinement, sweep away what lacks force, wear the look of being at play, and yet be tortured, just like a dancer who plays a Satyr, or a clownish Cyclops."

10. Especially given Ovid's advice on the fine line between elegance and overdoing it in *Ars* 3.129ff.: "vos quoque nec caris aures onerate lapillis, / quos legit in viridi decolor Indus aqua," "You, too, don't burden your ears with precious stones that the dark-skinned Indian gathers up from green water" (compare *Med.* 21–22: "induitis collo lapides oriente petitos, / et quantos onus est aure tulisse duos"). The woman who "wants, wants, wants" in *Medicamina* 18ff. has clearly not heeded Ovid's warning in *Ars* 3 and checked her reflection in the mirror before going out (*Ars* 3.136: *speculum consulate ante suum*). Again, our critical gaze functions as her missing looking glass, showing her how hideous she *really* looks.

11. See Downing 1999.249 n. 17.

12. See, for example, Plautus *Mostellaria* 274ff., Horace *Epode* 12.7–10, Martial 2.41.11–12, 9.37, Juvenal 6.457–73. These and other sources are catalogued by Rosati 1985.

13. As Bulloch 1985.130 notes, commenting on Callimachus's contrast of Athene with Aphrodite: "Aphrodite's coquettishness and mirror were an early feature" of the judgment of Paris. In Claudian, Venus's palace is literally a house of mirrors, so that *rapitur quocumque videt* ("She is captured wherever she looks,"

Nupt. Hon. 108). Juno, by contrast, does not wield or control a mirror (or her mirrored image).

.14. Cf. *Ars* 1.646: "in laqueos quos posuere, cadant," "Let them fall into the snare they themselves have laid"; 1.655–58: "neque enim lex aequior ulla est / quam necis artifices arte perire sua. / ergo ut periuras merito periuria fallant, / exemplo doleat femina laesa suo," "For there is no law more just, that the contrivers of death should perish by their own contrivances, so that perjurers deceive the perjured, as they deserve, and woman feels the wound she first inflicted."

15. Jane Harrison compares the Gorgon's head to primitive ritual masks (1903.187–88): "They are the natural agents of a religion of fear and 'riddance' ... the function of such masks is permanently to 'make an ugly face' *at* you if you are doing wrong, breaking your word, robbing your neighbour, meeting him in battle; *for* you if you are doing right."

16. Downing 1999 stresses the point that *Ars* 3 is, similarly, a systematic counterpoint to *Ars* 1 and 2.

17. For discussion of *Remedia Amoris* as a poem of seduction, see Sharrock 2002b.160–61; Sharrock also suggests here that the close way in which the *Remedia* participates in the discourse of the *Ars* has contributed to the poor critical appraisal of it in much modern reading ("it is 'more of the same,'" and presents itself as poetry *parvo discrimine*). This statement might equally apply to the *Medicamina*.

18. Medusa causes death-by-erection: the state of being petrified is a kind of priapism (as well as, paradoxically, a state of impotence). Ferenczi 1926 postulates, in addition to the idea that Medusa's snaky hair is a mass of castrated penises, that "the fearful and staring eyes of the Medusa head also have the secondary meaning of erection."

19. *Attonitus* ("astonished") is the adjective used to describe the effect of Medusa's snake-hair, worn as an image on Minerva's breast, in *Met.* 4.802 ("ut attonitos formidine terreat hostes").

20. While it highlights some basic contrasts, Downing's argument (1999.235) that, in the *Ars Amatoria*, men (in *Ars* 1 and 2) "mechanize" and replace their inner lives, whereas women (in *Ars* 3) "mechanize" and replace their superficial, surface appearance, oversimplifies the opposition of male and female in this text. Ovid's advice to men in the *Ars* is contradictory; at first (1.509), *forma viros neglecta decet*, "It's good for men to not obsess over looks," but at the same time, appearances, and the use of mirrors to attempt to control how one is seen, are just as crucial for men as they are for women.

21. In *Amores* 2.17.21–22, Ovid compares the unequal partnering of hexameter with pentameter to his relationship with Corinna, which he then likens to Vulcan's courtship of Venus (Vulcan also incarnates the uneven elegiac couplet since he walks with a limp): "carminis hoc ipsum genus inpar; sed tamen apte / iungitur herous cum breviore modo," "This kind of verse is itself unequal; and yet the heroic line is suitably joined to the shorter."

22. "Ad multas lupa tendit oves, praedetur ut unam, / et Iovis in multas devolat ales aves. / se quoque det populo mulier speciosa videndam," "The wolf draws near to many sheep so that she might prey on one, and Jupiter's eagle swoops down on many birds. So, too, the beautiful woman should offer herself to the people to be seen."

23. Irigaray 1974 argues that woman is the negative required by the male subject's "specularisation," and that Western philosophical discourse depends for its effect on its specularity, or self-reflexivity, and is incapable of representing femininity/woman as anything other than a negative of its own reflection.

24. As Plato observes in the *Sophist*, mirror images share with semblances of all kinds an ambiguous mixture of being and non-being (240a). McCarty 1989.162 comments: "The mirroring vision is precisely something that is *there* yet also *not there*, hence it challenges the mentality that thinks in terms of here and there, or self and non-self." It is "ontologically ambiguous as well as fascinating."

25. See Eur. *Or.*111f., Dion. Hal. *Ant. Rom.* 7.9, Diog. Laert. 7.17, Gellius *NA* 6.12.5, Juv. 2.99–101, Lucian *Pisc.* 45, Macrob. *Sat.* 3.13.4, Mart. 9.16, Sen. *Nat. Quaes.* 1.17.10 (this links the development of mirrors with vice generally).

26. E.g., *Ars* 1.613–14: "sibi quaeque videtur amanda; / pessima sit, nulli non sua forma placet," "Every woman thinks she's loveable, even if she's hideous. There is no woman who doesn't like the way she looks."

27. "Ergo age et iratae medicamina fortia praebe: / illa feri requiem sola doloris habent: / illa Machaonios superant medicamina sucos: / his, ubi peccaris, restituendus eris," "Come then, bring powerful medicines for an angry woman; they alone can suppress savage rage; those drugs surpass the juices of Machaon; when you've sinned, it is with these that you must be restored to favor" (*Ars* 2.489–92)

28. See Siebers 1983.11 and Ovid *Met.* 4.793–803; cf. Lucan 9.669–70. Note that the idea of reflection as a defense against and boomeranging of Medusa's power is conspicuously absent from early sixth- and fifth-century Greek representations (where Perseus simply looks away as he cuts off the head), but develops later and is emphasized particularly in Ovid and Lucan; see Gantz 1993.307. In art, Medusa's image ranges from extreme ugliness to serene beauty.

29. The same simile is used at *Ars* 3.231–32 ("aurea quae pendent ornato signa theatro, / inspice, contemnes: brattea ligna tegit," "Look closely at the images that hang all golden in the decorated theater and you'll think them worthless; foil covers up wood"). *Ars* 1.70 also refers to Rome's "marble-effect" architecture (*externo marmore dives opus*).

30. See Kaplan 1997 for discussion of the inseparability of the male/imperialist gaze in the history of Western culture.

31. A colonized woman is implicitly a *nigra terra* at *Med.* 8, while in the *Remedia Amoris*, calling your girl *nigra* when she is *fusca* is the perfect way to give offense and to make her seem ugly (327).

32. Barnes 1974.36. Pegasus is born from drops of blood from Medusa's severed head. Paglia 1990.51 draws attention to the parallel birth of the Furies, who, according to Hesiod, sprang from drops of blood falling to earth from Uranus's castration by his son Cronos—"cruel chthonian emanations of the soil"—and suggests that this "motif of seminal splashes" that recurs in Pegasus's birth hints at the Gorgon's half-maleness.

33. See Hardie 2002a.180–81 on Astyages' petrification.

34. *Ars* 3.219–20: "quae nunc nomen habent operosi signa Myronis / pondus iners quondam duraque massa fuit," "The statues of industrious Myron, which are now famous, were once a hard mass and lifeless weight." Downing 1999 reads Ovid's role in *Ars* 3 as an anti-Pygmalion, turning real women into artifacts.

35. E.g., *Met.* 10.247ff.: "interea niveum mira feliciter arte / sculpsit ebur formamque dedit," "Meanwhile, with wondrous art, he successfully carves a figure out of snowy ivory."

36. For further discussion of how "Narcissus' erotic delusion merges into artistic illusion" in Ovid, see Hardie 2002a, especially 143–72.

37. As Rosati notes (1985 ad loc.), *pendere* suggests a political-administrative metaphor; see Pliny 16.1.

38. The metaphor that associates woman with earth and sex with plowing is as old as Homer. For a recent summary, see Keith 2000.36–64 or Dougherty 1998, and du Bois 1988.39–85. It is also the metaphor used of aging women in particular in *Ars* 3 (e.g., *continua messe senescit ager*, "The field gets old with constant harvesting," 3.82).

39. Compare the passage at *Ars* 2.489ff., when Ovid advises men to treat an angry woman with *medicamina* that "surpass the juices of Machaon" ("illa Machaonios superant medicamina sucos"). Ovid's (poisonous, medicinal) juices are added to, or in competition with, hers. The warning not to trust mixtures of juices in *Med.* 37 ("nec vos graminibus nec mixto credite suco") might well read as a tip not to trust *medicamina* generally.

40. Aeschylus's *Eumenides* (52–54) pictures the eyes of the Gorgon dripping a foul ooze that Jane Harrison identifies with the Gorgon's petrifying power. Wilk 2000 argues that this element of Medusa's image (along with the protruding tongue, bloated round face, and separating hair) suggests a stylized representation of a newly decaying body. The Gorgon, in other words, provokes and embodies the fear of death—and of good looks gone to rot.

41. As Camille Paglia suggests (1990.47): "The Greek Gorgon was a kind of *vagina dentata*: in Archaic art, she is a grinning head with beard, tusks and outthrust tongue."

42. Paglia 1990.14; see also 48: "Woman's genital wound is a furrow in female earth. Snaky Medusa is the thorny undergrowth of nature's relentless fertility." As Downing 1999 on *Ars* 3 puts it: "It is the natural woman . . . who especially repulses" (241).

43. See also *Ars* 3.59 and the advice that follows: women are to be mindful of encroaching old age and live life today, for the years pass like flowing water and cannot be called back (cf. *Med.* 40: "nec redit in fontes unda supina suos," "Nor does the wave stream backwards to its font"). Yet later on in the book, they are told that old age can be cheated: Ovid works his magic, doing the equivalent of precisely that which he denies can be done—turning back rivers to their sources.

44. "Motus uterque parens nati rata verba biformis / fecit et incesto fontem medicamine tinxit," "His parents heard the prayer of their two-formed son and charged the waters with that uncanny power," *Met.* 4.387–88.

45. Cf. Medea in *Her.* 12.97: "ipsa ego, quae dederam medicamina," "I myself, who had given the charmed drug."

46. The Gorgon herself, in her gory death, may be said to incarnate or produce a *pharmakon-medicamen*, which befits her double, contradictory identity as a beautiful/ugly, creative/deadly creature. Apollodorus 3.10.3. narrates how Asclepius took blood from one of her veins to revive the dead, and from another to cause harm. Compare Zenobius *Cent.* 1.18. According to Euripides (*Ion* 999ff.), Pallas gave Erichthonius two drops of the Gorgon's blood: one a deadly poison, the other a powerful medicine for the healing of diseases.

47. "Anguibus exuitur tenui cum pelle vetustas, / nec faciunt cervos cornua iacta senes," "Serpents shrug off their age with their frail skins, nor are stags aged by casting off their horns," *Ars* 3.77–78.

48. This is, of course, spelt out in *Am.* 1.1.17–18 ("cum bene surrexit versu nova pagina primo / attenuat nervos proximus ille meos," "My new page of song rose well with the first verse in lofty mode, when the next one unmans my vigor").

49. Note that part of Actaeon's punishment is having to look at himself in the mirror when he has been metamorphosed ("ut vero vultus et cornua vidit in unda . . .," "But when he saw his features and his horns in a clear pool . . . ," 200), and the transformation is triggered when Diana throws water in his face, disturbing the reflective stillness of her pool.

50. Ovid's obsessive return to Narcissus performs a Mulveyan critique of the male gaze, turning it back upon itself, making it visible, and, at that moment, disturbing it. See, e.g., Mulvey 1989a.

51. See Persius 4.35–36 for the use of *bulbi* to mean "balls" and Adams 1982.183 on the use of *tero* to infer masturbation (see, especially, Priapea 83.34).

52. I'd like to thank Emily Gowers for offering extremely helpful comments on a draft of this essay.

The Lover as a Model Viewer

Gendered Dynamics in Propertius 1.3

Hérica Valladares

Propertius's visual imagination and subtle handling of myth in depicting everyday experience have often been noted by scholars. It is, then, not surprising that Elegy 1.3, a gem-like synthesis of Propertian characteristics, occupies a special place in the vast corpus of commentary on the poet's style and technique. The poem's conceit is quite simple: Propertius, returning home late one night, finds Cynthia asleep. Afraid of disturbing her rest and provoking her anger, the lover contents himself with gazing upon the sleeping beauty and compares her to a series of mythological heroines: Ariadne, Andromeda, and a Bacchante. But his voyeuristic pleasure is suddenly interrupted when, awakened by the light of the Moon, Cynthia usurps the role of narrator and inverts the tableaux sketched by him in an irate diatribe. The text's most obvious poetic model is Catullus 64, whose retelling of Ariadne's abandonment and divine rescue on the shores of Naxos becomes the frame through which Propertius's protagonists see and act out their own erotic drama. However, the fact that a number of first-century frescoes represent the moment of Theseus's desertion and Dionysus's arrival has led critics to search not only for the textual but also for the pictorial sources of Propertius's invention.

Latin love elegy is a deeply self-conscious literary genre. Not only do elegiac poets constantly allude to the conventions within which they are writing and to their debt to and/or difference from earlier authors, but the subject of their poems (ostensibly, the poet's love for his mistress) often serves a metaphorical function. Elegy is poetry about poetry and so, as many scholars argue, the poets' love affairs are a means for writing about writing: the mistress, in this case, being nothing more than text.[1] This method of carefully tracing literary resonances and borrowings informs most philologists' approaches to Elegy 1.3, and has been wittily summarized by James E. G. Zetzel with a succinct analogy. He explains the poem's indebtedness to Catullus 64 by describing Propertius and Cynthia as seemingly inept readers of Catullus's work, whose own relationship is on a par with that between the two texts (Zetzel 1996.86–91). And, indeed, there is no better simile for the Latin elegiac tradition as it has been represented by a great number of critics than the tense bond between two lovers that occasionally flares up with the predictable threat of separation.

Within this debate on the relationship between the poet's individual style and the conventions of Latin love poetry, the question of Propertius's "realism" presents a thorny problem for literary scholars. One of Propertius's most prominent stylistic traits is his use of mythological exempla. As Jean-Paul Boucher observed almost forty years ago, mythology is for Propertius far more than a narrative subject matter: it functions as a poetic means of expression through which he communicates his feelings, triggering in the reader a chain of associations and emotional responses. The poet's ability to evoke familiar characters from well-known, established stories as validation for his feelings and, paradoxically, as an assertion of their uniqueness has spurred long discussions on how he juxtaposes the conventional and the personal so that a convincing representation of lived experience emerges from the blend.[2] In the case of Elegy 1.3, this problem has been compounded by the possible allusion to contemporary works of art portraying the same mythological scenes mentioned in the text. Yet despite general agreement that Propertius is a visual poet and that his exempla recall pictorial compositions, current scholarship on this poem has failed to explore the parallel with the visual arts more profoundly. For instance, the implications of Propertius's choice to express emotions through visual comparisons and what these comparisons reveal of a first-century visual culture and aesthetics are questions that have yet to be addressed by scholars who remain, primarily, text bound.

What this essay offers, then, is a close reading of Propertius 1.3. But unlike most studies of this text, it pays great attention to the poet's references to the visual arts, seeing them as central to his construction of a compelling representation of the typical aspects of being in love. As the title indicates, my approach owes much to the work of Mikhail Bakhtin and Umberto Eco, who have trained us to see literary production as not just the fruit of an individual, isolated unconscious but as the result of a dialogue between members of a community that is inevitably colored by a number of cultural and historical facts (Bakhtin 1994.44–63). It is fair to say that, when writing love elegy, Latin poets had an ideal or Model Reader in mind, that is, a reader who would not only respond to the text's message according to the terms already determined by the work but also recognize those terms and appreciate the way in which they were made to convey meaning (Eco 1990.49–50, 55). In the case of Propertius 1.3, three interrelated codes inform the author's portrayal of a simple bedroom scene: first, of course, the conventions of elegiac love poetry; second, a notion of realism, going as far back as Aristotle, that prescribes an empathetic dynamic of identification as essential to the illusion of life-likeness; and, third, a characteristically Roman practice of describing and defining the present through references to Greek myth. Interwoven with these conventions is the evocation of well-known pictorial types, which serve as a shared visual vocabulary for depicting what is purported to be a subjective and intransferable experience.

Two questions are at the core of this analysis: how does Propertius manipulate pictorial models to express moods and experiences perceived to be ineffable? And what does he accomplish by making the act of gazing the central metaphor for the dynamics between the poem's lovers? It is significant that the entire sequence of *illustrationes* used by the narrator focuses on moments of suspended erotic action: it is a drama of enthrallment, not possession, that the images recalled by the poet represent. And while lingering might be seen as a typical elegiac form of action, I would argue that, in the context of 1.3, the choice of hanging back, of arresting narrative development at the moment of looking and longing is central to Propertius's strategies of realism.[3] More than a Model Reader, the author is here constructing a Model Viewer. And as s/he lets him/herself be drawn into the text, into the image, the Reader/Viewer comes to realize that s/he and the Lover are, essentially, one. For a Roman audience, this transformation of the reader into an elegiac *amator* would undoubtedly have carried strong generic connotations. As we will see, the lover's gradual surrender of power before his beloved is designed to provoke a similar and simultaneous surrender in the reader. It is, then, in this negotiation of the poet's and our own subjective positions in relation to the text and the object of desire that we finally recognize the truth in Propertius's amorous fiction.

Towards an Understanding of Propertius's Visual Culture

Two articles are the principal sources for the repeated statements that, in composing Elegy 1.3, Propertius had pictorial representations of myth in mind: Theodor Birt's study of the so-called Vatican Ariadne and Karl Keyssner's survey of references to the visual arts in the poet's oeuvre.[4] Birt's essay on what he calls the *Ariadnemotiv* tries to connect the poem to a strictly defined iconographic type, seeing the entire elegy as a commentary on this image (1895.43, 58). Keyssner, on the other hand, adopts a broader approach. For him, it is impossible to tie Propertius's exempla to secure pictorial sources. So his goal is not to prove the poet's knowledge of any single, specific work of art (a point that has escaped many later critics), but to show how he adapts a certain category of images, reworking them within the body of his texts. Although Keyssner offers a list of extant visual representations of the Ariadne myth, he insists that one should not expect accurate reproductions of any work of art in the texts of Propertius, since Propertius's *illustrationes* are a mix of myth and art, molded in each instance to evoke different moods and bring a scene to life.[5]

Jean-Paul Boucher has followed a similar line of argument. Like Keyssner, he stresses the synthetic, pastiche-like nature of Propertius's visual references and suggests that, because of the ubiquity of mythological images in antiquity, the mention of a gesture, a pose, even a small detail could easily call to mind a name, while a name could evoke pictorial associations with a force that we can hardly fathom (Boucher 1965.42, 266). The advantage of Boucher's and Keyssner's methods is that they allow us to imagine, based on the works of art we know, the kinds of images comprising the visual currency shared by poet and audience. It is true that most of these works, especially in the medium of wall painting, are dated to a period after Propertius's death and that a wide gamut of variation appears possible for each mythological type.[6] Yet it is also true that the mythological paintings of the later first century C.E. that have been compared to the poet's *imagines* belong to a venerable pictorial tradition harking back to classical Greek and Hellenistic prototypes and that these prototypes began to exert a greater, wider influence on Roman visual culture around the time he was composing his first book of elegies.[7]

Propertius's youth (he was born c. 50 B.C.E.) coincides with an important shift in the history of Roman art, particularly Roman painting. Since the second century B.C.E., masterpieces of Greek art had been filtering into Italy, especially into Rome, where they were often set up in temples and public porticoes—marks of the Roman triumph abroad, marvels to be wondered at by the populace. A great number of these works of art also entered the private collections of Roman aristocrats. But in the last decades of the first century B.C.E., under the direction of Augustus and Agrippa, there was a new push for the restitution of such treasures to the public eye. As Bettina Bergmann argues (1995.105–06), the emergence of a new style of painting circa 20 B.C.E., characterized by its focus on figurative representation often in the form of mythological subjects, may well have been connected to the elite's desire to circumvent Augustus and Agrippa's mandate by replacing their "lost" originals with copies done in fresco on the walls of their houses. Two results of this change are significant for our understanding of Propertius's *sensibilité visuel*, as Boucher would put it, and his expectations regarding the reader's ability to recognize pictorial references: first, the proliferation of mythological images in Roman public and private spaces during the last quarter of the first century B.C.E.; and second, the accompanying boom in creative reinterpretations of Greek masterpieces on the part of Roman artists.

Bergmann writes eloquently on the question of the diversity of Roman pictorial types associated with particular titles and/or artists and the difficulty of extracting a Greek "original" from these multiples. According to her, what mattered most for a Roman audience was not the work's fidelity to its model but the recognizability of the composition's signal value. Thus the variations one finds in representations of such popular subjects as Theseus abandoning Ariadne and Perseus and Andromeda should not be seen as indications of a lack of skill and precise knowledge of the "originals" but of the artists' talents as translators and interpreters of an inherited tradition. Far from being slavish, mechanical copyists, Roman artists approached the Greek classics as "handy building blocks." As they translated received types from one medium to another and combined elements from different compositions in a new work, well-known images became "artful quotations" intended to express cultural sophistication and elicit in viewers the pleasure of connoisseurship (Bergmann 1995.81, 94–98).

Still, even though no Roman painting is ever exactly like another, a few compositional elements remain constant in the mythological representations produced between circa 20 B.C.E. and 69 C.E. If we take, for instance, the depiction of the mythological episodes mentioned by Propertius in 1.3 as they appear on monuments such as the Portland Vase (fig. 1), the paintings from Livia's House on the Palatine (fig. 2), and a num-

Figure 1 Portland Vase, late first century B.C.E., British Museum (Photo: Hirmer Verlag).

ber of later variants (fig. 6), one common feature becomes immediately apparent: the prominent placement of a scantily clad or nude female figure at the heart of the composition. This fascination with nudity in first-century B.C.E. poetry and visual arts has been explained by Christine M. Havelock as reflecting the impact on the Roman imagination of the various types of female nudes that were then being invented and widely distributed. Nudity, she argues, was on everybody's mind.[8] Clearly, it remained so, and became an essential characteristic of how myths were portrayed and thought of, evoking each time an atmosphere of intimacy and sensuality. One should also notice that these images are constructed around a similar compositional structure: a central pair, with either one of the protagonists looking at the other's sleeping form or with the two looking at each another. I will argue, then, that Propertius, engaging in a game of mythological name-dropping, intended not only to recall cer-

Figure 2 Io, Argus, and Mercury, House of Livia, Palatine Hill, Rome, c. 30 B.C.E.
(Photo: Deutsches Archäologisches Institut, Rome).

tain iconographic features (nudity and the presence of a central pair of
protagonists) but also to remind the reader of a specific mode of viewing. Central to the poem is an analogy between the plight of the lover
and the emotional dynamics elicited by the experience of viewing works
of art. For a poet who thought of the eyes as the guides to love ("oculi
sunt in amore duces," 2.15.12), there could be no better paradigm for the
amorous experience than the longing provoked by the contemplation of
mythological idylls.

On the Power of Images and Realism

The power of images to provoke an emotional response in the
viewer had been a topic of philosophical debate since the fifth century
B.C.E. In an intentionally controversial apology for Helen's betrayal of

Figure 3 Polyphemus and Galatea, House of Livia, Palatine Hill, Rome, c. 30 B.C.E.
(Photo: Deutsches Archäologisches Institut, Rome).

Menelaus, the sophist Gorgias used an analogy with painting to explain
how it is characteristic of human nature to be deeply moved by the sight
of beautiful objects (*Encomium of Helen* 18–19):

> ἀλλὰ μὴν οἱ γραφεῖς ὅταν ἐκ πολλῶν χρωμάτων καὶ σωμάτων ἓν σῶμα καὶ
> σχῆμα τελείως ἀπεργάσωνται, τέρπουσαι τὴν ὄψιν· ἡ δὲ τῶν ἀνδρίαντων
> ποίησις καὶ ἡ τῶν ἀγαλμάτων ἐργασία ⟨ν⟩όσον ἡδεῖαν παρέσχετο τοῖς
> ὄμμασιν. οὕτω τὰ μὲν λυπεῖν τὰ δὲ ποθεῖν πέφυκε τὴν ὄψιν. πολλὰ δὲ
> πολλοῖς πολλῶν ἔρωτα καὶ πόθον ἐνεργάζεται πραγμάτων καὶ σωμάτων.
>
> εἰ οὖν τῶι τοῦ Ἀλεξάνδρου σώματι τὸ τῆς Ἑλένης ὄμμα ἡσθὲν
> προθυμίαν καὶ ἅμιλλαν. ἔρωτος τῆι ψυχῆι παρέδωκε, τί θαυμαστόν;

But painters delight our eyes whenever they represent, out of so many colors and bodies, one body and one form. And pleasant is the affliction that

the depiction of human figures and well-crafted statues provoke in our vision. Thus it is in the nature of some things to cause grief in the observer, and in that of others, desire. Indeed, there are many things that arouse love and desire for both deeds and bodies in many. Then is it any wonder that Helen's gaze, having taken delight in Alexander's body, produced yearning and eagerness for love in her soul?[9]

In pushing for a justification of Helen's behavior, Gorgias offers great insight into how the ancients perceived the relation between spectator and work of art. Integral to the delight painters offer to our eyes is not just the satisfaction of gazing upon the skillful arrangement of colors and forms, but also the experience of a pleasant affliction (⟨ν⟩όσον ἡδεῖαν) that may take the form of either grief or desire. Clearly, sight is a powerful sensory gateway, since the perceptions collected through it can affect us at our core: the soul (ψυχή), seat of the emotions and of reasoning. The type or subject of the images observed is, of course, what determines our reactions to them and whether our longing will be for bodies or deeds. So in a passage preceding the one quoted above (*Encomium of Helen* 16–17), Gorgias describes how the sight of arms and warriors may arouse fear in the spectator. But, interestingly, in all the examples he cites for proving the irresistible force of the emotions incited by vision, the encounter between viewer and object appears accidental. It is not until Aristotle that we find a consideration of the emotional dynamics elicited by the contemplation of a representation in a predetermined setting.

In the *Poetics*, Aristotle continues the discussion on the pleasure we derive from representation, μίμησις.[10] Although his treatise focuses primarily on tragedy, many of his observations could easily be applied to an analysis of the emotional reactions elicited by the visual arts. Indeed, in first addressing the problem of why it is that we experience pleasure (ἡδονή) from the depiction of sights and events that would be either painful or repulsive to us in everyday life, he relies on a comparison with the visual arts. For him, the pleasure of μίμησις lies essentially in the fact that it is through imitation that man first comes to an understanding of the world around him. As an effective pedagogical tool, μίμησις always carries with it the delight of learning, so that, when looking at a portrait, a viewer will feel pleasure in making the connection between the image and the subject, saying "this is he" (*Poetics* 4.1–5). Thus it is not a first-hand knowledge that μίμησις offers to the viewer but the confirmation of something apprehended previously through experience that is now made comprehensible through representation. The pleasure offered by μίμησις is, then, that of moving from the realm of unexamined occurrences to knowledge. This is why recognition (ἀναγνώρισις) is one of the essential elements of tragedy. Yet two types of recognition seem to be interconnected in Aristotle's description of ἀναγνώρισις: one is the protagonist's own process of understanding himself and his situation; the other is the spectator's recognition of a tragic type in the character on stage and the subsequent realization of that character's impending fate.[11] For the viewer, then, the painful realization (ἀναγνώρισις) experienced by a tragic character is a source of pleasure because, although his suffering is within the realm of the probable, it is always at a remove from reality: the character, unlike the viewer, is always a king or a hero (*Poetics* 11.2–5, 13.8–9).

The tragic character's experience is, therefore, always mimetic, since it is always possible for the viewer to analyze and interpret his suffering from a safe distance. Although Aristotle does not use the Greek term for recognition in this sense, I would argue that the pleasure of tragedy he describes depends on the viewer recognizing, or at least identifying himself with, the characters in the situation represented. That is why he insists that authors should construct their plots around events that have happened, and that, even if they do not use the best-known names from myth, the action of the drama should be within the realm of the probable, for what is possible is credible (*Poetics* 9.1–9). Yet it is essential that the distance between representation and reality be maintained, a point Aristotle drives home by drawing one more analogy with painting: just as the best portrait artists, when making a likeness, take care to capture an individual's distinctive qualities but depict them as more beautiful than in everyday life, so tragedians must create characters that are lifelike, yet greater than ordinary people.[12]

This model of projection and identification, resulting in an empathetic viewing on the part of the spectator, continued to hold sway over how the ancients thought of the dynamics elicited by representation and how they judged a work's realism for centuries after Aristotle. Granted, the word realism is one that must always be defined according to context, so that a general definition encompassing all the different media and genres in which works of art were produced during the five centuries separating Aristotle and Propertius might not only be inaccurate but simply not possible. Yet I would argue that certain expectations regarding how a work of art might hook the viewer into the desired dynamic of identification and projection remained pretty much unchanged during this period.

Writing on realism in Alexandrian poetry, Graham Zanker argues that the goal of Hellenistic poets was to bring representation "into the closest possible contact with the sensory, intellectual, and emotional experience" of their audience (1987.3–8, 14, 197–98). There were, of course, several ways in which this approximation might be achieved. Still the concern to relate art to experience, and the fundamental methods for achieving this approximation, are consistent with Aristotle's remarks in the *Poetics*. For instance, the Alexandrians' practice of evoking the theme of love—an emotion that all of us experience or wish to experience—as a way of relating representation to reality recalls Aristotle's suggestion that tragic plots involve individuals who are near or dear to one another so that pity and fear might be more effectively aroused as a result (*Poetics* 14.4–5). Furthermore, the frequent appeal to the sense of vision in Hellenistic texts and the Roman rhetoricians' exhortations that, when listening to a description (ekphrasis), the public should be turned into eyewitnesses through the skillful use of language are in line with Aristotle's admonition that tragic poets should not rely too heavily on spectacle: for although it may be effective, spectacle requires less skill than invoking horror and pathos through words alone.[13]

Enargeia, or the quality of pictorial vividness in a text, did not, however, limit itself to the translation of a visual experience into words. For the goal of *enargeia* was not simply to make viewers out of listeners but to transform them into involved spectators who not only saw in their mind's eye what was being described, but felt the same emotions that had been experienced by the original witnesses (Zanker 1987.41–42). So what we see is that, at least since the time of Aristotle, there was in antiquity a perception that a work of art, whether poetic or pictorial, was effective if it engaged the audience in an empathetic emotional response elicited by the vividness of the representation and the familiarity of the depicted situation. That the provocation of an empathetic response was both expected by ancient audiences and perceived to be a source of pleasure is clear from the commentators' remarks on how this effect should be achieved. The power of a work of art to produce an emotional response was, then, a mark of its greatness. It was also what made representation and reality relate to one another in the eyes of the spectator. In other words, it was what made it realistic.[14]

Two passages from different works produced during the Roman empire illustrate the value of this realism and offer a less broad frame within which to place Propertius's approach in Elegy 1.3. The first comes from Book 1 of Vergil's *Aeneid*—a work not too far in date from Propertius's

Monobiblos.[15] Upon arriving in Carthage, Aeneas sets out accompanied by a few men to reconnoiter. In their wanderings, they happen upon a grove where a temple to Juno has been recently built. On its bronze doors, Aeneas is surprised to find the representation of scenes from the Trojan War. His reactions to these images are poignantly described: he feeds (*pascit*, 464) his soul with the empty forms (*pictura . . . inani*, 464); he wets his face with a flood of tears (*largoque umectat flumine vultum*, 465); he moans and weeps as he recognizes each of his lost friends (*multa gemens*, 465; *agnoscit lacrimans*, 470), but most deeply at the sight of Priam ("tum vero ingentem gemitum dat pectore ab imo," 485); and, finally, he sees an image of himself amidst the fray (*se quoque . . . agnovit*, 488). The intense pathos of this scene lies in the way that Vergil cleverly manipulates the Aristotelian notion of recognition and the Hellenistic tradition of *enargeia*: Aeneas's emotional reaction to any depiction of war would have sufficed to fulfill the tragic mechanism of ἀναγνώρισις. However, because it is indeed his own life that Aeneas sees represented before him, the poignancy of the recognition is intensified: unlike the reader, the hero is not granted any distance between representation and experience. His action of viewing the bronze doors corresponds to the reader's mental viewing of this work of art through Vergil's vivid description; and his tearful reaction to these images becomes a model for the reader's response: a model easily adopted since it mirrored contemporary practice (Aeneas reacts to works of art as a first-century Roman would) and placed the reader between two very familiar *corpora* of myths, forcing him/her to complete the tableau by recalling episodes from the Homeric epics and Roman mythological history.

The *locus classicus* of this model of what I would call empathetic realism is, however, an oft-cited passage from Plutarch's *Life of Brutus*. Written in the late first to early second century C.E, Plutarch's text is a significant successor of the tradition we have been tracing. In one of the most touching moments of his account of the tyrannicide's life, Plutarch describes how Porcia, Brutus's wife, as she was about to return from Greece without her husband, grew into the habit of visiting a gallery of paintings several times a day. In this gallery, there was a painting of Hector's adieu to Andromache that, according to the historian, presented to Porcia an image of her own suffering (ἡ τοῦ πάθους εἰκών), causing her to weep before it every time. On one of these occasions, a friend of the couple, Acilius, is said to have recited the corresponding lines from Homer (*Iliad* 6.429ff.). But as he finished doing so, Brutus amended his friend's literary reference by saying that he would never instruct his wife to occupy herself solely with domestic tasks (*Brutus* 23.2–6). For Paul Zanker (1999.41), the two phenomena described in this text are anachronistically juxtaposed: while the recognition of a specific, often personal, situation in a mythological scene was an ancient form of behavior, the fictional dialogue between the two men is representative of an interpretive practice characteristic of the late republican and early imperial Roman elite, namely the habit of articulating their own current concerns through episodes from Greek myth. If so, Plutarch, like Vergil before him, is intensifying the poignancy of his narrative by presenting the reader with a layered form of realism: first, he describes a domestic situation one might easily relate to: the impending separation of two spouses. Then he describes Porcia's reaction to a work of art, wherein she sees a depiction of her own suffering. Because this reaction is not dissimilar from that which the reader might experience in real life, Porcia's response to the painting becomes a mirror for the reader's own response to her story. Finally, Plutarch includes the commentary of the two men who explain Porcia's response by relating representation and experience through the medium of a literary citation—an addition that anticipates what the reader him/herself might do in relation to *his* text by referring to a contemporary cultural practice.

So let us return to the problem of Propertius's realism in Elegy 1.3. Most analyses focus on his use of mythological exempla and his debt to other poets, seeing these as either complementary or antithetical to the project of composing love elegy in a personal, persuasively lifelike voice. Even when critics try to take into account possible references to contemporary works of art, such considerations are peripheral to their discussion of poetic technique and style. In one of the most lucid studies of the problem of Propertian realism, Archibald W. Allen proposes that we look at it through Quintilian's concept of *fides*. Latin *fides* has both a subjective and an objective element: in one case, it may be translated as "sincerity" and, in the other, as "persuasiveness." But if one speaks of a writer's or an orator's *fides*, the word may indicate "the impression of sincerity resulting from persuasiveness." In ancient criticism, then, sincerity "involves a relation between the artist and the public . . . The personality of the artist, except as it appears to the public in the work of art, is irrelevant to the question of sincerity" (Allen 1962.109–10). Artistic *fides*, then, is the result of the manipulation of recognized conventions. Although Allen limits his study to the literary conventions that contribute to Propertius's effect of sincerity, his model is a useful one for thinking about the role of images or references to the visual arts in Elegy

1.3. It is not just the pictorial resemblance between the poet's mythological parallels and the visual representations of these episodes that would have lent the former a gloss of realism. More importantly, it was the conventions of viewing works of art and emotionally responding to them that made Propertius's sustained visual simile a convincing device, making the expression of his feelings for Cynthia appear truly sincere.

Talis—Qualis

Qualis Thesea iacuit cedente carina
    languida desertis Cnosia litoribus;
qualis et accubuit primo Cepheia somno
    libera iam duris cotibus Andromede;
nec minus assiduis Edonis fessa choreis   5
    qualis in herboso concidit Apidano:
talis visa mihi mollem spirare quietem
    Cynthia non certis nixa caput manibus,
ebria cum multo traherem vestigia Baccho,
    et quaterent sera nocte facem pueri.   10

Like Cnossian Ariadne, as she lay languid on a deserted shore while Theseus's ship sailed away in the distance; and like Cepheus's daughter, Andromeda, as she lay in her first sleep, just then set free from hard rocks; and no less like a Thracian maenad who, exhausted from the ceaseless dances, collapsed on the grassy banks of the Apidanus, so Cynthia seemed to me to breathe soft quiet, her head resting on unsteady hands, when I came dragging my feet, drunk with much wine, and the slave boys shook out their torches late at night.[16]

Undoubtedly, the most commented-on feature of Propertius 1.3 is the triad of similes in the poem's opening couplets. The witty originality of the structure merited parodying by Propertius's closest, most critical reader, Ovid (see *Amores* 1.10.1–6). But while Ovid used the evocation of mythological heroines (Helen, Leda, and Amymone) to illustrate Corinna's peerless beauty, Propertius uses his exempla in a far more subtle way: the names are intended to recall pictorial associations through which the reader could both visualize an otherwise unknown and unseen woman and immediately learn the nature of the relationship between the two protagonists—at least as that relationship is initially perceived by Propertius upon his drunken entrance. The assignment of roles is clear from the very beginning: Cynthia is Ariadne (verse 2) and Propertius is Bacchus (verse 9). So why stretch the comparison as he does? If he

Figure 4 Bacchus and Ariadne on Naxos, House of the Citharist, Pompeii, after 62 C.E., (Photo by Alinari: Art Resource, N.Y.).

wanted his reader to think of visual representations of a hero gazing upon the sleeping form of a scantily clad woman, would not just one such example have sufficed?

As has often been noted, the motifs of Bacchus finding Ariadne and that of a sleeping maenad about to be "discovered" by a male "passerby" were frequently represented in Roman art. Two paintings from the House of the Citharist, (I4, 25; figs. 4 and 5), although several decades later than the poem, give us an idea of the compositions Propertius might have had in mind.[17] The image of the inebriated god of wine, followed by a tumultuous thiasos, as he happens upon the recumbent maiden and falls in love with her, closely corresponds to Propertius's description of himself returning home accompanied by a cortege of torch-bearing slaves (Curran 1996.196). The Pompeian painting's composition, a popular type in the first centuries B.C.E. and C.E., had a long iconographic pedigree, possibly going back to a Greek, fifth-century panel described

Figure 5 Sleeping Maenad, House of the Citharist, Pompeii, after 62 C.E. (Photo by Erich Lessing: Art Resource, N.Y.).

by Pausanias as hanging in the temple of Dionysus in Athens.[18] But in Roman times, the two episodes described by Pausanias as having been represented in the same painting—Theseus's abandonment and Dionysus's arrival—were depicted separately by artists who transformed a continuous visual narrative into the depiction of isolated moments (Badoni 1990). Their emphasis on the moment is significant: by either blocking out or relegating to a secondary position the other stages of a well-known narrative sequence, the Roman tableaux of Dionysus and Ariadne dramatize the instant of the *coup de foudre*. It is through vision that the god is captivated. And although it may be argued that the amorous gaze is often a prelude to possession, nothing in the paintings of Dionysus finding Ariadne or of similar scenes involving satyrs and maenads confirms that this will occur. Fascination, not possession, is the true subject of these images.[19]

It is, then, within this pictorial paradigm of representations of enthrallment that we must imagine the painting of a sleeping Andromeda referred to in the second couplet (3–4). No work of art has been found depicting this moment in Andromeda's story, when, after her liberation, she rests under Perseus's desirous gaze. There is, however, no need to think that Propertius's words describe a lost masterpiece.[20] It is quite possible that he is here inventing a composition that could be easily visualized by his audience, especially since it was intended to fit into a triad whose uniting iconographic motif is that of a sleeping, seductively disrobed woman being watched by an avid admirer ("talis visa mihi mollem spirare quietem," 7).[21] Still the poet's choice of subject for his imaginary painting is a significant one: the mention of Andromeda asleep brings to mind a domestic setting. No longer bound to the rocks, Cepheus's daughter has been brought back to the comforts of the royal palace. The sensuality of the framing comparisons: *iacuit* (1), *languida* (2), and *fessa* (5)—words with strong sexual overtones—is sustained by the choice of the verb *accubuit* that also carries an erotic charge (Baker 1980.250). As Leo Curran suggests, the moment of Perseus's discovery of Andromeda and that of their wedding night are here boldly fused together.[22] Yet unlike the example of Ariadne and the Bacchante, that of Andromeda appears to locate the scene of enthrallment in a bedroom. This implication of a domestic setting forces the reader's mind away from distant Naxos and Apidanus back to the home, to the familiar.[23] Without leaving the structure of the priamel, Propertius brings myth and everyday life close together by evoking the space of a *cubiculum* as the setting for seduction—of Andromeda by Perseus and of Cynthia by the poet himself. Thus he elevates the *cubiculum* to mythical grandeur by making it the backdrop of a conquest worthy of vigorous gods and heroes.

One motif, three pairs of mythological lovers; should we suppose that the images evoked were identical, differing only in the set of characters represented? As the paintings from Pompeii mentioned above make clear, most certainly not. Boucher proposes that we see the evocation of different images in the three examples as a mark of the passage of time: while a love-struck Propertius stands at the threshold of action, Cynthia moves on the bed, taking on different poses (1965.54). It is a nice idea. Yet it is his comment on the inherent, peculiar logic of images that comes closest, I believe, to the poet's intentions in coining the initial triad of mythological similes. Boucher writes (1965.63):

> Les images n'ont pas l'enchaînement logique des idées: elles disposent d'unecertaine autonomie par rapport à celles-ci et possèdent des liens avec

d'autres images, et ainsi une puissance d'évocation qui a plus de lien avec la sensibilité qu'avec la logique. Aux grandes explosions de sensibilité corre-spond un déchaînement de l'imagination, une libération d'images qui s'ap-pellent par similitude ou par contraste. On aboutira donc dans certains cas à une composition par images successives, symboliquement identiques ou contraires.

Images do not follow the logical sequence of ideas: they enjoy a certain au-tonomy in relation to them and are linked to other images, so that their power of allusion is more closely connected to sensibility than to logic. To these great outbursts of sensibility corresponds a triggering of the imagi-nation, a liberation of images that recall one another through either simil-itude or contrast. In some cases, one will arrive at a composition through successive images, either symbolically identical or symbolically dissimilar to one another. (The translation is my own.)

Indeed, it is precisely an unchaining of the imagination that Proper-tius wants to trigger in the reader as he uses each image not only to em-phasize a similar theme but to comment on it and offer a different nuance of meaning each time. So in the first series of exempla, the poet compares his beloved to three ravishing, vulnerable beauties, casting himself first as Bacchus, then as Perseus, and finally as a third character who might be either a satyr or Pentheus. These two last interpretive possibilities open up the comparison to two different denouements, both of which point to the lover's disappointment at the end of the poem. If we see Propertius in the guise of a satyr, then the final simile implies that his discovery of the sleeping Cynthia will result in risible sexual frustration. Such is the case with Pan who, in a miniature of the Apollo and Daphne saga, pursues Syrinx only to embrace an armful of reeds without even having the chance to say who he is or speak of love; and also with Faunus who, misled by Hercules' and Omphale's exchanged finery, climbs into the wrong bed, is violently repulsed, and winds up a laughingstock.[24] But if we understand the maenad's admirer to be the Theban prince, then this last parallel foreshadows Cynthia's furious accusations and Propertius's quasi-tragic transformation from heroic conqueror to shattered lover.[25]

In any case, the structure of associations, based as it is on similari-ties and contrasts, is exactly that underlying the arrangement of mytho-logical panels on the walls of Roman houses. As Richard Brilliant and Bettina Bergmann show, this allusive technique is common to both poems and paintings of the first centuries B.C.E. and C.E.[26] And by invoking interconnected modes of viewing and metaphorical thinking, the poet brings his creation even closer to the reader's experience. From this point on, the comparison between the intimate, mundane experience of watching one's beloved sleep and that of standing in a *pinacotheca* and viewing works of art will inform the reader's perception of Propertius's narrative. And this comparison between *cubiculum* and *pinacotheca* is one of the most effective ways in which the poet appeals to convention to represent the personal most faithfully.

Io and Argus

hanc ego, nondum etiam sensus deperditus omnis,
    molliter impresso conor adire toro;
et quamvis duplici correptum ardore iuberent
    hac Amor hac Liber, durus uterque deus,
subiecto leviter positam temptare lacerto   15
    osculaque admota sumere [et arma] manu,
non tamen ausus eram dominae turbare quietem,
    expertae metuens iurgia saevitiae;
sed sic intentis haerebam fixus ocellis,
    Argus ut ignotis cornibus Inachidos.   20

I had not yet lost all my senses and, pressing softly on the couch, I tried to approach her. Although I was seized by a double flame, and Love and Bacchus, both harsh gods, were ordering me on this side and that to make an attempt on her as she lay there and, by slipping an arm gently beneath her, to lay my hands on Cynthia and steal kisses, still I did not dare disturb my lady's sleep, fearing the castigation of her well-known fierceness. Instead, I stood transfixed, my eyes stuck on her like Argus on the strange horns of Io.

In the next segment of the poem, the confident Bacchus of the priamel, who confesses to be burning with desire (13: *correptum ardore*, a Catullan echo),[27] is suddenly frozen in his tracks. Afraid of igniting his mistress's wrath (17–18), Propertius gives up on his attempt to approach her (12, 15–16). From this point on, watching is all he will do. Gazing, then, will be his only pleasure, and the static distance between himself and Cynthia the only trace of his longing.

The first mythological parallel that follows his change from potential ravisher to fearful sentinel is a rather unusual one. Describing both how his eyes are fixed upon his beloved and how he has been transfixed by her beauty, Propertius compares himself to Argus (19–20). Although the fierce monster of a thousand eyes is an astonishing comparison, the

Figure 6 Io and Argus, House of Meleager, Pompeii, after 62 C.E. (Photo: Soprintendenza Archeologica di Napoli e Caserta).

meaning of this exemplum is clear: Argus's intent gazing, traditionally a surrogate of Hera's own jealous watching, has been transformed into the fascinated stare of a lover. As R. O. A. M. Lyne points out, the choice of *fixus* to characterize Propertius's stance (19) is indicative of the amatory tone of the simile. The verb *figo* is commonly used to express the act of piercing through something, as when Cupid's arrows pierce through or transfix his victims. Moreover, the word *ocellus* is redolent of love poetry, so that the juxtaposition of *fixus* and *intentis ocellis* leads to an intensification of meaning that leaves the reader no doubt that what is being described is a fixed, amorous gaze.[28] Confronted with the new, strange vision of Inachus's horned daughter, Argus is now bound to Io not because of the decrees of an angry goddess but because of her own irresistible charms.[29] To our surprise, this unlikely romance is the subject of a number of paintings.[30] The earliest example, a panel from the House of Livia on the Palatine now rather damaged but preserved in a drawing (fig. 2), already shows Io in what will become her standard form in later Pompeian works: she is a young maiden, bearing diadem-like little horns, whose dress has seductively slipped off one shoulder (cf. fig. 6).[31] Argus's pose and placement in the composition vary a little in each instance, but in all the surviving examples, he is portrayed as a youthful hero.

As with the paintings evoked in verses 1–6, the settings in which the paintings of Io and Argus were found exploited the polysemic potential of the image through provocative combinations of pendants. In the House of Livia, for instance, where the panel of Io and Argus appeared in the same room as a panel of the young Polyphemus venturing into the sea for the sake of lovely Galatea (fig. 3), the works showed monstrous lovers (not so monstrously portrayed), comically in love, and incapable of physically traversing the distance separating them from the objects of their desire. In the House of Meleager (Pompeii VI 9, 2), on the other hand, the composition gained a more salacious tone, as it "hung" across the room from a painting of Mars and Venus being undressed by *amorini* in preparation, one imagines, for a lamp-lit "battle" (fig. 7).[32] Clearly, one is meant to see a correspondence between Io and Argus's exchange of glances and Mars and Venus's intimate embrace. And just as Mars has been disarmed, so has Argus been rendered harmless by *amor*. Yet the message of love's triumph is dimmed in both cases by our knowledge of the stories' inevitable outcome: Argus will be killed; Mars and Venus entrapped and ridiculed.

It is possible, then, that Propertius, by invoking this pictorial parallel, intended to recall not only the essential elements of an iconographic type (an enticingly disrobed woman being watched by a petrified voyeur), but also to unchain symbolic associations familiar to the reader from the experience of seeing such paintings in conjunction with others. In the context of Elegy 1.3, the poet's comparison to Argus carries the gamut of meanings described above: he, too, is a melancholically humorous *amator*, frozen in place, for whom the gaze has become the primary locus of eroticism and sole source of pleasure. But as a pendant to the tableau of Bacchus, Argus serves to counterbalance Propertius's initial overconfidence, stressing the ambiguous power of the gaze: the cause of enchantment, briefly perceived as a prelude to possession, is now shown definitely to be the source of an enervating fascination. After all, the one and only thing Argus can do is watch. As Curran puts it: "In spite of the constant proximity, indeed intimacy, the relationship of Io and Argus is nothing but one long unreciprocal confrontation of watcher and watched, nothing but the mere process of gazing and being gazed at" (1996.204). This last exemplum thus demonstrates vision's contradictory effects as it shifts power from the subject to the object of desire. Yet in the full/empty space of the gaze, the promise of fulfillment is kept safe—at least, for a while.

In the next section of the poem, Propertius dares to move closer to Cynthia; gently, he crowns her with garlands, arranges her disheveled hair, places an offering of apples in her hands—gifts that, sooner or later,

Figure 7 Mars and Venus, House of Meleager, Pompeii, after 62 C.E. (Photo: Soprintendenza Archeologica di Napoli e Caserta).

roll off her inert body as if from that of a sculpted, inanimate maiden (21–26). The ponderous use of imperfects in verses 19–24 (*haerebam, solvebam, ponebam, gaudebam*), the anaphora (*et modo . . . et modo*, 21, 23), and the epanalepsis (*munera . . . munera*, 25–26) all indicate the slow, heavy passing of time (Curran 1996.203). But what is the point of this passage? One way to read it is to see Propertius playing the role of artist, a Pygmalion *avant la lettre*, who literally turns the sleeping Cynthia into *materia* for his fantasies.[33] Another possibility is to see him as a timid, overly cautious worshipper who gingerly approaches the image of a goddess. Or even as a paradigmatic elegiac lover who, with a growing sense of impotence and isolation, approaches the unconscious, unresponsive beloved as he would the closed, unfeeling gates of her house upon which he leaves traces of his *paraklausithyron*.[34] This new description of Cynthia's simultaneous proximity and inaccessibility reverberates with the earlier *illustratio* of Argus. Nor is the power of vision to provoke strong emotional responses in the observer at all diminished here. Indeed, Propertius describes how he is dumbstruck (*obstupui*, 28) every time Cynthia draws a deeper breath and seems by her movements to be on the verge of waking up (27–28).

But there is another fear that informs Propertius's reactions to Cynthia's rare, occasional movements: the fear that she may be having nightmares and that, in these nightmares, she may be dreaming that she is being raped by another man (29–30). Curran sees the poet's description of Cynthia's possible dreams as a perverse projection of his own earlier intentions. Yet reintroduced at this point in the poem, the image of a divine or semi-divine ravisher of nymphs appears as a bitterly ironic comparison to the passive lover. Incapable of performing the traditional role of the conqueror, he can neither play the maiden's rescuer nor preserve her from being desired and even possessed by another.[35] Once the source of an attenuated pleasure, the spectacle of Cynthia's sleep is now darkened by the lover's feeling of uncertainty and jealousy. At the same time, his fantasies about what his beloved may be dreaming shows a degree of empathetic projection that echoes the ancient notions of realism discussed above: Propertius oscillates between being a character in a representation, the male protagonist of a mythological couple, and an observer who has become entangled in the emotional dynamics of viewing a work of art, Cynthia. And, at the peak of his distress, as he shifts from the status of dramatis persona to that of spectator, Propertius begins to fear that the bittersweet pleasure of gazing is not his alone as he discovers a new rival: the Moon.

The Moon

donec diversas praecurrens luna fenestras,
    luna moraturis sedula luminibus,
compositos levibus radiis patefecit ocellos.   33

Until the Moon, rushing past the opposite windows—the meddlesome Moon with light that would linger—opened your closed eyes with gentle rays.

The mythical parallel with Selene is the most symbolically complex of Propertius's analogies. On the one hand, the Moon is just the moon: the source of the patches of light that, in the words of R. J. Baker, have moved "inch by flickering inch" across the space of the room. Because the Moon and its projected light seem to travel in opposite directions, Propertius describes the latter as lingering (*moraturis . . . luminibus*, 32). But *lumina* may, of course, be also understood as "eyes."[36] In that case, the Moon is a potential competitor who, unwilling to part from Cynthia, a new, female, Endymion, looks longingly back as she moves along her path (*praecurrens luna*, 31). So instead of the benevolent ἐπίσκοπος of

Figure 8 Selene and Endymion, House of the Ara Massima, Pompeii, after 62 C.E. (Photo by the author).

Hellenistic epigrams, she becomes *luna sedula* (32): an officious, intruding presence who eventually disrupts Propertius's gazing by rousing Cynthia.[37] Perhaps here, too, the poet has been influenced by familiar representations of the myth. In a common compositional formula such as we see in an example from the House of the Ara Massima in Pompeii (VI 16, 15; fig. 8), the goddess tiptoes towards the sleeping shepherd, who is shown reclining, seductively disrobed—a beautiful object for *her* gaze. In formal terms, this iconography closely resembles that of Dionysus finding Ariadne. What to make, then, of this visible reversal of gender roles, especially if we take the Moon to be another parallel for Propertius?

In Catullus 68.135–41, we encounter a similar act of "cross-dressing," where the poet compares himself to Hera: if Lesbia, like Jupiter, is unfaithful, then Catullus, like the Olympian spouse, must endure her misdemeanors. Thus gender and hierarchy are used to illustrate the poet's helplessness. Of course, Selene's gender and divine nature are also important elements in Propertius's lunar exemplum. But while Catullus blurs the difference between mortals and immortals without truly problematizing that between genders (i.e., the supremacy of the male deity remains unquestioned by the poet's identification with a goddess), Propertius destabilizes both boundaries. In 1.3, what is being expressed is not just the lover's degree of demasculinization but the leveling force of desire as it shifts power from the gazing subject to the dormant object, temporarily blurring strictly defined gender roles.

Propertius's choice of Selene as an exemplum points to his interest in exploring the instability of gender boundaries more profoundly than his predecessor. After all, the myth of her love for Endymion contains in itself a dual inversion of established hierarchies. As Eva Stehle puts it (1990.94):

> The pairing of a goddess and a human man poses, within Greek [and, one might add, Roman] hegemonic discourse, an irreconcilable conflict between the two established hierarchies, the hierarchy of male and female and that of divine and human. In human relations, the female is "tamed" by sexual intercourse, and the subordinate position is identified with the female one. But in divine-human relations the human is subordinate to divine desire. Sexual intimacy between a human male and a goddess is therefore impossible to think in simple terms because the relative status of the two cannot be determined. The relationship must be adjusted somehow to make it conceivable.

What usually makes the desire of a goddess for a young man conceivable in ancient narratives is the suspension of sexual fulfillment. Unlike the encounters between male gods and their human beloveds, which invariably result in conquest and impregnation, the mortal paramours of goddesses are fated to a perpetual state of listlessness. With very few exceptions, the young men are said to be enclosed in a faraway place, forever sleeping (Endymion), aging without dying (Tithonos), or breathing their last (Adonis).[38] Thus Selene is a very fitting parallel for the elegiac lover who can do nothing more than watch over his beloved's sleep, and who, like her, has been displaced from a traditional position of power to fall into a generic and hierarchical conundrum. If, on the one hand, the goddess is masculinized by her role as the active, desiring subject, this masculinization is strongly countered by the impossibility of fulfillment and the mortal nature of her love object. Propertius, then, in comparing himself to Selene, is doubly feminized. For he not only "puts on" the feminine garb of a goddess (as had Catullus), he also describes the temporary suspension of erotic action as a kind of castration that prevents him from performing the one act that would define him as a man. The lack of resolution implied by Selene's narrative makes Propertius's "cross-dressing" even more radical than that of Catullus because it implies more than a

Figure 9 Bacchante and Ariadne (?), House of the Ara Massima, Pompeii, after 62 c.e. (Photo by the author).

simple reversal of gender roles, it suggests that admiring subjection and unsatisfied longing are the common lot of all those who desire—whether man or woman, whether god or mortal.

Yet Propertius's comparison to Selene carries with it another, even more daring implication. It invites the reader to imagine lesbian desire. For not only is the feminized poet like a woman desiring another woman, Selene herself is described as giving up her love for a young man to lust after Cynthia. It is significant that Roman male poets think of female homoeroticism in the same terms as those used to describe men's desire for either women or other men. Passages such as these few verses in Elegy 1.3 and Ovid's longer exploration of the topic in his account of the myth of Iphis in the *Metamorphoses* were certainly not intended as genuine attempts to understand lesbian love.[39] Quite the contrary; these texts betray a rather prurient fascination with lesbianism, turning this "deviant" sexuality into an element of titillation. And it is possible that it was an interest in the perceived exoticism of such a liaison that inspired the artist(s) of the House of the Ara Massima to place the painting of a maenad who approaches a sleeping woman (fig. 9), a composition similar to those of Dionysus's arrival on Naxos, as a pendant for the image of Endymion and Selene discussed above (fig. 8). Thus in texts and images, the elegiac game of gender bending role-reversal unfolds, expanding the range of parts to be played by the lover beyond the usual dichotomies between male versus female, active versus passive, and subject versus object.

Besides serving as a reminder of the generic flexibility of mythical models, this lunar parallel also points to the reader's position as someone who looks into this bedroom drama as if onto a painting. Let us go back once more to the Moon's *lumina* in verse 32. It is very possible that, in writing these lines, Propertius was inspired by an epigram of Philodemus that insinuates that the Moon shines because she is inflamed with love (*A.P.* 5.123). If so, Propertius has taken the connection between light and desire a step further by linking the ancient metaphor of love as an internal fire and the image of the eye as a lantern whose cone-shaped stream of light made objects visible.[40] Thus the Moon who, with her enamored eye, illuminates Cynthia's room is a proxy for the reader—a reader who, by following the poet's example, has become a viewer of mythological tableaux representing the typical and essential aspects of being in love. But if the power of looking upon this text, this work of art, from an objective position lies ultimately with us, the spectators, Propertius implies that we are not entirely safe from being affected by this seemingly passive object. Following the logic of the poem's example, we are led to conclude that, if we see, it is because an object has triggered our vision. In the case of Propertius and the Moon, it is desire for Cynthia that makes them burn and gaze. But in the case of the reader, what entices him/her to keep his/her eyes on the page?

Cynthia's Ariadne

sic ait in molli fixa toro cubitum:
"tandem te nostro referens iniuria lecto   35
    alterius clausis expulit e foribus?
namque ubi longa meae consumpsti tempora noctis,
    languidus exactis, ei mihi, sideribus?
o utinam talis perducas, improbe, noctes,
    me miseram qualis semper habere iubes!   40
nam modo purpureo fallebam stamine somnum,
    rursus et Orpheae carmine, fessa, lyrae;
interdum leviter mecum deserta querebar
    externo longas saepe in amore moras:
dum me iucundis lapsam sopor impulit alis.   45
    illa fuit lacrimis ultima cura meis."

And then, having set her elbow on the soft couch, she said: "So, at last, has another's scorn brought you back to my bed, having driven you out and shut the doors on your face? Where have you spent the long hours of my night, limp, alas for me, now that the stars have put out their fires? May you, scoundrel, endure such nights as you always condemn wretched me to have! For just now I was trying to deceive slumber by spinning purple thread, and then, though exhausted, with a song of Orpheus's lyre. Meanwhile, all alone, I softly bemoaned to myself your long delays, often in an illicit love: until Sleep stroked my weary body with pleasant wings. That was my tears' last care."

The Moon's lingering rays finally rouse Cynthia from slumber (33). And there is something rather disquieting about this coming-to-life (or, at least, consciousness) of a woman who has been, up to now, almost as still as a statue. It is as if the realism of the representation and its concomitant dynamic of identification between viewer and object had been taken just a little too far. Another comparison with Ovid makes clear Propertius's intention of not attenuating the shock of this bizarre turn of events. In Book 10 of the *Metamorphoses*, when Pygmalion's ivory maiden is finally transformed into a woman of flesh and bone, the strangeness of the situation is offset by the sweetness of the girl's reaction. Awakened by the artist's kisses, the maiden blushes and timidly lifts up her eyes ("erubuit timidumque ad lumina lumen / atollens," 293–94) to see at once the sky and her lover for the first time ("pariter cum caelo vidit amantem," 294).[41] Nothing could be farther from Cynthia's angry awakening, as she sits up on the bed to engage immediately in a violent denunciation of Propertius.

For many scholars, her irate performance is the cause of great frustration. To them, her behavior seems stereotypically shrewish: a harsh contrast between mythical ideal and unpleasant reality, which puts an end to Propertius's tender, idyllic musings (Lyne 1970.61). Although Cynthia may be shrewish, her protestation is hardly a simple comparison between myth and reality. Her final "lament" not only evokes several of the same images mentioned earlier by Propertius, it also mirrors his own words, so that she effectively turns his metaphors against him. Her first charge against Propertius—that he has come back to her after having been shut out from another woman's house (35–38)—is, of course, an evocation of the elegiac *exclusus amator*. But as Lyne points out, her use of *languidus* in verse 38, intensified as it is by *exactis sideribus* ("extinguished stars"), implies that Propertius has actually returned to her in an

Figure 10 Ariadne on Naxos, House of the Vettii, Pompeii, after 62 C.E. (Photo by the author).

"advanced state of sexual exhaustion" (1970.77). From Cynthia's point of view, whatever may have happened between him and this presumed girl-friend, Propertius has only come home after spending the night in the arms of another. Thus *languidus* and *exactis sideribus* both recall and in-vert the meaning of *languida* (2) and *sera nocte* (10) in the opening cou-plets, where the adjective, applied then to Cynthia, evoked a state of se-ductive frailty and abandonment, while the temporal expression held the promise of erotic dalliance. Similarly, *fessa* in verse 42 echoes the use of the same adjective in verse 5. But while, in its first occurrence, the word describes the ecstatic exhaustion of a Bacchante after a trance, Cynthia's *fessa* depicts a state of domestic solitude: like Penelope and faithful Roman wives, she has passed the time spinning (41), fighting off sleep (*somnum*, 41; cf. *somno*, 3), waiting for Propertius. Finally, the mention of her *Orphea lyra* (42) implies that, like the prototypical love poet, she has attempted to sublimate the pain of desertion through song. And by referring to this last attribute, she effectively usurps the role of *vates* and claims control of the text.[42]

It is, however, with Ariadne that Cynthia most fully identifies her-self, as she returns to the image of the Cnossian in the poem's final couplets. The *talis-qualis* structure of her curse (39–40) both parallels the poem's initial series of mythological comparisons and recalls the structure of the heroine's curse in Catullus 64 (Curran 1996.205–07). Her self-pitying claim of having been deserted by Propertius makes the *deserta* of verse 43 reverberate with *desertis . . . litoribus* in verse 2; while her description of how she softly bemoaned his delay until Sleep (*sopor*), with soothing wings (*iucundis . . . alis*), pushed her into unconsciousness (45) completes the opening panel of the priamel by evoking Ariadne on Naxos before Dionysus's arrival. Indeed, it is tempting to see in the iconography of Roman paintings of the abandoned, awakening Ariadne, such as the one in the House of the Vettii in Pompeii (VI 15, 11; fig. 10), the model for Cynthia's final vision of herself.[43] It is as if she had placed herself in the very role, in the very scene, in which the poet had first cast her. And she has done so without omitting a single detail—neither the image of Hypnos (cf. fig. 4), nor that of Theseus's vanishing ship (fig. 10). While Propertius is recast as the execrable Athenian prince, Cynthia becomes the poem's active, speaking subject. Yet she does not reject her position of vulnerable desirability. Instead, she exploits it, forcefully tugging at our heart strings and demanding that we shift our allegiances to her. As well-versed in elegiac conventions and mythological lore as the poet-lover, the *docta puella* turns the tables on him not by denying her status as an object of desire and fantasy but by pointing to *his* own status as *materia* for her imagination as well as the readers'. Surely, Cynthia may well be pure fiction—the fruit of the poet's mind and of his pen, a figure in a painting or just a figure of speech. But, as she points out, so is Propertius. Thus her speech ultimately has an adverse effect on the poem's mechanisms of illusion that, up to now, had aimed at closing the gap, ever so gradually, between viewer and object, between reader and text. Through her angry words, Cynthia reminds us of what these characters truly are: constructs, metaphors, signs standing in for what was perceived as the "real" symptoms and moods of being in love—a recognition that is essential if the audience is to appreciate the lifelikeness of the representation.

Coda: Gendered Identifications in Propertius 1.3

As in the Aristotelian theory of realism, identification and detachment are the key emotional responses that sustain the reader's interest in and involvement with the drama of Elegy 1.3. Although we have already considered at length Propertius's various means of triggering identification—his use of myth, his evocation of pictorial types, and the delineation of a love triangle that negates the reader's role as a passive observer—we must now turn our attention to the possible implications of the gender role-reversals and cross-gender associations elicited by the poem. In a society such as ancient Rome, where a strictly defined, generically coded hierarchy pervaded every level of an individual's existence, Propertius's playful bending of boundaries was only truly possible within the fictional world of elegy, where characters, both men and women, always appear outside the patriarchal social structures of real life. Thus the generic fluidity that characterizes amatory relationships in elegy was not only confined to the realm of poetic fantasy but also very often redirected within the poems themselves towards an ending that reasserted the accepted order of things.[44] Still the temporary, even minimal, destabilization of these established structures in the works of the elegiac poets was not, I believe, entirely without effect or significance.

In a now classic essay on cinema, Laura Mulvey argues that the "grammar" of Western narrative structures "places the reader, listener, or spectator with the *hero*," requiring that women spectators constantly perform an act of trans-sex identification (1989.32–33). More recently, other critics have elaborated on her observations to propose that a (film) text produces different gendered positions, and that identification is shifting, mobile, multiple, and fractured. In other words, men do not identify themselves exclusively with the heroes on the screen, just as women—as had already been recognized by Mulvey—do not identify solely with their diegetic counterparts. Instead, spectators can project themselves onto the various positions involved in the narrative: hero and heroine, villain, bit player, active and passive character.[45] It is precisely these shifting and multiple identifications that elegy elicits and requires of its readers: in general, because it portrays feminized men who have renounced the affairs of the state and the family to pursue, hopelessly, the love of a *domina* and, in the case of Propertius 1.3 in particular, because the poem constantly undermines the masculinity of its male narrator to the point that it substitutes him for Cynthia at the end.

In Elegy 1.3, trans-sex identification is further facilitated by Propertius's subtle use of poetic and pictorial clichés. The poem's exempla are, indeed, what Roland Barthes would call a series of figures, that is, familiar "scenes of language" in which Romans could recognize certain "truths" about love because they recalled a "reality" apprehended through things read, heard, seen, felt (Barthes 1978.4). In the course of the poem, these figures take on material form through a sustained simile between *cubiculum* and *pinacotheca*. And as we follow the sequence of images Propertius arranges before us, we are made aware of their essential similarity. Writing on the iconography of mythological romantic idylls, such as those evoked by Propertius, Paul Zanker observes that paintings that dramatize the moment of fascination triggered by vision articulate male and female desire through similar poses and gestures: it was the intensity of the characters' passion rather than their gender that determined their form and served as a primary means of identification.[46]

However, unlike tragedy, where the destabilization and crossing of traditional gender boundaries is, in most cases, rectified through harsh punishment, elegiac cross-dressing brings with it no dire consequences to the protagonists. In a genre where suffering is deprived of gravity, the elegiac reversal of gender roles served as a trope through which the reader was invited to transcend the reality of conservative social norms to participate in a fantastical world of heightened emotions and romantic love. Yet at the same time that it idealized the lover's feminized position as a devoted servant at the command of his mistress, elegy also countered this idealization through mockery. As Natalie Kampen shows in relation to the Augustan poets' treatment of the myth of Hercules' enslavement to Omphale, the hero's transvestism and the Lydian queen's eastern luxuriousness offered grounds for a self-conscious exaggeration of this literary generic play that carried with it strong social and political messages.[47] Given that, within Roman culture, the effeminization of the masculine was not balanced by a corresponding masculinization of the feminine, elegy's potentially subversive game was always offset and restrained by its own insistence that, although the lover might at times occupy the position of a woman, he retained the option of being a man.[48]

Caught in a mesh of pathos and bathos, of liberation and repression, the elegiac fantasy of unbounded passion and tenuously fulfilled desire thus lent a great semantic richness to the poems and paintings on the loves of gods and heroes. It did not, in any way, level the disparity between (male) lover and (female) beloved—whether in the poetic or in the real world. In fact, what is striking about elegy as a genre is how dependent it is on the disparity of power between its protagonists to structure its narrative of pursuit and longing. As David Konstan argues, this "dependence" had its basis "in the conception or nature of *eros* itself, conditioned as it was by the conventions that governed Greek and Roman social life." For at the same time that eros was seen as a demeaning, disreputable, disruptive emotion, it had also an aggressive, competitive aspect and was the sign of virile force and prowess (Konstan 1994.178–81). What poems such as Elegy 1.3 and mythological paintings such as those evoked by Propertius's exempla suggest is that, by focusing on enthrallment, not possession, these works of art made identification with the different roles of an amatory drama accessible across traditional gender lines. The oscillation triggered by the demasculinization of the *amator* allowed, then, for a temporary parity of accessibility to the positions of subject and object of desire. For a brief moment, before laughter punctured the illusion of equality, men and women could be transported to a world where all were equal before desire, where roles were fluid and interchangeable, and all that mattered was that passion burned.[49]

Notes

1. For a history of Latin love elegy and the conventions of the genre, see Conte 1994.321–66, Fedeli 1989.143–76, Konstan 1994.150–59, Lyne 1980. On the mistress as a metaphor for text, see Wyke 1987b.47–61 and Zetzel 1996. 73–100, especially 81ff.

2. Boucher 1965.227–63, 432–38. See also Allen 1962 and Whitaker 1983.11–18, 87–123.

3. For an interpretation of the symbolic meaning of *mora* and *limen* in Propertius, see Pucci 1978.

4. Birt 1895, Keyssner 1938. For later references to these two works as offering authoritative evidence of Propertius's knowledge and recollection of contemporary works of art, see Dunn 1985.242–43 and Whitaker 1983.91.

5. Keyssner 1938.172–75, 183. A number of scholars have missed Keyssner's central point. For less subtle readings of the relation between image and text in Propertius 1.3, see Curran 1966.195, 199, Harmon 1974.155, Whitaker 1983.91. Whitaker is so attached to the idea that there is an original pictorial source for each of Propertius's parallels that he goes so far as to claim that the image of the sleeping Andromeda had to be inspired by a painting now lost.

6. The date of Propertius's death is not certain, but line 764 of Ovid's *Remedia Amoris*, published in 1 C.E., implies that Propertius is dead by this time. Most of the mythological frescoes we have are from the fourth style, dated to c. 30–69 C.E.

7. The date of publication of Propertius's *Monobiblos* is c. 29 B.C.E. On Roman visual culture in the late first century B.C.E., see Pollitt 1979.

8. Havelock 1995.103ff., especially 118–21. She cites Ovid *Amores* 1.5 and Propertius 2.15 as examples of the poets' fascination with nudity. At least one type of nude can be said to have become a Roman "pop" icon: Apelles' Aphrodite Anadyomene, brought from Cos by Augustus and exhibited in the Forum of Caesar. See Bergmann 1995.89, Havelock 1995.118, Pollitt 1979.169 n. 15. For references to Apelles' painting in Latin literature, see Cicero *Orat.* 5, Ovid *Ars* 2.401–02, Propertius 3.9.11.

9. The translation is my own.

10. The following section of my discussion of Aristotle's concept of μίμησις

and the pleasures it evokes in an audience shares a number of similarities with Stephen Halliwell's lengthier study of these matters. His book, *The Aesthetics of Mimesis: Ancient Texts and Modern Problems* (Princeton 2002), had not yet been published at the time I wrote this essay. See, especially, his Introduction (1–33) and chapters 5–7 (151–233).

11. David Konstan has suggested to me that what Aristotle means by saying that the pleasure of μίμησις resides in the realization that "this is that" is not just the recognition that the image on stage is a representation of a particular individual (e.g., "That's Creon"), but that it stands in for a character or personality type. "Thus, mimesis teaches us something about the nature of reality, and not just a concrete instance of *tode ti*," Private correspondence, June 6, 2002. For a different interpretation of *Poetics* 4.4–19, see Halliwell 2002.178 n. 3, 189–90.

12. *Poetics* 13.8–9. Cf. *Rhetoric* 2.5, 1382b24–25; 2.7, 1385b11–12; 2.8, 1386a28–29. See Konstan 2001.128–36 for a discussion of Aristotle's definition of pity, in which the need for distance is again put forth as a requisite for empathetic identification, at least as it is delineated in the *Poetics*. "[Aristotle] specifies that we pity people we know, provided that they are not very close kin, since in that case we feel about them as we do about ourselves . . . A consequence of this qualification . . . is that pity is not directly proportional to intimacy, but requires a certain distance" (Konstan 2001.132). See also Halliwell 2002.227–30.

13. *Poetics* 14.1–3, Zanker 1987.39–42.

14. Elsner 1995 offers a different conception of realism in ancient art. For a discussion of the term and in its significance in later periods, see Fried 1990 and Novak 1969.

15. Vergil died in 19 B.C.E. The unrevised *Aeneid* was published by literary executors soon thereafter. The *Monobiblos* was published c. 29 B.C.E.

16. The translations of Propertius 1.3 that appear throughout this article are my own.

17. The two paintings are now in the Museo Archeologico Nazionale, Naples: fig. 4 = inv. 9286; fig. 5 = inv. 11283.

18. Pausanias 1.20.3. See also Bernhard and Daszewski 1986.1050–70, especially 1062.

19. For a different view of the meaning and function of depictions of mythological love stories in Roman wall painting, see Fredrick 1995.

20. On extant representations of Perseus and Andromeda, see Schauenburg 1981.774–90 and Philipps 1968. Whitaker 1983 assumes that Propertius is referring to a lost pictorial original; so does Boucher 1965.54.

21. For a similar view, see Cairns 1977.325–53.

22. Curran 1996.197. Propertius has purposely ignored the gruesome interlude during which Perseus was forced to deal with Andromeda's suitors and kinsmen. For an account of this part of the myth, see Ovid *Met.* 5.1–249.

23. In Roman painting, the myth of Perseus and Andromeda is given a far more proper iconography than other love stories involving gods and heroes. In

a well-known fresco from a villa in Boscotrecase, dated to the last quarter of the first century B.C.E. and now in the Metropolitan Museum in New York (20.192.16), two key moments of the narrative are simultaneously portrayed: at the center is Andromeda, bound to a cliff, being attacked by a sea monster below and about to be rescued by Perseus, shown hovering above. On the upper right corner of the painting, in a smaller scale, one sees a scene that precedes that of her rescue: Perseus and her father, Cepheus, shake hands before the royal palace, marking their agreement on the hero's reward for his services: Andromeda's hand in marriage. Another popular type, preserved in a number of monuments including a painting from the House of the Dioscuri in Pompeii (now Naples, Museo Archeologico Nazionale, inv. 8998), shows Perseus helping Andromeda step away from the rocks. Significantly, he holds up her left arm, which is still in chains. The gesture of holding the bride's left wrist, referred to in Greek as ἐπὶ καρπῶ, harks back to images from the late archaic period where it symbolizes marriage (see, for instance, the metope of the sacred marriage of Hera and Zeus from Hera's temple at Selinus, dated to the fifth century B.C.E.; Bergmann 1994, infra n. 48, fig. 15). It is, then, unlikely that a Roman audience would have imagined Perseus and Andromeda's wedding night taking place in any setting other than one of legitimate, domestic intimacy. For a reproduction of the painting in New York and a detailed discussion of it, see von Blanckenhagen and Alexander 1990.33–37.pls. 43, 46, 47. For the fresco from the House of the Dioscuri, see Phillips 1968.fig. 7.

24. For the myth of Pan and Syrinx, see Ovid *Met.* 1.689–712. For Faunus's failed attempt to rape Omphale, see Ovid *Fasti* 2.283–358. On the comic representations of satyrs' frustrated sexual assaults in Roman painting and their relation to Ovid's account of the story of Faunus's love for Omphale, see Kampen 1996.242–43. The only exception to the narrative pattern of satyrs' comic failures as lovers is the myth of Jove's rape of Antiope, where he impregnates the nymph while in the guise of a satyr; see Ovid *Met.* 6.110.

25. For indications that Propertius is thinking of Pentheus in the last couplet of the priamel, see Curran 1996.197 and Dunn 1985.241–42, 244.

26. Brilliant 1984.66, 71–75, Bergmann 1994.225–56, and 1996.199–218. See also Thompson 1961 and Schefold 1972.

27. See Curran 1996.196, who compares the expression to *incensus amore*, Catullus 64.253.

28. See Lyne 1970.71. In Propertius's oeuvre, and the *Monobiblos* in particular, the term *ocellus* carries programmatic meaning. Cf. Propertius 1.1.1: "Cynthia prima suis miserum me cepit *ocellis*" ("Cynthia first seized wretched me with her eyes"). The word's recurrence in 1.3 was quite likely intended to recall the initial account of the poet's *coup de foudre*.

29. "The use of *ignotus* here in the sense of 'strange' or 'out of one's experience' is exactly right in a simile illustrating his attitude to the sleeping girl . . . Lyne's discussion shows how appropriate the word is to the *illustratio* (horns on

the girl Io were decidedly *ignota* to Argus) . . . It seems to me that Propertius has clearly indicated that relevance by making *ignotis* (v. 20) answer so well to *expertae* (v. 18). The Cynthia on whom he gazes now, whom he has left unmolested, and who is silent and asleep as he first found her, is indeed a *Cynthia ignota* contrasted with the all too familiar *saeva domina* whom he feared to have confronting him . . . should she awake" (Baker 1980.254).

30. Karl Keyssner was the first to point out that this parallel, so strange to post-antique eyes, is far more comprehensible when one thinks of the representations of the myth in Roman painting; see Keyssner 1938.182.

31. This painting from the House of Meleager, Pompeii (fig. 6), is now in the Museo Archeologico Nazionale, Naples, inv. 9556. For a discussion of the six extant examples of this type and the hypothesis of their connection to a fourth-century original by Nikias of Athens, see Bergmann 1995.95.

32. The painting from the House of Meleager, Pompeii, depicting Mars and Venus (fig. 7) is now in the Museo Archeologico Nazionale, Naples, inv. 9256.

33. According to Jàs Elsner, the version of the Pygmalion myth we know best, where he appears as a sculptor who falls in love with his work, is an Ovidian invention (Elsner 1991.154–68). See also Greene 1995b and 1998.37–66.

34. For a similar view of this passage, see Curran 1996.203.

35. Curran 1996.203–04. Harmon also argues (1974.159–60) that Propertius's mention of Cynthia's dreams evokes Aeschylus's description of Io as being overtaken by nightly visions that terrified her "virgin soul" (Aesch. *Prometheus Vinctus* 645).

36. Baker 1980.248–49, Lyne 1970.75, Konstan 1977.56.

37. Lyne reads *sedula* as referring to the Moon's diligence in sticking to her timetable (Lyne 1970.75).

38. In the Homeric *Hymn to Aphrodite*, Anchises, after he finds out with whom he has slept, begs the goddess not to render him impotent (188–90). Aphrodite acquiesces, but his prayer shows that impotence was perceived as the common lot of the men who shared a goddess's bed. In the *Odyssey*, Odysseus's involvement with Calypso deviates somewhat from the standard mythical pattern. The goddess does not render him impotent, but does keep him on the edges of civilization in a state of emotional and physical dependency that effectively negates his status as a man. Although Odysseus spends his nights in her arms, Homer stresses that he does so unwillingly, under compulsion, at Calypso's command, so that the act that normally denotes male authority is here turned into another form of subjection (5.154–55); see Stehle 1990.88–95.

39. Iphis was the daughter of Ligdus. While her mother was still pregnant, her father vowed to expose the child if she were a girl. In order to protect Iphis, her mother raised her as a boy. But as she grew up, Iphis fell in love with Ianthe, the daughter of one of her father's friends. Both fathers, not knowing, of course, Iphis's true gender, decided to marry their children to one another. On the day of the wedding, Isis miraculously transformed Iphis into a man; see Ovid *Met.*

9.666–796. On the "unnaturalness" of lesbian love and its particular obstacles to fulfillment, see verses 720–59.

40. For descriptions of the eye as a lantern whence flowed a luminous stream and of sight as a kind of touching, see Plato *Timaeus* 45B–46C, Galen *On the Doctrines of Hippocrates and Plato* 7.5.42–6.4, 7.18–8.14, Lucretius 4.26–352. A useful discussion of these passages can be found in Simon 1988.21–56. Konstan traces the idea of the eye as containing a refined fire to Empedocles frag. 84b Diels-Kranz, and proposes that it may go back to the Pythagoreans. He also points to a similar conceit in the *Ass* ascribed to Lucian; see Konstan 1977.56–57 n. 130.

41. "[she] blushed and, raising her timid eyes to the light, / saw the sky and her lover at the same time."

42. For the lyre as an attribute of the "lonely lover of olden days," see Lyne 1970.76. Curran interprets *purpureo . . . stamine* (41) as a reference to Ariadne's thread, thus recalling the second heroine of the priamel (1996.206). See also Baker 1980.257–58 and Dunn 1985.249–50.

43. Badoni argues that the pictorial type of the abandoned Ariadne is a Roman or possibly Campanian invention. All the existing examples date to the fourth style and may be artistic responses to the popularity of Catullus 64 and Ovid's later reworking of it in *Heroides* 10; see Badoni 1990.83–87.

44. Konstan 1994.153–59, Hallett 1973.

45. Ellis 1982, Doane 1992b.227–43, Stacey 1992.244–60, Neale 1992.277–90.

46. Zanker 1999.45–47; see also Bergmann 1996.207ff.

47. Kampen 1996.235ff.; see also Wyke 1989.39ff.

48. I owe this insight to Paul Allen Miller's eloquent response to my paper on Propertius 1.3 at the Women's Classical Caucus Panel at the annual meeting of the American Philological Association on January 6, 2001.

49. I would like to thank Ronnie Ancona and Ellen Greene for their support in this project. For their helpful comments, I am grateful to Bettina Bergmann, Richard Brilliant, Natalie Kampen, Barbara Kellum, David Konstan, Paul Allen Miller, Matthew Roller, Tara Welch, and Gareth Williams. I must also thank the University Seminars at Columbia University for their help in publication. The ideas presented here have benefited from discussions in the University Seminar on Classical Civilization. Lastly, I thank Paola D'Agostino for her help in obtaining photographs from the Soprintendenza Archeologica in Naples. All remaining mistakes and misinterpretations are, of course, my own.

10 The Lover's Gaze and Cynthia's Glance

Kerill O'Neill

Let me beware of the fascination that lurks in Catherine Heath-cliff's brilliant eyes.

It's yon flaysome, graceless quean, ut's witched ahr lad, wi' her bold een, un' her forrard ways . . .—Brontë, *Wuthering Heights*

In recent years, the application of feminist theory to the study of Latin literature has generated provocative new perspectives on ancient texts. An intriguing part of this interaction has been feminist psychoanalytic theory's confrontation with Freud. Feminist engagement with Latin authors under the harsh light of Freud's theory of the gaze has spawned particularly fruitful lines of inquiry. The focus of gaze studies is the representation of the act of looking, and usually a woman is the object of that look. While this theoretical perspective is most often applied to film and the visual arts, various scholars have subjected literary and psychoanalytical texts to the same kind of scrutiny. For Freud, the gaze is a phallic activity, enacting the voyeur's desire for sadistic power. Consequently, the gaze casts its object as a passive, masochistic, feminine victim. Under Freud's gaze, a woman is a negative, mirror image of the male observer, a reflection of his desires (Moi 1985.132–35 and note 8). The process of female specularization, in which the woman can only reflect the male's desires, turns her into a statue under the ever-present male gaze. Thus the gaze presupposes a dominant male ideology and consigns women to its margins (Irigaray 1997.364–67).

This conception of woman under the male gaze coincides with the image of the elegiac woman generated by feminist readings. Thus Barbara Gold sees Cynthia as a relational other, a foil for the lover (1993.88–89). This kind of theoretical critique of the elegiac woman has gained still wider currency through the work of Maria Wyke. She has written extensively on the literary construction of the elegiac woman: the woman written as *materia* (substance or literary material) for the elegiac poet.[1] Wyke also draws attention to the common metaphorical association of women's adornment with the embellishment of a literary text (1994a.144–45). Thus Cynthia's body forms the poetic corpus that the male narrator articulates; she is defined in terms of his requirements. More recently, Ellen Greene has demonstrated that reading Propertius through Luce Irigaray can be very revealing. In 1.3, the lover's sexual arousal seems to hinge on treating the sleeping Cynthia like a pictorial object, a spectacle. Devoid of voice and agency, she is completely subject to the male gaze and, therefore, most desirable (Greene 1995b). She becomes a blank canvas onto which the lover can project his own voyeuristic fantasies. Thus recent readings of elegy have employed gaze theory to illustrate how elegy's male lovers objectify the women who ostensibly dominate their male admirers. Any apparent power attributed to the mistress is, therefore, illusory.

These readings are very valuable for our appreciation of gender hierarchy in love elegy and encourage us to look at the fictive, or deceptive, nature of the elegiac world. We must be careful, however, not to oversimplify the gendered relations of the lover and *puella* (the girl or mistress of elegy), nor to undervalue the power of the elegiac woman. The lover's gaze does, indeed, secure her as the *materia* of his poetry, but her own mastery of the look makes her his *domina* (she attains the role of mistress over the lover-poet as her slave). Rather than rejecting the validity of gaze theory for the elegiac arena, I employ a reformulated theory of the gaze to offer here another reading of the problematized hierarchy of male and female in Propertian elegy. Thus instead of discounting recent scholarship, I cast Gold, Wyke, and Greene as my own relational others as I argue that Propertius's elegiac woman does not submit quietly to the lover's objectifying gaze. To redraw the struggle for dominance in the elegiac relationship as a more evenly contested battle, I make reference to another perspective on gaze theory that emphasizes the power gained from intercepting the lover's gaze.

An influential alternative to the Freudian theory of the gaze is offered by Jacques Lacan (1977.67–119). My own understanding of Lacanian gaze theory is based on the more accessible work of Slavoj Zizek, a long-time expositor of Lacan.[2] For Lacan, there is an antinomic relationship between the eye and the gaze: the eye belongs to the spectator and the gaze belongs to the spectacle. The object can be a sardine can or a painting, but because a sight line connects the spectator and the object viewed, the object of the gaze is, in a sense, looking back at the spectator. Lacan's version of the theory of the gaze does not require an animate object. There is no sense that the (feminine) object is challenging the (masculine) spectator by usurping his prerogative of looking.[3] Nevertheless, Lacan remains relevant to this reconsideration because of another scholar's response to his theory of the gaze. In an important study of Emily Brontë's *Wuthering Heights*, Beth Newman engages some of the basic assumptions of gaze theory and confronts the issue of the power of the spectator in a compelling way. Through a reading of Lacan, Newman contends that "the gaze can serve to destabilize the viewer as well as to confer mastery, especially if the gazer is caught looking by another subject who sees the gaze and perceives it as an expression of desire." Newman goes even further, arguing that Brontë envisions "not a simple inversion in which the woman is permitted to turn the tables with an appropriating look back but a destruction of the hierarchical positioning of male and female that the gendered gaze entails." Newman suggests that Brontë's experiments with the gaze lay the foundation for a "feminist poetics of the novel."[4]

In this paper, I apply to Propertius Newman's redistribution of the power implicit in an intercepted objectifying gaze. I argue that Cynthia perceives that she is the object of the lover's gaze and recognizes it as an expression of his desire. This recognition then empowers Cynthia because she realizes that she alone controls access to what the lover wants and, therefore, that she is in a position to claim the dominant role in their relationship. I do not contend that Propertius is delineating a feminist poetics of elegy, but I propose that, through consideration of the gaze, we may gain a more informed perspective on elegy's distortion of traditional gender relations. I argue that the *puella*'s perception of desire in the lover's objectifying gaze is one key to the elegiac destabilization of traditional Roman gender hierarchy, which constructs the woman as unable to intercept the man's gaze. My paper thus acknowledges the value of identifying the objectification of Cynthia in Propertius. I also attempt, however, to reconcile that objectification with the construction of the relationship between *puella* and lover as that of mistress and slave. That this construction of love and gender is offered in the founding moment of Propertian elegy, the first poem of the *Monobiblos*, encourages us to subject the rest of his work to a similar reading through "the gaze."

From the very beginning, Propertius makes looking a crucial part of the lover's interactions with the *puella*. The opening lines of Book 1 immediately establish that the poet's subject is love and that the traditional gender hierarchy does not apply to the relationship constructed in this book. Both Cynthia's eyes and the lover's feature prominently in the non-traditional dynamics of their affair (1.1.1–8):

Cynthia prima suis miserum me cepit ocellis,
   contactum nullis ante cupidinibus.
tum mihi constantis deiecit lumina fastus
   et caput impositis pressit Amor pedibus,
donec me docuit castas odisse puellas
   improbus, et nullo uiuere consilio.
et mihi iam toto furor hic non deficit anno,
   cum tamen aduersos cogor habere deos.

Cynthia first, with her eyes, caught wretched me
   Smitten before by no desires;
Then, lowering my stare of steady arrogance,
   With feet imposed, Love pressed my head,
Until he taught me to hate chaste girls—
   The villain—and to live aimlessly.
And now for a whole year this madness has not left me,
   Though I am forced to suffer adverse gods.[5]

The Propertian lover declares that it is with her eyes that Cynthia captured him, that it is his desire for her that has cast down his once proud stare. Cynthia's assumption of the dominant position in their relationship turns normal gender relations on their head. The lover's passion for her forces him to be reckless, to focus his desire away from respectable women, women who could be expected to accept the traditional patriarchal values and hierarchy of Roman gender relations. The centrality of the eyes of both Cynthia and the lover in this paradigmatic description of their relationship encourages us to consider the construction of this relationship in terms of the gaze. The male gaze that seeks to deprive women of subjectivity seems to find a match in the lover's "stare of steady arrogance," *constantis . . . lumina fastus*, even though the lover's gaze fails to delimit Cynthia as object of the gaze. Cynthia's interception of that gaze is signaled by the military metaphor alleging the lover's capture by her eyes.

So what exactly does it mean that Cynthia captures the lover with her eyes? In 1.9, the narrator assumes an eroto-didactic role, warning Ponticus that his initial feelings of triumph will soon give way to submission when he realizes he cannot tear his eyes away from her (25–30). Here, perhaps, we may think of the Lacanian idea that the gaze belongs to the object.[6] In the Propertian lover's case, however, both the gaze and his eyes seem to belong to the object of the gaze. In 1.19, the narrator declares that Love cleaves to his eyes (*haesit ocellis*) to such an extent that, even as dust, he will remember his beloved (5–6). Theodore Papanghelis analyzes this poem to illustrate what he calls the visual slant of Propertius's conception of love. Cynthia's *forma* ("beauty") proves superior to the *formosae heroinae* ("beautiful heroines") of Troy, and, for Propertius, *forma* is "nothing but what meets the eye."[7] Thus the lover is unable to separate his eyes and gaze from the beauty of Cynthia. In another passage reminiscent of 1.1 (2.30A.7–10), Love stands over the head of the lover and acts as a sentry over the lover's imprisoned eyes (*lumina capta*). These captured eyes have been subjugated to the point that they cannot be raised from the ground. We may also compare the effect that Penthesileia achieved when she removed her helmet and exposed her beautiful face to the gaze of Achilles; she conquered her conqueror (3.11.15–16).

To these illustrations of captivating and captured eyes we may add another passage that recalls 1.1. A later poem purports to tell us more about the initial encounter between the lover and his mistress (3.10.15–18):

> dein qua primum oculos cepisti ueste Properti
> indue, nec uacuum flore relinque caput;
> et pete, qua polles, ut sit tibi forma perennis,
> inque meum semper stent tua regna caput.

> Then put on the dress you wore when first you caught Propertius's
> Eyes, and do not leave your head ungarlanded;
> And pray that the power of your beauty never fails,
> And that your dominion will stand forever over my head.

As the lover prepares to celebrate his mistress's birthday, he asks his mistress to wear the dress she was wearing the first time he saw her. Are we to envision that this is the sort of dress that leaves much of the breast exposed? In 2.22A, the lover admits that he seeks out women in such attire, even though this act of looking does him harm (7–8). In 3.10, the lover goes on to encourage the girl to pray for lasting beauty so that her dominion will always stand over his head (18). This phrase recalls Love pressing down with his feet on the lover's head in 1.1 and 2.30A. The combination of eyes, a captive lover, and someone standing on his head encourages us to consider these poems together and create a fuller picture of the event they purport to describe. The lover sees Cynthia. Maybe he even tries to see down or through her dress (if it is of the diaphanous Coan silk she favors).[8] Finally, Cynthia catches his eyes with her eyes, that is, sees him looking at her and, by looking back, forces him to drop his gaze. Propertius's model for these lines is an epigram of Meleager in which the active part of the love object's eyes is more explicit: ὄμμασι τοξεύσας, "having shot me with his eyes."[9] Cynthia's bold return of the lover's gaze constitutes her assumption of the male role of gazer. As Newman observes, a woman's assumption of traditionally masculine roles typically earns her the title of witch or monster (1997.450–53). It is therefore interesting that Alison Sharrock sees in Cynthia's capture of the lover the performance of a binding spell by means of her magically charged eyes.[10] Lawrence Richardson comments that Propertius makes the mistress's eyes a point of beauty at 2.3.14 and 2.12.23, but observes that, in 1.1.1, "her eyes are almost a weapon, and one is reminded of the evil eye."[11] The lover is caught not because of the beauty of Cynthia's eyes, but because she employed them aggressively to catch the lover looking and return his gaze.

The idea that the object of the gaze may catch the observer and profit from his attention is not a modern invention. The third book of Xenophon's *Memorabilia* records how Socrates used to help ambitious people thrive in their various professions, be they military men, orators, painters, sculptors, or courtesans. Xenophon recounts a visit made by Socrates and his friends to the home of Theodote, a beautiful courtesan of considerable renown.[12] Socrates questions his friends about who is gaining more from the act of looking (3.11.2): "My friends, ought we to be more grateful to Theodote for showing us her beauty, or she to us for looking at it? Does the obligation rest with her, if she profits more by showing it, but with us, if we profit more by looking?"[13] Socrates answers the question himself, declaring (3.11.3): "She already has our praise to her credit, and when we spread the news, she will profit yet more; whereas we already long to touch what we have seen, and we shall go away excited and shall miss her when we are gone. The natural consequence is that we become her adorers, she the adored."

In the ensuing conversation with Theodote, Socrates learns that this beautiful woman has enriched herself through the generosity of her admirers. Socrates seizes the opportunity to educate and assumes the posture of *praeceptor amoris* ("instructor in love"). He suggests that she could catch even more wealthy lovers if she had an agent to chase likely candidates into her "net," but as the subsequent exchange illustrates, his hunting metaphors confuse Theodote (3.11.10):

> "Nets! What nets have I got?"
>
> "One, surely, that clips close enough—your body! And inside it you have a soul that teaches you what glance will please, what words delight, and tells you that your business is to give a warm welcome to an eager suitor, but to slam the door upon a conceited playboy."

Socrates grows increasingly comfortable in his eroto-didactic role. His advice foreshadows that of the elegiac bawds Acanthis and Dipsas,[14] as he admonishes Theodote to keep her suitors eager for more by never making herself too available. He is so convincing that Theodote asks him to become her partner in the hunt for suitors, a nice euphemism for her pimp. Socrates, however, in an increasingly flirtatious manner, suggests that she must do all she can to persuade him to assist her, as he is often kept busy by other women who are studying erotic magic with him! He claims mastery of spells, potions, and the magic wheel (*iunx*) that lovers spin to draw their beloved to them.[15] Theodote then begs him to let her use his magic wheel on him, but Socrates counters that he wants to use the wheel and have her come to him. Theodote coyly promises to come, but wants his assurance that he will welcome her. This Socrates promises to do, but only if he is not with a girl more dear to him! It seems that Socrates is giving Theodote a lesson in the value of withholding access to increase a suitor's desire.[16]

In this early exposition of specular economics, Socrates suggests that both the bearer and object of the gaze have something to gain from the act of looking. Indeed, Socrates' audit establishes that the object gains more from the desiring gaze than the observer. At the same time, the female object's ability to look back, and her innate knowledge of how to make that look advantageous, is acknowledged as an important part of her arsenal. Xenophon's Theodote has much in common with Cynthia. Both profit from the gifts of the admirers who gaze at them. Both use their own glances to win further advantage. Both crush admirers who display excessive arrogance. Both are associated with magical practices as agents and victims. Both receive mercenary advice from a pimp or procuress who is also presented as a witch.[17] Thus there is much in the social context of Theodote that anticipates the elegiac world that Propertius creates for the lover and his elegiac woman. The specular economy is a phenomenon already acknowledged in antiquity.[18]

My reading of the lover's relationship with Cynthia through the gaze gains credibility from other key references to the scopic nature of elegiac love in Propertius. In the programmatic opening poem of the second book, the speaker explains why his mistress, rather than Calliope or Apollo, is the inspiration of his love poems (2.1.5–8):

> siue illam Cois fulgentem incedere uidi,[19]
>   totum de Coa ueste uolumen erit;
> seu uidi ad frontem sparsos errare capillos,
>   gaudet laudatis ire superba comis;

> If I have seen her step out glittering in silks from Cos,
>   Her Coan gown speaks a whole volume.
> If I have seen an errant ringlet on her brow,
>   Proud, she takes pleasure in going about with praised hair.

Looking emerges as the crucial factor in the speaker's account of his poetic inspiration. The woman is reduced to an object of the gaze, but we are told that she profits from serving as a spectacle to the poet-spectator. As Ellen Greene puts it, "The images of Cynthia as both joyful and *superba* derive syntactically from the speaker's actions of looking at her and being able to describe what he sees" (2000.245). Furthermore, the mistress's pride in going about reveals that she may also want to expose herself to the gaze of others.

The mistress can take pride in her hair because the spectator-poet has confirmed that she has something that others want, but how does the spectator respond to her eyes, her looking in return? In this case, it the mistress's failure to return the gaze that gains attention (2.1.11–14):

> seu compescentis somnum declinat ocellos,
>   inuenio causas mille poeta nouas;
> seu nuda erepto mecum luctatur amictu,
>   tum uero longas condimus Iliadas:

> Or if she closes her eyes exigent for sleep,
>   I have a thousand new ideas for poems.
> Or if, stripped of her dress, she wrestles with me naked,
>   Why then we pile up lengthy Iliads.

Greene observes that the narrator's poetic talent is enhanced by the mistress's position of vulnerability, either asleep or naked. These lines certainly confirm that the lover is capable of an objectifying gaze and that he is inspired to write by what he sees. Nevertheless, they do not preclude the possibility that his gaze can be answered and subdued, nor should we conclude that inspiration would fail him if Cynthia should intercept and return his gaze.

Concern about controlling the elegiac woman's appearance permeates the Propertian text. The poet-lover tells us that Cynthia deliberately sets out to elicit the male gaze, and he exhorts her to avoid winning further lovers by declining to expose herself to their attention (2.32.1–2):

> qui videt, is peccat: qui te non viderit ergo
>   non cupiet: facti lumina crimen habent.

> Whoever sees you falls; so he who has not seen you
>   Will not desire you. Eyes are the guilty parties.

Any man who sees Cynthia will fall under her spell, so the lover appeals to his mistress not to put herself before other men's eyes.[20] That Cynthia is empowered by the gaze of the lover's competitors is made clear later in the poem when he lamely defends her from the charge that she is enriching herself through the gifts she solicits from these men as they attempt to gain access to her. The beautiful, he says, are always targets of malicious tongues (25–26). In answer to questions he says are being asked about Cynthia's wealth and about the identity of her benefactor, the lover hollowly replies that she is not as bad as her (poetic) model Lesbia, who was the first Roman woman to amass riches from the gifts of lovers. He adds that Greek and Roman women have been doing wrong for a long time now.

The lover's own delight in gazing upon Cynthia is lasciviously exemplified when he implores her to come to bed without any clothing (2.15.11–16):

> non iuvat in caeco Venerem corrumpere motu:
>   si nescis, oculi sunt in amore duces.
> ipse Paris nuda fertur periisse Lacaena,
>   cum Menelaëo surgeret e thalamo.
> nudus et Endymion Phoebi cepisse sororem
>   dicitur et nudae concubuisse deae.

> But moving blind spoils love-making;
>   In love it's the eyes that lead.
> Paris fell for Helen naked
>   As she left Menelaus' bed.

> Endymion naked caught Selene's eye
>> And lay with the naked goddess.

Here, as so often, the lover eagerly embraces his enslavement, wishing to satiate his gaze even though it just fires the passion that binds him to his mistress. For while he threatens to tear off any clothing the *puella* might wear to bed and to bruise her if she defies him, the subordination to her wishes is apparent when he reveals that it is she who decides how often they should spend the night together. Moreover, for all his threats and posturing, the overall tone of his address to the girl is pleading and ingratiating. It is also noteworthy that, in this same poem, Cynthia actively demands that the lover gaze upon her. The opening lines link the lover's delight in a night of sexual pleasure to what he could see of his partner's body. The *puella* is unwilling to relinquish her hold over him (2.15.5–8):

> nam modo nudatis mecum est luctata papillis,
>> interdum tunica duxit operta moram.
> illa meos somno lapsos patefecit ocellos
>> ore suo et dixit: "sicine, lente, iaces?"

> Breasts naked, she would wrestle with me—then
>> Stall by covering up.
> She kissed open my drowsy eyes, saying,
>> "Are you just going to lie there, slowpoke?"

The girl's position here is very different from the one she holds in 2.1, where her vulnerability in nakedness and sleep is emphasized. In 2.15, the *puella* alternately conceals and reveals her nudity to tease the lover to new heights of passion. The second couplet in this passage may seem to present the familiar spectacle of a man immediately falling asleep after sex while his female partner wants to talk or cuddle. Nevertheless, Cynthia's insistence that the lover continue to gaze upon her indicates that she knows very well how to maintain control of her man. The query that accompanies her efforts to open his eyes seems flirtatiously to question the lover's manliness, establishing a connection between the phallic act of looking and the lover's ability to perform.[21] Despite that connection, it is the mistress, not the lover, who demands that phallic activity and, through her demands, adumbrates that looking and desiring by the lover grant her power in their relationship.

Within the same poem, the lover subsequently pleads that he and Cynthia should gaze upon each other (2.15.23–26):

dum nos fata sinunt, oculos satiemus amore:
> nox tibi longa venit, nec reditura dies.
atque utinam haerentis sic nos uincire catena
> uelles, ut numquam solueret ulla dies.

Let us sate our eyes with love while Fate allows.
> The long night comes and the day of no return.
I wish you were willing to bind us in this close embrace
> With a bond that time could never break!

This request reflects the lover's acknowledgement of the importance of the gaze. In the context of his greater affection for her, he hopes that reciprocal gazing will diminish the inequality in their love. In the course of his earlier plea that the *puella* come to bed, the lover cites two mythological precedents for naked beauty capturing the (eyes and) love of the beholder (13–16). Paris caught sight of Helen rising naked from the bed of Menelaus, and the naked Endymion captured (*cepisse*) Selene's love and slept with her in the nude. The example of the male Endymion capturing the gaze and love of the goddess resonates a little more now that the lover asks that each look at the other. The lover proposes an exchange of gazes quite different from the intercepted gaze or the discomfiting return gaze envisaged in 1.1. Endymion was the object of a desiring female subject's gaze. If even a goddess can look with love upon a mortal man, surely this *domina* can allow her gaze to fall with favor upon the lover.[22]

The lover is well aware that it is through his own gaze that he opens himself up to suffering. In 2.22A, he confides to Demophoon that he has been beset by problems with numerous girls because he falls for whatever beautiful girl he sees (2.22A.7–10):

interea nostri quaerunt sibi uulnus ocelli,
> candida non tecto pectore si qua sedet,
sive uagi crines puris in frontibus errant,
> Indica quos medio uertice gemma tenet.

And all the while my eyes are seeking to be wounded
> By a pretty girl in the audience with bare breast
Or wandering curls adrift on a smooth forehead,
> Clasped at the crown by an Indian gem.

The lover's gaze lingering on a smart hairdo or scandalously clad bosom certainly objectifies the women who catch his eye at the theater, but the lover asserts at the start of the elegy that his interest in these women brings him many troubles.[23] Despite this declaration that he has a problem, the lover seems happy with his weakness and declares that he will never change (2.22A.17–20):

> uni cuique dedit uitium natura creato:
>> mi fortuna aliquid semper amare dedit.
> me licet et Thamyrae cantoris fata sequantur,
>> numquam ad formosas, inuide, caecus ero.

> To everyone at birth Nature allots a failing;
>> Mine happens to be always to have an object for my love.
> Even if the fate of singer Thamyras befell me,
>> I'd never be blind, my envious friend, to pretty girls.

The link between falling in love and the gaze is affirmed in a new way by the lover's refusal to succumb to blindness. After defeating the bard Thamyras, who had arrogantly challenged them to a competition, the Muses punished him with blindness. The lover's boast that not even god-sent blindness will keep him from ogling beautiful women raises the question of what a blind man can see. Is this another case where the gaze belongs to the object? Perhaps the lover just means that the Muses could make him blind to all else but that he will still be able to see women of exceptional beauty, claiming this ability as a self-defining characteristic. Reading this passage is made more complicated because the lover reveals himself, even more than usual, to be an unreliable narrator here. For example, the lover's claim that his partiality to beautiful women is a fault seems disingenuous given the boastful tone of this elegy and his suggestion that Demophoon envies his predicament. Poem 22A of Book 2 offers an unusual solution for the lover's dependency on the object of his affections. He declares to Demophoon that he will maintain relations with more than one woman so that, if one rejects him, he may console himself with the other, thereby reducing the power of either woman over him. If blindness to his mistress's charms is not an option, perhaps a more diffuse gaze that encompasses more than one woman is the answer to his troubles.

This posture of self-protecting promiscuity is not one that the lover maintains elsewhere, which contributes to the air of false bravado that permeates this elegy. Three poems later, the lover seems to criticize his own advice when he chides those who encourage multiple partners (2.25.39–48):

> at, uos qui officia in multos reuocatis amores,
>> quantus sic cruciat lumina nostra dolor!

uidisti pleno teneram candore puellam,
  uidisti fuscam, ducit uterque color;
uidisti quandam Argiua prodire figura,
  uidisti nostras, utraque forma rapit;
illaque plebeio uel sit sandycis amictu:
  haec atque illa mali uulneris una uia est.
cum satis una tuis insomnia portet ocellis,
  una sat est cuiuis femina multa mala.

But you who recommend attentions to many loves,
  What pain you force your eyes to suffer!
You see a pretty girl with fair skin and fair hair,
  You see a brunette—both colors attract.
You see some girl of Grecian build walk by,
  You see our girls—both shapes grab you.
One wears plebeian dress, another scarlet—
  Either way you are badly wounded.
Since *one* can bring your eyes sleepless nights enough,
  One woman is trouble enough for any man.

In the first couplet of this passage, the eyes serve as a conduit between love and pain.[24] *Vidisti* ("you see") stands at the start of the next four consecutive lines, and the pounding emphasis of this quadruple anaphora makes it impossible to ignore the fact that looking is the medium of love. Listing complexion, body type, beauty, and adornment as the inspirations for love reaffirms the visual bias of the Propertian conception of love. The violent effect of these sights on the observer is signaled by the wound they cause. In 2.22A, the lover, in an act of playful masochism, seeks out the wounds that beautiful women inflict, but implies that one woman can salve the hurt that another imposes. Here, however, the playful tone is gone, and the lover seems more distraught. He concludes that one girl brings enough trouble to his eyes; additional women would just do more harm.

The lover's most explicit testimonial to the role eyes and the gaze play in his love for Cynthia comes in 3.21. In this elegy, the lover plots his escape from a near joyless love that he still cannot set aside. He reasons that seeking distractions in Athens is his best course of action, and explains why going abroad is necessary (3.21.1–10):

magnum iter ad doctas proficisci cogor Athenas,
  ut me longa graui soluat amore uia.

crescit enim assidue spectando cura puellae:
    ipse alimenta sibi maxima praebet amor.
omnia sunt temptata mihi, quacumque fugari
    possit: at ex omni me premit ipse deus.
uix tamen aut semel admittit, cum saepe negarit:
    seu uenit, extremo dormit amicta toro.
unum erit auxilium: mutatis Cynthia terris
    quantum oculis, animo tam procul ibit amor.

I am forced on a great journey to learned Athens
    To rid myself by travel of love's burden.
One's care for a girl grows by constant gazing;
    Love is its own chief nourishment.
I have tried every means of putting him to flight
    But after all, the God still presses me down.
She never admits me, or only once after many refusals,
    And if she comes, sleeps clothed on the edge of the bed.
The only cure will be foreign travel. Then love
    Will go as far from mind as Cynthia from my eyes.

Trading his learned girl for learned Athens, the lover acknowledges that as long as he can gaze upon Cynthia, he will never be free.[25] This observation recalls some of his other characterizations of the effect of looking at a beautiful woman: to see her is to fall. Once you set eyes upon the one you love, you cannot tear them away. Personified Love is pressing him down now with as much determination as he described at 1.1.4. The compulsion (*cogor*) he feels to travel recalls the compulsion (*cogor*) he once felt to endure the hostile gods that presided over his relationship with Cynthia. Cynthia's name occurs here for the first time in the third book, and the pairing of her name with *oculis* makes the first poem of the *Monobiblos* resonate anew. In the earlier poem, the lover declares that it is too late for his friends to find a cure (*auxilia*, 1.1.26) for him. Now the lover claims there is one cure (*auxilium*, 3.21.9), and he goes on to call on his friends to help him set sail (11–16). Out of sight, out of mind; the lover's solution is drastic. He must tear himself away from gazing at the compelling spectacle that Cynthia offers.

    The lover fantasizes about the different pursuits that will reform his mind and banish thoughts of his obsessive love. He sets himself some lofty philosophical, rhetorical, literary, and aesthetic goals, but the terms in which he casts these imagined studies hint that old habits die hard (3.21.23–30):

inde ubi Piraei capient me litora portus,
  scandam ego Theseae bracchia longa uiae.
illic uel stadiis animum emendare Platonis
  incipiam aut hortis, docte Epicure, tuis;
persequar aut studium linguae, Demosthenis arma,
  librorumque tuos, docte Menandre, sales;
aut certe tabulae capient mea lumina pictae,
  siue ebore exactae, seu magis aere, manus.

Next, when the shores of Piraeus' harbor will catch me,
  I'll mount the long arms of Theseus' Way.
There I'll begin to improve my mind in the training ground
  Of Plato or learned Epicurus' Garden.
Or I'll pursue the study of the tongue, Demosthenes' weapon,
  And the wit of smart Menander's books.
Or at any rate painted panels will catch my eyes,
  And work in ivory or, better, bronze.

Once in Athens, the lover will travel, appropriately enough, along the road named for Theseus, who swore eternal devotion to a woman (Ariadne) and then left her gazing at his departing ship.[26] Philosophy and rhetoric do not immediately seem likely subjects for the lover. The possibility of reading the comic poet Menander moves him onto more familiar ground. The study of art, however, will allow the lover to recreate some of the life he supposedly wants to escape. The painted panels or artworks in ivory and bronze will catch his eyes much as Cynthia did. He already envisions that the shores of Piraeus will catch him, too. The lover can envision a life without Cynthia but not without the gaze. Someone or something must trap his eyes.

At the close of Book 3, when the lover is bidding a bitter farewell to Cynthia and amatory elegy, he attacks the *puella*'s self-confidence. Whether we print them as one poem or as two, together 3.24 and 3.25 constitute a "designed repudiation of 1.1" (Goold 1990.301 n. 70), so it is fitting that the gaze should return as an important theme (3.24.1–4):[27]

falsa est ista tuae, mulier, fiducia formae,
  olim oculis nimium facta superba meis.
noster amor talis tribuit tibi, Cynthia, laudes:
  uersibus insignem te pudet esse meis.

Woman, you're wrong to be so sure of your good looks;
  It's my eyes long since made you proud.

> Such praises, Cynthia, my love accorded you
>> That I'm ashamed my verses made you conspicuous.

Here the lover once again explicitly asserts that Cynthia was made proud by the knowledge that he was gazing lustfully at her. The elegy continues with an acrimonious disavowal of his prior enslavement to Cynthia. In this context, it is clear that the power she exerted over him sprang from her recognition of the desire in his gaze. The lover's *oculis* ("eyes") recall Cynthia's *ocellis* ("eyes"). Cynthia's excessive pride and false confidence echo the erstwhile arrogance that the lover records losing in 1.1 when Cynthia caught his eyes with hers. The position Cynthia has occupied over the lover ever since will disappear if he stops looking.

The lover's bitterness at his mistress finds an outlet in the curse with which he ends the book. He envisions Cynthia as an ugly old woman, no longer able to enslave her admirers (3.25.11–18):

> at te celatis aetas grauis urgeat annis,
>> et ueniat formae ruga sinistra tuae!
> uellere tum cupias albos a stirpe capillos,
>> a! speculo rugas increpitante tibi,
> exclusa inque uicem fastus patiare superbos,
>> et quae fecisti facta queraris anus!
> has tibi fatalis cecinit mea pagina diras:
>> euentum formae disce timere tuae!

> But you—may age and the years you've hidden weigh you down
>> And wrinkles come to spoil your beauty!
> May your desire then be to root out the white hairs,
>> While the mirror, alas, accuses you of wrinkles.
> Excluded in your turn may you suffer arrogance's disdain,
>> A crone complaining you're done by as you did!
> These curses my prophetic page has sung for you;
>> So learn to dread your beauty's aftermath!

As a final indignity, the poet fantasizes that Cynthia will endure the suffering to which she subjected others. She who used love to cast down the lover's *lumina fastus* ("gaze of arrogance"), now must experience *fastus superbos* ("arrogance's disdain") in her turn. In 1.1, Cynthia intercepted the lover's gaze and used her understanding of the lover's desire to subjugate him. Here at the close of Book 3, the lover tries to turn the tables. In order to break with Cynthia, to tear his eyes away from her, the lover must picture her as an ugly old woman. Her beauty, his eyes, and the phenomenon of *servitium amoris* ("the slavery of love") are inextricably bound together. The lover takes malicious glee in imagining Cynthia as both spectator and spectacle. He envisions the once beautiful woman staring at herself in the mirror only to find that she has become a wrinkled, white-haired old woman. In other words, he imagines the girl subjecting herself to the objectifying, critical male gaze. These lines illustrate perfectly Luce Irigaray's view of the specularization of women, their marginalization by a dominant male ideology.

The lover's fantasy of the reflection that will destroy Cynthia recalls Maria Wyke's analysis of literary and visual texts that cast the female form as an image constructed in a mirror. The male-authored texts she considers present women's cosmetic efforts before the mirror as the preparation of a male-directed sexual identity: "Woman is constructed and constructs herself as a physical appearance, an object to be gazed upon by men" (Wyke 1994a.138). Earlier in the Propertius poem (3.24.5–8), the narrator alludes to his poems praising Cynthia's beauty. With bitter hindsight, he claims that her loveliness was not natural but the product of her efforts to beautify herself, a cosmetic deception. In this curse and dismissal of Cynthia, the lover conceives of another moment before the mirror, with his now-old mistress still seeking to prepare herself for the male gaze. Her own gaze, however, will reveal to her that she can no longer be the object of desire. She will no longer enjoy dominion over the men she catches looking because no one will want to look at her. In this context, we may recall Wyke's observation that the adornment of the elegiac woman is designed to attract the gaze of the lover in the same way that the poet's text is designed to attract the attention of the reader (1994a.144–45). At the close of Book 3, the narrator imagines this *scripta puella* ("written girl"), who was constructed to satisfy the requirements of elegiac verse, attempting to recapture her former self before a mirror. Her days of bewitching loveliness, however, are long gone. In the lover's malevolent vision, the mirror serves only to remind her that her wrinkles and white hair will make her the victim of arrogance instead of the object of desire. The destruction of Cynthia's physical appearance is a necessary step to prepare for the change in the poetic focus of his final book. In 3.21, the lover considers fleeing to Athens to put Cynthia out of sight, but this is the man who could see pretty women even if he were blind. The solution he settles upon here is to destroy Cynthia's beauty in order to make her invisible.

In the final book of elegies, we meet the elegiac mistress in only three poems. The first two appearances present evidence that the destruction of Cynthia's looks at the end of the previous book brought her reign to an end. In 4.5, the elegiac woman who receives advice from the bawd Acanthis is not named, but, as Kathryn Gutzwiller observes, the ugly, old bawd represents "an older version of what the reader knows Propertius will abandon Cynthia to become" (1985.111). In 4.7, Cynthia returns as a ghost disfigured by the pyre, complaining that the lover did nothing to call her back as death closed her eyes (23–24), and that he has found a woman to replace her so soon (39–40, 71–72). Is this an indication that the lover was happy to be free of those eyes? There is a macabre humor in the fact that Cynthia, even in death, is concerned with specular matters. She asks that her favorite slave never be called upon to hold a mirror for a new mistress (75–76). Cynthia can tolerate being replaced in the lover's bed, but does not want her reflection displaced from her mirror. It seems that she is content to wait for the lover's death, at which point she will grind his bones against hers in an eternal, deathly embrace. Cynthia's hair and eyes, the lover observes, are the same as the day she died (7–8), and that may be the reason that the lover, willing to anticipate her fatal clasp, tries to embrace her as her shade flits away (95–96).

The last time we encounter Cynthia is in the eighth poem of Book 4. The lover is attempting to enjoy the company of Phyllis and Teia, two promiscuous women, as he suspects that Cynthia's attendance at a rustic religious festival at Lanuvium is simply a cover for further infidelities on her part. Lanuvium is mentioned elsewhere in Propertius only in 2.32, where it features among a list of distant places that Cynthia claims she must visit (3–6). The lover, however, believes that she is leaving Rome only to evade his watchful eyes (*lumina nostra fugis*, 17). In 2.32, we encounter the lover's eyes trying ineffectively to hold onto the privilege of the controlling gaze. In 4.8, the lover knows he cannot control Cynthia and watches her leave, commenting on the spectacle (*spectaclum*, 21) she provides, which reminds us of the scopic nature of his love for her. He appears, however, to have all he needs for a raucous night of debauchery: good wine, musical accompaniment, a couple of promiscuous women, and a misshapen dwarf. Nevertheless, the party is ill omened and the lover is not himself (4.8.47–48):

> cantabant surdo, nudabant pectora caeco:
>   Lanuuii ad portas, ei mihi, solus eram;

> I didn't hear the singing, I was blind to naked breasts,
>   I was on my own alas at Lanuvium's gates.

The lover has been emasculated; he is no longer capable of the phallic gaze. His vainglorious claim to Demophoon in 2.22A that he will never be blind to beauty proves an empty boast. At least with these girls, he is not the man he wants to be. In his mind's eye, he is once again a pathetic *exclusus amator* ("locked-out lover"), now shut out by the gates of Lanuvium.

In the context of the dialogue between 2.22A and 4.8, an Ovidian elegy that conflates allusions to both offers an interesting perspective. In *Amores* 3.7, the lover laments a bout of impotence that has ruined an evening with a beautiful woman (61–62):

> quid iuuet, ad surdas si cantet Phemius aures?
> quid miserum Thamyran picta tabella iuuat?

> What good would it do if Phemius were to sing to deaf ears?
> What good is a painting to blind Thamyras?

The idea of singing to deaf ears and showing something beautiful to a blind man forges a link with Propertius 4.8. Citing Thamyras, in particular, as that blind man forces us to recall that the Propertian lover has contradicted what he said in 2.22A.[28] We may well be tempted to interpret the link between Ovid's poem and the two Propertian elegies as an ancient testimonial that the Propertian lover's loss of the phallic gaze is tantamount to a bout of impotence.

The gaze is not the only realm in which Cynthia contests her male lover. The lover's desire for his absent mistress leads him to envision himself as an *exclusus amator* at the gates of Lanuvium. What happens next, however, shatters any expectations of a fantasized *paraklausithyron* (the song of the locked-out lover), for Cynthia's sudden return briefly puts *her* in the unexpected position of shut-out lover. Cynthia, though, does not follow the parameters of the role. The lover's reverie is disturbed by a commotion at the entrance to his home. No door or gatekeeper, however, can keep Cynthia shut out for long (see Richardson 1977 ad loc.). Cynthia bursts in on the would-be revelers (4.8.51–58):

> nec mora, cum totas resupinat Cynthia ualuas,
>   non operosa comis, sed furibunda decens.
> pocula mi digitos inter cecidere remissos,
>   palluerantque ipso labra soluta mero.
> fulminat illa oculis et quantum femina saeuit,
>   spectaclum capta nec minus urbe fuit.

Phyllidos iratos in uultum conicit unguis:
   territa uicinas Teia clamat aquas.

Next moment Cynthia flung the folding doors wide open,
   Her hair a mess, but lovely in her fury.
My fingers lost their grip and dropped the glass,
   And loosened by the wine my lips turned pale.
Her eyes flashed and she raged as only a woman can;
   The spectacle was as frightful as a city's sack.
She directed her angry talons against Phyllis' looks;
   Terrified Teia shouted, "Neighbors, fire!"

Immediately, the lover's power to see and evaluate a woman reappears. Cynthia's disordered hair does not detract from the beauty (*decens*) of her anger in the lover's eyes. Lawrence Richardson points out that the phrase *furibunda decens* ("lovely in her fury") allows us to see that Cynthia's disordered hair made her look like a Fury. Furies and Gorgons have their snaky hair in common. In considering the gaze, we cannot forget that looking at the Gorgon, the emasculating woman who looks back, is the ultimate objectifying gaze. But it is the spectator who is made into an object, a stone statue. Cynthia here seems like a precursor of Freud's "Medusa's Head."[29] Meanwhile, the lover's pallor and slackened grip scarcely constitute a return to manly vigor. His reference to his own paleness reveals that the lover, too, is subject to specularization; as if gazing into a mirror, he envisions how he looks to others, even while he stares at Cynthia. In 1.1, the lover refers to his pallid cheek as he appeals to witches to make Cynthia's cheek paler than his as a sign that she returns his feelings of love. The *mollitia* ("softness, effeminacy") of the poet-lover sometimes allows him to claim the woman's position as object of the ever-present gaze. Nevertheless, the lover is still very much a spectator, too, staring again at a spectacle (4.8.56) offered by Cynthia. His infuriated mistress cements her triumph over her rivals by slashing at the *uultus* ("face") of Phyllis and putting the girls to flight. *Vultus* often indicates the eyes as the part of the face associated with looking and the gaze.[30] In the context of this last poem, where the eyes of Cynthia and the lover once again contest with one another, it seems appropriate to let the sense of looking in *uultus* resonate. Cynthia will not countenance the possibility that another woman's eyes might catch the lover looking.

Even as the roles of spectator and spectacle are contested in 4.8, it is Cynthia's eyes that seem dominant, shooting sparks of rage as she sees what the lover has been doing. Strikingly, however, when Cynthia reaches the apex of her power, taking control of the lover's home, slaves, and girlfriends, she is still a *spectaclum*. Cynthia seizes the role of city-sacker, but the very force of her agency once again subjects her to the gaze of the lover. The lover, by contrast, seems paralyzed by what he sees.[31] Having mastered the battlefield, however, Cynthia addresses this inequity (4.8.63–66):

> Cynthia gaudet in exuuiis uictrixque recurrit
> > et mea peruersa sauciat ora manu,
> imponitque notam collo morsuque cruentat,
> > praecipueque oculos, qui meruere, ferit.

> Pleased with her trophies, Cynthia rushed back victorious
> > And slashed my face with a back-handed slap
> And stamped her mark on my neck, biting till it bled,
> > And especially struck at my eyes, which deserved it.

If Cynthia is pleased now (*gaudet*), it is not because the poet-lover has praised her hair. She puts her mark on the lover for all to see. Scratches and bite marks will make *him* a spectacle.[32] The lover's brutal punishment reaches its climax with Cynthia's pointed assault on his eyes, which he had dared to turn upon another woman, and which are now fixated upon his original mistress. The lover recognizes that his eyes deserve this attack; he has violated the rules of looking. Cynthia will no longer allow him to impose his gaze upon her. Tired of beating the lover, Cynthia turns her anger on the slave Lygdamus. When the hapless Lygdamus appeals for help, the lover is powerless to do anything (4.8.70): "Lygdame, nil potui: tecum ego captus eram," "Lygdamus, I couldn't do a thing; I had been captured just like you." The *servitium amoris* has never seemed more absolute than when the lover addresses Lygdamus as slave to fellow slave. As in 1.1, Cynthia has captured the lover, and her more potent eyes have bested his. Now, however, gouged eyes and bloody gashes have been added to the metaphorical wounds the lover received from looking in 1.1, 2.22A, and 2.25. He is as battered and sore as 1.1's mythological exemplum, Milanion, the lover of Atalanta, who suffered serious injuries when fighting a centaur for her (1.1.9–16).

Cynthia takes full advantage of her triumph when the lover sues for peace. He grovels at her feet, which she will scarcely let him touch. He must accept all her conditions if he is to win her forgiveness (4.8.75–78):

> tu neque Pompeia spatiabere cultus in umbra,
> > nec cum lasciuum sternet harena Forum.

colla caue inflectas ad summum obliqua theatrum,
     aut lectica tuae se det aperta morae.

You shall not strut about dressed up in Pompey's Porch
     Or when they strew sand in the ribald Forum.
Take care you don't turn around and stare at the upper Theatre
     Or allow an open litter to offer itself to your gaze.[33]

The specularization of the lover now seems complete, as Cynthia out-
laws excessive attention to his appearance, thus reminding us that the
lover previously begged, rather than ordered, his mistress not to adorn
herself too much. Concern with the lover's whereabouts focuses on limiting his ability to display himself to a desiring gaze in areas frequented
by the lascivious.[34] Turning to sneak a glance towards the back of the theater, where the women sit, is also proscribed. Allowing his gaze to linger
on a woman in her litter who has her curtains drawn back to display herself is likewise forbidden. These conditions are imposed on the lover who
is prostrate before her and, therefore, in no position to gaze even upon
her.[35] In order to be forgiven, the lover must agree to surrender the right
to be a spectator and accept that Cynthia will control to what degree he
can be a spectacle. This *scripta puella* ("written woman") is being credited
with rewriting the rules of the game.

     Cynthia's final condition is the sale of Lygdamus, whom she appears
to blame as the go-between in procuring the lover's promiscuous companions (Fedeli 1965 ad loc.). The lover capitulates completely
(4.8.81–82):

     indixit leges: respondi ego "Legibus utar."
          riserat imperio facta superba dato.

     Such were her terms. I answered: "I accept the terms."
          She laughed, made proud by the power I gave her.

When Cynthia was made proud before, it was because the poet-lover had
praised her hair and, by doing so, had publicly recorded her exalted value
in the specular economy of his poetry. At the end of Book 3, in words
that 4.8 here recalls (*facta superba*, "made proud," is in the same metrical position in each poem), Cynthia was also said to be made proud, too
proud, by the lover's eyes. In 4.8, the lover's eyes are scratched and poked
by a Cynthia who no longer seems constrained by the scopic value system of the earlier elegies. The lover's eyes have lost the aesthetic credibility to make anyone proud. The lover himself has agreed to abandon

the privilege of the gaze, whose solitary focus on Cynthia once exalted her above all others (including, we are repeatedly told, the lover himself). Now Cynthia is made proud by the transfer of power from lover to mistress, from former spectator to erstwhile spectacle, and perhaps, too, from poet to *materia* ("literary material"). Cynthia was once proud to be a compelling spectacle, and the lover delighted in being a compulsive spectator. By giving up the right to see or be seen, the lover gives Cynthia the power to laugh at him and lays aside the antagonism that is a prerequisite for erotic elegy. Cynthia is absent from the rest of the book, which closes with a poem to the matron Cornelia, a paragon of chaste monogamy and, therefore, the antithesis of the elegiac woman.

In this essay, I have drawn upon conceptions of gaze theory formulated by Freud, Irigaray, Lacan, Newman, and even Socrates, and applied to elegy by Gold, Wyke, and Greene. Gaze theory permits us to apprehend more completely the construction of the elegiac woman as the relational other, the *materia* required by the poet. It also enables us to understand how Cynthia, this foil for the lover, can convincingly assume the dominant position in the disrupted gender hierarchy of Propertian elegy. Cynthia is a "looker," defined simultaneously by her beauty and by the look with which she intercepts the phallic gaze of the lover, catches him looking at her with desire, and uses that knowledge to emasculate him and hold his gaze captive.[36] Throughout the Propertian text, the eyes of lover and mistress frequently engage in a struggle for control, what Ellen Greene identifies as the contest for erotic domination (1998.37–66). The lover sometimes embraces, sometimes chafes against the discomfiting gaze that Cynthia's captivating eyes employ to cast down his eyes. Knowledge of her power beneath and through the gaze is attributed to Cynthia, and she is shown to revel in it. By controlling access to her beauty, sometimes naked, sometimes clothed, Cynthia is shown to inflame and manipulate the lover's elegiac passion. From the beginning, Cynthia is made proud of her looks by the affirming gaze of the spectator-poet-lover who deems her a fitting spectacle to record in his poems. Yet the woman who looks back is a monster or a witch, and the lover eventually cannot endure to stay caught in her trap. Having tried ineffectively to escape their exchange of looks, the poet-lover has to destroy the specular value of this constructed beauty. But the monster will not die. She reappears first in the guise of an ugly old crone, and then she comes back from the grave to reclaim her specular value. Finally, in her ultimate appearance, she comes back as an impassioned beauty, spectacle and spectator all in one, more alive than the incapacitated lover. She routs her competitors for the lover's gaze and punishes his eyes for losing their focus on her. By agreement, she then blinds the lover to all other women and rescinds his rights to see and be seen. This absolute rout of the male gaze by the Gorgon-like female object constitutes the transcendent triumph of Cynthia's annihilating gaze, but the victory of the woman looking back spells the death of amatory elegy in Propertius.

Notes

1. Wyke 1987b and 1989a. See also Konstan 1994.150–59, who emphasizes that the mistress must be fickle, greedy, and "more the object than the subject of erotic passion" to enable elegy as a literary form.

2. See Zizek 1991.107–22, especially 110, 114, and 118. For aspects of the Lacanian gaze less relevant to this paper, see Zizek 1992.15 and 126–27 and 2001.247–52.

3. The closest Lacan comes to addressing gender dynamics in the gaze explicitly is in answer to a question about the apprehension of the gaze in the direction of desire (1977.9): "If one does not stress the dialectic of desire one does not understand why the gaze of others should disorganize the field of perception."

4. Newman 1997. I selected the two quotations from Brontë's *Wuthering Heights* at the start of this chapter from among the numerous passages Newman cites in her article to illustrate the power of the woman's gaze.

5. All Propertius translations are from Lee 1994. I have occasionally made some minor changes of phraseology to emphasize the vocabulary of looking, to permit the recognition of an intertextual link, or to create a more literal translation.

6. "In this matter of the visible, everything is a trap," opines Lacan 1977.92–93, by which he means that something that is there to be looked at is designed to catch the observer in its trap.

7. Papanghelis 1987.10–19. See also Nakayama 1963–64.62–73.

8. On the association of Cynthia with Coan silk and its transparent qualities, see O'Neill 2000.269 and notes 33 and 34.

9. "Myiscus, shooting me, whom the Loves could not wound, under the breast with his eyes, shouted out thus: 'It is I who have struck him down, the overbold, and see how I tread underfoot the arrogance of sceptred wisdom that sat on his brow,'" *A.P.* 12.101.1–4.

10. Sharrock 1994b.57–58. Winkler states that eye contact can play the part of an erotic binding spell and quotes Sophocles' *Oinomaus* frag. 474 as an example of the erotic magical potential of the eyes (1990.85).

11. Richardson 1977 ad loc. Eyes are also associated with beauty at 1.18.13–16, 2.26A.13–14, and 2.28.9–12.

12. I am grateful to Cindy Benton for drawing this passage to my attention.

13. All Xenophon translations come from Marchant and Todd 1979.

14. On the literary relationship between Propertius's Acanthis and Ovid's Dipsas, see O'Neill, 1999.

15. For the bawd as witch, see Sharrock 1994b, O'Neill 1998, and Myers 1996.

16. Vivienne J. Gray interprets Socrates' words as a playful comparison of his own trade with Theodote's (1998.146).

17. I note in passing that the hunting metaphors that characterize Theodote's pursuit of admirers find a parallel in Cynthia's association with Atalanta in Propertius 1.1. Theodote's shutting out (*apokleiein*) of an arrogant lover could also be seen as setting the stage for a *paraklausithyron*. Socrates makes a convincing elegiac bawd.

18. The Propertian lover expresses a desire to study that other expositor of Socratic thought, Plato, at 3.21.25–26.

19. *Vidi* (I saw) in line 5 is the most widely accepted emendation for the obviously corrupt *cogis* or *togis* of the mss.

20. Richardson explains the first four words: "Every man who sees you is your victim" (1977 ad loc.).

21. The question attributed to the girl undermines the lover's boast to Demophoon that he is an indefatigable lover (2.22A). I have tried to capture the sexual challenge in Cynthia's words by translating *lente* as "slowpoke." Note that, in *Amores* 3.7, where the poet bemoans an incident of impotence, the verb *iacere* ("to lie prostrate") is repeatedly used to convey the excessive *mollitia* ("softness") of his member (4, 15, 65, and 69).

22. It is tempting, perhaps, to see an echo of the Endymion and Selene story in the lover's subsequent emphasis (37–40) on the possibility of gaining immortality through spending nights with his mistress like the one he just spent. Out of love for Endymion, Selene extracted a promise from Zeus to grant him one wish, and the young man asked to be granted eternal sleep, thus remaining young and beautiful forever. Some versions of the story have Selene fall in love with him during his eternal sleep; like the lover, he would have been lying there, inert, while Selene tried to coax him into making love.

23. In an elegy that may allude to this passage from 2.22A, the lover extols the less corrupting lifestyle of Sparta; among other improvements, expensive clothing does not tempt eyes to wander (*errantia lumina*, 3.14.27).

24. Lines 39–40 mirror the structure and vocabulary of 1.1.25–26. Self-reference is common in Propertius, but the links between poems where scopic matters feature prominently seem constructed with particular care.

25. The position of *doctas* ("learned") earlier in the line than *Athenas* allows us, however briefly, to anticipate that the lover is traveling to see learned women of Cynthia's ilk (1.7.11, 2.11.6, 2.13.11).

26. Catullus's version of the story refers frequently to the gaze and eyes of Ariadne as she recalls her lover's false promises (64.50–250). The combination of Theseus with *litoribus Piraei* in neighboring lines of the Catullan text (64.73–74) establishes a link with this Propertian text.

27. Goold notes that 3.24 and 3.25, which he prints as one poem, share the same themes, structure, and even the same number of lines (38) as 1.1 (1990 ad loc.).

28. Richard Thomas dubs this kind of reference to a number of antecedents "conflation" (1986.193–98). For another example of Ovid referring to two contradictory passages in Propertius, see O'Neill 1999.297–98.

29. See Newman 1997.450–53 and Freud, "Medusa's Head," in *The Complete Psychological Works of Sigmund Freud*, vol. 18, ed. Strachey (1955.273–74).

30. Cp. Verg. *Aen.* 3.320, Ov. *Am.* 3.6.28, *Met.* 10.601, V. Fl. 7.105, Stat. *Theb.* 11.700, *Silvae* 14.400.

31. Note that Tarpeia (*obstipuit*, 4.4.19–22) and the lover (*obstipui*, 2.29.3–4) are *immobilized* by looking or by the desire for what they are looking at. In 1.3, the lover's response (*obstupui*, 28) may stem more from the sleeping girl's sighs than from the effect of his gaze. Nevertheless, the lover's gaze upon the sleeping mistress is so all-consuming that he compares himself to Argus, whose many eyes kept watch on the transformed Io (1.3.19–20). He describes himself as spellbound with his eyes intent upon her (*intentis . . . fixus ocellis*, 19).

32. At 4.5.39–40, the old bawd Acanthis counsels the elegiac woman always to have fresh bite marks on her neck for the lover to see.

33. For the last line of this passage, I have drawn on the text and translation as printed by Goold 1990, who accepts Gruter's *se det* ("offers itself") for the surely corrupt *sudet* of the mss.

34. W. A. Camps notes that Ovid later identifies Pompey's Portico and the Forum, among other public places, as locations where flirts of either sex went to meet (1965 ad loc.). See *Ars* 1.67ff., 89ff., and 163ff.

35. At 2.30A.7–10, Love presses down the head and neck of the lover and will not let him raise his captured eyes from the ground.

36. I borrow this bivalent word from Newman, who plays with the colloquial sense of a "good-looking woman" and the more literal "someone who looks."

Female Subjectivity
and Silence

Hermeneutic Uncertainty and the Feminine in Ovid's *Ars Amatoria*

The Procris and Cephalus Digression

Phebe Lowell Bowditch

The ghost of Cynthia delivers a chilling harangue to Propertius for his cheap funeral arrangements and infidelity after her death (4.7); Ovid, in turn, launches two poems mixing prayer and reproof of Corinna for aborting a child (2.13, 14). In one case, the poem depicts with grisly realism a woman's voice and perspective; in the other, the feelings, motives, and cultural context of the woman are suppressed.[1] Indeed, the subject status and agency of the women featured in Latin love elegy have been disputed since the 1970s: early feminist criticism on elegy saw the often dominant role of the elegiac mistress as evidence of a countercultural empowerment of women that sought to challenge the ideological power structures of the Augustan regime (Hallett 1973). Today, many scholars see the elevation of the elegiac woman's status in relation to her lover as merely textual inversion on the part of the male poet, who nonetheless maintains discursive mastery over the beloved.[2] But those writing from perspectives influenced by French feminism and Lacanian psychoanalysis see the elegiac representation of the concepts of woman and the feminine subject in terms of disruption and instability in a text: that is, despite the elegiac poet's seeming mastery and control of the mistress as textual object, there are spaces in the narrative whose logical inconsistency or semantic indeterminacy reveal the mark of the feminine as an otherness that a masculine system—in this case, the discourse of love elegy—can neither control nor repress. These spaces may be logical disjunctions, textual problems, or thematic incoherencies that result from the attempt to represent the concept of woman or from conflicting representations of feminine subject positions.[3]

While much has been written about these problems in relation to elegy proper, there are few gendered readings that directly address the question of women's subject status and constructions of the feminine in the *Ars Amatoria*.[4] Perhaps this critical neglect derives from the unsettling view of elegy unmasked by the *Ars*: that is, the various conventions and topoi of elegy are revealed as a semiotic (often behavioral) system, one whose principles become, in the *Ars*, objective material to be taught and manipulated for the purposes of seduction. The social power with which a woman is invested in elegy is shown to be merely a strategy for masculine control over her. Moreover, for all its urbane wit, there is something chilling, even monstrous about the *Ars*, a text that asserts that a woman's "no" in fact means "yes," that force is permissible to make an erotic conquest (1.664–80), and whose narrator observes women in pain as aestheticized objects. In a text that is all about control, both of the self and of women, the concept of a female subject independent of masculine discourse seems moot. And yet I will argue that, even in this most cynical of works, it is possible to discover evidence of resistance to such control in both the logical disjunctions of the narrative itself and in the role that women occupy as unpredictable readers—of semiotic systems, of myth, and of Ovid's own poem.

Reading this text with a view to recovering the potential for a feminine subject position not fully controlled and constructed by masculine discourse must begin with a recognition that the *praeceptor*, who so conspicuously flaunts his intent to manipulate women, is a figure whose own status is made problematic by the premise of his argument: the idea of the self as a rhetorical construction. The *Ars Amatoria*, or at least its narrator, presents a view of the self that subverts what a recent critic identifies as the typical "relationship of cause and effect . . . in Platonic ontology and *mimesis*." In Ovid's erotic handbook, Duncan Kennedy argues, this relationship is reversed: representations, rather than being degenerative versions of the "real," in fact create it, bringing about "the possibility of truth, knowledge, and progress" (2000.168–72). Ovid's pedagogical verse equates didacticism with mimesis, so that the citation of prior texts authorizes the knowledge of the *praeceptor* even as such texts become the means by which the student realizes his self. But we should note that, even in Plato, although imitations *are* ontologically inferior to what they imitate, mimesis, in some instances, can be a cause as well as an effect. Thus when we consider the *praeceptor*'s claim in Book 1 of the *Ars* that the lover who plays the part and imitates the effects of love often begins to experience as real the very attitudes and postures he invokes as conventions (1.615–16), we are reminded of Socrates' warning in the

Republic that impersonation can profoundly alter a person's character (3.395d). In the ontological context of the *Ars*, when Ovid lends his "signature" to the end of Books 2 and 3, *Naso magister erat* ("Naso was your teacher"), he flirts with the boundary that separates the *praeceptor*'s system from the poet's own biography. For he archly tempts the reader to collapse the distinction between an authorial self and the *praeceptor*[5] and to speculate whether, by the laws of his creation, the author who adopts in his own name a persona that devalues women with a cynical Don Juanism risks acquiring the identity of a misogynist. And for all that Ovid here plays a sophisticated game of self-impersonation in adopting the role of *praeceptor*, the recognition of that literary game makes it no easier to determine whether he seeks to expose, to perpetuate, or cleverly to satirize the power dynamics of gendered relations in Augustan Rome.[6]

All the same, if the self is refashioned, even created, through the representations it assumes and projects, this "constructionist" view of subjectivity opens up a space for deconstruction of certain edifices of gender and for women's resistance to accepting the role of object that the narrator's system in the *Ars* assigns them. Like the "many faces of fear" that the narrator remarks in the victims' attitudes during the rape of the Sabine women (1.121–26), the objectified status of the female in Ovid's text has many manifestations: she is the *quod* or "that which" the lover must discover (1.35); she is the animal to hunt down in the natural world; she is the *materia* or "matter" for a long love (1.49); and, finally, she is both a visible surface of pain that excites the sadistic and erotic gaze of the narrator and a cosmetic surface, the narrator's ideal woman of Book 3.[7] As we shall see, however, the very premise of the *Ars*—that prior texts, paradigms, and conventions of behavior serve to mediate, indeed generate, the "real"—provides the antidote or *pharmakon*, as it were, to such constructions of gender.

To be sure, this objectification of women is often metaphorical, not only part of the classical treasury of tropes for the concept of woman but also an index of how the "feminine" serves as a metaphor in its own right. Thus the elaboration of what is feminine in Book 3 becomes, on closer analysis, a figure for the aesthetic process. Moreover, such object status is necessarily belied in Ovid's text by certain attributes *puellae* ("girls," slang for female love-interests) possess and that they must possess in order to respond to the narrator's systematic manipulation of erotic conventions: for women are also viewed as readers and writers in dialogue with a literate male (3.438–86, 2.395–97). They may refuse a first epistle, but a persistent suitor will have his letters read, and a woman who has wished to read, will wish also to reply (1.469–70, 479–82). The woman must read about and respond to her potential lover before she sees him, thus engaging her imagination and sustaining a vision of both him and herself through the medium of writing and language—the very condition, some would argue, of subjectivity. The sense of private interiority may even be accentuated by the social context: out in public, because the lover is advised to beware of possible eavesdroppers, he communicates messages ambiguated by a riddling language that a woman must interpret (1.487–90). At dinner parties, she must decipher statements traced in wine (1.569–72) or, at the theater, be attuned to the less subtle if equally semiotic eyebrows that speak across a public space (1.497–500). In addition, there are all the tell-tale "signs" of love—the tears (real or simulated) (1.659–62), pale complexion (1.729–30), and underfed physique (1.733)—the physiological lexicon of elegiac passion that must be understood in its proper discursive context. Hence, although women may be objects to be shaped, they are also readers, writers, and decoders, and therefore subjects who participate in the interpretation of, and communication through, semiotic systems. Indeed, they are just as involved in the rhetorical construction of the self and the mediated nature of "truth" as their male counterparts. And yet whose subjectivity is this? That is, are women only subjects to be mastered by a manipulation of elegiac rhetoric, or does an inherent instability in the narrator's system effectively lend women, at least within the parameters of Ovid's *Ars Amatoria*, the potential to elude such domination?

Let us consider this last question by focusing on a few of the digressions in which constructions of femininity—either in metaphorical terms or explicitly as a subject position—pose interpretive problems. The digressions, as extended mythological tales intended to illustrate the *praeceptor*'s advice, must be interpreted in light of an implicit analogy: the parallel between the *praeceptor*'s relationship to the *materia* ("subject matter") or thematic content of his text and his, or his student-lover's, relationship to a woman.[8] There are two complementary levels of art in the *Ars Amatoria*: the art of seduction, which ensnares and holds the woman as *materia*, and the poetic art, which shapes the material of the narrator's didactic advice (serving to seduce the reader as well).[9] Given this analogy—that a woman parallels the text as unformed material—it follows that where the *praeceptor* loses control of his narrative, where there are contradictions or betrayals of his intentions, where a digression resists or complicates, through overdetermination, the precepts that it is meant to illustrate, there is a place coded as "feminine" that seeks to elude full determination by masculine discourse. Seen from the perspective of a conflict between the objectivity of didactic verse as a literary mode and the subjectivity characteristic of elegy proper, these runaway digressions constitute the symbolic resistance to masculine control of a genre often characterized as feminine (because *mollis* or "soft").[10] The gendered dichotomy between the male as the controlling and privileged subject—that is, the *praeceptor* and his student-lover—and the female as an object to be caught, held, and molded is therefore replicated on the generic level in the contrast between masculine didactic and feminine elegy, the tropes and conventions of which are presented as a body of knowledge that can be objectively systematized.[11]

Such an approach would seem initially to bypass the representation of women in Ovid's text as individual subjects and favor instead the view of the feminine in French feminist thought: that "woman" signifies "a process that disrupts symbolic structures in male discourse."[12] And when we consider the *praeceptor* as a narrator whose relationship with his material is shown to be governed by emotional outbursts, all the fits and starts of a temperamental teller (one who is prompted, in the first place, by feelings of revenge [1.23–24]), such "disruptions" of his system could be read as so many confirmations of the symbolic structure that aligns the feminine with spontaneous emotion, nature, the corporeal and animal world, etc. For when a digression betrays the narrator's intentions or signifies beyond the precept meant to be illustrated, it often involves emotion or the forces of "nature" overcoming reason and art—and to understand such conflicts in gendered terms would only shore up conventional gender constructions. Indeed, as we shall see, the *praeceptor*'s own emotional involvement in the imaginative pictures that he develops in the digressions implies that he is giving in to the feminine elements of his psychological makeup.[13] Moreover, if we do understand Ovid as separate from his *praeceptor* (despite the potential consequences of his self-impersonation as discussed above), as an author staging this conflict between his narrator's masculine didactic system and the unruly spontaneity of his *materia*, then the feminine spaces that disrupt the constructionist premises of the *praeceptor* could be read as a reinforcement of the essentialist position of a "natural," pre-rhetorical self. And yet, even if we were to posit such authorial intention, these disruptions nonetheless create a space where the signifying excess, as it were, of the mythic tale prevents hermeneutic closure and allows for an instability of structures of gender as well as for interpretations that affirm the possibility of a feminine subject independent of masculine control. And for all that Ovid's text cannot be taken to represent historical women—after all, this is a text where mimesis does not reflect but rather creates "reality"—the female subject alluded to within Books 1 and 2 is paralleled by Book 3's audience of *puellae* ("girls," "potential mistresses"). In turn, the figure of Procris in the Procris and Cephalus digression is the mythic counterpart of this audience, even as she serves to focalize the experience of doubt in a more sophisticated reader. As I hope to show, her interpretive error (deriving from her status as a subject in language) points to the polysemous character of the tale as a whole (the unruliness of the digression), suggesting what may be characterized as a gendered, even feminine, reading of the text.

The construction of both textual and physical matter as feminine is prominent in the digression in which Ulysses must constantly retell the story of the Trojan war for a Calypso reluctant to let him go (2.123–42). As he traces his reductive *Iliad* on the shore, embellishing his own daring in the killing of Dolon and the theft of King Rhesus's horses, a wave rolls up and washes away these sandcastles of epic *kleos* ("glory").[14] Calypso, seizing the opportunity, draws an admonitory (and self-serving) conclusion: Ulysses should be wary of trusting waves whose force has wiped out such great *nomina* or names (2.141–42). Comic in its diminution of epic subjects to drawings in the sand, this scene alludes to the *Odyssey*'s thematic linking of the feminine with the sea and the hero's consequent fear of cultural anonymity. Calypso, ironically, here warns against the very loss of fame that she herself represents for the hero. But the destruction of *nomina* by such a fluid element also resonates with the *Ars Amatoria*'s own thematic exploration of the instability of semiotic systems. In this digression, we see the familiar binary opposition between nature as the realm of the feminine disrupting and effacing the realm of masculine culture, but the word *nomina* functions in an overdetermined way: not only does it refer literally to the names of heroes at Troy and thus to their cultural reputation and glory—the *kleos* of a name familiar through storytelling—but it also signals that the entire Homeric system of values is a cultural code, a semiotic system that, in keeping with the formulaic epic by which it is reinforced, constitutes a cultural construction—a castle in the sand, as it were—rather than a transcendent essential order. Moreover, in keeping with the ironic fact that staying with Calypso herself would ensure the hero's anonymity, the goddess's repeated requests for Homeric epic serve as a feminine strategy to keep Ulysses busy with storytelling, preventing his desired departure.[15] As such, her feminine wiles might be said to manipulate the masculine system of epic discourse for her own purposes, a kind of appropriation of Homeric *nomina* that, *mutatis mutandis*, recalls Sappho's recasting of epic discourse in the context of private passion (see Winkler 1990.162–87).

This instability of *nomina* (or of language more generally), and its relation to masculine cultural codes, appears as well towards the end of Book 1. After advising that love may enter a relationship disguised by the name of friendship (1.720), a strategy of deception whose Latin term is *dare verba*, "to give words," twenty lines later the *praeceptor* laments that right and wrong are presently confused and that both *amicitia*, "friendship," and *fides*, "trustworthiness," are "empty terms" or words: *nomina inania* (1.739–40).[16] A comic moment, to be sure, since although the *praeceptor* refers in this instance to the possibility that a trusted companion might steal his friend's mistress, the hypocrisy that contaminates the signifying function of these words applies not least to the narrator's own perversely corrupt exploitation of friendship and a woman's assumed credulity. However, from the perspective that meaning is produced through representation (thus the man who "plays" the lover becomes one), it is the so-called emptiness of such terms as *amicitia* and *fides* that permits them to be redeployed in a different discursive context than the network of male patronage and friendship to which they more generally refer.[17] That is, there is no essential connection between these *nomina* ("nouns," "names," "terms") as words or signifiers and the masculine social relations they signify—only accepted convention. All the same, when such cultural codes *are* manipulated, they still depend on the assumption of common references in order—even deviously—to function.[18]

The Ulysses and Calypso digression underscores the fragility of such cultural codes, although it is intended to emphasize the importance of eloquence. Presumably, because Ulysses had continually to retell the story of the Trojan war, he provides a positive model of linguistic invention and innovation: he is the Homeric bard engaged in oral formulaic improvisation—a paradigm for the lover who must improvise variations on a prior text. However, he is also the *praeceptor*, teaching through representation, relying on his imitative exempla in the sand. That these should be so easily dissolved by the waves hardly serves to illustrate the effectiveness of eloquence as a strategy in a system that aims to control wayward passion. But this "mythologem" signifies more than the potential for wild emotion, as symbolized by the sea, to overwhelm artifice. For the digression self-reflexively figures the way the *praeceptor*'s own material—coded as feminine—resists the masculine control of his didactic purpose.

A similar disruption of the coherent exposition of his system occurs later in Book 2, when the advice to rekindle a dying passion through the revelation of real (or fabricated) infidelities evolves into a meditation on the genesis or creation of the world (2.439–92). Not only does the *praeceptor* reveal his longing for a time of sexual spontaneity when men and women, in a primitive animal state, instinctually found their way without the need of instruction, but his erratic narration as a spontaneous emotional effusion belies the posture of narratorial control and necessitates the intervention of Apollo. Inasmuch as emotionality in Roman culture is aligned with women (it is contrary to Roman *gravitas*, "dignity," "solemnity" and masculine self-restraint), the *praeceptor*'s sentimental reverie as a "runaway" text again figures the resistance of his *materia* and is a mark of the feminine.[19] Indeed, it is precisely the passionate and violent behavior unleashed by jealousy in a woman that attracts the speaker and leads him to abandon his didactic posture. He wishes that he could be the lucky recipient of such rage—the sign of a woman's passion and a prelude to sweet reconciliation through lovemaking: "ille ego sim, cuius laniet furiosa capillos; / ille ego sim, teneras cui petat ungue genas" ("Let me be the one whose hair she rips out in fury; let me be the one whose soft cheeks she marks with her nails," 451–52).

The relationship between this situation and the following lines on genesis and animal sexuality lies in the concept of eros as a civilizing and taming force, a view with a long literary and philosophical pedigree.[20] Moreover, verbal echoes between the lines describing lovemaking after quarreling and the evolution of the world from chaos reinforce an analogy between the act of sex (if not specifically procreation) and the creation of the cosmos.[21] And yet this digression has predictably struck some critics as irrelevant Ovidian excess or as merely part of Ovid's game of "disproportion"—epic style and content set against the banal frame of erotic jealousy and infidelity.[22] Generic incongruity is no doubt meant to amuse and divert, but such disjunction also accords with the feminine disturbance of the *praeceptor*'s system—both in terms of the implicit rejection of reason and calculation that the passage displays and in the very details of the animal erotics that are emphasized (481–88):

> ales habet, quod amet; cum quo sua gaudia iungat,
> 　　invenit in media femina piscis aqua;
> cerva parem sequitur, serpens serpente tenetur;
> 　　haeret adulterio cum cane nexa canis;
> laeta salitur ovis, tauro quoque laeta iuvenca est;
> 　　sustinet inmundum sima capella marem.

in furias agitantur equae spatioque remota
  per loca dividuos amne sequuntur equos.

The bird has its love object; the female fish finds in the deep a mate with
which to couple; the deer pursues her stag, snake is embraced by snake; bitch
clings fast in wayward sex with another dog; the ewe is happily mounted, the
heifer rejoices in her bull; the flat-nosed she-goat sustains the stinking bil-
lygoat. Mares are driven into a frenzy and pursue stallions across the river,
through out-of-the-way places.

This passage has the reductive ring of a nursery rhyme, a kind of birds
and bees version of evolution, but it points up the female of the species
as the subject of the verbal action. And while one of the premises of Book
1 is affirmed—women, the female sex, are lustful and therefore ready for
the taking—these lines nonetheless give agency to the female in a way
that contradicts her object status in the *praeceptor*'s system. The female
fish, singled out with the adjective *femina*, actively discovers her mate,
and the gendered power relations of the fishing metaphor for "catching
a girl" at the poem's outset (1.47–48) thereby become neutralized, if not
in fact inverted, in this vision of harmonious animal sexuality. Mutual attraction governs here, a far cry from the violent coercion deemed legitimate by the *praeceptor* in the first book. And yet, despite this glimpse of
female agency, the alignment of emotion, nature, and animal instinct
with the feminine gender is, as I remark above, hardly an escape from
masculine discourse. The desire to give way to these attributes may signify the repressed feminine nature of the *praeceptor*, but the gendered
coding of such attributes *as* feminine is nonetheless a convention of a patriarchal culture and numerous male-authored texts. And from the perspective of tamed wildness, where a lover's soothing of a woman's anger
is paralleled by the transformation of chaos into cosmic order, the genesis passage here does, in the logic of the metaphor, imply the shaping of
the female sex.

This leads us to consider the implications of the Procris and
Cephalus digression, the only extended mythological exemplum in Book
3 (685–746). For Procris, it can be argued, also embodies contradictions
in the *Ars Amatoria*'s conception of the feminine, both reaffirming and
resisting such gendered coding. In order to fully understand the function
of this myth as recounted here, it is necessary to examine the intertextual backdrop of other versions and take into account the varied audiences for whom the *praeceptor* writes. Let me briefly review the major
components of the different tellings of the myth, starting with the bare

frame of this version, introduced by the narrator as a cautionary tale for women who too readily believe rumors about the philandering of their husbands or lovers. As narrated in the *Ars Amatoria*, Cephalus often leaves his home to hunt on Mount Hymettus, where, at noon, he habitually lies down in a *locus amoenus* ("pleasant spot") and summons the cool, "shifting breeze" (*mobilis aura*) to relieve him of his heat (3.697–98). An officious gossip overhears Cephalus and reports these *auditos sonos* ("overheard sounds," 3.700) to Procris, who understands them to refer to the name of a mistress, Aura. After losing and regaining consciousness, Procris first indulges in the conventional acts of despair: she rips her clothes, gouges her cheeks, and runs through the streets, hair outstrewn, like a possessed maenad. However, when she arrives at the grove, she has enough self-composure to conduct an empirical test and review of the evidence. Encouraging her suspicions, as the narrator relates, are the place, the name, and the informant (*index*), as well as the traces (*vestigia*) of bodies pressed on the grass (3.719–22).[23] But when she hides in the bushes and overhears her husband call on both the gentle Zephyr, or West wind, and *aura*, the breeze, she recognizes her mistake. Her *mens* ("mind") returns, and color comes back to her face. As she moves out of her hiding place, her rustling movements startle Cephalus, who, as he leaps up, thinks he sees an animal, and pierces her with a fatal cast of his spear.

Perhaps the most important difference from other versions of the myth in this telling is the complete absence of any overt reference to the goddess of the dawn, Aurora. Ovid does mention her briefly at the beginning of Book 3, as an immortal who enjoys Cephalus's youthful charms—"nec Cephalus roseae praeda pudenda deae" ("Nor was Cephalus a catch for which the rosy dawn-goddess felt shame," 84)—but he suppresses any mention of other details that appear in more extended permutations, such as his own account in the *Metamorphoses* (7.672–862). To be sure, the earliest rendition given by the scholiast at *Odyssey* 11.321, drawn from Pherecydes, does not feature any explicit infidelity on Cephalus's part but shows him as a neglectful, suspicious husband who, gone for eight years after his marriage to Procris, returns in disguise and successfully tempts her with jewelry to sleep with him. It is only after their reconciliation, when a slave reports that he has heard his master calling Νεφέλη ("Cloud") on his repeated hunting expeditions, that Procris investigates by following Cephalus to his mountain top, only to be killed by him as in Ovid's telling.

Thus although the account attributed to Pherecydes does figure possible confusion over an anthropomorphized natural phenomenon—is

Νεφέλη simply a cloud?—it is only in the more fleshed-out versions of this myth in Antoninus Liberalis, Hyginus, and Ovid's *Metamorphoses* (and Servius) that the figure of Ἠώς/Aurora plays a part, falling in love with and abducting Cephalus.[24] Her later incitement of Cephalus's suspicions about Procris is then implied in Antoninus (whose sources are Hellenistic, e.g., Nicander), while both Ovid's epic version and Hyginus have the dawn-goddess actively transforming the young man's appearance and encouraging him to test his wife's fidelity. Excepting Servius, in all these accounts, Procris departs for exile out of shame for having given in to the "stranger's" temptation (although in the Ovidian *Metamorphoses*, she only shows signs of weakening before Cephalus reveals himself). Antoninus recounts that Procris goes into exile on Crete, where she devises a remedy for King Minos's sexual infertility, and he rewards her with a javelin that never misses its mark and a similarly magical hound.[25] In Ovid's epic and Hyginus, these are gifts from Diana, to whose company Procris devotes herself as a huntress, abjuring contact with the opposite sex. Most significant for the question of gender identification is the homosexual and cross-dressing motif that occurs in both Antoninus and Hyginus and that Ovid, arguably, hints at in Cephalus's own narration of his experience in the *Metamorphoses*.[26] In this twist to the story, Procris, disguised as a man, returns to Cephalus's house and joins him in the hunt. When Cephalus witnesses the extraordinary powers of the javelin and hound, he asks for them as a gift from Procris. She is willing to grant his request only on the condition that he have sex with her—"Give me what boys are wont to give" ("da mihi id quod pueri solent dare") as Hyginus *Fabulae* 189.7 puts it.[27] Despite the somewhat periphrastic expression, it is clear that Procris's demand puts Cephalus in the feminized position of the ἐρώμενος ("beloved boy"), even as she takes on a masculine role—a point to which we will return. When Cephalus agrees, Procris reveals herself in the bedroom, but still gives him the weapons. At this point Procris no longer figures in Antoninus's narrative, but, in Hyginus, she meets her tragic end as she does in Ovid's two renditions—following Cephalus into the forest only to be killed by his javelin. It is only in Ovid and Servius, however, that Cephalus's calls to *aura* produce confusion and suggestively echo the name of the dawn-goddess, Aurora.[28]

Now to what degree Ovid in the *Ars* is assuming knowledge on his reader's part of an intertext of material included in other versions of the myth is a vexed question. Peter Green argues (1975) that Ovid has deliberately chosen one of the most tawdry tales of Greco-Roman mythol-

ogy and suppressed many of the details. This widely disseminated interpretation of the Procris and Cephalus episode (appearing in condensed
form in the notes of the Penguin translation) reads it as a cynical manipulation of the third book's notional female audience that, unlike its
male counterpart, is culturally unsophisticated: in this view, such readers
possess no sense of intertextuality and are thus ignorant of the more extended permutations of the myth, where Cephalus is blatantly unfaithful to his wife, and Procris, in turn, not only is successfully seduced—or
at least tempted—by her husband in disguise, but also takes vengeance
in the basest fashion. According to Green, Ovid's selective fashioning of
the myth reinforces double standards, whereby the male audience views
Procris as a "conniving little trollop who deserved all she got" (1975.24),
and the naïve female readership is duly warned by Procris's rash behavior to disregard hearsay (thus conveniently enabling the infidelities of
men). Such a critical reading has been faulted for wrongly assuming both
a single master version of the myth, an Ur-text that supersedes all other
versions, and that myth is primarily passed down through writing
(Fontenrose 1980).

These objections are also relevant to the question of audience and,
ultimately, to a female reader as a gendered subject position. For if myth
is recognized as first and foremost an oral phenomenon, reinforced by
literature as well as by visual media, and if we recognize that literate
women—those who would qualify as readers of the *Ars Amatoria* in the
first place—would have read the literary classics as part of their elemen-
tary education, then it becomes more difficult to view Ovid's female audience—implied or actual—as necessarily any less mythologically sophisticated than his male one.[29] Indeed, we know that Sophocles wrote
a play Πρόκρις, that Nicander was probably the source for Antoninus,
and that the figures of Procris and Cephalus were part of the repertoire
of Attic vase painting.[30] And no fewer than eighty-one extant Attic vases
depict Cephalus with Ἡώς (Dawn or Aurora).[31] Clearly there were
plenty of visual and literary reminders of other elements or permutations
of the myth. Moreover, *any* reader could have picked up on the allusion
to Cephalus's affair with Aurora, goddess of the dawn, in line 3.84 and
realized that the later extended digression may be only part of the story.[32]
Thus while the idea of a single Ur-text of the myth should be discarded,
the presence of Aurora and a complex intertextual backdrop to the digression should not.

Such an intertext is clearly operative if, as one commentary suggests,
Ovid invites his reader to jump to conclusions similar to those of Pro-

cris: just as she believes *aura* to refer to a woman Aura, so we suspect that *aura* may very well conceal the name Aurora (Gibson 2003.358). And though we should realize our error just as Procris does, the uncertainty that the *praeceptor* has introduced with his mention of the "rosy goddess" (3.84) is, I believe, never fully put to rest. Such doubt and uncertainty accompany the process of interpretation, and Procris, inscribed as a reader within the poem, becomes emblematic of a reader's experience of subjectivity as effected by the actual process of reading.[33] Alison Sharrock deftly analyzes the role of readers of the *Ars Amatoria*, particularly in reference to Book 2, and she makes the important distinction between the addressee of didactic as necessarily naïve—the "Reader"—and readers (you or I or anyone) who observe the progress of the education of this Reader. Reading didactic poetry is a complicated process of "readers watching Readers," and it is this "duplicity of readership" that is key to an understanding of the *Ars* (Sharrock 1994b.8). Such duplicity, I would add, inasmuch as it involves a recursive rereading in which we learn to distance ourselves from the naïve Reader, the "you" to whom the *praeceptor* addresses his advice and for whom he intends Procris as a negative exemplum, contributes to the subjectivity effect produced by reading.[34]

Situated between these two levels is the implied readership or audience of the *Ars*, a culturally sophisticated male group: "educated Roman men of a detached and mildly subversive frame of mind, contemporary with Ovid" (Sharrock 1994b.10). The female readership described above, those who might have read the work under the Augustan regime, would have shared, I believe, the education and subversive temperament of their implied male counterparts.[35] However, there is no denying that the addressee of the third book, like the prospective lovers of Books 1 and 2, is a naïve Reader and, however hard her gullibility might be for us to imagine, one who would qualify as a member of Green's easily manipulated female audience. But Green's interpretation clearly constitutes a "male" reading that too readily identifies with the praeceptor's point of view:[36] the male audience is in the know and the female audience is the dupe of that knowledge—the very didactic goal of Books 1 and 2. Translated into Sharrock's terms, it means that the implied male readers are watching the foolish, naïve female Reader—so that educated females who recognize the intertext perform a male reading all the same. The problem, again, is that this male—or rather masculine reading—depends on a uniform Ur-text that would provide interpretive mastery. A feminine reading, by contrast, is experienced by a reader who first identifies with Procris's suspicions and then resists the manipulations of the *praeceptor* by sustaining the hermeneutic uncertainty that many of the details in the digression encourage. Unlike a male or masculine reading, this critical position views the text as polysemous and eschews the need for control by recognizing that the text precludes any certainty through allusions that create an "irreducible conflict between . . . two meanings, contextual and intertextual"—that is, between the story as told in the *Ars* and the allusions to other versions that undermine that telling.[37]

Procris's role as a reader and interpreter of signs, a role in keeping with the *Ars Amatoria*'s thematic emphasis on semiotic manipulation, becomes clear when we compare the descriptions of the same events as narrated in Ovid's epic and didactic versions.[38] Thus only in the *Ars* do we have Procris herself interpreting what are reported merely as "overheard sounds" (*auditos sonos*, 700), a phrase absent from the *Metamorphoses'* version; and it is Procris who construes them first as referring to a proper name, suggesting another woman, and then further interprets this name as signifying betrayal in the context of marital infidelity. Indeed, Procris raises these sounds from the level of a mere "aural" experience to one of semantics, hermeneutics, and human cognition.[39] While this makes Procris culpable in a way that she is not in the *Metamorphoses*, where her informant has already interpreted Aura as a mistress (Gibson 2003.365), such active construction on Procris's part points to her own status as a subject prey to the ambiguities of language. In keeping with the mimetic premise of the *Ars* that the citation and deployment of prior texts produce a reality that must be decoded, the *auditos sonos* constitute a reiterated text construed in a new context. We see Procris again engaging in active interpretation when she reads—albeit incorrectly—the signs or *vestigia* in the grass, another detail absent from the *Metamorphoses* version. Her misreading conforms precisely to the hermeneutic suspicions that a female reader of the third book might likely entertain in Procris's situation, given the first two books' treatment of erotic psychology and the sly allusion to Cephalus and Aurora at 3.84. Recalling this reference, the reader is led to seek out and interpret other *vestigia* (3.721) or traces of the intertextual backdrop in a way that parallels Procris's own search for certainty.

And Ovid does taunt the reader with this larger frame to the myth when, just before introducing the Procris exemplum, the *praeceptor* claims that a lover who has been flattered by a woman's jealousy, "particularly if he is well groomed and attractive in the mirror, may even— he believes—attract the love of goddesses" ("praecipue si cultus erit speculoque placebit, / posse suo tangi credet amore deas," 3.681–82).

The use of the term *deas* seems particularly designed to recall the earlier allusion to Aurora, where her proper name is suppressed in favor of "rosy goddess" (*roseae . . . deae*, 3.34). And there are other tantalizingly suggestive details at the beginning of the digression: the alluring description of the *locus amoenus* in which Cephalus is accustomed to rest casts an erotic aura, as it were, over the narrative. The ground is soft (*mollis*, 688), which of course allows for the imprint that Procris later perceives, but it also introduces amorous associations. Similarly, myrtle is a plant particularly associated with Venus, and both "laurel and dark myrtle provide a sweet fragrance" ("ros maris et lauri nigraque myrtus olent," 690), an atmospheric scent that may have signaled, for a Roman reader, the pleasures of the bedroom (Dalby 2000.244). Indeed, Varro claims that "those places are called *amoena loca* because they offer only love," and Servius explains the etymology of *amoena loca* as "places full of pleasure (*voluptatis*) alone, as it were 'without claims on one's services or duty' (*a-munia*)."[40] Hera's seduction of Zeus in Book 14 of the *Iliad*, for example, occurs in such a sensuously erotic setting.

Another "trace" of the presence of Aurora is found in Procris's final words as she dies in the *Ars* version: "You have pierced your lover's breast; this place always has wounds from Cephalus" ("fixisti pectus amicum: / hic locus a Cephalo vulnera semper habet," 737–38). Now, clearly, the overt reference here is to the emotional wound, in addition to the physical wound, that she suffered when she misconstrued *aura* as the name of Cephalus's mistress. However, given that she recognizes her error, it is perhaps suspect that she uses the adverb *semper* in a context where the source of the emotional wound has been proven a misinterpretation. Moreover, *semper* implies a longer period of time than the swift succession of events that leads to Procris's death. Whether or not Procris herself intends this allusion, *semper* may subtly hint at Cephalus's affair with Aurora in other versions. Ovid has dropped enough direct allusions that this greater intertextual context is inevitably borne in mind by an alert reader.[41]

For a reader whose hermeneutic uncertainty is focalized by Procris as emblematic of a subject's experience of language and literature, the question arises as to whether Procris herself represents a specifically gendered subject position. Although Procris's passionately self-destructive behavior when she first misinterprets the word *aura* enacts the conventional alignment of wild emotion with the feminine, the way she conducts an empirical test and, at least implicitly, assesses the evidence is more in keeping with masculine reason.[42] Of course the *praeceptor*, who casts Procris in the role of an irrational woman who jumps to conclusions, describes her as "scarcely sound" (*male sana*) and asks her where her *mens* or reasoning has gone (3.713–14). Comparing her to a Bacchant, he recalls the description of Dido in the *Aeneid* (4.301), thereby reinforcing gender stereotypes by invoking literary tradition. And yet we should read this editorializing not only as masculine self-interest, intended to discourage women from spying on husbands engaged in infidelities, but also as a reaction specifically directed at Procris's appropriation of a masculine subject position—that is, as subject rather than object of the gaze: she is a woman who observes, rather than one observed by, her husband.[43] Her experience of pleasure, though punctuated by regret as she anticipates the possibility of seeing her husband with Aura, suggests the scopophilia that critics of cinema attribute to the male spectator whose enjoyment derives from passive looking at the female form. More aggressive is the voyeurism of the *praeceptor* himself, who has demonstrated repeatedly the sadistic and erotic pleasure that he derives from his own gaze, as in his analytic focus on the pain of the Sabine women or of Ariadne in her abandonment;[44] his characterization of Procris as crazed reveals his desire to reassert the dominance and power inherent in such a gaze as he describes a woman who has transgressed into the territory of masculine subjectivity.

Indeed, such a transgression characterizes Procris's actual sojourn in the masculine space of solitary hunting and recreation, a point emphasized by the similar diction in the lines describing the separation of both husband and wife—he to relax from the hunt and she to observe—from their companions: Cephalus lies down, "his servants and dogs left behind" (*famulis canibusque relictis*, 695), and Procris, in turn, "leaves her companions in the valley" (*comites in valle relinquit*, 711).[45] While there is no explicit mention of Procris as a huntress here, the echo of Cephalus's own activity and the reference to her as *fortis* ("brave," "strong," 712)[46] constitute "traces" of this Procris from other versions, just as her adoption of masculine power inherent in the gaze parallels the dominance she exerts when, in Antoninus Liberalis and Hyginus, dressed as a man, she places Cephalus in a feminine position by her request for his sexual favors. Ironically, it is at that point in those authors that she gives up the weapon that arguably constitutes the ultimate signifier of her masculinity. And as Procris is visibly without arms or defense in the *Ars*, the reader cannot help but recall as retrospectively ironic the *praeceptor*'s claim at the outset of Book 3 that he is now equipping "Penthesileia and her crowd" with arms in this battle of seduction. The figure of Penthesileia, a mythic female who both represents female readership (in terms of the *praeceptor*'s metaphorical wit) and looks ahead to the "masculine" Procris, embodies the threat posed by women that the *praeceptor* seeks to contain through his selective manipulation of myth—his (and ultimately Ovid's) mythopoesis that undermines Procris's credibility by suppressing the larger context in which she operates.

Moreover, though she is driven by fear and apprehension, Procris's demonstration of agency—her conduct as an active subject—stands in pointed contrast to her complete loss of consciousness upon first hearing of *aura*, a mute condition that the *praeceptor* exploits by converting her into an aesthetic object in three successive similes: the pallor that signals her distress is likened to vine leaves chilled by an early frost, to ripe quinces, and to cornel-berries (3.703–06). The narrator's impulse to use Procris's pain as an opportunity to demonstrate his rhetorical skill mirrors the greater context of Book 3 in which women are encouraged to transform themselves into aesthetic surfaces so that as both text and body they function as *materia* that serves to exhibit the art of the *praeceptor*. In keeping with the overall alignment of the female with nature in the *Ars*, the substance of the narrator's simile compares Procris to natural, organic objects, whereas the aesthetic finish is the result of an application of masculine *cultus*. Procris's actions on her own behalf might thus be read as symbolic of the narrowly circumscribed space within which a female subject in Ovid's *Ars* may act—that is, she must wander into masculine territory in order to operate as an autonomous agent.

Yet, as I argue, Procris resists the narrator's objectification insofar as she employs her interpretive faculties and becomes a reader of signs. And although the *praeceptor* relates the myth as a cynical ploy intended to encourage the female audience to "turn a blind eye" to sexual infidelity, Procris's death as a result of her misinterpretation of the word *aura* signifies much more: it demonstrates the potential loss and tragedy that may result from the hermeneutic ambiguities of the narrator's system and should be viewed as a commentary on the inevitable slippage between signifier and signified, in this case, *aura* as "breeze" or, alternatively, as the name of a woman (a name phonetically resembling Aurora). The digression as a whole points up that the narrator's semiotic project of teaching potential lovers how successfully to seduce women through the manipulation of erotic conventions may founder on the unpredictability of the recipient of any communication, erotic or otherwise. Full control and mastery of the discursive system of *amor*, and therefore of women, is impossible, since signifiers have more than one referent, and signs are forever subject to different discursive contexts and thus to hermeneutic uncertainty. Cephalus's own misreading of the rustling movements of his wife's surprised realization of her mistake similarly points up the instability of any sign and the impossible project of controlling its reception by an audience: while Procris confused a natural phenomenon for a human, Cephalus reverses the process and thinks his wife's movements in the woods to be those of an animal. However, Cephalus's confusion about his wife's identity in the *Ars* does not point to the same degree of signifying ambiguity as does Procris's mistake: after being alerted to the presence of a living being by sound, Cephalus believes that he *sees* an animal when, in fact, it is Procris. The nature of this visual sign that is ontologically identical with his wife is of an entirely different order than the polysemous referentiality of the word *aura*.[47]

Indeed, Ovid stages an ambiguous allegory of an ancient debate with this digression: the argument between what has been called the "ontological and rhetorical positions on language" that arose with the Sophists and to which Plato's *Cratylus* is devoted (Thomson 1994.124). In this dialogue, Hermogenes stands for the rhetorical view, believing that names (and ultimately all words) refer to things by virtue of custom and usage; Cratylus, by contrast, believes that names have an a priori, ontological connection to their referents. On one level, Procris's own confusion clearly emanates from the conventional view of language, where the arbitrary connection between signifier and signified allows for semantic slippage depending on the context. And yet Ovid forecloses any comfortable conclusion that Procris should represent the rhetorical view by the very suggestiveness of her own name. Although one derivation of her name, in the sense of "chosen one," connects it to προκρίνω ("choose," "prefer"), Procris could also derive from that verb in its meaning "decide beforehand" (Gibson 2003.366). Insofar as Procris's initial assumptions could be said to exemplify that latter derivation, she herself becomes exemplary of Cratylus's view of the natural appropriateness of language to its referent.

Similarly, if one accepts that Cephalus has been faithful, an argument could be made that his correct understanding of *aura* also reinforces the natural view of language: *aura*'s breathy combination of liquid and vowel sounds makes it a fitting name for the natural phenomenon of the breeze and vindicates the ontological position, whereas Procris's understanding of it as a person's name enacts the view of language as a system of conventions governed by context and agreed upon usage. But if Procris's realization of her mistake (or at least the narrator's selective telling of her story) might seem to legitimize the ontological view and, in fact, to undercut the constructionist premises of the *Ars* as a didactic text, Cephalus's even more pronounced misperception of his wife as an animal underscores the inevitable role that context and hermeneutics play in human cognition—that is, he ironically reaffirms a constructionist position. Ultimately, just as there is more than one referent for *aura* depending on the context and recipient, so, too, are the meanings of the digression as a whole more than the message "beware rash credulity" that the *praeceptor* originally wishes to communicate.[48]

From the perspective of a digression that signifies beyond the *praeceptor*'s intentions, the Procris myth in the *Ars* once again reveals that his elegiac material, coded as a feminine genre, has overwhelmed the masculine control of didactic. That elegy is particularly woven into this digression in terms of its signifying resistance is apparent in several ways. Perhaps most pronounced is the *praeceptor*'s exclamation as he becomes emotionally involved in the imaginative content of his own narrative and cries out when Procris is pierced: "me miserum, iaculo fixa puella tuo est" ("Wretched me, the girl is struck by your spear!" 736). "Wretched me," is precisely the phrase that Ovid uses at *Amores* 1.1.25 when the speaker himself has been wounded by Cupid, indicating above all a shift in generic orientation from epic to elegy: "me miserum! certas habuit puer ille sagittas: / uror, et in vacuo pectore regnat Amor" ("Wretched me! That boy had good aim [sure arrows]: I burn, and Love rules in my empty breast"). In elegy, being the victim of erotic pain and subjugation indicates the feminized status of the lover-poet; here, in the *Ars*, the *praeceptor*'s cry suggests an identification with both Procris in her physical pain and Cephalus in what will be the emotional suffering of his loss. But the echo of *Amores* 1.1.25 particularly underscores the identification with the recipient of the spear's wound, Procris, even as it serves to feminize the *praeceptor* and to undermine his didactic posture. Echoes of Tibullus, too, appear in line 712, when Procris "boldly and stealthily enters the grove" ("ipsa nemus tacito clam pede fortis init"). While this line recalls Tibullus's pentameter on death's silent approach—"imminet et tacito clam venit illa pede" ("She is near and comes secretly, without a sound," 1.10.34)—and ominously anticipates Procris's end (Gibson 2003.368), it also resembles the statement that Venus "assists the brave" when she "teaches how to step without making a sound": "fortes adiuvat ipsa Venus . . . illa docet . . . pedem nullo ponere posse sono" (Tib. 1.2.16–20). And elegy is also marked in the digression by the use of the term *puella* ("girl," 736), as well as *domina* ("mistress") at the very end of the tale: "ille sinu dominae morientia corpora maesto / sustinet" ("He holds the dying body of his mistress at his mourning breast," 743–44). Both terms contrast with the lexical choice in line 732, "movit in amplexus uxor itura viri" ("The wife moves toward the embrace of her husband"), where Procris's married status and the conjugal context are emphasized. The narrator's interests and motive—to scare an audience of *puellae* from prying into a man's affairs—determine the use of elegiac terms to refer to Procris at one level: a tragic story of conjugal mistrust and misinterpretation must be tailored to fit as a didactic exemplum in a largely elegiac context (cf. Gibson 2003.359–60).

However, it is precisely as elegiac *materia* that the exemplum fails, insofar as the thematic nexus of longing, jealousy, and death that often pervades the elegiac sensibility, particularly in Tibullus and Propertius, overwhelms the narrative frame.[49] This results in the narrator's loss of didactic objectivity, revealing contradictions in the implicit and explicit premises of the digression and the *Ars* as a whole: that women, as both subjects and objects, may be manipulated by masculine discourse. Indeed, the various appellations for Procris and her female role—*puella, domina, coniunx,* and *uxor* ("girl," "mistress," "spouse," "wife")—reflect the three facets of Procris visible in the different versions that make up the mythic intertext to the *Ars*: she oscillates between virgin huntress (*puella*), sexually sophisticated and powerful woman (*domina*), and wife.[50] Thus not only do the elegiac terms point to the digression's resistance to masculine didactic as a gendered phenomenon, but taken together with the conjugal diction, they also imply an overall uncertainty about the nature of the feminine as explored by the *Ars*. Such ambiguity and uncertainty inform, then, the conflicting subject positions of Procris as a female as well as the hermeneutic status of the digression and its relation to the *Ars* as a whole.

Procris is indeed killed like a beast, an event that makes literal the metaphor of hunting in the previous two books and that parallels the rhetorical objectification involved in the narrator's descriptive gaze. But her death, in fact, signifies the very attribute that makes her human: her capacity for linguistic (mis-)interpretation may bring her ruin, but it ironically testifies to the potential for a feminine subject position that eludes masculine control. Although semiotic systems may be manipulated, the reception of signs can never be prescribed or fully determined. And just as Procris must construe the word *aura* that, on one reading, appears to have had the middle syllable *-or-* suppressed from *Aur-or-a*, so must the reader interpret a myth "missing" significant sections. And although Procris's initial "error" is subsumed by the narrator into the uniformity of a seeming "correct" interpretation, the digression as a whole resists hermeneutic closure: the connotative excess of the mythologem as sign—the digression's unruly subversion of the praeceptor's didactic control—enacts for the reader the very semantic slippage that Procris experiences, causing her to symbolize the feminine subject position of a reader whose relation to Ovid's text and semiotic discourse differs from a masculine reading that assumes interpretive mastery. Procris's error thus figures the instability of meaning as a gendered construction even as her character itself suggests that gender is a fluid concept. *Mobilis*, "shifting, nimble, or changeable," the epithet by which Cephalus invokes the breeze (3.698), underscores this semiotic instability, an overdetermined phenomenon here insofar as it is specifically a *nomen* as common noun that Procris interprets as a name. But just as *nomina* may refer to proper names, to common nouns, or simply to words as signifying sounds, thus enabling Procris's confusion, so it is the very fragility or slipperiness of language as a system of signifiers, or *nomina*, that reveal gender also to be a system of discursive conventions open to visions and revisions. That these conventions have real consequences, however, that rhetoric does not simply consist in a ludic play of signifiers, is tragically inscribed in the all-too-referential flesh of Procris.[51]

Notes

1. On Ovid's abortion poems, see Gamel 1989.

2. Greene 1998, Wyke 1994b.110–28; see Miller and Platter 1999a and b for additional relevant bibliography.

3. See Gold 1993, Janan 2001, and Miller 2001.

4. For a general discussion of gender in Ovid's poetry, see Sharrock 2002a.95–107. Downing 1999 compares the ultimate inhibition and immobility of the "constructed" woman in Book 3 of the *Ars* to the inverse result of the Pygmalion story. See Myerowitz 1985.113–28, 134–35, for the construction of women in terms of the artistic process.

5. Kennedy 2000.172. Kennedy remarks that by "splitting the poem's *ego* into poet and *praeceptor*," critics have distanced their "'humanist' Ovid from his *praeceptor*'s disturbing, disruptive, and otherwise dubious views."

6. If the self is a rhetorical construction, then autobiographical personae come dangerously close to being so many rhetorical postures taken up by, and possibly constituting, that self. On the complex self-impersonation that Ovid enacts in the *Ars Amatoria* and the importance for both the student's lovemaking and the poet's fiction-making that their "*persona* both seem the actual 'I' and is not the actual 'I,' but rather its literary equivalent, its literarily mediated re-presentation," see Downing 1993.48–50.

7. All citations are from the Oxford Classical Text and all translations are my own.

8. This analogy is implicit in the use of the term *materia*—"matter," "stuff"—to refer to a potential mistress in the first book (1.49), while, in the third book, the woman's body constitutes raw material to be aesthetically shaped and artificially remade by the narrator, even as she becomes the source of the poet's *fama*, causing text and body to become one. Ovid often uses the term *materia* in his other works to refer to the subject matter of a poetic text: cf. *Tristia* 2.70, 321, 382, 516; *ex Pont.* 3.4.40, 4.10.72. On Propertius's use of Cynthia as *materia*, see Wyke 1987b, 1989a.25–47, and Greene 1998.37–66.

9. See Sharrock 1994b.27–50 on the *praeceptor*'s relationship with the prospective lover, his addressee, as homoerotic instruction and seduction of a *puer delicatus* ("pretty boy," "beloved boy").

10. Writing of Propertian elegy in particular, Wyke 1994b.119–20 sees it not as a "feminine" genre but rather as "effeminate" because the speaking voice of the poet is inescapably male. However, poems such as Ovid *Amores* 3.1 present Elegia as an attractive woman, thus reinforcing the gender identity of the poet's textual matter as feminine even if the speaker himself is effeminate. Cf. Propertius 2.24A, where an imagined speaker refers to the *Monobiblos* as "Cynthia," who is read all over town. Wyke 1989b also argues that the figure of Elegia in Ovid's poem reinforces the other side of the equation: not elegy as feminine, but the figure of the mistress as a symbol of poetics.

11. Although the praeceptor announces that Amor is his subject—the unruly *puer* ("boy") who will yield to his instruction—the biological sex of Cupid does not disqualify him as a symbol of the feminine genre of elegy. Indeed, the principle of metonymic slippage (whereby Amor suggests Ovid's own *Amores* that, in the discourse of elegy, are both women and text) and the conventions of *amor* as distinctly elegiac both indicate that the *praeceptor*'s textual *materia* is typed as feminine even as a *puer delicatus* (colloquial for "beloved boy"; see notes 9 and 10 above) or ἐρώμενος ("beloved") occupies a feminine subject position.

12. Gold 1993.83; cf. Jardine 1985.42: "'Woman,' 'the feminine,' and so on have come to signify those *processes* that disrupt symbolic structures in the West." I am indebted to Gold's discussion of Jardine's theory in relation to Propertius and, in particular, to her idea of "a space in the text, an area of uncertainty that has feminine connotations . . . a space over which the narratives have lost control (Jardine 1985:25)" (Gold 1993.83).

13. See Williams 1999.138–42 for loss of control as "feminizing" a man in Roman culture.

14. Sharrock 1987.410 points out that Ulysses in Ovid's digression suppresses any mention of Diomedes' part in the night attack on Rhesus's camp.

15. Cf. Sharrock 1994b.81 on Calypso's manipulation of Ulysses's love of talking.

16. The sense of *nomina* here is that of *OLD* s.v. 5, where *nomen* indicates

simply a "word denoting an object of thought, a term or expression." In Ovid's passage, *nomina* are to be understood precisely as (corrupted) "signifiers" for the concepts of friendship and trust.

17. Cf. Conte 1994a.40: "In other words, those values elegy recuperates from the universe of the culture (within which it has cut out its own autonomy) cease to be signifieds and become signifiers of different signifieds." On the cultural discourse of *amicitia* in elegy, see Labate 1984.196–219.

18. That the *praeceptor* takes for granted women's subordination to his system of references appears in his trusting assumption of their gullibility: see the lover who makes up suitable *nomina* for captive leaders and peoples in the anticipated triumph of Gaius Caesar (1.219–28). Although this is constructionism at its most satiric, it nonetheless is in keeping with the view that representations serve to create the real.

19. See Cic. *Tusc.* 2.47–48 and the discussion in Williams 1999.132–35.

20. See Lucretius 5.1011–18; more generally, one senses echoes of Plato's *Symposium* and *Phaedrus.* On the parody of Lucretius, see Janka 1997.477–78.

21. 2.457–58: "candida iamdudum cingantur colla lacertis, / inque tuos flens est accipienda sinus" ("Immediately embrace her white neck with your arms, and take her, weeping, into your lap"); and compare with lines 469–71: "mox caelum impositum terris, humus aequore cincta est / . . . silva feras, volucres aer accepit habendas" ("Soon the sky was set over the earth, the land was surrounded with water . . . the woods took in beasts, the air received birds to keep").

22. See Janka 1997.346–47 and the critics cited there.

23. As Gibson 2003.371 points out, the narrator refers to *vestigia corporis* or the "traces of [one] body," but this is the privileged perspective of the *praeceptor* in the know.

24. The major accounts and sources are Pherecydes 3.34J *ap. Schol. in Od.* 11.321, Ovid *Met.* 7.690–862, Ant. Lib. 41, Apollod. 3.15.1, Hyg. *Fab.* 189, and Serv. *Aen.* 6.445. For an excellent discussion of the varying representations of Procris as good wife, chaste huntress, or sexually active and clever woman, see Davidson 1997.

25. In Apollod. 3.15.1, Procris herself has sex with Minos, an event that Ovid refers to in *Remedia Amoris* 453.

26. For an argument against such "hints," see Tarrant 1995.99–111.

27. Cf. Antoninus 41.6 for the same request worded differently.

28. Servius's commentary on *Aeneid* 6.445 extends the confusion to Aurora herself, who thinks she is being called and falls in love with Cephalus as a result.

29. On Roman women's education in literary classics, see Habinek 1998.123.

30. We have only a fragment of Sophocles' play (*TrGF*, vol. 4 [Radt] frag. 533), so it is unclear what version of the story he told. For images of Procris and Cephalus, see *LIMC*, vol. 6, Kephalos 26, 28; for Procris as huntress, see *LIMC*, vol. 7, Prokris 1.

31. See *LIMC*, vol. 3, Eos 46–126.

32. Ovid also mentions Cephalus and Aurora at *Am.* 1.13.39–40.

33. For the idea that subjectivity is experienced in such a situation of "suture" or identification, see Silverman 1983.194–236. The experience is generally held to occur when mediated, in the context of literature, through the first person pronoun "I" employed by the "speaker," or, in the case of cinema, through the implied gaze of the camera/male viewer, which is often linked through the "shot / reverse shot formation" to a character in the film. In Ovid's text, the *praeceptor's own* subjective identification with Procris's feelings and thoughts invites the reader similarly to participate in (read into) her subjectivity but not always as the *praeceptor* directs.

34. See Miller 1994.73–77 on rereading and the "subjectivity-effect."

35. Certainly Augustus's daughter, Julia, who was exiled under the adultery laws, would have been representative of such a possible female audience. Cf. Sharrock 1994a.111: "Reading the *Ars* implies playing a certain political role: respectable women simply cannot be admitted as readers but excluded as students— and therefore they are inevitably drawn into the subversive culture."

36. Cf. Gamel 1989.185 on the *Amores*: "The *amator's* 'reading' of events is conspicuously marked as male, and those readings by critics who see the world of the text through his eyes and who accept his reading may be characterized as 'male readings.' A reading which questions that perspective and offers a different one, thereby putting the adequacy of univocal readings in question, can thus be called a 'female reading.'" On the unquestioned privileging of the male narrator's view in traditional readings of Horatian love poetry, see Ancona 1994.

37. On the problem of recognizing boundaries when the allusions in a text are to the system of myth, see Edmunds 2001.147–48. His discussion of Riffaterre's theory of intertextuality as a conflict between contextual and intertextual meaning (150–51) allows for greater uncertainty than in Riffaterre (cf. 1979.497, 1980.629).

38. For a useful comparison of Ovid's two versions that argues for the prior composition of the tale in the *Metamorphoses*, see Anderson 1990.

39. Ovid underscores the ambiguity of phonemes as signifiers with the echo of *auditos*, "heard," and *aures*, "ears," in *aura*, even as he puns maliciously on the "aural" source of confusion. Cf. Gibson 2003.366.

40. *Isid.* 14.8.33: "amoena loca dicta Varro ait, quod solum amorem praestant"; *Serv. Aen.* 5.734: "'amoena' sunt loca solius voluptatis plena, quasi 'amunia.'"

41. See Edmunds 2001.74 on a character's "unknowing" allusion and the poet's irony at his or her expense.

42. Davidson 1997.182 would claim the opposite, that "the emotionalism of her response to the belief that she has a rival . . . pushes her towards the 'irrationality' of the natural world." And yet, as I argue, it is precisely her capacity to interpret language that causes her predicament, even as her empirical examination and implicit assessment of the evidence, as suggested in line 719, constitute the use of reason. As the narrator himself comments, fear can also be involved

in the mind's calculations: "credere quae iubeant, locus est et nomen et index / et quia mens semper, quod timet, esse putat" ("There is the place, the name, and the informant that compel belief, and the fact that what the mind fears to be, it thinks is true," 719–20). Responding to an earlier draft of this paper delivered at the 2001 Annual Meeting of the American Philological Association, Ronnie Ancona observes that Pyramus similarly "misreads" the signs when he comes upon Thisbe's bloody garment in Ovid *Met.* 4.105–08.

43. Kaplan 1983b.319 asserts that the "gaze is not necessarily male (literally), but to own and activate the gaze, given our language and the structure of the unconscious, is to be in the masculine position." For the distinction between scopophilia and voyeurism, see Mulvey 1997.432–42. For analyses of elegy in terms derived from the cinematic theory of the gaze, see Greene 1998.67–92, 1999.409–18, and Fredrick 1997.172–93. See, too, the essays in Fredrick 2002a.

44. Describing the fear of the Sabine women in a paratactic list of their discrete responses to their abductors, the *praeceptor* comments finally on how much their terror became them (1.121–26). Similarly, when he depicts Ariadne, he finds her weeping alluring (1.533).

45. In the *Ars* version, Cephalus appears to leave his companions when he goes to recline in the *locus amoenus*; in the *Metamorphoses*, however, he explicitly hunts alone.

46. See Gibson 2003.368–69 on *fortis*.

47. As Gibson 2003.366 points out, the name Aura, though not common, does appear in the story of the virgin huntress, Aura, in Nonn. *Dion.* 48.24ff.

48. Verducci 1980.37–38 observes that "there is no digression in the *Ars Amatoria* which does not somehow conspicuously go awry, whether by poetic suggestion or by logical inapplicability, or both" and that "the details of the [Procris digression] . . . have an ambiguity lost in the spare hypothesis which might easily make Procris guilty of rash credulity."

49. See Tib. 1.3, Prop. 1.19, 2.8, 2.9, 2.13B, 4.7.

50. See Davidson 1997.183, who quotes J-P Vernant's observation that, in Greek myth and society, the "position of the . . . legitimate wife is in between that of . . . the young girl defined by her virginal status and that of the . . . courtesan entirely devoted to love."

51. I am grateful to Ronnie Ancona, Ellen Greene, and an anonymous reviewer for comments on earlier drafts of this essay, and to Louise Bishop, Cristina Calhoon, Mary Jaeger, and Elizabeth McCartney for their helpful suggestions, as well as to the Center for the Study of Women in Society at the University of Oregon for providing valuable research time.

12   *Amor* versus Roma

Gender and Landscape in Propertius 4.4

Tara S. Welch

In his fourth and final book of elegies, Propertius sets out a new artistic program: etiological poetry explaining Rome's origins. Leaving behind love elegies addressed to the elusive Cynthia, a program defiant for its insistence on a life of love rather than public duty, he turns his polished poetic voice to the celebration of Roman institutions (4.1.67–69):

> Roma, fave, tibi surgit opus, date candida cives
>   omina, et inceptis dextera cantet avis!
> sacra diesque canam et cognomina prisca locorum.

> Rome, approve: this work rises for you. Grant favorable omens, O citizens, and may the bird of prophecy sing propitiously at what I have begun! I shall sing of the rites and festivals of Rome, and of the hallowed names of her places.[1]

Recent scholarship demonstrates that these etiological poems are as heavily marked with problematic gender dynamics as Propertius's more traditional love elegies.[2] But two factors complicate the gender dynamics in Book 4. First, the poet's first-person voice is replaced by third parties, external characters who model various gender identities.[3] The submissive poet and his dominant mistress remain in this book, but they are joined by submissive women, virile heroes, and cross-dressing men. The second factor is the mapping of elegy's complex gender roles onto specific parts of the city of Rome. This paper explores the interactions of gender identity, displaced subjectivity, and the urban landscape in Propertius's etiological elegy on the Tarpeian rock.

According to legends of Rome's foundation, Tarpeia was a maiden who betrayed the Capitol to enemy Sabine forces. In the popular version of her myth found in Livy, Plutarch, Dionysius of Halicarnassus, and Varro, and reflected in all extant visual representations of her story, Tarpeia is a Roman maiden who betrays the Capitol to Tatius, commander of the Sabine forces besieging Rome in response to the rape of the Sabine Women.[4] Her motivation, whenever expressed, is greed; in return for her betrayal, she demands what the Sabines wear on their arms. She means, of course, their bracelets and rings, but the Sabines reward her instead by crushing her with their shields, which they also wear on their arms. At the end of the war, the Sabines and the Romans join together to form a stronger, combined state, but, as a grim reminder of Tarpeia's betrayal, the Romans christened the Tarpeian rock on the Capitol, over which, as legend has it, traitors were thrown to their deaths. Her story, and the rock named for her, came to represent the threat posed to the state by the selfish pursuit of private goals over public needs.

To be sure, Tarpeia's myth was not monolithic, and variations appear in other, more idiosyncratic versions of her story. Like the mutable identity of Vertumnus in Elegy 4.2, these variations in Tarpeia's myth point to tensions in Roman ideology. Though her betrayal was memorialized by the Tarpeian rock, for example, Tarpeia was also venerated at her tomb in the city, no longer extant.[5] These twin Roman places—Tarpeia's rock and her altar—create an ideological crisis: her betrayal of Rome is to be condemned (the symbolism of the rock), while her contribution to the newly expanded state is to be commended (via worship at the tomb). Similar tensions arise from her status in Rome: Tarpeia was either a daughter of the Roman commander, with no other social role, or a Vestal Virgin. If the former, as in most versions, her transgression was a private act, while if the latter, as in Varro's telling, the state's very institutions were tainted with the crime (*DLL* 5.41). She may not even have been Roman.[6] Another variant, preserved in Simylus's elegy of unknown date, has Tarpeia betray Rome to the Gauls rather than the Sabines; in this case, there is no resulting assimilation of the invaders to palliate her guilt.[7] Another oddity appears in Simylus's version: the girl acts out of love, not greed. This variant raises questions about the extent to which these two personal desires are interchangeable in the threat they pose to the state.[8]

Propertius's version draws attention to Tarpeia's alterity and to this alterity's confrontation with (and contribution to) Roman ideology by exploiting the tensions of gender and landscape in Tarpeia's myth. Propertius's telling veers sharply from the popular version in a number of ways. For one, the elegist's Tarpeia is no simple maiden. Following

Varro's version, Propertius's Tarpeia is a Vestal Virgin, a public priest-hood that emphasizes her duty to the state and raises the stakes of her treason. Second, in an innovation (if Simylus's elegy postdates his), Prop-ertius motivates Tarpeia not with greed but with love for Tatius—a mo-tive she elaborates in the long monologue she delivers at the heart of the poem. This changes the conflict of the poem from private gain against the interests of the state to emotion directed against the state, *amor* ver-sus Roma. This emotional motivation generates sympathy for Tarpeia, and we see her in this poem searching for a way to reconcile her private desire with her duty to the state. Third, and the main focus of this paper, Propertius intimately connects her story with places in the Roman city. Though the poem is ostensibly an *aetion* of Tarpeia's tomb, the spatial scope of the action is much wider, ranging across the Capitol and the Forum valley, two areas rich with patriotic resonance. Tarpeia spends most of her time between these two areas, comfortable in neither and ul-timately unwelcome in each. The elegist's mapping of Tarpeia's strug-gle onto Rome's most symbolic locales emphasizes her predicament as a feeling individual within a state that subsumes all to itself. As we shall see, his combination of Tarpeia and the city comments not only on Tarpeia's situation but on the city as well.

The Elegiac Tarpeia: *Amor* versus Roma

In good Alexandrian fashion, the elegist lends Tarpeia extra sympathy by granting her a subjectivity lacking in other sources. Proper-tius is unique in focusing the narrative through Tarpeia's perspective. Like Ovid's elegiac heroines (who are patterned, in part, after her), Tarpeia tells her own story, and the reader is allowed a glimpse into her complex feel-ings and motivations. Propertius's Tarpeia is not greedy, nor does she think only of herself, nor is she naively blind to the implications of her desire.[9] Rather, in her long monologue—over a third of the poem—Tarpeia demonstrates that she is aware of the potential consequences of her de-sire and loath to do harm to the state. Her oscillation between desire and duty gives her a moral dimension she lacks in other sources.

Throughout Tarpeia's speech, her mind flickers back and forth be-tween following her desires (marked as *amor* below) and noting the costs of these desires to herself and the state (marked Roma) (4.4.31–46):[10]

Ignes castrorum et Tatiae praetoria turmae	*amor*
et formosa oculis arma Sabina meis,	
o utinam ad vestros sedeam captiva Penatis,	Roma

> dum captiva mei conspicer ora Tati!   *amor*
> Romani montes, et montibus addita Roma,
>   et valeat probro Vesta pudenda meo: Roma
> ille equus, ille meos in castra reponet amores,   *amor*
>   cui Tatius dextras collocat ipse iubas!
> quid mirum in patrios Scyllam saevisse capillos,
>   candidaque in saevos inguina versa canis?   Roma
> prodita quid mirum fraterni cornua monstri,   *amor*
>   cum patuit lecto stamina torta via?
> quantum ego sum Ausoniis crimen factura puellis,   Roma
>   improba virgineo lecta ministra foco!
> Pallados exstinctos si quis mirabitur ignis,
>   ignoscat: lacrimis spargitur ara meis.   *amor*

O fires of the camp and headquaters of Tatius's squadron and Sabine weapons lovely to my eyes, O, would that I might sit at your hearth as a captive, as long as, captive, I might look upon the face of my Tatius! Roman hills, and upon the hills, Rome, and you, Vesta, who must be shamed by my sin, good-bye: that horse, let that horse carry my passions back into his camp, that horse whose mane Tatius himself smoothes to the right. Why wonder that Scylla violated her father's hair, and her pale groin was changed into vicious dogs? Why wonder that the monstrous brother's horns were betrayed when the twisted path lay revealed by a gathered thread? How great a crime am I about to commit for Italian girls, I, a sinful girl chosen to be minister to a virgin's hearth! If someone should wonder that the fires of Pallas have gone out, let him forgive me: the altar is wet with my tears.

As quickly as a new line unfolds, it seems, Tarpeia's thoughts shift; she is searching for solutions to her dilemma and finding none so far. For example, she first expresses her desire to be a member of Tatius's household (a testament to her *amor*), but realizes that she can only do so as a captive (a capitulation to Roma). Even in her choice of mythical exempla, Tarpeia sees tensions: both Scylla and Ariadne choose love over fatherland (*amor*, 4.4.39, 41–42), but not without punishment (Roma, 4.4.40). At 4.4.43–46, she recognizes not only a general danger posed by her desire (*quantum crimen*) but even the specific transgressions caused by that desire: she violates the virginal chastity of her priesthood (*improba ministra*, 4.4.44) and lets the sacred fire of Vesta go out (*exstinctos ignis*, 4.4.45). Her tears reveal her perplexity at her impasse: with her mind searching for explanations and solutions, she realizes she is caught in an irreconcilable situation. Her very pain is a sacrifice at Vesta's altar.

At 4.4.53, her mind takes a sudden turn. With a balanced case for *amor* and Roma, Tarpeia instead justifies her transgression by condemning Rome (4.4.53–54):

> te toga picta decet, non quem, sine matris honore
>   nutrit inhumanae dura papilla lupae.

It is you the *toga picta* befits, not that one whom the harsh nipple of a wolf nursed, without the honor of a mother.

Tatius, she says, is more worthy of her loyalty than wolf-suckled Romulus, who is unaccustomed even to a mother's love. Tarpeia questions the loveless state that she serves. Her resentment toward Rome does not last long, however, as her flickering mind soon seizes upon a solution that would benefit Rome, the Sabines, and herself: namely, her legitimate marriage to Tatius would bind Romans to Sabines (4.4.55–62):

> hic, hospes, patria metuar regina sub aula:
> dos tibi non humilis prodita Roma venit.
> si minus, at raptae ne sint impune Sabinae,
> me rape et alterna lege repende vices!
> commissas acies ego possum soluere nupta:[11]
> vos medium palla foedus inite mea.
> adde, Hymenaee, modos: tubicen, fera murmura conde:
> credite, vestra meus molliet arma torus.

Here, as a guest, I will be revered as queen in your country's palace: Rome betrayed comes as no humble dowry to you. If not, so the Sabine women weren't raped without punishment, capture me and settle the score by the law of reciprocity! I, as a bride, am able to dissolve the battles that have begun. Enter into a compromise through my wedding gown! Hymenaeus, add your strains! Trumpeter, stop your wild sounds! Believe me, my marriage bed will soften your weapons.

Like the Sabine women, Tarpeia envisions herself combining marriage and peacemaking. Her mention of the Hymenaeus, dowry, wedding dress, marriage bed, and the reference to herself as *nupta* all reveal Tarpeia's hope for a legitimate marriage with the Sabine king.[12] Indeed, she foresees the solution that eventually does bring peace—the reconciliation brought about by the Sabine women through their marriages. Tarpeia wants to facilitate, not undermine, this process, an interesting comment since Tarpeia and the Sabine women are so often foils for each other in the sources, such as Livy's history and the relief sculptures in the Basilica Aemilia. Tarpeia's hopes for a treaty with the Sabines and an end to the war, seen in *soluere* and *foedus* and encapsulated in the chiastic *arma torus* (4.4.59, 60, and 62, respectively), embody a hope of all Roman marriages: to blur the distinctions between families and strengthen the community, rather than sever community ties. Tarpeia's hopes are noble; Rome betrayed will become Rome triumphant. In envisioning a winning situation for all parties, the elegist's Tarpeia would become a positive example for all time.

The extended moral debate she has with herself in which she tries to reconcile her private desires with her public duty makes Tarpeia human and makes her sympathetic to us. Propertius further complicates her situation by presenting her as a Vestal Virgin. In no other version of her story is Tarpeia so ambivalent; Propertius alone combines Tarpeia's ritual chastity and her desire. For some interpreters, Tarpeia's status as a Vestal Virgin increases her shame (Beltrami 1989). In this view, for a girl whose ritual chastity is so beneficial to the state, Tarpeia's love constitutes an especially selfish and heinous crime. The combination of chastity and love in the poem and the resultant erotic *frisson* would therefore produce a more rousing condemnation of the girl than had appeared in earlier versions of her legend. On the other hand, this combination highlights the barrenness imposed on Tarpeia's life by the cult of Vesta and throws into high relief the conflict between Tarpeia's private desires and her public duty. This conflict aligns her with the elegiac poet and lover, who disdains public institutions, especially those that mandate or limit sexual activity.[13] Tarpeia recognizes the tension inherent in her situation: her criticism of unmothered Romulus at 4.4.53–54 hints that, for her, love (even motherly love) is incompatible with the Roman state. Indeed, her mention of the wolf recalls the story of another Vestal Virgin, Rhea Silvia, whose sexuality was activated (albeit by a god) and who was punished for it (Livy 1.3). Like Tarpeia, Rhea Silvia was performing her Vestal duties when she was caught by *amor*.[14]

This tension between *amor* and Roma is emphasized by Vesta's disconcerting appearance in the poem (4.4.67–70):

> et incerto permisit bracchia somno,
>   nescia se furiis accubuisse novis.
> nam Vesta, Iliacae felix tutela favillae,
>   culpam alit et plures condit in ossa faces.

And she gave her arms to fitful sleep, not knowing that she was going to bed with new demons. For Vesta, propitious keeper of the torch from Troy, feeds her sin and plants more fires in her bones.

Vesta is thus the goddess who mandates Tarpeia's chastity as a Vestal Virgin *and* makes that chastity impossible by fanning the flames of her love. Some editors, at a loss to explain Vesta's perplexing behavior, emend this line to read "Venus."[15] As one editor states: "The fires of torches and love are the province of Venus and Amor, and for Vesta to arrogate them to herself to compass so cruel a purpose as the further undoing of her votary is monstrous" (Richardson 1977 ad loc.). Indeed it is, but in my view, the reading stands: the poem's malicious Vesta is a distilled and potent image of Tarpeia's own predicament.[16] As Vesta is the focus for Tarpeia's public duties, this goddess's intervention makes all the more problematic the tension between *amor* and Roma that Tarpeia feels: the very state the maiden serves fosters her transgression against it. The problem is not only Tarpeia's, and this poem dramatizes the contradictions inherent in the broader cult of Vesta. This goddess's priestesses guaranteed Rome's growth and fertility via their own unfruitfulness, an ideological conundrum manifest in the ambiguous sexual status of Vestal Virgins in Roman thought (see Beard 1980 and 1995). Such contradictions indicate a Roman attempt to negotiate sexual identity and to tease out permutations of gender. Tarpeia's elegiac story, therefore, speaks not only to the difficulties of her own situation but to deeper fissures in Roman ideology, "fault lines . . . in the larger architectonics of Roman ideology" (Miller and Platter 1999b.453).

In this way, Propertius's Tarpeia is caught, confined in her public role, and confounded in her desire. Tarpeia rejects her priestly virginity and convinces herself that proper service to Rome requires the sexual union of man and woman. She envisions a solution that would restore her fertility and serve the state: a marriage with Tatius that would unite the two peoples. By exposing her tormented inner thoughts and by emphasizing the contradictions in her priesthood, Propertius causes the Roman reader to question both the suppositions behind Tarpeia's negative legend and the way her story is memorialized in the cityscape. Tarpeia's love, therefore, constitutes a subtle challenge to the traditional status and use of her legend.

Caught in the Middle: Tarpeia and the Capitol

Tarpeia's monologue reveals to the reader that she is fully aware of the untenable situation in which she is caught and of the ramifications of her decision. She is pulled in opposite directions by two forces: her loyalty to the state of Rome and her love for the Sabine king Tatius. This tug of war between state and love is played out in her movements in the city as well, as she is pulled toward the Capitol, on the one hand, temporary home of Rome's forces, and toward the Forum, on the other hand, the site of Tatius's Sabine encampment. A decade ago, Ann Vasaly, studying topographical references in Ciceronian oratory, demonstrated how much meaning a place's "metaphysical topography" could add to the text that mentioned it or otherwise engaged with it (1993.41). Just as deliberately as Cicero in his orations, Propertius evokes places as a way to add nuance to his poetry: Tarpeia's emotional struggle is to be found in places with strong Roman ideological signification.

Setting Tarpeia in the city center was not new. The Tarpeian rock on the Capitol eternalized her betrayal, and Julius Caesar, and later Augustus, chose the Forum as a fitting place to commemorate her punishment with a relief sculpture (to be discussed below). In Propertius's poem, Tarpeia is an example not of how the individual threatens the state but of how the state threatens the individual. The poet emphasizes this perspective by rewriting the girl's relationship to the city center, by repositioning Tarpeia within the Roman cityscape. Hans-Peter Stahl, a critic concerned with the tension between public and private in this and all Propertius's poems, touches on the importance of place: "Thus her conflict, expressed in local terms in that, though physically on her state's territory (in the neighborhood of Jupiter Optimus Maximus), she emotionally longs to be in the enemy's camp. It is worth noting how once more Propertius chooses the scenic as a vehicle for the emotional."[17]

We begin, as does Propertius, with the Capitol, temporary home for Tarpeia and the Roman state. Tarpeia descends the Capitol daily to fetch sacred water and to gaze upon her Tatius. Evenings she ascends again, scratched by brambles, into the Roman camp. She delivers her monologue while sitting on the edge of the hill, overlooking Tatius's camp. This hill, Rome's steepest and most ancient according to legend, was the religious and ideological head of the Roman empire.[18] Rome's most important temple, that of Jupiter Optimus Maximus, lay on its crest, as did its oldest, the temple of Jupiter Feretrius. The triumphal ceremony, a splendid celebration of Roman military victory, reached its climax atop the Capitol in the great temple to Jupiter. Regalia from these ceremonies were dedicated in the temple and displayed along the triumphal route up the hill, making it a permanent museum of Rome's dominion. The temple to Jupiter Feretrius housed *spolia opima*, the state's rarest and highest military honors. Both of these temples had long figured prominently as symbols of Rome's imperial domain; restored by Augustus, they became totems of his might. Finally, the Capitol testified to Rome's eternity.[19]

It was so much a symbol of Roman dominion that most colonial outposts, even those built on flat land, featured a Capitol.[20] To revise Bede's popular maxim, as long as the Capitol will stand, so will Rome stand.[21]

With these associations, the Capitoline hill forms a pointed setting for Tarpeia's unhappy situation and an extraordinarily resonant site for her betrayal. Tarpeia's crime is multifaceted. She violates the city religiously by transgressing the rules of her priesthood; by ignoring the sacred fire, a crime she mentions in 4.4.45, she opens Rome to possible disaster. She violates the city militarily by revealing its defenses to the enemy, literally opening a path for the enemy to enter. Finally, she violates Rome symbolically by betraying the Capitol, Rome's strongest symbol of itself. Her last journey down the Capitol reverses the Roman triumph in which victorious generals would bring foreign resources into the city. Tarpeia, exiting the Capitol, leads those very resources out of the city, away from its head.[22] These many layers of her betrayal heighten the damage she does to the state.

Her final departure from the Capitol emphasizes her rejection of Rome's public realm. In choosing Tatius, she rejects cult, state, and urban center, fleeing the pervasive public presence in her life in order to achieve her private desires. In short, her private desires cannot be met on the Capitol, a place where her actions are interpreted as treason and permanently enshrined as such in the establishment of the Tarpeian rock. Propertius expresses Tarpeia's crime against the community in topographical terms that raise the stakes for both betrayed and traitor, a point he underscores in the poem's introductory lines (4.4.1–2):

> Tarpeium nemus et Tarpeiae turpe sepulchrum
>   fabor et antiqui limina capta Iovis.

> I shall tell of Tarpeia's grove and Tarpeia's shameful grave, and how the threshold of ancient Jove was once captured.

The Temple of Jupiter gets captured, and Tarpeia gets a grave.[23]

Caught in the Middle: Tarpeia and the Forum

Tarpeia violates the Capitol to bring to fruition her love for Tatius, who is encamped in the Forum valley below. In so doing, she hopes to escape the restrictions placed on her by Rome and by her public role as a Vestal Virgin. However, in her escape, she rushes into another urban area loaded with symbolic meaning for Rome's political dominion. Tatius has stationed his troops in the grand Forum Romanum, the area that would become the political, commercial, social, and religious center of Rome. Not only was the Forum the locus of republican statecraft and the seat of senatorial authority, it also housed one of the most rousing and condemnatory versions of Tarpeia's demise in all of Rome. After its refurbishment of 55–34 B.C.E.—a refurbishment funded by Julius Caesar—the Basilica Aemilia, next to the Curia, boasted paired relief sculptures of Tarpeia's punishment and of the rape of the Sabine women.[24] Augustus, who restored the building in 14 B.C.E. after a fire, retained Tarpeia and the Sabine women as part of the building's decorative program. As Natalie Kampen argues, Tarpeia's presence alongside the Sabine women in the heart of the Forum, center of Rome's public traffic, sent a powerful message about the role of women in the evolving state.[25] When Roman women behaved appropriately, as did the Sabine women, they acted as social mediators between men and even facilitated Roman expansion. Tarpeia's perfidy, on the other hand, represented the danger of unregulated female conduct and the ability of women to undermine the proper relationships between men. This message, Kampen notes, would have been especially pointed in the years after Augustus's legislation on marriage and adultery, passed in 18 B.C.E.—legislation that sought to regulate female behavior in more official ways.[26] Focusing as it does on Tarpeia's death rather than her life, the Basilica Aemilia relief suggests that the Forum Romanum was not a place that would welcome the maiden's love.

Though she imagines it will be otherwise, Tarpeia's fate in this urban sector will be no better than it was on the Capitol under Rome's jurisdiction. Tatius is encamped in the northeastern portion of the Forum Romanum, in an area stretching from the Tullian spring (his water source, 4.4.3 and 13) to the Curia (4.4.13). This whole area was visible from the Arx on the southeastern edge of the Capitol.[27] Propertius pays careful attention to his description of this locale (4.4.1–14):

Tarpeium nemus et Tarpeiae turpe sepulchrum
    fabor et antiqui limina capta Iovis.
lucus erat felix hederoso conditus antro,
    multaque nativis obstrepit arbor aquis,
Silvani ramosa domus, quo dulcis ab aestu
    fistula poturas ire iubebat ovis.
hunc Tatius fontem vallo praecingit acerno,
    fidaque suggesta castra coronat humo.
quid tum Roma fuit, tubicen vicina Curetis

cum quateret lento murmure saxa Iovis?
atque ubi nunc terris dicuntur iura subactis,
stabant Romano pila Sabina Foro.
murus erant montes: ubi nunc est Curia saepta,
bellicus ex illo fonte bibebat equus.

I shall tell of Tarpeia's grove and Tarpeia's shameful grave, and how the threshold of ancient Jove was once captured. There was a propitious copse, hidden in an ivy-clad cave, and many a tree rustled with native waters. It was the leafy house of Silvanus, where the sweet pipe used to bid sheep to come and drink away from the summer heat. Tatius surrounded this valley with a maple palisade, and he topped his trusty camp with earth heaped up. What was Rome then, when the nearby flute player of the Sabines shook the stones of Jove with a light rumbling? And where now laws are pronounced for conquered peoples, Sabine javelins used to stand in the Roman Forum. The mountains formed a wall: where now the Curia lies, there used to be sheep pens, and the warhorse used to drink from that fountain.

Propertius begins his poem with a mention of Tarpeia's grove (*nemus*, 4.4.1). This reading is contested, however, and some editors emend *nemus* to read *scelus*.[28] Though *scelus* is attested in no manuscripts, the primary problem these editors find with *nemus* is that there is no monument known as Tarpeia's grove. I believe *nemus* should stay, for several reasons. First, the poem spends much time describing proto-Rome's natural, undeveloped landscape. Springs, trees, plants, and flowers abound on Tarpeia's path, features that fit the description of a grove quite well. Second, as Paul Allen Miller describes, the poem's tricky elision of the *nemus* with the *sepulchrum* of 4.4.1 and the *lucus* of 4.4.3 parallels the transformation of the Golden Age *locus amoenus* that opens the poem into the site of the transgression that destroys that very Golden Age (2003.200–01). Third, the juxtaposition of nature and the built environment is prominent in Elegy 4.4, emphasizing the various Romes on the spot; so, too, in the first line, the natural (*nemus*) stands in sharp contrast with the constructed (*sepulcrum*). Fourth, the lack outside this poem of a formally attested Tarpeia's grove in the cityscape—indeed, its replacement by the Tarpeian rock—testifies to the city's ability to organize its myths according to its need. The durable Tarpeian rock, like the reliefs in the Basilica Aemilia, focus attention on Tarpeia's punishment rather than her motivations or intentions. Propertius's Tarpeian grove, on the other hand, painted in pastoral terms, focuses attention on the girl's predicament. Tarpeia's grove can be seen as a "topographical crystallization point from which . . . Tatius and Tarpeia can now be measured . . . by reference to their attitude towards peaceful pastoral landscape."[29] In short, Tatius makes the *lucus* a *locus* for warfare, while Tarpeia makes it a *locus* for her love.

Tatius's camp is a perversion of the pastoral landscape as he turns a *locus amoenus* into a military locale. Trees appear not as a source of pleasant shade (as in Vergil *Eclogues* 1.1) but rather as a military barricade. The hills, too, are defenses, rather than comfortable places to relax and sing (Vergil *Eclogues* 1.82–83). Tatius's camp disrupts the normal sounds of the pastoral world; instead of singing shepherds and piping goatherds who pass peaceful days (Vergil *Eclogues* 1.10), we hear the trumpeter call the Sabines to war. Even the animals in Tatius's realm are militarized: the fountain sates not sheep but the warhorse (cf. Vergil *Eclogues* 7.11–13). The first half of poem 4.1 similarly blends a pastoral proto-Roman landscape with its future monuments of military might and with the men who made Rome great.[30] In that portrait of early Rome, the poet adopts what Stahl calls the "Palatine viewpoint"—not so much a focalization from the Palatine as an evaluation according to the values of the Augustan state (1985.254–55). Tatius adopts this same Palatine viewpoint, seeing Tarpeia's grove as a place where he can prepare for war.

Tatius's encampment reveals the Palatine viewpoint in another way as well. Tatius has chosen as his base the northeast corner of the Forum Romanum, an area whose resonance with the Palatine viewpoint Propertius makes clear. Propertius names the Forum particularly as a place where laws are pronounced for conquered lands (4.4.11–12), but, at the narrative time of the poem, as an area for Sabine weapons. This identifies the Forum as the center for the exercise of military power—whether Roman or Sabine does not really matter, since this war will unite the two into a single military force; Propertius's use of the Sabine-Roman name Curetes in 4.4.9 underscores the assimilation. The poet also brings before our eyes the senate house (Curia, 4.4.13), the seat of republican political power, rebuilt and rechristened the Curia Iulia by Caesar and his adopted son in ominous concert with their appropriation of its former functions. An even starker urban symbol of the *princeps*'s appropriation of the Curia's functions would be realized in his transfer of these functions to the Forum Augustum at the end of the century.[31] The warhorse mentioned in 4.4.14, though certainly referring to Tatius's Sabine horse, also evokes the future equestrian monument of Julius Caesar that would adorn the Forum Iulium.

With these details (the laws for the conquered, the Curia, and the warhorse), Propertius draws attention to the Forum as a place symbolic of Rome's manifest destiny, particularly its Augustan manifest destiny. Unfortunate Tarpeia seeks out this locale in order to escape the pressure put on her by the Capitol. Misguided, her view of the proto-Forum landscape is much softer, it is not Stahl's "Palatine viewpoint." For her, the place is a playground for Tatius's erotic sport and for her desiring gaze (4.4.19–30):

> vidit harenosis Tatium proludere campis
>   pictaque per flavas arma levare iubas:
> obstipuit regis facie et regalibus armis,
>   interque oblitas excidit urna manus.
> saepe illa immeritae causata est omina lunae,
>   et sibi tingendas dixit in amne comas:
> saepe tulit blandis argentea lilia Nymphis,
>   Romula ne faciem laederet hasta Tati:
> dumque subit primo Capitolia nubila fumo,
>   rettulit hirsutis bracchia secta rubis.
> et sua Tarpeia residens ita flevit ab arce
>   vulnera, vicino non patienda Iovi.

She saw Tatius exercise on the sandy fields and raise his painted weapons above his golden crests. She stood fast, struck by the face of the king and by his royal arms, and her urn fell through her forgetful hands. Often using omens of the blameless moon as a pretext, she said she had to wash her hair in the river. Often she carried silver-white lilies to the softhearted Nymphs, praying that Romulus's spear not harm Tatius's face. When she ascended the Capitol, hazy at the first smoke of night's fires, she returned with arms cut by bristling thorns, and Tarpeia, sitting down, thus wept her wounds from the citadel, wounds that nearby Jove would not tolerate.

Looking at Tatius's activities, Tarpeia sees not military exercises but the poetic and amatory activity that is a hallmark of elegiac poetry: *pro-ludere*. She pays attention to Tatius's adornment (*picta arma, flavas iubas*) and to his face (*facie*), and she prays to pastoral rather than patriotic or martial deities to preserve her beloved's face (*Nymphis*).[32] She is transfixed by her gaze, and, like the Propertian lover of 1.3 before her, her perception of the landscape matches her erotic fantasies.[33] Also like that lover, Tarpeia's vision is proven to be illusory. Just as the sleeping Cynthia awakens and shatters the lover's fantasy, so, too, Tarpeia finds not love in the Roman landscape but death. She escapes the Capitol, believing that with Tatius her private desires will be fulfilled and the good of the state will be served by reconciliation between the two peoples, accomplished by her (4.4.59–60):

> commissas acies ego possum soluere nupta:
>   vos medium palla foedus inite mea.

> I, as a bride, am able to dissolve the battles that have begun. Enter into a compromise through my wedding gown!

However, in joining the Sabine commander in the Forum, she enters into an arena equally marked out for Roman public life, equally resonant with Roman public institutions, successes, and policies. There she finds herself in a predicament similar to the one she faced on the Capitol: she is faced with a military leader unwilling to sanction her love. Like the Capitol, Tatius's encampment is an unsafe place for her personal goals: the Sabine king kills her on the spot (4.4.91–92), reinforcing the Roman values that mandated her public service and facilitating a pact between the two peoples, a pact entered into not because of Tarpeia's love, as she had hoped, but because of her death. Tarpeia's grove thus becomes not a nostalgic glance that privileges the "lost and irretrievable natural innocence of the populated pre-urban community," as has been suggested (see Fantham 1997.135). Rather, her grove forebodes the meaning and power of the future city.

Though Tarpeia believes that by joining Tatius she is reconciling her love with the needs of the state—a reconciliation ominously resonant with the new state Augustus was trying to create through his moral legislation—her actions are, to the traditional Roman eye, criminal and doomed to fail. Her departure from one site of Roman power, the Capitol, enacting as it does the reverse of a triumph, nevertheless leads her to the other urban axis of Roman dominion, the Forum Romanum. She departs from one center of Roman ideology to rush into another where she is equally bent to the will of the state—where, indeed, her story will be enshrined by the *gens* Iulia as a negative example in the Basilica Aemilia. She is caught, if you will, between a rock and a hard place.

The Perils of the Threshold

Tarpeia, as we have seen, spends most of her time moving between the Capitol and the Forum, from the edge of the precinct of Jupiter Optimus Maximus to the edge of Tatius's camp below.[34] Each day she descends the hill on the pretext of washing her hair, drawing water,

gathering lilies, or expiating omens (4.4.15, 23–25, and 27); and each
night she climbs the hill again (4.4.27). Her exact path is of little concern; all approaches to the Capitol, the steepest hill in Rome, are abrupt,
even with modern paving.[35] More important is the way Propertius presents the area through which she moves. It is dark and threatening.

Tarpeia describes in her soliloquy the path that she travels, the path
that she eventually reveals to Tatius (4.4.48–50):

> tu cape spinosi rorida terga iugi.
> lubrica tota via est et perfida: quippe tacentis
>   fallaci celat limite semper aquas.

> You seize the dewy back of the thorny crest. The whole path is treacherous
> and slippery, for everywhere it hides silent waters in its deceptive track.

She does not describe a pleasant locale but one difficult to maneuver,
beset with hidden dangers, and perilously wet. Micaela Janan and Paul
Allen Miller both read the water imagery in this poem as an indication
of indeterminacy; for Miller, this indeterminacy is the result of the contradictions inherent in Roman identity, especially in the Augustan age,
while for Janan, the indeterminacy represents a feminine logic that defies rigid masculine categorizations.[36] When read as a feature in the
urban landscape that is Tarpeia's domain, the water becomes an ominous
symbol of Tarpeia's predicament as a woman displaced from her wom-
anhood by the demands of the Roman state.[37] It is important to note that
these lines come from Tarpeia's own speech, revealing a self-consciousness about her dilemma framed in topographical terms.

The poet later confirms her evaluation: "mons erat ascensu dubius
festoque remissus" ("The mountain was difficult to climb and unmanned
because of the festival," 4.4.83); the difficulty of the ascent is one reason
Romulus could leave the hill unattended during the celebration of the
Parilia. Tarpeia, moreover, is wounded by thorns and brambles along the
way (4.4.27–30):

> dumque subit primo Capitolia nubila fumo
> rettulit hirsutis brachia secta rubis
> et sua Tarpeia residens ita flevit ab arce
> vulnera, vicino non patienda Iovi.

> When she ascended the Capitol, hazy at the first smoke of night's fires, she
> returned with arms cut by bristling thorns, and Tarpeia, sitting down, thus wept
> her wounds from the citadel, wounds that nearby Jove would not tolerate.

Indeed, her dangerous path is similar to that negotiated by Ariadne, who also, Tarpeia argues in 4.4.41–42, used her womanly resources (thread, the implements of weaving) to help a man travel a tricky route:

prodita quid mirum fraterni cornua monstri
cum patuit lecto stamine torta via?

Why wonder that the monstrous brother's horns were betrayed when the twisted path lay revealed by a gathered thread?

Both Tarpeia and Ariadne betray their families for the sake of love by making accessible to men the contorted, dangerous paths they them-selves have mastered and maneuver regularly. The women are masters of paths neither straight nor straightforward. On either end of Tarpeia's travels, where men dwell, the ground is level—the Forum valley below and the crest of the hill above.[38] Her in-between area, the slope of the hill she treads daily and where she sits nightly, is steep and hazardous.

Tarpeia's literal marginality echoes her emotional marginality.[39] She is threatened on both sides; on the one—the top of the hill—she is con-strained to be unnaturally barren as a Vestal Virgin; on the other—the bottom—she expresses her desire, but is killed for it. Propertius presents Tarpeia's internal emotional struggle between *amor* and Roma in topo-graphical terms, using, as he frequently does, the physical to convey the emotional. Yet his landscape invites us to consider Tarpeia's social situa-tion as well, that is, her position in society with respect to others. We have seen how the areas between which Tarpeia travels are ideologically charged, urban shorthand for Rome's masculine power and glory and for the divine favor it enjoys. Tarpeia's assigned feminine area is empty, lim-inal, un-urban, and untamed in its lack of future monuments to Rome's glory.[40] To be sure, two "monuments" were located on the slopes of the Capitol, but both of them are testimonials to marginality, to exclusion from the Roman state: the Tarpeian rock and the Carcer Tullianum. Like the Carcer's prisoners and those condemned to the Tarpeian rock, Tarpeia is confined to Rome's no man's land. Once the woman exits her liminal area, Rome suffers violence, a point underscored in the opening couplet of the poem (*antiqui limina capta Iovis*, 4.4.2). She must therefore be contained there or, if she escapes, punished.

Her liminal area is the only place Tarpeia can speak. Tarpeia's entire soliloquy is delivered from the threshold of the hill (*flevit ab arce*, 4.4.29–30). On either side of her liminal area, she is muted by indirect discourse. Furthermore, at the top of the hill, she must tell lies, inventing pretexts for her visits to Tatius's camp: "saepe illa immeritae causata est omina lunae" ("Often using omens of the blameless moon as a pretext," 4.4.23) and, at the bottom, she is silenced by death: "ingestis comitum super obruit armis" ("He overwhelmed her with the heaped up weapons of his comrades," 4.4.91). Her confinement is replayed in the structure of the poem. Tarpeia's soliloquy lies in the middle of the poem between the descriptions of her situation and of her demise. Her subjectivity, therefore, is poetically bracketed by the voice of the omniscient narrator, just as she is bracketed by the urban axes of Rome's dominion.

Conclusion

Tarpeia's topographical confinement is more than a metaphor for her situation. By making her liminality central—Tarpeia has the poem's most extensive voice, speaking thirty-six lines of the poem (4.4.31–66)—the poet invites us to consider her point of view. The reader is led to sympathize with Tarpeia. From her space on the margins, her perspective is drawn, and it proves to be unlike the snapshot of her in the traditional version. In Propertius's poem, Tarpeia disagrees with the state's appropriation of her sexuality for its own benefit, and this is expressed in her desire to marry Tatius and in her negative evaluation of Romulus, child of another Vestal Virgin whose sexuality was activated. From the margin, Propertius's Tarpeia also dreams of the best effects of personal affection: her affection would dissolve the boundary between warring states, increasing Rome's greatness. From the margin, however, Tarpeia can only ascend into one area of public, masculine control and values or descend into another.

Yet Propertius allows Tarpeia to voice dissent against Rome's mandates and leaves the reader with a sense of shock at her quick dispatch. The poet thereby creates an opportunity for recovering women's perspectives. Barbara Gold speaks (1993) of Propertius as opening up a space where the woman's voice can be heard. She argues that having a woman (Cynthia) as anchor for his text already destabilizes traditional gender roles, and that Cynthia's multiple roles in the text (as lover, literary critic, friend, etc.) further complicate the status quo between men and women, opening up a space for consideration of the asymmetry of gender roles. Tarpeia's complicated gender perspective is underlined by the placement of this poem between Elegy 4.3, in which a woman physically confined within the city comments on the mobility of men and the locations available to them alone (see, e.g., 4.3.35–40 and 45), and Elegy 4.5, in which an angry man (the poet?) seeks to confine a threatening woman (a *lena*) in the ultimate controlled, marginalized, and circumscribed space: a tomb under the earth itself (4.5.1–5). Like Tarpeia, the *lena* resists her confinement with an inset speech.

In 4.4, Propertius creates an actual physical space for Tarpeia's voice, a location where she can speak, though one riddled with problems, interstitial, and apart from the areas claimed by men. The fact that Tarpeia's space lies between the spaces that men have claimed for themselves draws attention to the imbalance of power with respect to gender in Rome. The characterization of Tarpeia's liminal space as dangerous and treacherous punches a hole in the construction of Roman gender relations that prizes traditional masculinity, for it shows the cost of this construction to anyone who is other.

Propertius was one such other, and, in this, he displays a great affinity with Tarpeia.[41] Both poet and *puella* are pressured by the state to abandon their love affairs. Both try to reinterpret their own and others' social roles within the state. Both are accomplished elegiac poets; Tarpeia's monologue reenacts the traditional *paraklausithyron*, complete with weeping and complaining. Her song-before-the-gates employs the sorts of learned mythical exempla and rapid shifts in thought that are the hallmarks of elegiac poetry.[42] She performs it in a setting strongly resonant of Callimachean aesthetics.[43] Indeed, both Propertius's poetry and Tarpeia's poem look to the model of Parthenius, whose Ἐρωτικὰ Παθήματα presents the psychological torment of love through first-person narrative in elegiac verse.[44]

Given the displacement of the poet's subjective voice onto the *puella*, it is tempting to see in Tarpeia's situation a commentary on the relationship between elegiac poetry and the Roman cityscape. Elegy, like Tarpeia, dwells on Rome's margins and is vulnerable to the authority imposed by the city. By attaching Tarpeia's story to Rome's urban places, Propertius works a double purpose. First, he underlines some of the problems of Tarpeia's particular situation, torn as she is between public and private duties. The second and subtler point is that, through Tarpeia's punishment, the poet comments forebodingly about the topographical markers of Roman identity and power. Threatened by the disorder she represents, the city silences Tarpeia.

Notes

1. All translations are the author's own.
2. See, for example, Wyke 1987a, Janan 2001, and O'Neill 2000.
3. Miller 2003.184–209 investigates this feature of Propertius's fourth book,

opening up new directions for exploring the implications of the poet's ventriloquism.

4. Varro *DLL* 5.41, Livy 1.10, Dionysius of Halicarnassus 2.38ff. (who cites Fabius Pictor [frag. 8P] and Cincius [frag. 5P]), and Plutarch *Romulus* 17 (citing Antigonus *FGH* 816 F2) all support the traditional version. The traditional version also appears in relief sculptures from the Basilica Aemilia from the first century B.C.E. Finally, Tarpeia appears on two coins: one that dates from the Social War by the moneyer L. Titurius Sabinus (*RRC* = Crawford 1974.344.2a–2c with plate 45.7) and one from 19 B.C.E. by the moneyer P. Petronius Turpilianus (*BMCRE* = Mattingly 1965 [1923].1.69.29–31 with plate 1.16).

5. Calpurnius Piso apud Dionysius of Halicarnassus 2.40, the first source to mention her veneration, puzzles over it. In order to explain the discrepancy between Tarpeia's treason and her veneration at Rome, Piso exonerates Tarpeia by making her a double agent. Also, Festus 496L mentions a statue to Tarpeia in the vicinity of the temple of Jupiter Stator, but no vestiges of this remain and its date is unknown; Festus's statue indicates a version of the myth that does not condemn Tarpeia.

6. Plutarch *Romulus* 17 offers this option without attributing it to anyone in particular.

7. Simylus's elegy is quoted in Plutarch *Romulus* 17.5.

8. The "betrayal-for-love" motif, analogous as it is to many Greek myths, seems older than the "betrayal-for-greed" motif found in the traditional Roman version and perhaps even attests to Greek origins for Tarpeia's myth. See Bremmer and Horsfall 1987.68–70.

9. Here I disagree with Tissol 1997.149, who sees Propertius's Tarpeia as a naïve girl who deceives herself by ignoring Scylla's punishment, even though she acknowledges her own illicit love.

10. Unless otherwise noted, all citations are from Barber 1960.

11. I prefer Camps' emendation of *nuptae* to *nupta* at 4.459 and his revised punctuation; the meaning remains the same while the grammar is decidedly less awkward (Camps 1965 ad 4.4.59–60).

12. As DeBrohun 2003.194 points out, Tarpeia's elision of her wedding clothes with her Vestal costume illuminates her own precarious situation and the uneasy mingling of *amor* and Roma in Book 4 generally.

13. Elegy 2.7 is the most explicit statement of this disdain.

14. Ovid *Fasti* 3.11 and Dionysius of Halicarnassus 1.77.1.

15. Richardson 1977 and Goold 1990.

16. So, too, is Tarpeia's broken water jar, according to Janan 2001.74. Like the water that slips out of the broken jar, Tarpeia's sexuality escapes the confines of her priesthood. For Stahl 1985.283, the tension is best expressed in Propertius's description of Tarpeia as a *mala puella* (4.4.17). The elegiac *puella* (as opposed to a *virgo*) has sexual potential that she devotes to her lover. Were Tarpeia to break faith with the goddess she serves, she would be a bad (i.e., disobedient)

mistress. Reading *mala puella* another way, as unable to fulfill this sexual potential, Tarpeia is a bad (i.e., unaccomplished) mistress.

17. Stahl 1985.285 and, for Propertius's amatory landscape in Books 1–3, see also Scivoletto 1979.

18. Livy 1.55.5 gives an etymology for the name Capitol: an actual head was found there. Catharine Edwards, in her chapter "The City of Empire" (1996.69–95), discusses the religious and military messages the hill delivered to Romans, their subjects, their clients, and their enemies.

19. Though the Gauls had come close, the Capitol had never been occupied by enemies (Livy 5.33ff.). Horace even describes eternity in terms of this hill in his famous Ode 3.30.7–9: "usque ego postera / crescam laude recens, dum Capitolium / scandet cum tacita virgine pontifex" ("I shall grow fresh with future praise, as long as the Pontifex with the silent Vestal Virgin climbs the Capitol").

20. For this phenomenon, see Stambaugh 1988.243–86. Cosa boasts an *arx*-style Capitol; Timgad, a flat version.

21. Bede's formulation: "quandiu stabit colyseus, stabit et Roma. Quando cadit colyseus, cadet et Roma. Quando cadet Roma, cadet et mundus."

22. Stehle 1989 discusses the "triumphal" arrival of two goddesses, Venus Erycina and Cybele, into Rome. The symbolic procession of these goddesses into the city to their new Roman sanctuaries—in Venus's case, on the Capitol—resembled the triumphal ceremony in form and purpose. Tarpeia's journey down the Capitol reverses that procedure.

23. There may be multiple puns in this first line. Boyd 1984 sees *se-pulchrum* as its own etymological play on *turpe*. *Tarpeiae turpe sepulchrum* may also refer to the name of the moneyer Turpilianus, who minted coins of Tarpeia in 19 B.C.E. (Mattingly 1965 [1923].1.69.29–31). Wallace-Hadrill 1986.77 sees the pun operating in the other direction: Tarpeia's appearance on his coin puns Turpilianus's own name.

24. A full description of all parts of the frieze is given in Carettoni 1961. For the dating of the frieze to the Aemilian/Julian restoration of 55–34 B.C.E., see Carettoni 1961.65, Arya 1996, and Albertson 1990.

25. Kampen 1991. Kampen argues for an Augustan date for the frieze, but her compelling arguments about its resonance in the Augustan age do not require that the frieze be newly sculpted in the teens B.C.E. Even if he reused the relief sculptures, Augustus's renovation of the building would have rewritten their meaning in the new context; see Favro 1996.189. Paul Zanker 1988.82 comments on the new Julian flair of the building, without dating the frieze, and see also Evans 1992.129–34.

26. Raditsa 1980.339. This legislation spoke to the same concern as the legends: the ability of women to undermine proper relationships between men. The laws on marriage and adultery sought to stabilize families via children, social classes via restricted intermarriage, and female conduct via the punishment of adultery. They also established a new relationship between the individual and the

state, subordinating private desires and personal liberties to public needs and state authority.

27. The location of Tatius's camp is disputed. It is either in the northeast corner of the Forum near the Tullian spring or the northwest corner of the Forum Romanum around the Lacus Iuturnus. For the former, see Richardson 1977 ad 4.4.3–4. For the latter, see Camps 1965 ad loc. Richardson's reasons for choosing the northeast corner are more compelling: the Tullian spring lay right at the base of the hill and would be a better water source for Tarpeia, whereas the Lacus Iuturnus lay further into the Forum. Grimal 1953.211 also points out that Tatius's location in this poem calls to mind the future location of his descendant Julius Caesar's forum.

28. Camps 1965 and Goold 1990 both offer *scelus* in the opening line.

29. Stahl 1985.282–83. He finds the same contrast between "(Julian) arms and (pastoral) lover" in Elegy 2.34, a poem that values Vergil's *Eclogues* higher than his *Aeneid* (p. 283).

30. Specific military and political monuments are situated in the proto-Roman pastoral landscape: the temple to Palatine Apollo (4.1.3), the Curia (4.1.11–12), and the house of Romulus (4.1.9–10). The characters that appear in 4.1's first half are all male figures from Roman history (Romulus, Remus, Caesar, Tatius, Decius, Brutus). As for women, only Venus, stripped of her femininity as arms-bearer for Caesar, and the virginal goddess Vesta are present (4.1.46 and 4.1.21). Even Tarpeia occurs in masculine form as *Tarpeiusque pater* (4.1.7), a name for Jupiter. The primary female presence in 4.1's first half is the she-wolf, the wolf of Mars (*lupa Martia*, 4.1.55).

31. Suetonius *Augustus* 29.2. See Richardson 1992 s.v. Forum Romanum for a discussion of the functions of the Forum.

32. It is tempting also to see here a pun on *nubilis* ("marriageable") in the description of the Capitol as *nubila* ("hazy," 4.4.27).

33. In Elegy 1.3, the lover adorns the sleeping Cynthia so as to create an erotic tableau that matches his feelings. He, like Tarpeia, is transfixed by his gaze upon the tableau. See Valladares in this volume and Gioia 2002.

34. From the Capitol: 4.4.29–30: *ab arce . . . vicino . . . Iovi*. To the Forum: *hinc*, 4.4.15.

35. The hidden waters Tarpeia describes along the way (4.4.48–50) suggest that she takes the path along the southeastern edge of the hill that leads past the Tullian spring.

36. Miller 2003.192–93, Janan 2001.72–76.

37. These lines hint at elegy's predicament as well, for the words Tarpeia uses to describe her (feminine) portion of the Roman city resonate with the terms Propertius has used to describe his own poetry and the love affair that generates it (*fallax*, 4.4.50 and 4.1.135; *perfidus*, 4.4.49 and 4.7.13; cf. *perfidia*, 4.7.70).

38. *murus erant montes* (4.4.13) evokes the flatness of the valley where Tatius is camped, and *patriamque iacentem* (4.4.87) hints at the flatness of the Capitol where the Romans are encamped.

39. For DeBrohun 2003.146–49, the *limen* in this poem as elsewhere in Book 4 acts as a powerful symbol of the tensions exerted upon the elegiac genre by Propertius's new etiological program. In this poem, she focuses on the fact that Tarpeia's actions lead to the capture of Jove's threshold (4.4.2).

40. Stahl 1985.285 says this of Tarpeia's urban incongruity: "Tarpeia's thoughts are not at home in her country, but in an apolitical, individual, lyrical and pastoral world of her wishes." Janan 2001.78 discusses the contribution the maenad/Amazon simile (4.4.71–72) makes to the poem's surreal landscape. Why, Janan wonders, is a woman from the region of the river Strymon running along the banks of the Thermodon? "Always, before thought can overtake it in this poem, the feminine is already elsewhere" (78). Warden also sees a spatial dimension to this simile, for the maenad "bursts forth from her house into the streets, the movement expressing as it were the making public of private emotions" (Warden 1978.181). In her urban incongruity, Tarpeia is like the women of the second half of poem 4.1. Arria loses her sons to warfare (4.1.89–97), Iphigeneia loses her own life to expedite the Trojan war (4.1.109–14), and Cassandra is raped in the context of that same war (4.1.114–18). The fourth woman mentioned in Horos's catalogue of his own prophetic achievements is Cinara, who had trouble at childbirth. These women find themselves in a poem whose climax and primary message is "avoid the Forum" (4.1.134).

41. Stahl 1985.285–98 offers the lengthiest and most satisfying treatment of the similarities between Propertius and Tarpeia, but see also Wyke 1987a.

42. She cites Ariadne and Scylla, blending variants of Scylla's myths to suit her amatory purposes. Her frequently shifting thoughts and her abrupt transitions are the result of her heightened emotion and the tensions of her situation.

43. Her path is narrow and difficult, and she pursues trickling, not gushing, water; cf. Callimachus *Hymn* 2.108–12. For a fuller discussion of these nuances, see King 1989–90.

44. Other models include Ariadne's extended complaint in Catullus 64 and some of Dido's speeches in the *Aeneid* (such as *Aeneid* 4.590–629). Indeed, Tarpeia's mention of Ariadne may be an allusion to Catullus's poem. Boyd 1984.86 with note 6, Tissol 1997.143–53, and Wyke 1987a.163 all discuss the literary pedigree of the Tarpeia elegy.

Silenced Subjects

Ovid and the Heroines in Exile

Efrossini Spentzou

Silence and the Self

Already three years in exile, Ovid opened his fifth and last book of the *Tristia* with an address to "his devoted reader" (*nostri studiose*, 1) that draws a clear and explicit distinction between his old, frivolous poetry and the new, sober verses (5.1.15–24):

> delicias siquis lascivaque carmina quaerit
> praemoneo, non est scripta quod ista legat.
>
> . . . .
>
> ille pharetrati lusor Amoris abest.
> quod superest, animos ad publica carmina flexi,
> et memores iussi nominis esse mei.

If anyone wants frivolous amusement and frisky poems, I warn him, he is not to read writings such as these . . . That poet who played with Love and his quiver is gone. For what is left of my life, I have turned my spirit to public poems and ordered them to remember my name.[1]

The renunciation of Ovid's earlier literary taste is firm and unequivocal. Only a few lines earlier, he had already made it plain: "talis erit, qualis fortuna poetae / invenies toto carmine dulce nihil" ("The poem matches the fortune of the poet, you will find nothing pleasurable in the whole of it," 5.1.3–4). By denouncing the frivolities of his youth, Ovid attempts to ingratiate himself with Augustus. The ultimate hope, of course, is a recall from exile. So far so good; but Ovidian critics have learned to be always on their guard.

Ovid's unequivocal renunciation of the frivolous tropes and manners

318

of his love elegy in *Tristia* 5.1 is but one more trope in this ceaselessly protean collection, a collection whose inclusion within the elegiac genre depends on more than its meter. The exile poetry is the final and most spectacular twist to elegiac love. Ovid is now the real excluded lover, and *Tristia* 3.1 is an impressive lament before the closed door of Rome (the closed door of Augustus), sung not by a rejected lover but by the bleak and stumbling book of the exile.[2] In this inverted love elegy, Augustus is a remarkably unapproachable and unusually dangerous *puella*.[3] Rome is Ovid's desperate, unrequited, and ultimate love.

The situation is typically Ovidian. Declarations of inadequacy and failure, together with loss of talent and nerve, are intricately coated with skilled and subtle allusions to the very art whose death is deplored. Patricia Rosenmeyer notes that, in *Tristia* 1.5.79ff., Ovid explicitly differentiates himself from Odysseus's mythical persona ("quod illius pars maxima ficta laborum, / ponitur in nostris fabula nulla malis," "The greater part of his labors is fictitious, my sufferings contain no element of fiction"), though she refuses to be dragged to this positivistic dead end (1997.50–51):

> Here we confront the great conundrum of Ovid's poetic innovations: what is *ficta* and what is *nulla fabula*? . . . In such an emotionally laden situation as exile, and in the genre of autobiography, we expect the "truth"; but does not truth demand multiple, complex meanings with an author so committed to rhetorical posturing, to clever wit, and to intertextual allusion? One response is that truth and fiction for Ovid function less as polar opposites and more as points on a continuum. Is it "truer" to show fictional characters acting out "honest" and lifelike emotions, or rather to limit oneself to what actually happened in a recorded (auto)biography or history?

Sharing this notion of "artful reality," the present study explores the story of the (largely metaphorical) silence imposed on the disgraced Ovid following his removal from Rome and traces its twists and turns throughout the *Tristia*. I would claim that this story is of central importance for the poetics not only of the Ovidian exile but of Ovidian self-projection in general. Silence brings Naso into direct contact with his other creatures of exile, the heroines of the *Heroides*, half-forgotten creations of his youth who now join him in his latest twist of fortune, a twist that may have been less unpredictable than he would have us believe.

In her recent discussion of Ovidian exilic silence, Elizabeth Forbis stresses the significance of verbal authority and draws attention to characters of remarkable eloquence who regularly control the speech of other defenseless and muted characters (1997.261, 263). Her readings chart the map of speech and silence, but mainly provide a functional understanding of speech and its deprivation in the *Tristia* and the *Epistulae ex Ponto*. She rightly notices that Ovid laments his loss of voice and desperately tries to sustain an illusion of speech in his tired, exilic books. He is clearly ashamed of his removal from the center and of the loss of the admiration he used to enjoy; but, as Forbis suggests, above all, he is increasingly weighed down by the realization that his written words are not enough to persuade Augustus to recall him from Tomis (1997.261, 257–59).

My exploration of silence probes less immediate and pragmatic themes. Certainly, silence often denotes weakness and submission; but, as I explain in the last section of my paper, it can also signify strength and lurking danger. I will trace a number of interrelated polarities: silence versus speech, but also spoken versus written words, presence versus absence, strength versus weakness, control versus powerlessness, security versus danger, and even, briefly, voice versus body, activity versus inertia. Though based on such polarities, my discourse will be far from polarized itself and will often explore the meeting points between different pairs. Indeed, the real significance of my subject is to be found with a study of such polarities and, especially, at the moments of instability within them: for example, those moments when silence acquires a voice and inertia is power. At least two Ovidian personae will emerge from this study: one who struggles against and another who appropriates silence, one who resembles and another who is drastically different from the exiled heroines of the *Heroides*. As we shall see, the heroines explain as well as expose Ovid's exilic self. Ovid's personae in the *Tristia* live within the force field of these creative tensions.

In his encounter with silence, Ovid finds himself implicated in a complex questioning of power, control, presence, and communication. These questions have an obvious functional value for the exiled poet, but they also form part of the core of his self-definition as an educated Roman male in close touch with the political center in the imperial period.[4] They are also all highly gendered concerns not only within Greco-Roman culture but in many contemporary discourses. There is a final twist in the gendered dynamics of Latin love elegy as Ovid confronts his ultimate love: Rome (and/or the emperor).

Presence and Prestige

Even a cursory reading of the *Tristia*[5] uncovers numerous signs of Ovid's despair at the latest twist to his life. The tone and mood of the collection are far from even. The poems tend to progress toward increasingly bleak forms as time passes and the hope of a recall inexorably diminishes. Yet the main reason for Ovid's plight is clear from early in *Tristia* Book 1. In *Tristia* 1.3, as Ovid recollects with overwhelming sentimentality his final night at Rome, we get a clear sense of his deprivation. He is abandoning Rome, the center of power, the site of the only way of life he has ever chosen and enjoyed. His concerns are rather inappropriate, shallow one might say. Exile terrifies him because he has no clue how to "present" himself in it: no idea what protocols to apply to the new situation: "non mihi servorum, comites non cura legendi, / non aptae profugo vestis opisve fuit" ("I had no mind for choosing slaves and companions, clothes and the kit fit for an exile," 1.3.9–10). Grief clouds his mind (13–14); more than the vast unknown that stretches ahead, it is precious Rome that makes his heart ache: it is his house, right in the center of power by the Capitol (29–30), and the society of his loyal friends and fellow intellectuals, this group that marked his presence in the bustle of the metropolis, that he misses.

The loss is even more poignantly marked in 1.5. Such is Ovid's despair at the parting that not even the legendary Odysseus and his helpless wanderings can match it. The difference is not so much the toil, not even the exile itself, but that which is left behind. In Odysseus's case, it is just a Greek island, Ithaca, but in Ovid's case, it is Rome, the center of empire and seat of the gods (1.5.67–70):

nec mihi Dulichium domus est Ithaceve Samosve,
poena quibus non est grandis abesse locis:
sed quae de septem totum circumspicit orbem
montibus, inperii Roma deumque locus.

My home was neither Dulichium, nor Ithaca, nor Samos—to leave such places is no great punishment—but what overlooks the world from its seven hills, Rome, place of gods and power.

Barely a year after these lines were written, the mood is distinctly and progressively more somber in Book 3 of the *Tristia*. If Ovid initially nursed the thought that his fate would be similar to that of Cicero, his famous republican counterpart who was exiled in 58 B.C.E. and back in Rome in 57 B.C.E., this hope was rapidly proving illusory. Critics note that in Book 3 (and more emphatically in Books 4 and 5 of the *Tristia*), Rome fades from view, displaced by Ovid's laments about the freezing cold, the dullness, and the hostility of Tomis. By 5.12, Ovid's endless complaints would seem to have exhausted the patience of even the most loyal of friends. And yet these complaints should not obscure the single obsession of the displaced poet: Rome, its everyday life, its seasonal cycles, and its momentous events, which the poet strives to relive in his mind's eye. As the traumas of life dull Ovid's (and perhaps the reader's) mind, 3.2.21–22 encapsulates his plight:

> Roma domusque subit desideriumque locorum,
> quicquid et amissa restat in urbe mei.

> Rome and home and the desire for all the places I know surge up within me, whatever of me has stayed back in the city I have lost.

This is far from a passing reference. Rome is "under Ovid's skin," no matter how afflicted his mind and spirit are. It comes back to haunt him again in 3.3.11–14, as he lies ill and lonely, sorely missing a proper doctor's care and his friends' comforting conversation. And in 3.12, one of the most gentle elegies of the whole collection, the onset of warmer weather in Tomis brings colorful memories of the bustling life in the eternal city as spring sends its signals of awakening. His mind may have been dulled by grief and cold, as he repeatedly protests,[6] but Ovid never forgets the details of life in Rome. Twice nostalgic descriptions make mention of spring festivals such as the Megalensia and the Floralia, when the law courts were closed (3.12.17–24):[7]

> otia nunc istic, iunctisque ex ordine ludis
>   cedunt verbosi garrula bella fori

> . . . .

> scaena viget studiisque favor distantibus ardet,
>   proque tribus resonant terna theatra foris.

> There is a holiday now over there; the garrulous battles of the wordy Forum have yielded to a row of successive game-days . . . The stage thrives, rival efforts are blazing, three theaters now roar instead of the three Fora.

Ample critical attention has been paid to Ovid's reminiscences of life in Rome. As with every line of the exile poetry, such memories have been mined for covert messages, their appropriateness (or lack thereof), their subversive potential, and, conversely, their flattering effect on Augustus. Whatever their value for the above concerns, such memories share a common feature: the longing for physical presence and, even more importantly, the trust in physical presence and immediate communication as guarantees of Ovid's intact Roman identity. Ovid languishes in the wilderness of Tomi; the distance, the cold, the lack of culture, his wife's absence all contribute to the steady plummeting of his morale. But above all, he misses the mingling of people, the proximity of his house to the Capitol, the "live" conversations in the street, the word-battles whose intermissions he diligently ticks off on his calendar. It is the lack of presence, of any physical association with the culture, and, ultimately, the lack of "live" speech that makes Ovid's silencing so hard to bear. He is a male Roman citizen—in a metaphorical sense, a hero of his own time—and thus preconditioned to react badly to reticence and even worse to enforced reticence.

Sonority and Silence: Writing in the Greco-Roman World

Silence as the absence of presence was regarded with discomfort from as early as the Homeric epics. This was a culture of orality; people talked in order to communicate. Writing was yet to be established as a medium of communication;[8] voice and speech in the archaic world were the major channels of status and power. Voice conveys determination and reveals strength in the military universe of the *Iliad*; silence blocks action and exemplifies anti-heroic behavior. The heroes of the *Iliad* fill the last moments of their lives with speech: it is, after all, what determines presence, and presence is the only mode of heroic existence (the only real mode of existence) in the Iliadic world[9]—a kind of peculiar reassurance that the heroic code is honored up until the moment of the hero's death.[10]

There is obviously much that separates the closed archaic society of Homer and Ovid's contemporary, cosmopolitan world, but similar attitudes to silence and speech bring the two worlds into dialogue. Ovid repeatedly places himself in the company of archaic and classical heroes such as Odysseus, Orestes, or Philoctetes, to name but a few of his mythical impersonations in the *Tristia*. In their capacity to serve as diachronic exempla, the vocal heroes of Greek myth established direct links between speech, presence, and status that still held, even if the gradual passage from orality to literacy and the different media of expression and creation had transformed the social and cultural context of literary production.[11]

Plato spells out clearly the advantages of speech over writing. Close to the end of the *Phaedrus*, having just been asked to comment on the qualities of writing, Socrates recollects the myth of Theuth, the inventor of writing (274c–275d), and, in doing so, casts doubt on the efficiency of writing (275d):

Δεινὸν γάρ που, ὦ Φαῖδρε, τοῦτ᾽ ἔχει γραφή, . . . δόξαις μὲν ἂν ὥς τι
φρονοῦντας αὐτοὺς [τοὺς λόγους] λέγειν, ἐὰν δέ τι ἔρῃ τῶν λεγομένων
βουλόμενος μαθεῖν, ἕν τι σημαίνει μόνον ταὐτὸν ἀεί. ὅταν δὲ ἅπαξ γραφῇ,
κυλινδεῖται μὲν πανταχοῦ πᾶς λόγος ὁμοίως παρὰ τοῖς ἐπαΐουσιν, ὡς δ᾽
αὔτως παρ᾽ οἷς οὐδὲν προσήκει, καὶ οὐκ ἐπίσταται λέγειν οἷς δεῖ γε καὶ μή.
πλημμελούμενος δὲ καὶ οὐκ ἐν δίκῃ λοιδορηθεὶς τοῦ πατρὸς ἀεὶ δεῖται βο-
ηθοῦ· αὐτὸς γὰρ οὔτ᾽ ἀμύνασθαι οὔτε βοηθῆσαι δυνατὸς αὑτῷ.

Writing, Phaedrus, has this wondrous quality . . . You might think that [writ-
ten words] spoke as if they could reflect, but if you ask them, wishing to find
out more about their sayings, they always point out one and the same thing.
And every word, once written, tumbles alike amongst those who understand
and those who have no concern about it. And it does not know to whom it
ought to speak and to whom it ought not. And when wronged and unjustly
reviled, it always needs its father to help it; for, on its own, it has power neither to protect nor to help itself.

All the imaginative metaphors used here to describe writing seem to
add up to one major observation: writing is uncontrollable and/or helpless. Writing travels without escort and may meet the "right" people, but
may also meet inappropriate ones, those unable to perceive the original
meaning of the words they read. Writing may thus be abused and so
needs a father to help this original meaning to emerge and to educate
those capable of misunderstanding it.

The reactionary nature of the above passage cannot pass unnoticed
in an age that has lived through—and survived—the Death of the Author. These lines from the *Phaedrus* can legitimately be said to provide
an apparatus of male hegemony that underpins Greek and Roman culture. Meanings are to be controlled, stray ideas can be dangerous, and so
can the unpredictable receptions of original ideas, as they undermine the
power of the Author/Father/Creator, to use Jacques Derrida's frequently
quoted imagery.[12] The values from which power is derived in the above
vision are presence and control, and, through these, certainty, firm guid-
ance, and assertion.

Whatever other differences there may be from the age of Plato, the
same nexus of interconnected values drives the world that engendered
Ovid. Note, for example, Horace, whose life and career also presented
complex questions and choices relating to dependency and independence
in all forms. Physical togetherness and hegemony are given special emphasis in *Odes* 1.1, when Horace imposes his presence as a lyric bard by

inserting—rather asserting—an image of himself as a giant reaching the stars with his lifted head (1.1.37–38). The *Odes* negotiate subtle and often dangerous territories of ambition and poetic vision that fall beyond the scope of the present article. It is significant, though, that as his poetic self-confidence increases (proportionately to Horace's own place in Roman public life), we notice an increased emphasis on the voice. Equally significant is the rare and troubled presence of book and writing imagery in the *Odes*. Alison Sharrock explores the book imagery of *Odes* 2.20 and the story of Daedalus (1994b.117–22), and Joseph Farrell, in a forthcoming work, discusses at length the dominance of voice in the collection.[13] Horace seems to be fully aware of the irreplaceable force of being present and speaking one's own words.[14]

The urge to defeat death and destruction is most emphatic in *Odes* 3.30, a deeply ambiguous poem. Horace proudly speaks about his own books of poetry, denouncing their perishable materiality at the very moment he claims to assert it. He has achieved a monument more lasting than bronze, a creation that neither countless years nor the passage of the ages can destroy, an achievement whose voice will be heard forever. A rather idiosyncratic presence, more like a disembodied memory, Horace's imagery in *Odes* 3.30 radiates remarkable self-confidence, control,[15] and the poet's impressively solid belief in his ability to signify forever his own meaning, the very thing that writing cannot guarantee.

The triumph of the voice becomes even more transparent in the epilogue of Ovid's *Metamorphoses*, another intriguing passage, one of the most self-confident pieces of Latin poetry and a widely acknowledged intertext of *Odes* 3.30. Having instilled doubts and confusion about the inspirational qualities of Roman history in the last two books, Ovid surprises us once more and for the last time in his epic. The moral of the last two books has been that even history can be prey to contradictory, and even skewed, readings (especially after Ovid has tampered with it). Ovid's voice, though, will never stop emitting its crystal clear message, a bardic voice with never diminished strength. "Ore legar populi, perque omnia saecula fama, / siquid habent veri vatum praesagia, vivam," "I shall be heard on people's lips, and my fame will live through all centuries, if there is any truth in the prophesies of the bards," 15.878–79. As in Horace's Ode 3.30, the relationship between human and textual body, voice and artistic creativity throughout the *Metamorphoses* and culminating in the epilogue seems a hard one to define. Critics have chosen to emphasize different aspects of these amazingly delicate interrelationships.[16] Placing the emphasis of my own reading on the remarkable self-confidence that characterizes these passages rather than on other imagery and concerns, I would like to add the following question to the ongoing debate: could it be the case that, in moments of confidence, the male Roman poets retreat instinctively to images of a coherent, controlling voice, always nursing a certain suspicion (perhaps even with hints of contempt) toward writing and its feeble constitution, something instilled in them as part of their own "classical" heritage?[17] Such prejudices lie at the heart of the exiled Ovid's predicament[18] and condition his rhetoric in manifold ways, accounting to a large extent for the unresolved conflicts of tone that have been repeatedly observed by critics.

Ovid and the Books

A few lines into the *Tristia*, the need for a surrogate presence has already been eagerly expressed. Ovid wishes well and also envies his little book of exile verse that heads to Rome instead of him. "Parve (nec invideo) sine me, liber, ibis in urbem; / ei mihi, quod domino non licet ire tuo!" "Little book—and I do not begrudge it to you—you're off to the city without me, where it is not allowed to me, your master, to go!" 1.1.1–2. Hardly has this farewell wish ended than heaps of advice follow the small book on its way to the Big City. I paraphrase Ovid's words: "Off you go, little book, but avoid adornment and polish (as befits my state as an exile)," 3–5; "Speak to those who used to like me," 17–19; "Avoid awkward questions," 20–22; "Try to discover readers well-disposed and willing to be moved by you," 27–28.[19]

The rest of the elegy revolves around Ovid's consternation at his enforced absence from Rome, yet it is constantly interlaced with injunctions to the book on its behavior in the big city. Ovid visualizes, preempts, frets about, even attempts to manipulate the reception of his little book. It may be that his self-assurance was steadily corroded as the months passed by. Poem after poem was dispatched without achieving the much desired change of the imperial mind. Nonetheless, the little book on its own is little trusted by Ovid. He can hardly bear giving up control; what hurts the poet most is the loss of that influence and persuasive power achievable, in his mind, solely through his immediate, bodily presence, an evaluation perhaps not surprising in the vocal, competitive, and confrontational culture in which he was brought up.[20] Writing is, after all, helpless and weak willed, as we saw in the *Phaedrus*. It needs a father to help it through.

Such preferences for control and presence figure prominently in Ovid's earlier poetry. His attitude to letters and writing in the *Ars Ama-*

toria, especially Book 1, reveals a rather limited appreciation of the letter as a means of self-expression. The catalogue of tricks and devices for men who wish to seduce a woman is long and impressive. Sending a letter is included in Ovid's list. As he suggests, it should be sent ahead to predispose the woman with sweet words (1.437–86). It can test the ground, give empty promises, and be filled with flattery that amounts to nothing. It can fold the sender's persona in its twists and prevent his[21] real self from being deciphered: it is a perfect and relatively safe medium for duplicity.[22] The message is totally in tune with Ovid's overall playfulness in the *Ars*, where love and life are a game in which the cleverest and wittiest wins.

At this confident moment, Ovid feels at his most comfortable in the heart of the city; the history, monuments, triumphs, and landmarks in the public life of Rome all transform, in his mind, into apt spots for private indulgences (1.163–228). Once again, it is the dynamics of presence, integration, and participation that empower Ovid. From his firm standpoint at the heart of the empire, Ovid presents letters as lacking spirit and energy, poor relatives to the formidable spoken words that his male lovers possess but are advised to hide (1.464) behind plain speaking. Letters may be the perfect medium of dissimulation, but their potential when it comes to self-disclosure is strikingly limited in male hands.

Not that Ovid himself considers this dishonesty a handicap—rather the opposite. He relishes the dissimulating capacity of aspiring male lovers. For them, duplicity is another clear sign of masculine superiority over women. Despite the fact that his advice to women on writing letters in *Ars* 3 (479–82) is quite similar in tone to his admonitions to his male readers in Book 1, in his poetry, women letter writers almost invariably use their tablet to lay bare their selves and release their emotions without reservation. The letters of the *Heroides* instantly spring to mind, and I will return to them in the next section.

The same complex relationship between duplicity and emotional truth in speaking and letter writing is thematized in the *Metamorphoses* 9 story of Byblis, who is, in her scorned love, a mirror image of the other Ovidian heroines. Byblis attempts to present her case to Caunus, her brother and unwitting beloved, through writing. Initially, she tries to adhere to Ovid's advice, formulating and reformulating her words to the maximum effect (523–27). But, gradually, typical female abandon takes over, and her letter brims to the margins with her barely contained grief (563–64)—with the well-known tragic results.[23] However, is there not something that Byblis, like the heroines of the *Heroides*, also gains, even if her letter condemns her to death (by metamorphosis) and her brother to life in remote exile? As I argue elsewhere, there is a great deal to recuperate and release from the heroines' self-exposure in the *Heroides* (see n. 21). Some of the advantages of such "weakness" will also become apparent in the next section of this analysis.

The Multiple Faces of Absence

A brief contrast between the heroines of the *Heroides* and Ovid in exile clarifies the dynamics of speech and writing, presence and absence in the *Tristia*. The relationship between the *Heroides* and *Tristia* puzzles critics, but Patricia Rosenmeyer has recently convinced us of the artificial nature of any "life versus art" distinctions in the two collections,[24] providing also the most thorough comparative reading to date. Her close inspection reveals that Ovid and the heroines experience similarly intense feelings of isolation, relegation, and self-deprecation. All of them struggle with the emotional as well as physical hindrances of writing; they feel similarly harshly treated by life; they admit the same debilitating sense of abandonment; and they express the same "access" anxieties (Rosenmeyer 1997.33–34, 36, 37–38, 41–42).

Yet the attitudes of Ovid and his heroines about silence—and more crucially the power relations behind it—are fundamentally different. Several similar topoi are used in both cases, as already noted; yet take a step back, and an altogether different context is revealed. Ovid comes to writing having lost everything; the heroines come to writing with the hope that it will help them break out of the silence in which they were traditionally imprisoned in "official" myths. In Alessandro Barchiesi's reading, the *Heroides* letters occupy certain blank spots, filling in silences in the narratives of the established myths. In other words, the heroines' letters are stories in the interstices.[25] If Ovid comes to writing having lost his ability to be heard in Rome (as we saw in the previous sections), the heroines *find* a voice through their writing, and thus escape the silence to which they were resigned in earlier, male-dominated narratives.[26] Last, but not least, Ovid writes back to the world he thinks he knows and belongs to. Most of the heroines, however, address a world in which they never occupied a central, and often not even a marginal, position. Heroines such as Medea (12.105–11) but also, in a more limited but crucial way, Phaedra, who does not hesitate to call Troezen (the place that would shelter her imagined life with Hippolytus) a country dearer than her own land (4.105–08), speak about the departure from their homes in a very poignant way.

Ovid the castaway feels that he and his poetry are an integral part of the world he has just lost, and he struggles hard with the multiple signs of his isolation and the absence of action and participation. In the freezing cold of Tomis, there is nobody to recite his poems to, none with a comprehending ear to rely on (3.14.39–40).[27] Therefore, he writes incessantly and repeatedly to a long series of friends,[28] asking for favors, but also sustaining a connection with the latest events in Rome. Even though the strongest motive behind the composition of these letters appears to be the gathering of support for his appeal to Augustus, these letters have also been seen as a desperate attempt by Ovid to fulfill some, at least, of the duties of *amicitia:* mingling with and trying to sustain a society of citizens and friends severed by exile (cf., e.g., Williams 2002.234). In fact, in his repeatedly declared eagerness to be a part of the society from which he was forced to withdraw, Ovid seems to undermine the elegiac persona of his youthful poetry. Back then, he used to relish his friction with the establishment.[29] Whatever we make of this reinvention of Ovid's own self, several elegiac topoi have had an elevated reworking in the exilic poems, not least among them the figure of the elegiac mistress, who is replaced by Ovid's respectable matron-like wife in poems such as 1.6 or 4.3. There his wife is likened to Andromache or Evadne, famous chaste figures from the world of epic.[30]

If Ovid's existence in exile involves relinquishing the duties of a Roman citizen, this is not a burden that the heroines are asked to carry. Many of them are the typical Other (figures rather distant from power due to ethnicity, status, age, or other marginalizing factors). Contact with that Other seems to alarm Ovid so much that he even resents his learning some Getan and Sarmatian:[31] "dicere saepe aliquid conanti (turpe fateri) / verba mihi desunt dedidicique loqui," "I often lack the words (shameful to confess) as I try to say something, and I have unlearnt how to speak," 3.14.45–46. It has been noted that his distress at the fading of Latin from his mind and at having to speak these barbaric languages is connected to his fear of losing not only his Roman identity but, in a more extreme reading, his very humanity, like Actaeon in *Metamorphoses* 3 (Forbis 1997.262–63).

Things are certainly different for the heroines. Their relationship to language appears looser, more permissive, but also less debilitating. Briseis of *Heroides* 3 is an eloquent case study as a barbarian who tries to write herself into the established literature and culture but without denying her difference. Her letter speaks about (and to) a culture that was, and will always be, foreign to her. Lack of linguistic competence bothers her much less than it bothers Ovid: she knows her Greek is weak (3.1–2), but she does not waste a single line worrying that her message may not get through. On the contrary, she appears remarkably confident that she can do better where Odysseus, Phoenix, and Ajax (the Homeric delegation) failed (3.129–30). But even though she ultimately asks for permission to visit Achilles (for presence), she does not seem to draw her confidence from eloquent words and cunning rhetoric (3.131–34):

> est aliquid collum solitis tetigisse lacertis,
> praesentisque oculos admonuisse sui.
> sis licet inmitis matrisque ferocior undis,
> ut taceam lacrimis conminuere meis.

> It is of some avail to have touched his neck with familiar arms and to have reminded his eyes of my existence. Even though you are cruel and fiercer than your mother's waves, you will be broken down by my tears, even if I stay silent.

For Briseis, physical touch and even the complete absence of words are judged perfectly capable of conveying her message. Deprived of the verbal authority usually associated with the male, she is also less damaged by its absence.

This may all have to do with the female inability to contain feelings and thoughts when writing, a serious flaw according to Ovid's injunctions to male lovers in *Ars Amatoria* 2. Letters obviously had their crucial uses in the art of seduction, but self-expression was not among them. If Ovid believed any of his own lessons, then being left with letter writing as the only device for calling attention to himself must have seemed dire indeed. On the other hand, the heroines turn to the letter to find a self and a voice previously denied to them. Phaedra's case is paradigmatic; no matter how many times she has tried, her voice is not her ally; writing, however, brings to her a freedom of expression that she has never experienced before (4.7–10):

> Ter tecum conata loqui ter inutilis haesit
> lingua, ter in primo restitit ore sonus.
> qua licet et sequitur, pudor est miscendus amori;
> dicere quae puduit, scribere iussit amor.

> Three times I tried to speak to you, three times my tongue was tied, unable to be of any use, three times the sound ceased at the very edge of my lips. Wherever modesty may accompany love, love should be mixed with propriety. In my case, what modesty forbade me to say, love forced me to write.

Unlike Ovid, who is hardly able to come to terms with the limitations of letter writing, the heroines use letters to build up an unprecedented presence. Bursting into writing—like Byblis in the *Metamorphoses*, who poured out her forbidden feelings for Caunus in a letter—might not be a handicap after all.[32] Whatever the results of such outbursts—and in the cases of both Byblis and Phaedra the results were destructive—the heroines find a self and a means of expression that the live and immediate instrument of the voice would never give them. Most of the heroines of the *Heroides* share this profound sense of liberation. Isolated or undermined in the past, their hitherto largely unnoticed existence acquires weight and significance. Especially young and marginal heroines, like Oenone, Hermione, Hero, and Cydippe (in *Heroides* 5, 7, 19, and 21 respectively), cling to letter writing when the world around them collapses; fearful and hesitant as it may be, this is the best and the clearest voice they have ever had.

Cydippe's story betrays Ovid's resigned attitude in the *Tristia* with remarkable clarity. Smitten by Acontius and his insidious apple-love message, but betrothed to another man she no longer loves, she wastes away, languishing in bed with a broken heart (21.13ff.). But her corporeal infirmity does not interfere with writing. She is scarcely able to raise her hand to write (14–15), and she is also consumed by fear of her relatives discovering her letter and the love she so diligently hides (17–30). Yet she manages a long and powerful letter before her strength abandons her in line 246.[33]

Ovid's bodily infirmity, however, has a much more profound effect on him. He starts *Tristia* 3.3, yet another letter to his wife, accounting for its different handwriting: he is so gravely ill and so uncertain about his survival that he can no longer write and, therefore, has to resort to dictating (1–4). It is not clear to whom he dictates the letter, but this dictation undermines his very message, that is, his complaints about his utter isolation and absence of conversation (11–12). In spite of his protestations, *someone* cares enough to attend to him and write his letter for him. The passage deserves more attention for its symbolic rather than its literal significance; Ovid manages to return to this means of expression that has given him authority in the past: the voice. Writing seems never to register properly as a potent medium of self-realization in this moment of intense self-doubt—the lessons of the *Ars* have gone deep into Ovid's consciousness. Even when his sees his letter off to Rome at *Tristia* 1.1.60–62, he still does not believe it needs to speak up "on its own": "ut titulo careas, ipso noscere colore: / dissimulare velis, te liquet esse meum," "Even if you lack a title, you will be known by your hue; dissimulate as you like—it is evident that you are mine," 1.1.61–62. Alternate stories are being hinted at beneath the surface narrative of the poem, but they remain the preserve of those with hidden (and silent) knowledge, raising the specter of radical differences in the interpretative strategies to be adopted by different readers. The style is the man, or, rather, the man is the style, writing features nowhere in the equation, and this conviction is superbly exposed in 3.3.5: "scribere plura libet: sed vox mihi fessa loquendo," "I would like to write more, but my voice is tired of speaking." Voice is what really matters. Acontius in *Heroides* 20 knows that well, and therefore forces Cydippe to speak the oath written in the apple—a letter masterfully controlled but also deeply deceitful (a letter worthy of the spirit of *Ars* 1).

In their plight, the heroines turn to the silent words of the letter. They have come to it from a past shrouded in neglect and have no established verbal authority to cherish. In his plight, Ovid still longs for his voice, reading his poems aloud to himself. To return to earlier discussions, could control, and the lack thereof, be a crucial factor in shaping the differences between Ovid's and the heroines' attitudes to their malaise, to speech and to silence? As we have seen, exiled Ovid in the opening poem of the *Tristia* strives to prearrange, protect, monitor, and preempt his letter's journey to and around Rome; the opening, programmatic letter of the *Heroides* is a striking contrast: Penelope puts her own letter in a bottle and entrusts it to the sea explicitly soliciting unknown, intercepting readers to carry her message across to Odysseus. Her letter, like many of the letters of the *Heroides*, appropriates the weak constitution of writing deplored in the *Phaedrus* (see p. 324). Unnoticed and uncontrollable, the heroines' letters send the voice of their neglected authors across (to the heroes and the readers). And these stories survive *precisely* because they are neither assertive nor dominating; they are, instead, furtive and do not draw attention to themselves.

The Subversive Sound of Silence

Given that this is a study of silence, I have been concentrating to a remarkable extent on the spoken. Yet there is much that is "not said" in the collection, and turning our attention to the unspoken reveals another aspect of silence and Ovid's relation to it; it is with this aspect that I wish to conclude.

In spite of the angst readily available for inspection in the *Tristia*, Ovid was no novice on the question of freedom of speech. Throughout his life and career, he constantly challenged and was challenged by concerns about constraints on speech and the vulnerability of presence. The very subject matter and the numerous figures deprived of speech (as well as their human form) that feature in the *Metamorphoses* reveal deep-seated anxieties about the precariousness of autonomy and control as Augustus's regime became increasingly authoritarian. The message that permeates the *Metamorphoses* is that a physical surface, however beautiful or dynamic, is all too easily violated or destroyed—an index of the precariousness of the human condition.[34] In fact, Ovid himself calls his exilic state his last metamorphosis. He bids his exilic book to find the fifteen books of his earlier epic in his library at home and ask them to include the new face of his fortune among their bodily changes: "his mando dicas, inter mutata referri / fortunae vultum corpora posse meae," "I bid you to say to them that my fortune's face can now be numbered among their changed bodies," 1.1.119–20. In her exploration of silencing in the *Metamorphoses*, Judith De Luce notices several similarities between Ovid in exile and the distorted epic figures she examines, not least the paradigmatic case of a mutilated self, Philomela.[35]

What all this suggests is that Ovid was not exactly unprepared for his harsh change of fortune. On the contrary, for all his life, he perceived the ongoing signs of authoritarianism, flouted them when possible, and fought them with cunning and subtlety. As Denis Feeney puts it, "At no period of Roman history was it possible simply to say what you liked, when you liked it" (1992.10). Yet the problems surrounding (free) speech reach a climax in the *Fasti*, and there Ovid recognizes openly the increasing domination of silence: "tempora labuntur, taciscisque senescimus annis," "Time elapses, and we grow old in silent years," 6.771.[36] Respect and resistance coexist in the *Fasti* as Ovid attempts to take some control over Augustus's increasingly controlling regime. The balance between power and powerlessness, center and periphery, is an intricate one. Most critics of the *Fasti* have noticed the blend of determination and disappointment, as well as the manipulative and subversive nature of silence in this pseudo-religious epic.[37] Ovid ceases his didaxis just as we were getting ready to learn about Julius Caesar's very own month. No wonder: Ovid knew well the sort of faithful silence favored by Augustus that protects sacred things from being vulgarized; it was an issue discussed in the *Fasti*.[38] And yet, he did not hesitate to appropriate this faithful silence for his own (less than sacred) purposes in the *Ars Amatoria* 2.601 ff. when refusing to talk about Venus and Mars's story of illicit sex; his silence is clearly threatening to those in power, as he draws attention to those very uncomfortable topics he refuses to talk about.[39]

Is it really possible that this subversiveness, so fundamental to Ovid's poetry and persona, has vanished from his exile poetry? If Ovid in the *Tristia* is a raped, mutilated Philomela,[40] does he not share any of her resourcefulness or resistance?[41] He surely does. Let us read the poems once again. *Tristia* 1.1 is dominated by Ovid's efforts to manipulate the life of his book at Rome. In a collection whose singular purpose, we are repeatedly told, is to reach Augustus and obtain parole, a brief admonition jars: "ergo cave, liber, et timida circumspice mente, / ut satis a media sit tibi plebe legi," "So be careful, my book, be timid in your heart and content with readers of the common sort," 1.1.87–88. A similar desire for withdrawal from the public stage is expressed at the very end of *Tristia* 3.1, once Ovid realizes that he is no longer welcome in public places (3.1.79–82):

> interea, quoniam statio mihi publica clausa est,
> > privato liceat delituisse loco.
> vos quoque, si fas est, confusa pudore repulsae
> > sumite plebeiae carmina nostra manus.

> In the meantime, since a public resting place is shut for me, may it be allowed to me to hide in some private retreat, and you hands of the people, if it is lawful, take up my poems, confused by the shame of their rejection.

The poem ends by drawing a clear distinction between state authority and private friendship.[42] Another question arises: in the light of Ovid's shame over his removal from the political center, how valued is this private friendship? Do we get any indications as to what it involves? Searching for the answer reveals a long series of silences. First and foremost, most of Ovid's partners in this private alliance are not named, in spite of his urge to include them as stated time and again throughout the collection (perhaps most explicitly in 4b.63–67), due to fear of possible recriminations once their support of the disgraced Ovid becomes publicly known. And then, the most cherished feelings of Ovid regarding these friends are those not actually stated in his poems to them. The most valuable thoughts are so private that they are not actually uttered in 3.4b.69–70: "intra mea pectora quemque / alloquar, et nulli causa timoris ero," "In my heart, I will address each one of you, and I will be no source of fear to anyone." More (lack of) description of another such previous relationship ensues at 3.6. The first fourteen lines abound in gratitude for the bond between Ovid and his anonymous friend. But nothing concrete is laid out, other than that they shared their secrets (3.6.9–12):

nil ita celabas, ut non ego conscius essem,
    pectoribusque dabas multa tegenda meis;
cuique ego narrabam secreti quicquid habebam,
    excepto quod me perdidit, unus eras

> There was nothing that you kept hidden in such a way that I was not aware of it, and gave much to my heart that had to be concealed; you were the only one to whom I would reveal all my secrets except the one that destroyed me.[43]

However, if the public cannot know, this coterie of friends do not need telling. They know all the details, just like the friend of 1.5 who is told at 8–9 that he knows well the debt of friendship owed to him by the exile and is only given clues so that he might realize that he was the addressee.[44] According to Ellen Oliensis, this suppression of names and feelings obstructs the "smooth work" of *amicitia*.[45] Yet from a different point of view, through this reticence, stories are getting written in the interstices of official reality, such as, for example, the story of another anonymous friend and Ovid's benefactor, (not) laid out in 4.5, suspected to be M. Valerius Cotta Maximus, a person frequently vilified in other sources. If Cotta was indeed the addressee of this poem, another private story is being deposited in the margins of the official histories of people such as Tacitus and Pliny the Elder, who seemed to have thought of Cotta much less highly than Ovid.[46]

On account of this reticence and compression, Ovid starts coming across more like the heroines. As a matter of fact, his own life and story appear to be slipping through the net. In earlier sections, we studied his plentiful complaints at the loss of verbal authority. Among the many devices for its retrieval, he used parallels with epic heroes. In 4.4.69–87, he was an Orestes; in 5.1.61–62 and 5.2.13–15, he was a Philoctetes; in 1.9.27–35, he was a Pylades or a Patroclus or a Nisus rejoicing at his friends' success at Rome. Last but certainly not least, he was an Odysseus to his wife's Penelope (see, especially, 1.5 and 1.6, though the poet complains that he and his wife both deserved a better fate than that famous Homeric couple). Being an epic hero, that is, being part of the official myth, keeps him in the system, the Roman world he so misses, and also saves him from silence: as we have seen, epic heroes shout till the moment of their death. But the signals we get are not consistent. Already in *Tristia* 1.5, still on the way to Tomi, Ovid questions the ability of his voice to convey adequately his story (1.5.53–56):

si vox infragilis, pectus mihi firmius aere,
   pluraque cum linguis pluribus ora forent:
non tamen idcirco complecterer omnia verbis,
   materia vires exsuperante meas.

Even if I had an unbreakable voice, lungs stronger than bronze, multiple
tongues in many mouths, still I would not be able to encompass my whole
story with my words, as my subject exceeds my powers.

Shortly after this admission, he tries to reinsert himself into the official language of myth. He is a figure taking after Odysseus. But actually—Ovid proceeds to inform us—he is not: Odysseus's journey was a
short haul, he enjoyed loyal companions, he was returning victorious to
his homeland, and he was a physically strong man—a proper epic hero
(1.5.59–72). On the other hand, Ovid himself is "accustomed to quieter
endeavors": "adsuetus studiis mollibus ipse fui," 1.5.74. Does this mean
that Ovid is no more part of the official myth than marginal heroines
such as Oenone, Hermione, Hero, or Cydippe wanted to be in *Heroides*
5, 8, 19, and 21, respectively? Does seclusion and enforced silence make
Naso closer to the heroines? While reflecting on this, let us read
5.1.37–38, where Ovid points to his misfortune as the sole proprietor of
his poetry:

quod querar, illa mihi pleno de fonte ministrat
   nec mea sunt, fati verba sed ista mei.

My complaints well up and serve my writing. The words I write now are not
mine, but come from my fate.

And 5.1.71–72, where Ovid gives up the previously imperative need for
a final polishing of his production: "ipse nec emendo, sed ut hic deducta
legantur," "I do not amend these scribbles. Let them be read as they are
written on the spot." Is it a mere coincidence that despite his orchestrated efforts to control the journey of this writing (see p. 326), in the
passages just mentioned, words flood over the margins of the pages he
so frantically and uncontrollably fills, thus eerily reminding us of Byblis
in *Metamorphoses* 9?

Afterword

This study has triggered at least as many questions as those it
tried to answer—an appropriate conclusion to a study of silence. It has
tried to trace some of the contours of speech and silence in the *Tristia*

and their capacity to reflect the uncertainties of power and identity throughout the collection. Ovid was poorly equipped, but ready, to face silence a long time before it came upon him. Silence terrified him because it deprived him of the verbal authority available to important men in his culture. And yet, losing control, he comes face to face with the freedom of powerlessness, of not belonging to the system, and with a language that labels and specifies. His exilic poetry is scarred by his enforced separation from speech, and yet it is also marked by his refusal to speak up and explain his error, the fatal mistake that led to his disgrace. By not speaking, Ovid refuses to fix realities with the dogmatic labels of language; he is also able to use other, less overt forms of manipulation. By not telling his story clearly, he avoids the necessity of negotiating it with Augustus. And all the way through, he reserves the right to insinuate, to draw attention to the unspoken, to threaten those in power who do not know what he is thinking or plotting next. In his complete and defenseless powerlessness, Ovid manages to resemble the emperor Tiberius, who famously raised anxieties and uncertainties by silence and cryptic words (Tacitus *Annales* 1.12). Both Ovid in exile and Tiberius in the purple use silence to create uncertainties and hint at their power. And yet, Ovid never manages to get over the loss of his public voice and existence at Rome. Defiance and resignation blend together in his exilic poems to the last line.

Silence is the final challenge for the elusive and puzzling figure of the Roman slave to and soldier of love. It addresses all the inherited dilemmas and famous ironies of power and impotence that have made love elegy such a uniquely unsettled and unsettling genre. Authority, presence, failure, success, and belonging are all important aspects in the gendered dynamics of elegy. Silence probes them all and still leaves them precariously propped against one another.

The silence of dying elegy speaks eloquently.

Notes

1. All translations are my own.

2. On the many affinities of the poem with an erotic *paraklausithyron*, see Newlands 1997.

3. Cf. Claassen 1999 passim and, esp., 211–14.

4. One might think that such concerns veil Ovid's (in)famous bookishness. I do not wish to refute this vital feature of his creations, but I take a different slant in this article, promoting concerns and anxieties that have, perhaps, been a little overlooked—not least because of the ingenuity of Ovid's writing.

5. To which I limit my exploration in this article.

6. See, e.g., *Tristia* 3.14.

7. Cf. *Fasti* 1.297–98.

8. Though, of course, the first mention of writing, Bellerophon's σήματα λυγρά should not pass unheeded; see *Iliad* 6.168.

9. It is enough to recollect the shame surrounding the forced absences from the action of Achilles, held back in disguise on Skyros after his mother's intervention, and of Philoctetes, who was forced to miss the war due to the wounded foot that kept him on Lemnos for almost the entirety of the Trojan War.

10. For examples and more discussion of the prominence of speech in the *Iliad*, see Montiglio 2000.

11. It would be too unwise to generalize about silence here. Montiglio 2000 is a good starting point for an exploration of the different incarnations, uses, and abuses of silence in a wide range of social situations in antiquity.

12. Cf. here Derrida 1976.141–64, 1981.95–117. On writing's poisonous nature and its significance for the heroines' own letters in the *Heroides*, see Spentzou 2003, esp. 40–51.

13. Farrell 2000.6–7. I am very grateful to the author for making this unpublished material available to me. Farrell's own main concern in this paper is rather different from mine: he traces significant changes in the imagery of the body (poetic and human) throughout the Horatian corpus. His attention is drawn by the disembodied voice of Horace at the climax of the *Odes*.

14. But he is also aware of the drive against it. Epistle 1.1 brims with the poet's self-sufficient presence, but at the other end of the collection, Epistle 1.20, Horace's book longs to expose itself to the city and its readers, and Horace wistfully recognizes his inability to monitor and protect this journey in space and time. The key word again is *control*, and this is what is being tested in a deeply self-conscious way in the *Epistles*. Cf. also Hardie 2002a.297–98, with further bibliography and discussion of the many allusions or parallels between the *Epistles* and the *Tristia* in note 36.

15. Still mixed with some underlying anxiety given that this *is* a silent book, even if Horace would prefer to remember the voice.

16. Contrast, e.g., Farrell 1999 passim, who reads triumph into the gradual disembodiment of the poetic voice in the *Metamorphoses*, with Theodorakopoulos 1999 passim, who reads abandonment of control and defeat into the same disembodiment. Hardie 2002a.94–96 sees in the epilogue to the *Metamorphoses* the textual triumph of Ovid's poetry, noting, at the same time, the re-embodiment of Ovid's voice on other people's lips. According to Hardie, then, writing and speaking coexist in the epilogue as modes of perpetuation: an interpretation consistent with his search for "present absences" throughout the Ovidian corpus.

17. As with Horace, whose confident disembodied voice in *Odes* 3.30 manages to overcome the troubled book of *Odes* 2.20.

18. And they are to be detected in the *Fasti* as well, also significantly affected

by exile. On the complex dynamics between original and subsequent readings, and Ovid's struggles against the endless proliferations of meaning that fictions such as Lala and Flora make possible in the *Fasti* and *Tristia*, see Di Lorenzo 2001, esp. 102–56.

19. Cf. here *Amores* 2.1.1–6, where Ovid invites the tender girl and the untutored boy to read his verse. Was he sensitized to the precariousness of (his) writing and the uncontrollable power of (his) readers from such a young and reckless stage in his career? *Tristia* 1.1 has, of course, been extensively discussed by Hinds 1985.13–32.

20. It is worth recalling the significant boom in rhetoric in the early empire. The voice, posture, and overall physical behavior of the citizen are increasingly scrutinized, moderated, and ultimately prescribed in a culture that believes more and more strongly in "making men" and promotes and valorizes the impact of words in gaining status. Gleason 1995 ably negotiates these complex matters.

21. Or, of course, *her* real self? On this, cf. Farrell 1998.307–38. Farrell also discusses the duplicitous character of the letter in the *Ars Amatoria* (esp. 311–17, 328–29), though his primary interest is in the relationship between passion and sincerity in the *Heroides*. For more on gendered modes of letter writing, see Spentzou 2003.123–60.

22. Though not without its risks: there is always the danger that the girl "might read more" than was intended for her—certainly if the man does not erase completely the letters to previous women—but the metaphorical sense of the risks of reading more should not pass unnoticed.

23. Farrell 1998 offers a close reading of the successive stages in Byblis's approach to writing and notices her mixed attitudes towards writing under the circumstances.

24. Rosenmeyer 1997 passim, esp. 29–30.

25. Barchiesi 2001b, esp. 29–31 and passim.

26. I write extensively about the heroines' discovery of their own voices in Spentzou 2003, esp. 1–42 and passim.

27. Similar complaints are uttered in 3.3.11 (where friends and conversation are missing), 4.1.89–90 (where the absence of a comprehending audience is noted), and 5.12.53 (again underlining the absence of audience and books).

28. Communications that are carried on with increased vigor in the *Epistulae ex Ponto*, which cover the last, and increasingly bleakest, phase of his exile.

29. Cf. here Hardie 2002a.303–04 on *Tristia* 5.3, written for the Liberalia, a festival of Bacchus of a rather private nature that Ovid sorely misses.

30. For more on this new respectability and "Romanization" of the exilic elegy, see Harrison 2002.90–92.

31. The language that only the animals and the Getans understand (*ex Ponto* 1.8.55). Cf. also *Tristia* 5.7b.55–60, with a repeat of the complaint.

32. Even if, when faced with Caunus's rage and rejection, Byblis seems to regret her reckless venture (9.580ff.).

33. Canace and Dido show similar bravery, writing during labor and when faced with the ultimate terror of an imminent suicide in *Heroides* 7 (Dido) and 11 (Canace).

34. Segal 1998 and Hardie 1999 discuss different aspects of these poignant anxieties concerning absent or vulnerable bodies.

35. De Luce 1993. Cf. here Di Lorenzo 2001, esp. 120–21, who observes the connection between the raped Lara of *Fasti* 2.571–616 and the *raptus* Ovid of *Epistulae ex Ponto* 4.16.1 (and, I would add once again, Philomela of the *Metamorphoses*); see also Sharrock 2002a, esp. 100–01, addressing female silencing in the *Metamorphoses*.

36. A phrase that will eerily resonate in Tacitus (*Agricola* 2–3), who considers the blanket of silence under which several generations grew old during Domitian's reign, deprived of speech and this exchange of opinions so critical for people's well-being.

37. See, especially, Feeney 1992, Boyle 1997.7–28.

38. Cf., e.g., Suetonius *Divus Augustus* 66.2, Horace *Odes* 3.2.25–30.

39. On this sort of subversive silence in the *Ars*, see Sharrock 1994a, esp. 117–21.

40. Cf. n. 35 above; see also *Tristia* 1.3.73–74: "dividor haud aliter, quam si mea membra relinquam / et pars abrumpi corpore visa suo est," "I am sundered, as if I have left behind my limbs and part of my body is severed."

41. A resourcefulness explored by Joplin 1984.

42. Cf. here Newlands 1997.74–75, who notices the religious solemnity bestowed on this private realm through the *si fas est* of 3.1.81 and its associations with imperial authority in *Fasti* 1.25.

43. Casali 1997 and Henderson 1997 probe several of these "unspoken statements" in Ovid's exile poetry.

44. Given that many of these anonymous addressees have been identified by modern scholars, I cannot help wondering: could they not be identified by ancient readers, too?

45. Oliensis 1997a. Cf. also Hardie 2002a.293–94.

46. Cf. Pliny *Natural History* 10.52, Tacitus *Annales* 6.5–7.

Bibliography

Abelove, H., M. Barale, and D. Halperin, eds. 1993. *The Lesbian and Gay Studies Reader*. New York.

Adams, J. N. 1982. *The Latin Sexual Vocabulary*. London.

———. 1983. "Words for 'Prostitute' in Latin," *RhM* 126.321–58.

Albertson, F. 1990. "The Basilica Aemilia Frieze: Religion and Politics in Late Republican Rome," *Latomus* 49.801–15.

Allen, A. 1962. "*Sunt qui Propertium malint*," in Sullivan 1962.107–48.

Ancona, R. 1989. "The Subterfuge of Reason: Horace, *Odes* 1.23 and the Construction of Male Desire," *Helios* 16.49–57.

———. 1994. *Time and the Erotic in Horace's* Odes. Durham, N.C.

———. 2002. "The Untouched Self: Sapphic and Catullan Muses in Horace, *Odes* 1.22," in Spentzou and Fowler 2002.161–86.

Anderson, W. S. 1966. "*Talaria* and Ovid *Metamorphoses* 10.591," *TAPA* 97.1–13.

———. 1972. *Ovid's* Metamorphoses: *Books 6–10*. Norman, Okla.

———. 1990. "The Example of Procris in the *Ars Amatoria*," in Griffith and Mastronarde 1990.131–45.

———. 1997. *Ovid's* Metamorphoses: *Books 1–5*. Norman, Okla.

Archer, L., S. Fischler, and M. Wyke, eds. 1994. *Women in Ancient Societies: An Illusion of the Night*. New York.

Ariès, P., and A. Béjin, eds. 1985. *Western Sexuality: Practice and Precept in Past and Present Times* (trans. A. Forrester). New York.

Armstrong, C. 1989. "The Reflexive and the Possessive View: Thoughts on Kertesz, Brandt, and the Photographic Nude," *Representations* 25.57–70.

Arthur, M. B. 1977. "Politics and Pomegranates: An Interpretation of the Homeric *Hymn to Demeter*," *Arethusa* 10.7–47.

Arya, D. 1996. "The Figural Frieze of the Basilica Aemilia: A New Perspective in Building Context and Pentelic Marble," Master's thesis, University of Texas at Austin.

Atkinson, C. W., C. H. Buchanan, M. R. Mills, eds. 1985. *Immaculate and Powerful*. Boston.

Badoni, F. P. 1990. "Arianna a Nasso: La rielaborazione di un mito greco in ambiente romano," *DArch* 8.73–87.

Baker, R. J. 1980. "Beauty and Beast in Propertius 1.3," in *Studies in Latin Literature and Roman History II*, ed. C. Deroux. Brussels. 245–58.

Bakhtin, M. 1973. *Problems of Dostoevsky's Poetics* (trans. R. W. Rotsel). Ann Arbor.

————. 1994. *The Bakhtin Reader* (ed. P. Morris). London.

Bal, M. 1997. *Narratology: Introduction to the Theory of Narrative* (trans. C. van Boheemen from the 1946 original). Toronto.

Balsdon, J. P. V. D. 1979. *Romans and Aliens.* Chapel Hill.

Barber, E. A. 1960. *Properti Sexti Carmina.* Oxford.

Barchiesi, A. 2001a. *Speaking Volumes: Narrative and Intertext in Ovid and Other Latin Poets* (trans. M. Fox and S. Marchesi). London.

————. 2001b. "Narrativity and Convention in the *Heroides*," in Barchiesi 2001a.

Barkan, L. 1986. *The Gods Made Flesh: Metamorphoses and the Pursuit of Paganism.* New Haven.

Barnes, H. E. 1974. *The Meddling Gods: Four Essays on Classical Themes.* Lincoln, Neb.

Barthes, R. 1978. *A Lover's Discourse—Fragments* (trans. Richard Howard). New York.

Bauer, D. F. 1962. "The Function of Pygmalion in Ovid's *Metamorphoses*," *TAPA* 99.1–21.

Beard, M. 1980. "The Sexual Status of Vestal Virgins," *JRS* 70.12–27.

————. 1995. "Re-reading (Vestal) Virginity," in Hawley and Levick 1995.166–77.

Beissinger, M., J. Tylus, and S. Wofford, eds. 1998. *Epic Traditions in the Contemporary World.* Berkeley.

Beltrami, L. 1989. "Properzio 4.4: La colpa della Vestale," in Catanzaro and Santucci 1989. 267–72.

Benton, C. 2002. "Split Vision: The Politics of the Gaze in Seneca's *Troades*," in Fredrick 2002a.31–56.

Bergmann, B. 1994. "The Roman House as Memory Theater: The House of the Tragic Poet in Pompeii," *Art Bulletin* 76.225–56.

————. 1995. "Greek Masterpieces and Roman Recreative Fictions," *HSCP* 97.79–120.

————. 1996. "The Pregnant Moment: Tragic Wives in the Roman Interior," in Kampen 1996a.199–218.

Bernhard, M-L., and W. A. Daszewski. 1986. "Ariadne," *LIMC*, vol. 3. Zurich.

Birt, T. 1895. "Die vaticanische Ariadne und die dritte Elegie des Properz," *RhM* 50.31–65, 161–90.

Bloomer, M. W. 1997. "A Preface to the History of Declamation: Whose Speech? Whose History?" in Habinek and Schiesaro 1997.199–215.

Bömer, F., ed. 1977. *P. Ovidius Naso: Metamorphosen*, vol. 4. Heidelberg.

Boswell, J. 1980. *Christianity, Social Tolerance, and Homosexuality.* Chicago.

Boucher, J-P. 1965. *Études sur Properce: Problèmes d'inspiration et d'art.* Paris.

Boyd, B. W. 1984. "Tarpeia's Tomb: A Note on Propertius IV.4," *AJP* 105.85–86.

Boyle, A. J. 1973. "The Edict of Venus: An Interpretive Essay on Horace's Amatory *Odes*," *Ramus* 2.163–88.

———. 1997. "Postscripts from the Edge: Exilic *Fasti* and Imperialised Rome," *Ramus* 26.7–28.

Braund, S., and B. Gold, eds. 1998. *Vile Bodies: Roman Satire and Corporeal Discourse. Arethusa* 31.3. Buffalo.

Bremmer, J., and N. Horsfall. 1987. *Roman Myth and Mythography*. London.

Brilliant, R. 1984. *Visual Narratives: Storytelling in Etruscan and Roman Art*. Ithaca.

Brooten, B. 1985. "Paul's Views on the Nature of Women and Female Homoeroticism," in Atkinson, Buchanan, and Mills 1985.61–85.

———. 1996. *Love Between Women: Early Christian Responses to Female Homoeroticism*. Chicago.

Bulloch, A. W. 1985. *Callimachus: The Fifth Hymn*. Cambridge.

Burnett, A. P. 1983. *Three Archaic Poets: Archilochus, Alcaeus, Sappho*. Cambridge.

Cahoon, L. 1985. "A Program for Betrayal: Ovidian *Nequitia* in the *Amores*," *Helios* 12.29–39.

———. 1988. "The Bed as Battlefield: Erotic Conquest and Military Metaphor in Ovid's *Amores*," *TAPA* 118.293–307.

Cairns, F. 1972. *Generic Composition in Greek and Roman Poetry*. Edinburgh.

———. 1977. "Two Unidentified *Komoi* of Propertius: 1.3 and 2.29," *Emerita* 45.325–53.

———. 1979. "Propertius on Augustus' Marriage Law," *GB* 8.185–204.

Calame, C., ed. 1988. *Métamorphoses du mythe en Grèce antique*. Geneva.

Cameron, A., ed. 1989. *History as Text*. London.

Campbell, D., ed. 1982. *Greek Lyric Poetry*. Bristol.

Camps, W. A., ed. 1965. *Propertius* Elegies *Book IV*. Cambridge.

———. ed. 1967. *Propertius* Elegies *Book II*. Cambridge.

Carettoni, G. 1961. *Il fregio figurato della Basilica Emilia: rinvenimento, dati tecnici, collocazione*. Rome.

Carson, A. 1986. *Eros the Bittersweet*. Princeton.

———. 1990. "Putting Her in Her Place: Woman, Dirt, and Desire," in Halperin, Winkler, and Zeitlin 1990.135–69.

Casali, S. 1997. "*Quaerenti plura legendum:* On the Necessity of 'Reading More' in Ovid's Exile Poetry," *Ramus* 26.80–112.

Case, S-E. 1993 [1988–89]. "Towards a Butch-Femme Aesthetic," in Abelove, Barale, and Halperin 1993.294–306.

Catanzaro, G., and F. Santucci, eds. 1989. *Tredici Secoli di Elegia Latina*. Assisi.

Cixous, H. 1975. "The Laugh of the Medusa," *Signs* 1.875–93.

Claassen, J-M. 1999. *Displaced Persons: The Literature of Exile from Cicero to Boethius*. London.

Clarke, G. 1997. "Defending Ski-Jumpers," in Gelder and Thornton 1997.175–80.

Clarke, J., S. Hall, T. Jefferson, and B. Roberts, 1997. "Subcultures, Cultures and Class," in Gelder and Thornton 1997.100–11.

Classen, C. 1988. "Satire—the Elusive Genre," *SO* 63.95–121.

Clover, C. 1992. *Men, Women, and Chainsaws: Gender in the Modern Horror Film*. Princeton.

Commager, S. 1962. *The Odes of Horace: A Critical Study*. New Haven.

Conte, G. B. 1989. "Love without Elegy: The *Remedia Amoris* and the Logic of a Genre," *Poetics Today* 10.3.441–69.

———. 1994a. *Genres and Readers* (trans. G. W. Most). Baltimore.

———. 1994b. *Latin Literature: A History* (trans. J. B. Solodow). Baltimore.

Copley, F. 1947. "*Servitium Amoris* in the Roman Elegists," *TAPA* 78.285–300.

Corbeill, A. 1996. *Controlling Laughter: Political Humor in the Late Roman Republic*. Princeton.

———. 1997. "Dining Deviants in Roman Political Invective," in Hallett and Skinner 1997.99–128.

———. 2002. "Political Movement: Walking and Ideology in Republican Rome," in Fredrick 2002a.182–215.

Crawford, M. H. 1974. *Roman Republican Coinage*. Cambridge.

Culham, P. 1990. "Decentering the Text: The Case of Ovid," *Helios* 17.161–71.

Curran, J., M. Gurevitch, and J. Woollacott, eds. 1977. *Mass Communication and Society*. London.

Curran, L. 1978. "Rape and Rape Victims in the *Metamorphoses*," *Arethusa* 11.213–41.

———. 1996. "Vision and Reality in Propertius 1.3," *YCS* 19.189–203.

Cyrino, M. 1995. *In Pandora's Jar: Lovesickness in Early Greek Poetry*. Lanham, Md.

Dalby, A. 2000. *Empire of Pleasures: Luxury and Indulgence in the Roman World*. New York.

Dalzell, A. 1996. *The Criticism of Didactic Poetry: Essays on Lucretius, Virgil, and Ovid*. Toronto.

Davidson, J. 1991. "The Gaze in Polybius' *Histories*," *JRS* 81.10–24.

———. 1997. "Antoninus Liberalis and the Story of Prokris," *Mnemosyne* 50.165–84.

Davis, G. 1991. *Polyhymnia: The Rhetoric of Horatian Lyric Discourse*. Berkeley.

Davisson, M. 1996. "The Search for an *Alter Orbis* in Ovid's *Remedia Amoris*," *Phoenix* 50. 240–61.

Day, A. A. 1938. *The Origins of Latin Love Elegy*. Oxford.

Dayagi-Mendels, M. 1989. *Perfumes and Cosmetics in the Ancient World*. Tel Aviv.

DeBrohun, J. D. 2003. *Roman Propertius and the Reinvention of Elegy*. Ann Arbor.

De Forest, M., ed. 1993. *Woman's Power, Man's Game*. Wauconda, Ill.

De Grummond, N. T., ed. 1982. *A Guide to Etruscan Mirrors*. Tallahassee.

De Grummond, N. T., and M. Hoff. 1982. "Mirrors of the Mediterranean," in De Grummond 1982.52–58.

De Lauretis, T. 1984. *Alice Doesn't: Feminism, Semiotics, Cinema*. Bloomington.

———. 1987. *Technologies of Gender: Essays on Theory, Film, and Fiction*. Bloomington.

D'Elia, S. 1959. *Ovidio*. Naples.

De Luce, J. 1993. "'O for a Thousand Tongues to Sing': A Footnote on Metamorphosis, Silence, and Power," in De Forest 1993.305–21.

Derrida, J. 1976. *Of Grammatology* (trans. G. Spivak). London.

———. 1981. *Dissemination* (trans. B. Johnson). London.

———. 1991. "Living On: Border Lines," in Kamuf 1991.254–68.

———. 1992. "The Law of Genre," *Acts of Literature*. New York. 221–52.

Devereaux, M. 1990. "Oppressive Texts, Resisting Readers, and the Gendered Spectator: The New Aesthetics," *The Journal of Aesthetics and Art Criticism* 48.4.337–47.

Di Lorenzo, K. 2001. "Looking Both Ways: Janus, Doubling, and Intertextuality in Ovid," Ph.D. thesis, University of Pennsylvania.

Dixon, S. 2001. *Reading Roman Women*. London.

Doane, M. 1987. *The Desire to Desire: The Woman's Film of the 1940s*. Bloomington.

———. ed. 1992a. *The Sexual Subject: A Screen Reader in Sexuality*. London.

———. 1992b. "Film and the Masquerade: Theorizing the Female Spectator," in Doane 1992a.

Donaldson Evans, L. K. 1980. *Love's Fatal Glance: A Study of Eye Imagery in the Poets of the École Lyonnaise*. Mississippi.

Dougherty, C. 1998. "Sowing the Seeds of Violence: Rape, Women, and the Land," in Wyke 1998b.267–84.

Dover, K. J. 1978. *Greek Homosexuality*. London.

Downing, E. 1993. *Artificial I's: The Self as Artwork in Ovid, Kierkegaard, and Thomas Mann*. Tübingen.

———. 1999. "Anti-Pygmalion: The *Praeceptor* in *Ars Amatoria*, Book 3," in Porter 1999.235–51.

duBois, P. 1988. *Sowing the Body: Psychoanalysis and Ancient Representations of Women*. Chicago.

———. 1995. *Sappho is Burning*. Chicago.

———. 1998. "The Subject in Antiquity after Foucault," in Larmour, Miller, and Platter 1998.85–102.

Dunn, F. 1985. "The Lover Reflected in the *Exemplum*: A Study of Propertius 1.3 and 2.6," *ICS* 10.233–59.

———. 1995. "Rhetorical Approaches to Horace's *Odes*," *Arethusa* 28.165–76.

Dupont, F. 1997. "*Recitatio* and the Reorganization of the Space of Public Discourse," in Habinek and Schiesaro 1997.44–60.

Eagleton, T. 1981. *Walter Benjamin, or Towards a Revolutionary Criticism*. London.

Eco, U. 1984. *Semiotics and the Philosophy of Language*. Bloomington.

———. 1990. *The Limits of Interpretation*. Bloomington.

Edmunds, L. 2001. *Intertextuality and the Reading of Roman Poetry*. Baltimore.

Edwards, C. 1993. *The Politics of Immorality in Ancient Rome*. Cambridge.

———. 1996. *Writing Rome*. Cambridge.

———. 1997. "Unspeakable Professions: Public Performance and Prostitution in Ancient Rome," in Hallett and Skinner 1997.66–95.

Eilberg-Schwartz, H., and W. Doniger, eds. 1995. *Off with Her Head! The Denial of Women's Identity in Myth, Religion, and Culture*. Berkeley.

Eldred, K. O. 2002. "This Ship of Fools: Epic Vision in Lucan's Vulteius Episode," in Fredrick 2002a.57–85.

Ellis, J. 1982. *Visible Fictions*. London.

Elsner, J. 1991. "Visual Mimesis and the Myth of the Real: Ovid's Pygmalion as Viewer," *Ramus* 20.154–68.

———. 1995. *Art and the Roman Viewer: The Transformation of Art from the Pagan World to Christianity*. Cambridge.

Ensor, E. 1902. "Notes on the *Odes* of Horace," *Hermathena* 28.105–10.

Esler, C. C. 1989. "Horace, Barine, and the Immortality of Words: *Odes* 2.8," *CJ* 84.105–12.

Evans, J. deRose. 1992. *The Art of Persuasion*. Ann Arbor.

Fantham, E. 1979. "The Mating of Lalage," *LCM* 4.47–52.

———. 1997. "Images of the City: Propertius' New-Old Rome," in Habinek and Schiesaro 1997.122–35.

Farrell, J. 1998. "Reading and Writing the *Heroides*," *HSCP* 98.307–38.

———. 1999. 'The Ovidian Corpus: Poetic Body and Poetic Text," in Hardie, Barchiesi, and Hinds 1999.127–41.

———. 2000. "Horace's Body: Horace's Books," unpublished paper delivered at D. Fowler's Memorial Conference, Oxford.

Favro, D. 1996. *The Urban Image of Augustan Rome*. Cambridge.

Fear, T. 2000. "The Poet as Pimp: Elegiac Seduction in the Time of Augustus," *Arethusa* 33.217–40.

Fedeli, P., ed. 1965. *Properzio Elegie: Libro IV*. Bari.

———. 1983. *Catullus' Carmen 61*. Amsterdam (orig. publ. in Italian [Freiburg 1972]; later editions revised).

———. 1989. "La poesia d'amore," in *Lo spazio letterario di Roma antica*, vol. I: *La produzione del testo*. Rome. 143–76.

Feeney, D. 1992. "*Si licet et fas est*: Ovid's *Fasti* and the Problem of Free Speech under the Principate," in Powell 1992.1–25.

Ferenczi, S. 1926. "On the Symbolism of the Head of Medusa," *Further Contributions to the Theory and Technique of Psychoanalysis*. London.

Fetterley, J. 1978. *The Resisting Reader: A Feminist Approach to American Fiction*. Bloomington.

Flynn, E. A., and P. P. Schweickart, eds. 1986. *Gender and Reading: Essays on Readers, Texts, and Contexts*. Baltimore.

Foley, H. 1993. "The Politics of Tragic Lamentation," in Sommerstein, Halliwell, Henderson, and Zimmerman 1993.101–43.

Fontenrose, J. 1980. "Ovid's Procris," *CJ* 75.289–94.

Forbis, E. P. 1997. "Voice and Voicelessness in Ovid's Exile Poetry," in *Studies in Latin Literature and Roman History* 8, ed. C. Deroux. Brussels. 245–67.

Foucault, M. 1980 [1976]. *An Introduction: The History of Sexuality*, vol. 1 (trans. R. Hurley). New York.

———. 1985 [1984]. *The Use of Pleasure: The History of Sexuality*, vol. 2 (trans. R. Hurley). New York.

———. 1986 [1984]. *The Care of the Self: The History of Sexuality*, vol. 3 (trans. R. Hurley). New York.

Fowler, B. H. 1984. "The Archaic Aesthetic," *AJP* 105.119–49.

Fowler, D. P. 1991. "Narrate and Describe: The Problem of Ekphrasis," *JRS* 81.25–36.

Fränkel, H. 1945. *Ovid: A Poet Between Two Worlds*. Berkeley.

Fredrick, D. 1995. "Beyond the Atrium to Ariadne: Erotic Painting and Visual Pleasure in the Roman House," *ClAnt* 14.266–87.

———. 1997. "Reading Broken Skin: Violence in Roman Elegy," in Hallett and Skinner 1997.172–93.

———. ed. 2002a. *The Roman Gaze*. Baltimore.

———. 2002b. "Introduction: Invisible Rome," in Fredrick 2002a.1–30.

Freud, S. 1955. "The Medusa's Head," in *The Standard Edition of the Complete Psychological Works of Sigmund Freud*, vol 18 (ed. J. Strachey). London. 273–74.

Freudenburg, K. 2001. *Satires of Rome: Threatening Poses from Lucilius to Juvenal*. Cambridge.

Fried, M. 1990. *Absorption and Theatricality: Painting and Beholder in the Age of Diderot*. Berkeley.

Frye, N. 1957. *Anatomy of Criticism: Four Essays*. Princeton.

Gale, M. 1997. "Propertius 2.7: *Militia Amoris* and the Ironies of Elegy," *JRS* 87.77–91.

Galinsky, K. 1975. *Ovid's* Metamorphoses: *An Introduction to the Basic Aspects*. Bristol.

———. 1996. *Augustan Culture*. Princeton.

Gamel, M. K. 1989. "*Non sine caede*: Abortion Politics and Poetics in Ovid's *Amores*," *Helios* 16.183–206.

———. 1998. "Reading as a Man: Performance and Gender in Roman Elegy," *Helios* 25.79–95.

Gantz, T. 1993. *Early Greek Myth*, vol. 1. Baltimore.

Gardner, J. 1986. *Women in Roman Law and Society*. Bloomington.

Geisler, H. 1969. *P. Ovidius Naso: Remedia Amoris, Mit Kommentar zu Vers 1–396*. Berlin.

Gelder, K., and S. Thornton, eds. 1997. *The Subcultures Reader*. London.

Genette, G. 1982. "Frontiers of Narrative," *Figures of Literary Discourse* (trans. A. Sheridan). New York. 127–44.

Gentilcore, R. 1995. "The Landscape of Desire: The Tale of Pomona and Vertumnus in Ovid's *Metamorphoses*," *Phoenix* 49.2.110–20.

Gibson, R. 2003. *Ovid: Ars Amatoria Book 3*. Cambridge.

Gioia, J. 2002. "Stop your Staring: The Destructive Gaze in Propertius 1.3 and 4.4," paper presented at the annual meeting of the Classical Association of the Middle West and South, Austin, Texas.

Gleason, M. 1995. *Making Men: Sophists and Self-Presentation in Ancient Rome*. Princeton.

Gold, B. K. 1992. "Openings in Horace's *Satires* and *Odes*: Poet, Patron, and Audience," *YCS* 29.161–85.

———. 1993. "'But Ariadne was Never There in the First Place': Finding the Female in Roman Poetry," in Rabinowitz and Richlin 1993.75–101.

———. 1998. "'The House I Live in is Not my Own': Women's Bodies in Juvenal's *Satires*," *Arethusa* 31.369–86.

Goldstein, J., ed. 1994. *Foucault and the Writing of History*. Oxford.

Goold, G., ed. 1990. *Propertius* Elegies. Cambridge, Mass.

———. ed. 1994. *Ovid* Metamorphoses. Cambridge, Mass.

Gordon, P. 1997. "The Lover's Voice in *Heroides* 15: Or, Why is Sappho a Man?" in Hallett and Skinner 1997.274–91.

Gowers, E. 1995. "The Anatomy of Rome from Capitol to Cloaca," *JRS* 85.23–32.

Grabes, H. 1982. *The Mutable Glass: Mirror-Imagery in Title and Texts of the Middle Ages and English Renaissance* (trans. G. Collier). Cambridge.

Graf, F. 1988. "Ovide, les Métamorphoses et la véracité du mythe," in Calame 1988.57–70.

Gray, V. 1998. *The Framing of Socrates: The Literary Interpretation of Xenophon's Memorabilia*. Stuttgart.

Green, P. 1975. "The Innocence of Procris: Ovid *Ars Amatoria* 3.687–746," *CJ* 75.1–24.

———. 1979. "*Ars gratia cultus*: Ovid as Beautician," *AJP* 100.381–92.

Greene, E. 1995a. "The Catullan *Ego*: Fragmentation and the Erotic Self," *AJP* 116.77–94.

———. 1995b. "Elegiac Woman: Fantasy, *Materia*, and Male Desire in Propertius 1.3 and 1.11," *AJP* 116.303–18.

———. 1998. *The Erotics of Domination: Male Desire and the Mistress in Latin Love Poetry*. Baltimore.

———. 1999. "Travesties of Love: Violence and Voyeurism in Ovid *Amores* 1.7," *CW* 92.409–18.

———. 2000. "Gender Identity and the Elegiac Hero in Propertius 2.1," *Arethusa* 33.241–62.

Griffith, M., and D. J. Mastronarde, eds. 1990. *Cabinet of the Muses: Essays on Classical and Comparative Literature in Honor of Thomas G. Rosenmeyer*. Atlanta.

Grimal, P. 1953. "Les intentions de Properce et la composition du livre IV des Elegies," *Collection Latomus* 12.5–53.

Gutzwiller, K. 1985. "The Lover and the *Lena*: Propertius 4.5," *Ramus* 14.105–15.

Habash, M. 1999. "Priapus: Horace in Disguise?" *CJ* 94.285–97.

Habinek, T. 1986. "The Marriageability of Maximus: Horace Ode 4.1.13–20," *AJP* 107.407–16.

———. 1998. *The Politics of Latin Literature*. Princeton.

———. 2002. "Ovid and Empire," in Hardie 2002b.46–61.

Habinek, T., and A. Schiesaro, eds. 1997. *The Roman Cultural Revolution*. Cambridge.

Hall, S. 1977. "Culture, the Media, and the 'Ideological Effect,'" in Curran, Gurevitch, and Woollacott 1977.315–48.

———. 1980. "Encoding/Decoding," in Hall, Hobson, Lowe, and Willis 1980.128–38.

Hall, S., D. Hobson, A. Lowe, and P. Willis, eds. 1980. *Culture, Media, Language*. London.

Haller, R. 1968. "The *Altercatio Phyllidis et Florae* as an Ovidian Satire," *Mediaeval Studies* 30. 119–33.

Hallett, J. P. 1973. "The Role of Women in Roman Elegy: Counter-Cultural Feminism," *Arethusa* 6.103–24 (reprinted in Peradotto and Sullivan 1984.241–62).

———. 1990. "Contextualizing the Text: The Journey to Ovid," *Helios* 17.187–95.

———. 1997 [1989]. "Female Homoeroticism and the Denial of Roman Reality in Latin Literature," in Hallett and Skinner 1997.255–73 (originally published in *Yale Journal of Criticism* 3.209–27).

Hallett, J. P., and M. Skinner, eds. 1997. *Roman Sexualities*. Princeton.

Halliwell, S. 2002. *The Aesthetics of Mimesis: Ancient Texts and Modern Problems*. Princeton.

Halperin, D. M. 1990. *One Hundred Years of Homosexuality*. New York.

———. 1994. "Historicizing the Subject of Desire: Sexual Preferences and Erotic Identities in the Pseudo-Lucianic *Erôtes*," in Goldstein 1994.19–34.

———. 1998. "Forgetting Foucault: Acts, Identities, and the History of Sexuality," *Representations* 63.93–120.

———. 2002. *How to do the History of Homosexuality*. Chicago.

Halperin, D. M., J. J. Winkler, and F. I. Zeitlin, eds. 1990. *Before Sexuality: The Construction of Erotic Experience in the Ancient World*. Princeton.

Hardie, P. 1999. "Ovid into Laura: Absent Presences in the *Metamorphoses* and Petrarch's *Rime Sparse*," in Hardie, Barchiesi, and Hinds 1999.254–70.

———. 2002a. *Ovid's Poetics of Illusion*. Cambridge.

———. ed. 2002b. *The Cambridge Companion to Ovid*. Cambridge.

Hardie, P., A. Barchiesi, and S. Hinds, eds. 1999. *Ovidian Transformations: Essays on Ovid's* Metamorphoses *and its Reception*. Cambridge.

Harmon, D. 1974. "Myth and Fantasy in Propertius 1.3," *TAPA* 104.151–65.

Harrison, J. 1903 [repr. 1955]. *Prolegomena to the Study of Greek Religion.* New York.

Harrison, S. 2002. "Ovid and Genre: Evolutions of an Elegist," in Hardie 2002b.79–94.

Hart, J. 1991. Review of Stephen Greenblatt, *Shakespearean Negotiations: The Circulation of Social Energy in Renaissance England, Textual Practice* 5.3.429–58.

Havelock, C. 1995. *The Aphrodite of Knidos and Her Successors: A Historical Review of the Female Nude in Greek Art.* Ann Arbor.

Hawley, R., and B. Levick, eds. 1995. *Women in Antiquity: New Assessments.* London.

Hebdige, D. 1997. "Subculture: The Meaning of Style," in Gelder and Thornton 1997.130–42.

Henderson, A. 1979. Remedia Amoris: *P. Ovidi Nasonis.* Edinburgh.

Henderson, J. 1989. "Satire Writes 'Woman': *Gendersong*," *PCPS* 35.50–80.

———. 1997. 'Not Wavering but Frowning: Ovid as an Isopleth (*Tristia* 1 through 10)," *Ramus* 26.138–71.

Hinds, S. 1985. "Booking the Return Trip: Ovid and *Tristia* 1," *PCPS* 31.13–32.

Hooley, D. 1999. "Horace's Rud(e)-imentary Muse: Satire 1.2," *Electronic Antiquity* 5.2. <http://scholar.lib.vt.edu/ejournals/ElAnt/V5N2/hooley.html> (9 January 2003)

Housman, A. E. 1931. "Praefanda," *Hermes* 66.402–12.

Hubbard, M. 1974. *Propertius.* London.

Hubbard, T. 2000–01. "Horace and Catullus: The Case of the Suppressed Precursor in *Odes* 1.22 and 1.32," *CW* 94.25–38.

Hutchinson, G. O. 2001. *Greek Lyric Poetry: A Commentary on Selected Larger Pieces.* Oxford.

Irigaray, L. 1974. *Speculum de l'autre femme.* Paris.

———. 1977. *Ce Sexe qui n'en est pas Un.* Paris.

———. 1997. "This Sex Which Is Not One," in Warhol and Herndl 1997.363–69.

Iser, W. 1974. *The Implied Reader: Patterns of Communication in Prose Fiction from Bunyan to Beckett.* Baltimore.

———. 1978. *The Act of Reading: A Theory of Aesthetic Response.* Baltimore.

Jaeger, M. 1995. "Reconstructing Rome: The Campus Martius and Horace, Ode 1.8," *Arethusa* 28.177–91.

James, S. 1997. "Slave-Rape and Female Silence in Ovid's Love Poetry," *Helios* 24.60–76.

———. 1998. "Introduction: Constructions of Gender and Genre in Roman Comedy and Elegy," *Helios* 25.3–16.

———. 2001. "The Economics of Roman Elegy: Voluntary Poverty, the *Recusatio*, and the Greedy Girl," *AJP* 122.223–53.

———. 2003. *Learned Girls and Male Persuasion: Gender and Reading in Roman Love Elegy*. Berkeley.

Jameson, F. 1981. *The Political Unconscious: Narrative as a Socially Symbolic Act*. Ithaca.

Janan, M. 1994. *When the Lamp is Shattered: Desire and Narrative in Catullus*. Carbondale, Ill.

———. 2001. *The Politics of Desire: Propertius Book IV*. Berkeley.

Janka, M. 1997. *Ovid Ars Amatoria: Buch 2, Kommentar*. Heidelberg.

Jansen, G. 1997. "Private Toilets at Pompeii: Appearance and Operation," in *Sequence and Space in Pompeii*, eds. S. Bon and R. Jones. Oxford. 121–34.

Jardine, A. 1985. *Gynesis: Configurations of Woman and Modernity*. Ithaca.

Jauss, H. R. 1982. *Toward an Aesthetic of Reception*. Minneapolis.

Jocelyn, H. D. 1980. "Horace, *Odes* 2.5," *LCM* 5.197–200.

Johnson, W. R. 1982. *The Idea of Lyric: Lyric Modes in Ancient and Modern Poetry*. Berkeley.

———. 1996. "The Rapes of Callisto," *CJ* 92.9–24.

———. 1997. "Vertumnus in Love," *CP* 92.367–75.

Jones, F. 1983. "Horace, Four Girls, and the Other Man," *LCM* 8.34–37.

Joplin, P. 1984. "The Voice of the Shuttle Is Ours," *Stanford Literary Review* 1a.25–53.

Joshel, S., and S. Murnaghan, eds. 1998. *Women and Slaves in Greco-Roman Culture*. London.

Kamen, D. unpublished ms. "Compulsory Heterosexuality and the Metamorphosis of Iphis."

Kampen, N. 1991. "Reliefs of the Basilica Aemilia: A Redating," *Klio* 73.448–58.

———. ed. 1996a. *Sexuality in Ancient Art*. Cambridge.

———. 1996b. "Omphale and the Instability of Gender," in Kampen 1996a.233–46.

Kamuf, P., ed. 1991. *A Derrida Reader: Between the Blinds*. New York.

Kaplan, E. A. 1983a. *Women and Film: Both Sides of the Camera*. New York.

———. 1983b. "Is the Gaze Male?" in Snitow, Stansell, and Thompson 1983.309–27.

———. 1997. *Looking for the Other: Feminism, Film, and the Imperial Gaze*. New York.

Kaster, R. 2001. "The Dynamics of *Fastidium* and the Ideology of Disgust," *TAPA* 131.143–89.

Katz, P. 2002. "'Marriage Catullan Style': Poem 61," unpublished paper delivered at American Philological Association Annual Meeting, Philadelphia, Pa.

Keith, A. 1994. "*Corpus Eroticum*: Elegiac Poetics and Elegiac *Puellae* in Ovid's *Amores*," *CW* 88.27–40.

———. 1997. "*Tandem Venit Amor*: A Roman Woman Speaks of Love," in Hallett and Skinner 1997.295–310.

————. 1999. "Versions of Epic Masculinity in Ovid's *Metamorphoses*," in Hardie, Barchiesi, and Hinds 1999.214–39.

————. 2000. *Engendering Rome: Women in Latin Epic*. Cambridge.

Kennedy, D. 1992. "'Augustan' and 'Anti-Augustan': Reflections on Terms of Reference," in Powell 1992.26–58.

————. 1993. *The Arts of Love: Five Studies in the Discourse of Roman Love Elegy*. Cambridge.

————. 2000. "Bluff Your Way in Didactic: Ovid's *Ars Amatoria* and *Remedia Amoris*," *Arethusa* 33.159–76.

Keynes, G., ed. 1966. *Blake: Complete Writings*. Oxford.

Keyssner, K. 1938. "Die bildende Kunst bei Properz," *Würzburger Studien zur Altertumswissenschaft* 13.169–89.

King, R. 1989–90. "Creative Landscaping in Propertius 4.4," *CJ* 85.225–46.

Koch, G. 1985. "Ex-Changing the Gaze: Re-Visioning Feminist Film Theory," *New German Critique* 34.139–53.

Konstan, D. 1977. *Catullus' Indictment of Rome: The Meaning of Catullus 64*. Amsterdam.

————. 1991. "The Death of Argus, or What Stories Do: Audience Response in Ancient Fiction and Theory," *Helios* 18.15–30.

————. 1994. *Sexual Symmetry: Love in the Ancient Novel and Related Genres*. Princeton.

————. 2001. *Pity Transformed*. London.

Labate, M. 1977. "Tradizione elegiaca e società galante negli Amores," *SCO* 27.283–339.

————. 1984. *L'arte di farsi amare: Modelli culturali e progetto didascalico nell' elegia ovidiana*. Pisa.

La Belle, J. 1988. *Herself Beheld: The Literature of the Looking Glass*. Cornell.

Lacan, J. 1977. *The Four Fundamental Concepts of Psycho-Analysis* (ed. J.-A. Miller, trans. A. Sheridan). London.

Laing, R. D. 1970. *Knots*. New York

Larmour, D., P. A. Miller, and C. Platter, eds. 1998. *Rethinking Sexuality: Foucault and Classical Antiquity*. Princeton.

Leach, E. W. 1993. "Absence and Desire in Cicero's *De Amicitia*," *CW* 87.3–20.

————. 1994. "Horace *Carmen* 1.8: Achilles, the Campus Martius, and the Articulation of Gender Roles in Augustan Rome," *CP* 89.334–43.

Leary, T. 1988. "Medicamina Recalled," *LCM* 13.140–42.

Lee, G. 1994. *Propertius: The Poems*. Oxford.

Lee, M. O. 1975. "Catullus in the *Odes* of Horace," *Ramus* 4.33–48.

Leitao, D. 1995. "The Perils of Leukippos: Initiatory Transvestism and Male Gender in the *Ekdusia* at Phaistos," *ClAnt* 14.130–63.

Lilja, S. 1965. *The Roman Love Elegists' Attitude to Women*. Helsinki.

————. 1972. *The Treatment of Odours in the Poetry of Antiquity*. Helsinki.

Lindberg, D. C. 1976. *Theories of Vision from Al-Kindi to Kepler*. Chicago.

Ling, R. 1991. *Roman Painting*. Cambridge.

Linthwaite, I., ed. 1987. *Ain't I a Woman? Poems of Black and White Women*. London.

Lyne, R. O. A. M. 1970. "Propertius and Cynthia: Elegy 1.3," *PCPS* 16.60–78.

———. 1979. "*Servitium Amoris*," *CQ* 29.117–30.

———. 1980. *The Latin Love Poets*. Oxford.

Macleod, C. W. 1979. "Horatian *Imitatio* and *Odes* 2.5," in West and Woodman 1979.89–102.

MacMullen, R. 1982. "Roman Attitudes to Greek Love," *Historia* 31.484–502.

Makowski, J. F. 1996. "Bisexual Orpheus: Pederasty and Parody in Ovid," *CJ* 92.25–38.

Marchant, E. C., and O. J. Todd. 1979. *Xenophon IV:* Memorabilia *and* Oeconomicus, Symposium *and* Apology. Cambridge, Mass.

Mattingly, H. 1965 [1923]. *The Coins of the Roman Empire in the British Museum*. London.

McCarthy, K. 1998. "*Servitium Amoris: Amor Servitii*," in Joshel and Murnaghan 1998.174–92.

McCarty, W. 1989. "The Shape of the Mirror: Metaphorical Catoptrics in Classical Literature," *Arethusa* 22.161–95.

McGinn, T. A. J. 1998. *Prostitution, Sexuality, and the Law in Ancient Rome*. New York.

McGrath, E. 1992. "The Black Andromeda," *JWI* 55.1–77.

McKeown, J. 1989. *Ovid* Amores: *A Commentary on Book One*, vol. 2. Leeds.

Mendell, C. 1935. "Catullan Echoes in the *Odes* of Horace," *CP* 30.289–301.

Metz, C. 1982. *The Imaginary Signifier: Psychoanalysis and the Cinema*. Bloomington.

Middleton, P. 1992. *The Inward Gaze: Masculinity and Subjectivity in Modern Culture*. London.

Millar, F., and E. Segal, eds. 1984. *Caesar Augustus*. Oxford.

Miller, P. A. 1994. *Lyric Texts and Lyric Consciousness: The Birth of a Genre from Archaic Greece to Augustan Rome*. London.

———. 1998. "The Bodily Grotesque in Roman Satire: Images of Sterility," *Arethusa* 31.257–83.

———. 2001. "Why Propertius Is a Woman: French Feminism and Augustan Elegy," *CP* 96. 127–46.

———. 2003. *Subjecting Verses: Latin Erotic Elegy and the Emergence of the Real*. Princeton.

Miller, P. A., and C. Platter. 1999a. "Introduction," *CW* 92.403–07.

———. 1999b. "Crux as Symptom: Augustan Elegy and Beyond," *CW* 92.445–54.

Miller, W. 1997. *The Anatomy of Disgust*. Cambridge.

Mills, S. 1994. "Reading as/like a Feminist," in *Gendering the Reader*, ed. S. Mills. New York. 25–46.

Minadeo, R. 1982. *The Golden Plectrum: Sexual Symbolism in Horace's Odes*. Amsterdam.

Moi, T. 1985. *Sexual/Textual Politics: Feminist Literary Theory*. London.

Montiglio, S. 2000. *Silence in the Land of Logos*. Princeton.

Mulvey, L. 1975. "Visual Pleasure and Narrative Cinema," *Screen* 16.3.8–18.

———. 1981. "Afterthoughts on 'Visual Pleasure and Narrative Cinema' Inspired by *Duel in the Sun*," *Framework* 15–17.12–15.

———. 1989a. *Visual and Other Pleasures*. Bloomington.

———. 1989b. "Afterthoughts on 'Visual Pleasure and Narrative Cinema,'" in Mulvey 1989a.

———. 1997. "Visual Pleasure and Narrative Cinema," in Warhol and Herndl 1997.432–42.

Murnaghan, S. 1998. "The Poetics of Loss in the Greek Epic," in Beissinger, Tylus, and Wofford 1998.203–20.

Murray, O. 1993. "Symposium and Genre in the Poetry of Horace," in Rudd 1993.89–105.

Myerowitz, M. 1985. *Ovid's Games of Love*. Detroit.

Myers, K. S. 1996. "The Poet and the Procuress: The *Lena* in Latin Love Elegy," *JRS* 86.1–21.

———. 1999. "The Metamorphosis of a Poet: Recent Work on Ovid," *JRS* 89.190–204.

Nakayama, T. 1963–64. "Schönheitsbegriff bei Catull und Properz," *AIGC* 1.61–74.

Neale, S. 1992. "Masculinity and Spectacle," *The Sexual Subject: A Screen Reader in Sexuality*. London.

Newlands, C. 1997. "The Role of the Book in *Tristia* 3.1," *Ramus* 26.57–79.

Newman, B. 1997. "'The Situation of the Looker-On': Gender, Narration, and Gaze in *Wuthering Heights*," in Warhol and Herndl 1997.449–66.

Nisbet, R. G. M., and M. Hubbard. 1970. *A Commentary on Horace: Odes, Book I*. Oxford.

———. 1978. *A Commentary on Horace: Odes, Book II*. Oxford.

Novak, B. 1969. *American Painting of the Nineteenth Century: Realism, Idealism, and the American Experience*. New York.

Oliensis, E. 1997a. "Return to Sender: The Rhetoric of *Nomina* in Ovid's *Tristia*," *Ramus* 26.172–93.

———. 1997b. "The Erotics of *Amicitia*: Readings in Tibullus, Propertius, and Horace," in Hallett and Skinner 1997.151–71.

———. 1997c. "*Ut arte emendaturus fortunam*: Horace, Nasidiensus, and the Art of Satire," in Habinek and Schiesaro 1997.90–104.

———. 1998. *Horace and the Rhetoric of Authority*. Cambridge.

———. 2002. "Feminine Endings, Lyric Seductions," in Woodman and Feeney 2002.93–106.

O'Neill, K. 1998. "Symbolism and Sympathetic Magic in Propertius 4.5," *CJ* 94.49–80.

———.1999. "Ovid and Propertius: Reflexive Annotation in *Amores* 1.8," *Mnemosyne* 52.3.286–307.

———. 2000. "Propertius 4.2: Slumming with Vertumnus?" *AJP* 121.259–77.

Otis, B. 1970 [1966]. *Ovid as an Epic Poet*. Cambridge.

Owen, S. 1949. "Ovid," in *The Oxford Classical Dictionary*. Oxford. 632.

Paglia, C. 1990. *Sexual Personae: Art and Decadence from Nefertiti to Emily Dickinson*. London.

Papanghelis, T. D. 1987. *Propertius: A Hellenistic Poet on Love and Death*. Cambridge.

Park, D. 1997. *The Fire within the Eye: A Historical Essay on the Nature and Meaning of Light*. Princeton.

Parker, H. 1997. "The Teratogenic Grid," in Hallett and Skinner 1997.47–65.

———. 2001. "The Myth of the Heterosexual: Anthropology and Sexuality for Classicists," *Arethusa* 34.313–62.

Parkin, F. 1971. *Class Inequality and Political Order*. London.

Pêcheux, M. 1977. *Language, Semantics, and Ideology*. New York.

Pedrick, V. 1986. "*Qui Potis Est, Inquis?* Audience Roles in Catullus," *Arethusa* 19.187–209.

Penley, C. 1989. *The Future of an Illusion: Film, Feminism, and Psychoanalysis*. Minneapolis.

Peradotto, J., and J. P. Sullivan, eds. 1984. *Women in the Ancient World: The Arethusa Papers*. Albany, N.Y.

Phillips, K. 1968. "Perseus and Andromeda," *AJA* 72.1–23.

Pinotti, P. 1988. *Remedia Amoris: Publio Ovidio Nasone*. Bologna.

Pintabone, D. T. 2002. "Ovid's Iphis and Ianthe: When Girls Won't Be Girls," in Rabinowitz and Auanger 2002.156–85.

Platter, C. 1995. "*Officium* in Catullus and Propertius: A Foucauldian Reading," *CP* 90.211–24.

Pollitt, J. 1979. "The Impact of Greek Art on Rome," *TAPA* 108.155–74.

Pomeroy, A. J. 1980. "A Man at a Spring: Horace, *Odes* 1.1," *Ramus* 9.34–50.

Porter, D. H. 1987. *Horace's Poetic Journey: A Reading of Odes 1–3*. Princeton.

Porter, J., ed. 1999. *Constructions of the Classical Body*. Ann Arbor.

Powell, A., ed. 1992. *Roman Poetry and Propaganda in the Age of Augustus*. London.

Pucci, P. 1978. "Lingering on the Threshold," *Glyph* 3.52–73.

Quinn, K., ed. 1980. *Horace:* The Odes. New York.

Rabinowitz, N. S., and A. Richlin, eds. 1993. *Feminist Theory and the Classics*. New York.

Rabinowitz, N. S., and L. Auanger, eds. 2002. *Among Women: From the Homosocial to the Homoerotic in the Ancient World*. Austin.

Rabinowitz, P. J. 1986. "Shifting Stands, Shifting Standards: Reading, Interpretation, and Literary Judgment," *Arethusa* 19.115–34.

Raditsa, L. 1980. "Augustus' Legislation Concerning Marriage, Procreation, and Adultery," *ANRW* 2.13.278–339.

Radt, S. 1977. *Tragicorum Graecorum Fragmenta*, vol. IV. Göttingen.

Raval, S. 2002. "Cross-Dressing and 'Gender Trouble' in the Ovidian Corpus," *Helios* 29. 149–72.

Rawson, B., and P. Weaver, eds. 1997. *The Roman Family in Italy*. Oxford.

Reckford, K. J. 1969. *Horace*. New York.

———. 1998. "Reading the Sick Body: Decomposition and Morality in Persius' Third Satire," *Arethusa* 31.337–54.

Rich, A. 1993 [1982]. "Compulsory Heterosexuality and Lesbian Existence," in Abelove, Barale, and Halperin 1993.227–54.

Rich, B. R., et al. 1978. "Women and Film: A Discussion of Feminist Aesthetics," *New German Critique* 13.83–107.

Richardson, L. ed. 1977. *Propertius* Elegies I-IV. Norman, Okla.

———. 1992. *A New Topographical Dictionary of Rome*. Baltimore.

Richlin, A. 1991. "Zeus and Metis: Foucault, Feminism, Classics," *Helios* 18.160–80.

———. 1992a [1983 New Haven]. *The Garden of Priapus: Sexuality and Aggression in Roman Humor* (rev. ed.). Oxford.

———. ed. 1992b. *Pornography and Representation in Greece and Rome*. Oxford.

———. 1992c. "Reading Ovid's Rapes," in Richlin 1992b.158–79.

———. 1993. "Not Before Homosexuality: The Materiality of the *Cinaedus* and the Roman Law Against Love Between Men," *Journal of the History of Sexuality* 3.523–73.

———. 1995. "Making Up a Woman: The Face of Roman Gender," in Eilberg-Schwartz and Doniger 1995.185–213.

———. 1998. "Foucault's *History of Sexuality*: A Useful Theory for Women?" in Larmour, Miller, and Platter 1998.138–70.

Riffaterre, M. 1979. "La syllepse intertextuelle," *Poétique* 10.496–501.

———. 1980. "Syllepsis," *Critical Inquiry* 6.625–38.

Rosati, G. 1983. *Narciso e Pigmalione: Illusione e Spettacolo nelle Metamorfosi di Ovidio*. Florence.

———. 1985. *Ovidio: I Cosmetici delle Donne*. Venice.

Rose, H. 1966³. *A Handbook of Latin Literature*. London.

Rosenmeyer, P. 1997. "Ovid's *Heroides* and *Tristia*: Voices from Exile," *Ramus* 26.29–56.

Ross, D. 1975. *Backgrounds to Augustan Poetry: Gallus, Elegy, and Rome*. Cambridge.

Rousselle, A. 1988. *Porneia* (trans. Felicia Pheasant). Oxford.

Rubin, G. 1975. "The Traffic in Women: Notes on the 'Political Economy' of Sex," in *Towards an Anthropology of Women*, ed. R. Reiter. New York. 157–210.

Rudd, N., ed. 1993. *Horace 2000: A Celebration—Essays for the Bimillennium*. Ann Arbor.

Salzman, P. 2001. "A Web of Fantasies: Gaze, Image, and Gender in Ovid's *Metamorphoses*," Dissertation, Oxford.

Santoro L'hoir, F. 1992. *The Rhetoric of Gender Terms: "Man," "Woman," and the Portrayal of Character in Latin Prose*. Leiden.

Sappa, M. 1883. "Ovidio umorista," *Rivista di filologia e di istruzione classica* 11.347–72.

Sartre, J. P. 1966. *Being and Nothingness* (trans. H. E. Barnes). New York.

Schauenburg, K. 1981. "Andromeda I," *LIMC*, vol. 1. Zurich.

Schefold, K. 1952. *Pompeianische Malerei: Sinn und Ideengeschichte*. Basel.

———. 1972. *La peinture pompéienne: Essai sur l'évolution de sa signification* (ed. and trans. J-M. Croisille). Brussels.

Schweickart, P. P. 1986. "Reading Ourselves: Toward a Feminist Theory of Reading," in Flynn and Schweickart 1986.31–62.

Scivoletto, N. 1979. "La città di Roma nella poesia di Properzio," *Colloquium Propertianum* 2.27–38.

Segal, C. 1969. *Landscape in Ovid's* Metamorphoses: *A Study in the Transformation of a Literary Symbol*. Wiesbaden.

———. 1998. "Ovid's Metamorphic Bodies: Art, Gender, and Violence in the *Metamorphoses*," *Arion* 5.3.9–41.

Shankman, S., ed. 1994. *Plato and Postmodernism*. Glennside, Pa.

Sharrock, A. 1987. "*Ars Amatoria* 2.123–42: Another Homeric Scene in Ovid," *Mnemosyne* 40.406–12.

———. 1991. "Womanufacture," *JRS* 81.36–49.

———. 1994a. "Ovid and the Politics of Reading," *MD* 33.97–122.

———. 1994b. *Seduction and Repetition in Ovid's* Ars Amatoria *II*. Oxford.

———. 1995. "The Drooping Rose: Elegiac Failure in *Amores* 3.7," *Ramus* 24.152–80.

———. 1998. "Re(ge)ndering Gender(ed) Studies," in Wyke 1998a.179–90.

———. 2002a. "Gender and Sexuality," in Hardie 2002b.95–107.

———. 2002b. "Ovid and the Discourses of Love," in Hardie 2002b.150–62.

———. 2002c. "Looking at Looking: Can You Resist a Reading?" in Fredrick 2002a. 265–95.

Shelton, J. 1998². *As the Romans Did: A Sourcebook in Roman Social History*. New York.

Shlain, L. 1998. *The Alphabet versus the Goddess: The Conflict between Word and Image*. New York.

Siebers, T. 1983. *The Mirror of Medusa*. Berkeley.

Silverman, K. 1983. *The Subject of Semiotics*. Oxford.

Simon, G. 1988. *Le regard, l'être, et l'apparence dans l'optique de l'antiquité*. Paris.

Skinner, M. 1993. "*Ego mulier:* The Construction of Male Sexuality in Catullus," *Helios* 20. 107–30 (reprinted in Hallett and Skinner 1997.129–50).

———. 1997. "Introduction: *Quod multo fit aliter in Graecia*," in Hallett and Skinner 1997.3–25.

Snitow, A., C. Stansell, and S. Thompson. 1983. *Powers of Desire: The Politics of Sexuality*. New York.

Snow, E. 1989., "Theorising the Male Gaze: Some Problems," *Representations* 25.1.30–41.

Snowden, F. M., Jr. 1970. *Blacks in Antiquity: Ethiopians in the Greco-Roman Experience*. Cambridge, Mass.

———. 1983. *Before Color Prejudice: The Ancient View of Blacks*. Cambridge, Mass.

Sommerstein, A., S. Halliwell, J. Henderson, and B. Zimmerman, eds. 1993. *Tragedy, Comedy, and the Polis*. Bari.

Spentzou, E. 2003. *Readers and Writers in Ovid's* Heroides: *Transgressions of Gender and Genre*. Oxford.

Spentzou, E., and D. Fowler, eds. 2002. *Cultivating the Muse: Struggles for Power and Inspiration in Classical Literature*. Oxford.

Stacey, J. 1992. "Desperately Seeking Difference," in *The Sexual Subject: A Screen Reader in Sexuality*. London.

Stahl, H. P. 1985. *Propertius: Love and War: Individual and State under Augustus*. Berkeley.

Stambaugh, J. 1988. *The Ancient Roman City*. Baltimore.

Stehle, E. 1989. "Venus, Cybele, and the Sabine Women: The Roman Construction of Female Sexuality," *Helios* 16.143–64.

———. 1990. "Sappho's Gaze: Fantasies of a Goddess and a Young Man," *Differences* 2.88–125.

Studlar, G. 1988. *In the Realm of Pleasure: Von Sternberg, Dietrich, and the Masochistic Aesthetic*. Bloomington.

Sullivan, J. P., ed. 1962. *Critical Essays on Roman Literature: Elegy and Lyric*. London.

———. 1972. "The Politics of Elegy," *Arethusa* 5.17–34.

Sutherland, E. H. 1997. "Vision and Desire in Horace's *Carmina* 2.5," *Helios* 24.23–43.

———. 2002. *Horace's Well-Trained Reader*. Frankfurt am Main.

———. 2003. "How (Not) to Look at a Woman: Bodily Encounters and the Failure of the Gaze in Horace's *Carmina* 1.19," *AJP* 124.57–80.

Syme, R. 1978. *History in Ovid*. Oxford.

Syndikus, H. P. 2001. *Die Lyrik des Horaz: Eine Interpretation der Oden*, vol. 1. Darmstadt.

Tarrant, R. J. 1981. "The Authenticity of the Letter of Sappho to Phaon," *HSCP* 85.133–53.

———. 1995. "The Silence of Cephalus: Text and Narrative Technique in Ovid, *Metamorphoses* 7.685ff.," *TAPA* 125.99–111.

Theodorakopoulos, E. 1999. "Closure and Transformation in Ovid's *Metamorphoses*," in Hardie, Barchiesi, and Hinds 1999.142–61.

Thomas, R. 1986. "Virgil's *Georgics* and the Art of Reference," *HSCP* 90.171–98.

Thompson, M. 1961. "The Monumental and Literary Evidence for Program-
    matic Painting in Antiquity," *Marsyas* 9.36–77.
Thomson, D. F .S., ed. 1997. *Catullus*. Toronto.
Thomson, D. S. 1994. "Plato's *Cratylus* in the Light of Postmodernism," in
    Shankman 1994. 122–33.
Tissol, G. 1997. *The Face of Nature: Wit, Narrative, and Cosmic Origins in Ovid's*
    Metamorphoses. Princeton.
Travis, R. 2000. "The Spectation of Gyges in P. Oxy. 2382 and Herodotus
    Book 1," *CA* 19.330–59.
Treggiari, S. 1991. *Roman Marriage*. Oxford.
Vasaly, A. 1993. *Representations: Images of the World in Ciceronian Oratory*.
    Berkeley.
Verducci, F. 1980. "The Contest of Rational Libertinism and Imaginative
    License in Ovid's *Ars Amatoria*," *Pacific Coast Philology* 15.2.29–39.
Vernant, J-P. 1991. *Mortals and Immortals: Collected Essays* (ed. F. I. Zeitlin).
    Princeton.
Veyne, P. 1978. "La famille et l'amour sous le haut-empire romain," *Annales*
    (E.S.C.) 33.35–63.
———. 1985. "Homosexuality in Ancient Rome," in Ariès and Béjin 1985.26–35.
———. 1988. *Roman Erotic Elegy* (trans. D. Pellauer). Chicago.
Volosinov, V. 1973. *Marxism and the Philosophy of Language*. Cambridge, Mass.
von Blanckenhagen, P., and C. Alexander. 1990. *The Augustan Villa at Boscotre-
    case*. Mainz am Rhein.
Walker, A. D. 1993. "*Enargeia* and the Spectator in Greek Historiography,"
    TAPA 123.353–77.
Walker, J. M. 1998. *Medusa's Mirrors: Spenser, Shakespeare, Milton, and the Meta-
    morphosis of the Female Self*. Newark, Del.
Wallace-Hadrill, A. 1986. "Image and Authority in the Coinage of Augustus,"
    JRS 76.66–87.
Walters, J. 1997. "Invading the Roman Body: Manliness and Impenetrability in
    Roman Thought," in Hallett and Skinner 1997.29–43.
———. 1998. "Making a Spectacle: Deviant Men, Invective, and Pleasure,"
    Arethusa 31.355–67.
Walters, S. D. 1996. "From Here to Queer: Radical Feminism, Postmodern-
    ism, and the Lesbian Menace (Or, Why Can't a Woman be More Like
    a Fag?)," *Signs* 21.830–69.
Warden, J. 1978. "Another Would-be Amazon: Propertius 4.4.71–72," *Hermes*
    106.177–87.
Warhol, R., and D. Herndl, eds. 1997². *Feminisms: An Anthology of Literary
    Theory and Criticism*. New Brunswick, N.J.
Watson, P. 1982. "Ovid and *Cultus: Ars Amatoria* 3.113–28," *TAPA* 112.237–44.
Werness, H. B. 1999. *The Symbolism of Mirrors in Art from Ancient Times to the
    Present*. Lewiston.

West, D., ed. 1998. *Horace* Odes *II: Vatis Amici*. Oxford.

West, D., and A. J. Woodman, eds. 1979. *Creative Imitation and Latin Literature*. Cambridge.

Wheeler, S. W. 1997. "Changing Names: The Miracle of Iphis in Ovid *Metamorphoses 9*," *Phoenix* 51.190–202.

Whitaker, R. 1983. *Myth and Personal Experience in Roman Love-Elegy: A Study in Poetic Technique*. Göttingen.

White, P. 1993. *Promised Verse*. Cambridge, Mass.

Wiedemann, T. 1989. *Adults and Children in the Roman Empire*. London.

Wilk, S. R. 2000. *Medusa: Solving the Mystery of the Gorgon*. Oxford.

Wilkinson, L. P. 1955. *Ovid Recalled*. Cambridge.

Williams, C. 1992. "Homosexuality and the Roman Man: A Study in the Cultural Construction of Sexuality," Ph.D. dissertation, Yale University.

———. 1995. "Greek Love at Rome," *CQ* 45.517–39.

———. 1998. Review of Hallett and Skinner 1997, *BMCR* 98.10.16.

———. 1999. *Roman Homosexuality*. New York.

Williams, G. 1996. *The Curse of Exile: A Study of Ovid's Ibis*. Cambridge.

———. 2002. "Ovid's Exile Poetry: *Tristia, Epistulae ex Ponto*, and *Ibis*," in Hardie 2002b. 233–48.

Williams, R. 1977. *Marxism and Literature*. Oxford.

Wilson, R. 1992. Shakespeare's Roman Carnival," in Wilson and Dutton 1992.145–56.

Wilson, R., and R. Dutton, eds. 1992. *New Historicism and Renaissance Drama*. London.

Winkler, J. J. 1990. *The Constraints of Desire: The Anthropology of Sex and Gender in Ancient Greece*. New York.

Wiseman, T. P. 1985. *Catullus and His World*. Cambridge.

Wittig, M. 1992. *The Straight Mind and Other Essays*. Boston.

———. 1993 [1981]. "One Is Not Born a Woman," in Abelove, Barale, and Halperin 1993.103–09.

Woodman, T. 2002. "*Biformis Vates*: The *Odes*, Catullus and Greek Lyric," in Woodman and Feeney 2002.

Woodman, T., and D. Feeney, eds. 2002. *Traditions and Contexts in the Poetry of Horace*. Cambridge.

Wyke, M. 1987a. "The Elegiac Woman at Rome," *PCPS* 33.153–78.

———. 1987b. "Written Women: Propertius' *Scripta Puella*," *JRS* 77.47–61.

———. 1989a. "Mistress and Metaphor in Augustan Elegy," *Helios* 16.25–47.

———. 1989b. "Reading Female Flesh: *Amores* 3.1," in Cameron 1989.111–43.

———. 1994a. "Woman in the Mirror: The Rhetoric of Adornment in the Roman World," in Archer, Fischler, and Wyke 1994.134–51.

———. 1994b. "Taking the Woman's Part: Engendering Roman Love Elegy," *Ramus* 23. 110–28.

———. ed. 1998a. *Gender and the Body in the Ancient Mediterranean*. Oxford.

————. ed. 1998b. *Parchments of Gender: Deciphering the Body of Antiquity.* Oxford.

————. 2002. *The Roman Mistress.* Oxford.

Yavetz, Z. 1984. "The *Res Gestae* and Augustus' Public Image," in Millar and Segal 1984.1–36.

Zanker, G. 1981. "*Enargeia* in the Ancient Criticism of Poetry," *RhM* 124.297–311.

————. 1987. *Realism in Alexandrian Poetry: A Literature and its Audience.* London.

Zanker, P. 1988. *The Power of Images in the Age of Augustus* (trans. A. Shapiro). Ann Arbor.

————. 1999. "Mythenbilder im Haus," *Proceedings of the XVth International Congress of Classical Archaeology.* Amsterdam.

Zetzel, J. 1996. "Poetic Baldness and Its Cure," *MD* 36.73–100.

Zizek, S. 1989. *The Sublime Object of Ideology.* London.

————. 1991. *Looking Awry: An Introduction to Jacques Lacan through Popular Culture.* Cambridge, Mass.

————. 1992. *Enjoy Your Symptom: Jacques Lacan in Hollywood and Out.* New York.

————. 2001. *Did Someone Say Totalitarianism? Four Interventions in the (Mis)Use of a Notion.* London.

Index